International Review of
Industrial
and Organizational
Psychology
1991 Volume 6

International Review of Industrial and Organizational Psychology 1991 Volume 6

Edited by

Cary L. Cooper
and
Ivan T. Robertson

*University of Manchester
Institute of Science & Technology UK*

JOHN WILEY & SONS

Chichester · New York · Brisbane · Toronto · Singapore

International Review of Industrial and Organizational Psychology
ISSN 0886-1528

Published annually by John Wiley & Sons

Volume 6 — 1991 $95 (Institutions)

Personal subscription at reduced rate
available for prepayment direct to the publisher.
For details telephone 0243 770 397 or write to
The Journals Subscriptions Department,
John Wiley and Sons Ltd,
Baffins Lane, Chichester, West Sussex, PO19 IUD, England.

Future volumes will be invoiced to subscribers prior to
publication, and subscriptions may be cancelled at any time.

The Library of Congress has cataloged this serial publication as follows:

International review of industrial and organizational psychology.
—1986—Chichester; New York: Wiley, c1986—
v.: ill.; 24 cm.
Annual.
ISSN 0886-1528 = International review of industrial and organizational psychology

1.Psychology, Industrial—Periodicals. 2.Personnel management—Periodicals.
[DNLM: 1.Organizaton and Administration—periodicals. 2.Psychology,
Industrial—periodicals.   W1IN832U]
HF5548.7.I57   158.7'05—dc19   86-643874
AACR 2   MARC-S
Library of Congress   [8709]

British Library Cataloguing in Publication Data:

International review of industrial and organizational
psychology 1991.
1. Industrial psychology
I. Cooper, Cary L. (C. Lynn), *1940–* II. Robertson,
Ivan T.
15877

ISBN 0-471-92819-4

Typeset in 10/12pt Plantin by Photo·graphics, Honiton, Devon
Printed and bound in Great Britain by Courier International, Tiptree, Essex

CONTRIBUTORS

Cary L. Cooper
Editor

Manchester School of Management, University of Manchester Institute of Science & Technology, UK.

Ivan T. Robertson
Editor

Manchester School of Management, University of Manchester Institute of Science & Technology, UK.

J. H. Erik Andriessen

Department of Work and Organizational Psychology, University of Technology, Kanaalweg 26, 2628EH Delft, The Netherlands.

Richard D. Arvey

Industrial Relations Center, 574 Management and Economics Building, University of Minnesota, 271 19th Avenue South, Minneapolis, Minnesota 55455, USA.

Deborah K. Buerkley

Industrial Relations Center, 574 Management and Economics Building, University of Minnesota, 271 19th Avenue South, Minneapolis, Minnesota 55455, USA.

Gary W. Carter

Industrial Relations Center, 574 Management and Economics Building, University of Minnesota, 271 19th Avenue South, Minneapolis, Minnesota 55455, USA.

D. R. Davies

Human Factors Research Unit, Aston Business School, Aston University, Aston Triangle, Birmingham B4 7ET, UK.

Jeffrey R. Edwards

Darden Graduate School of Business Administration, University of Virginia, Box 6550, Charlottesville, Virginia 22906, USA.

Andreas Guldin

Universität Hohenheim, Lehrstuhl für Psychologie, Postfach 70 05 62, D-7000 Stuttgart 70, Federal Republic of Germany.

Daniel R. Ilgen

Department of Psychology, Psychology Research Building, Michigan State University, East Lansing, Michigan 48824, USA.

G. Matthews

Department of Psychology, University of Dundee, Dundee, Scotland, UK.

E. D. Megaw

Ergonomics Information Analysis Centre, School of Manufacturing and Mechanical Engineering, University of Birmingham, Birmingham B15 2TT, UK.

Lawrence R. Murphy

Motivation and Stress Research Section, National Institute for Occupational Safety and Health, Robert A. Taft Laboratories, 4676 Columbia Parkway, Cincinnati, Ohio 45226, USA.

Jeffrey Schneider

Department of Psychology, Psychology Research Building, Michigan State University, East Lansing, Michigan 48824, USA.

Heinz Schuler

Universität Hohenheim, Lehrstuhl für Psychologie, Postfach 70 05 62, D-7000 Stuttgart 70, Federal Republic of Germany.

Naomi G. Swanson

Motivation and Stress Research Section, National Institute for Occupational Safety and Health, Robert A. Taft Laboratories, 4676 Columbia Parkway, Cincinnati, Ohio 45226, USA.

Zhong-Ming Wang

Department of Psychology, Hangzhou University, Hangzhou 310028, Zhejiang, People's Republic of China.

C. S. K. Wong

Human Factors Research Unit, Aston Business School, Aston University, Aston Triangle, Birmingham, B4 7ET, UK.

CONTENTS

EDITORIAL FOREWORD

With the publication of this sixth volume of the *International Review of Industrial and Organizational Psychology* the series is entering a new phase. One important change (signified by the use of a volume number as well as a year on this and future issues) is that it will now be possible to take out a subscription to the series, so that future volumes will be automatically forwarded to subscribers as soon as they are published. We feel that this is an important development which, together with a significantly lower subscription rate for personal subscribers, should help us to meet the goal of the series in becoming the main, authoritative source of state of the art reviews of topics in I/O psychology. These changes have come about partly through suggestions from colleagues and partly through a steady improvement and evolution in editorial and promotional policies for the series.

This volume retains the international nature of the series with contributions from several countries across a broad range of I/O psychology topics. This volume, with the chapter on I/O psychology in China, also contains the first of a planned series of chapters on I/O psychology in countries throughout the world.

As noted in previous editorial forewords, the success of this series relies heavily on the help and collaboration of colleagues concerning important topics, and we are always pleased to receive suggestions for topics and offers of contributions. As far as topic coverage is concerned, this year provides the first examples so far of the repeat coverage of a topic dealt with in an earlier volume; the topic of work motivation was dealt with in 1986. We expect to re-review other topics in future years but will always retain space for new and emerging areas of importance.

CLC
ITR
August 1990

Chapter 1

RECENT DEVELOPMENTS IN INDUSTRIAL AND ORGANIZATIONAL PSYCHOLOGY IN PEOPLE'S REPUBLIC OF CHINA

Zhong-Ming Wang
Department of Psychology
Hangzhou University
People's Republic of China

INTRODUCTION

In China, work psychology and recently managerial psychology have been used as the names for industrial and organizational psychology (I/O psychology). Managerial psychology and engineering psychology are considered as two major branches of industrial psychology. Another closely related branch of I/O psychology is personnel psychology. For convenience, the name I/O psychology will be used in this chapter to describe some recent developments in these areas in China.

Although psychology as a scientific subject did not start until the 1920s, the study and discussion of I/O psychological issues have had a long history. Many ideas such as intrinsic motivation, systematic performance evaluation, multi-level personnel selection and quality control have been applied for centuries in work situations in China. For instance, as early as 400 BC, some Chinese scholars proposed that workload and actual performance be the prerequisites for job evaluation and reward allocation. In the year AD 587, China started its national personnel examination and selection system for the Civil Service, which was the first such system in the world and lasted for about 1300 years (Li, Song and Li, 1989). To a large extent the approach and practice of modern Chinese I/O psychology is rooted in this tradition.

During the 1920s through 1940s, some Chinese scholars went to Europe and North America to study psychology. A few textbooks of psychology,

International Review of Industrial and Organizational Psychology 1991 Volume 6
Edited by C. L. Cooper and I. T. Robertson © 1991 John Wiley & Sons Ltd.

including industrial psychology, were then translated into Chinese and used in universities, although very few studies were conducted in this area. After the founding of the People's Republic of China in 1949, Chinese psychology was heavily influenced by Soviet psychology in the 1950s. In the early 1960s, a number of I/O psychology studies were carried out in China in areas such as technical skill training, technological innovations and signal design, work competition and accident analysis (e.g. Chen *et al.*, 1959; Chao *et al.*, 1966). However, very little organizational research was conducted. The study and practice of Chinese psychology then suffered greatly from the 10-year Cultural Revolution (1966–76).

Fortunately, I/O psychology has developed very rapidly since China launched her recent economic reform program and adopted an open-to-the-world policy in 1978. The Chinese Society of Industrial Psychology (including I/O psychology and engineering psychology) was organized in 1978. The Chinese Society of Behavioral Sciences, with many members who are managers and supervisors from enterprises, was established in 1985. Since 1980, I/O psychology has become a very popular subject in Chinese universities and enterprise management. China's first I/O psychology program was started at Hangzhou University (including BA, MA. and PhD.) in 1980, and approved as the National Key Program by the State Education Commission in 1988. A number of psychology programs and management programs at other universities (e.g. East China Normal University, Shanghai JiaoTong University and People's University) are now offering graduate training in I/O psychology or organizational behavior. Many textbooks on I/O psychology have been published in China. Among the popular ones are *Essentials of Industrial Psychology* (Chen, 1983), *Behavioral Sciences* (Yang, 1983), *Managerial Psychology* (Lu *et al.*, 1985), *Managerial Psychology* (Xu & Chen, 1988), *Work and Personnel Psychology* (Wang, 1988a) and *Psychology of Industrial Management* (Chen, 1988a). There are also two major Chinese journals (quarterly) in I/O psychology: *Chinese Journal of Applied Psychology* and *Chinese Journal of Behavioral Sciences*. Much I/O psychology research has been carried out in the organizational settings, which has greatly facilitated the development of Chinese I/O psychology.

SOME CHARACTERISTICS OF CHINESE WORK SITUATIONS

It is important to understand some unique cultural and organizational characteristics of Chinese work situations in order to understand I/O psychology in China. Ancient Confucian thinking, especially concerning the work ethic, has for long been influential in China. There is also a strong tradition of group work and collectivism in Chinese organizations. Group approaches to work, such as group goal-setting, group reward systems and team decision making are greatly valued. In the last 40 years, socialist ideology has also had great impact on work attitudes and behavior in China. Ideological work has been one of the major tasks for management. As the Chinese Enterprise Law states: 'While achieving socialist material growth, the enterprise must persistently promote socialist cultural and ideological progress and build up a contingent of well-educated and self-disciplined staff and workers with high ideals and moral integrity' (*China Daily Business Weekly*, 1988). For a period, equality was much emphasized in compensation systems as well as in general social life. Organizational commitment and a sense of mastery have been very much encouraged. Social recognition has been one of the most important motivators at work. Especially in the last 10 years, both social and material rewards were used to motivate employees, including workers and managers. One of the common practices in using social rewards is to organize national evaluation campaigns for awards to national excellent entrepreneurs or to national excellent enterprises. In many organizations a title of 'excellent worker' would be awarded to those employees who were most productive.

The organizational system in Chinese work units is unique. In most enterprises, there are three organizational systems: (1) Communist Party organization; (2) management responsibility system; and (3) trade unions and workers' congress. According to the recent Enterprise Law in China (*China Daily Business Weekly*, 1988), in the state-owned enterprises, the role of the party organization is to guarantee and supervise the implementation of the guiding principles and policies of the party; the director of management responsibility system shall be the legal representative of the enterprise and assume overall responsibility in production, operation and management; and the trade union and Workers' Congress shall represent and safeguard the interests of the staff and workers and organize participation in democratic management and supervision. The relationships among the above three groups characterize the Chinese approach of management.

Another important characteristic of Chinese organization is its community style of organizational life. In most of large- and medium-sized industrial enterprises and other organizations, housing and medical care are provided. Many organizations are also responsible for children's day-care and school education. Work organization is then not only a working unit, but also a type of community. Employees have closer connections or attachment with their organizations, even after their retirement. Therefore, the concepts of work, group and participation have broader meanings and implications in I/O psychology in China. For example, people talk about 'two-way participation', i.e. workers participating in top-level management decision making and managers participating in daily work at the shopfloor level.

Recent nationwide economic reform in China has brought great organizational changes in enterprises, schools and governmental organizations. The new emphasis on work efficiency, responsibility, competition and democratic management are changing Chinese work life. The reform has provided a kind of nationwide field laboratory for Chinese I/O psychologists to develop their expertise and apply I/O psychology principles.

RECENT DEVELOPMENT IN RESEARCH AND APPLICATIONS

Recent research and applications in I/O psychology in China have been very closely tied to economic reform. Most of the research has been conducted in organizations using workers and managers as subjects. Many Chinese I/O psychologists are involved in developing I/O psychological principles and models useful to the Chinese work situation.

Reward Systems and Work Motivation

A decade ago, I/O psychology studies in China emphasized the effects of contextual and cultural factors on organizational behavior. During the early 1980s the focus of Chinese reform was on developing more effective incentive or reward systems for motivating people. The idea was to design a reward system combining social rewards with material incentives, which were supposed to be more suitable to the Chinese situation. Some field experiments on reward systems were then conducted in enterprises. In one experiment, a flexible multi-reward system was developed and introduced in some departments. Employees who completed their production targets could choose an incentive from the following alternatives: (1) bonus (money); (2) opportunity for technical training; (3) early leave for home; (4) group vacation (sightseeing); (5) possessing titles such as 'excellent worker' on the company posters. The results showed that, in general, group vacation was a popular incentive and group social interaction was apparently more rewarding. There were, of course, some age differences. For instance, young employees preferred more opportunities for further training and group activities; middle-aged workers liked to have more bonuses or flexible working time; while among elderly workers social recognition was valued. Compared with the control group, the experimental group under the multi-reward system resulted in significantly higher motivation and productivity (Chen, 1987).

In another experiment, an effort was made to find out the effects of attributions on performance and subsequent work behavior under individual versus team reward systems in Chinese enterprises (Wang, 1986). It was shown that the attributions of failure or success, and their relationship with subsequent work behaviors in Chinese organizations, were somewhat different from the findings reported in Western countries. First, Chinese workers tended to make multiple attributions, i.e. giving several reasons for their performance and assuming that multiple factors interacted with each other and together contributed to their success or failure. Second, the attributions and their relationships with the subsequent behaviors very much depended upon the organizational context, especially characteristics of the Chinese reward system, e.g. whether one was working under a group reward system or an individual system. Under a group reward system, workers tended to make attributions related to their team collaboration and efforts which may, to a large extent, maintain or enhance their expectancy for further performance; whereas under the individual reward system, workers more frequently attributed their results to some personal factors or task difficulty which reduced their motivation.

In a quasi-experiment conducted at a large chain factory, Wang (1986) found that a team reward program with a clear team-goal structure and individual member responsibilities was more effective than an individual reward (piece-rate type) program. Based on these findings the team reward system was recommended, and a kind of team development program was designed for attributional training which proved to be very successful (Wang, 1988).

During the early and middle 1980s, several research projects were carried out to find out the needs structure of Chinese employees and the factors influencing work motivation (Xu & Wang, 1990). A needs hierarchy was categorized on the basis of about 2700 needs from a large-scale survey in the industries. It was shown that social needs (e.g. contributions to organizations and the country) were listed as most important. Moreover, Chinese employees tended to differentiate needs in terms of their ethical or moral nature, e.g. correct need or wrong need, rational or irrational needs (Xu, 1987). In another field survey it was found that decision-making power and organizational climate are among the significant factors affecting managers' work motivation in the Chinese industrial organizations (Liang, 1986). The results of these studies have important implications for the design of various incentive systems as well as the practice of organizational reform in China.

Group Development and Team Effectiveness

China has a long tradition of collectivism and team approaches to work. Togetherness has been very important among Chinese people throughout history. The team approach was greatly emphasized after the founding of the People's Republic of China in 1949. However, in the 1960s and 1970s, the concept of collective was misunderstood as equality without responsibility, which led to a decrease of team effectiveness. In the early 1980s, as a reaction against the 'iron rice bowl' (i.e. everybody was guaranteed equal pay and lifetime employment regardless of performance) and absolute egalitarianism, many Chinese companies started paying wages based on piece-rates or introduced individual incentive systems. The practice of more individualistic compensation systems resulted in a lower degree of group consciousness and cohesiveness (e.g. Jin, 1983). Therefore, enhancing the effectiveness of work groups has become one of the keys for the success of economic reform in China.

In recent years many Chinese I/O psychologists have been studying group development and team effectiveness. In a field study among 16 companies, Jin (1983) tried some sociometric measures in a group development study when workers were asked to choose those they most preferred as co-workers in the same group and to reorganize such groups autonomously. Managers and supervisors then gave some guidance and made a few adjustments in group assignments. The results showed that the experimental groups significantly increased their group cohesiveness and improved team performance when compared to a quasi-control group. About four years later, autonomous work groups under supervision became one of the major approaches in a nationwide practice called 'optimization through regrouping', an effort to enhance team effectiveness in both state- and collective-owned enterprises in China.

One important factor for team effectiveness is the social psychological climate in groups. Yu (1985) used a group climate scale in seven factories in Shanghai and found that relationships with the management and among fellow workers are the two major indicators of the social psychological climate. The study provided some useful evidence for improving team management in Chinese organizations. In another field experiment, Wang (1988b) demonstrated that team attributional training was an effective way of facilitating group consciousness and positive work behavior. Operating under a team responsibility (incentive) system, all team members met in the workshop once a week after work and joined in team attributional training session together with a psychologist as external facilitator. They discussed production and teamwork and made attributions about the performance in the previous week. It was found that the training session resulted in more objective attributions, fewer biases and better mutual understanding. Team attributional training enhanced positive attributional patterns, improved morale and, in turn, team effectiveness.

In recent years it has been a nationwide practice to develop and award 'excellent team' titles in Chinese organizations. Some I/O psychology research workers examined the characteristics of these excellent work teams and the goal-directed behavior in work groups (e.g. Lu, 1987; Wu, 1987). It was shown that the key to team excellence includes a high degree of group involvement and a good fit between task requirements and group goals with clear member responsibility. Team goal-setting activity could greatly strengthen a kind of team-goal-directed behavior and lead to a high degree of responsibility sharing, group cohesiveness and morale. Furthermore, because of strong formal organizational norms and the social desirability for pro-organization behavior in Chinese organizations, the informal group, where existing, was largely functioning as a friendship group and had relatively weak group norms

(Xu, 1986). Thus, this emphasis on teams did not lead to enhanced group norms.

Personnel Selection and Leadership Assessment

With the development of Chinese economic reform, enterprise management has been largely decentralized and managers have been given much more power in running their work units. As a result, selecting more qualified and competent managers has become a major concern in many enterprises. Since 1984, personnel selection and leadership assessment have been an active area of research and practice in I/O psychology in China.

During 1984 and 1985, a large-scale assessment of leadership behavior involving 53 factories with 16 260 respondents was carried out by a research group at the Institute of Psychology in the Chinese Academy of Sciences (Xu, 1987). Initially, a Japanese two-dimensional instrument for leadership assessment (Misumi, 1985; Misumi & Peterson, 1985) was adapted to measure task performance and relationship maintenance (the so-called performance–maintenance scale or PM scale). But Chinese research data soon revealed that a three-dimensional assessment of leadership was needed. In addition to the two dimensions (performance vs maintenance), there was a third dimension, i.e. moral. The moral factor generally includes some personal characteristics such as honesty, integrity and organizational commitment. Later, a three-dimensional scale (performance, maintenance and moral) was developed and implemented in a number of factories and proved to be a valid assessment of leadership (Lin, Chen and Wang, 1987).

There are other approaches to leadership assessment research in China. An assessment center with simulated tasks was used in Shanghai to select higher-level managers, e.g. directors for large enterprises or industrial bureaus. The results showed that group simulation tasks could provide better assessment of a candidate's ability and competence to work in groups, e.g. in a management team than the paper-and-pencil questionnaire survey (Wang, 1988a).

Wu (1986) conducted a different kind of leadership assessment based on a job analysis in 60 Chinese factories. She found that there were seven categories of management functions in Chinese enterprises: administration, ideological work, production, technical work, marketing, welfare and personnel. An assessment instrument was then developed and used for selecting managers in factories. An interesting method used in this research was role-set and multi-level measurement. Each role set involved the candidate, his/her previous supervisor, subordinates and peers. They individually made assessments regarding the characteristics and performance of the candidate. It was shown that such assessment produced more accurate and comprehensive information for personnel decisions.

Recently, the focus of research has shifted towards two different areas of personnel psychology:

1. Developing psychological instruments for selecting ordinary workers, especially for jobs with high requirements, e.g. power plant operators;
2. Examining the structure of personnel information and the information processing of personnel decisions (selection, classification and placement).

Some I/O psychologists are developing a number of specific selection instruments for industry as well as the national Civil Service system. A research group from the Psychology Department of Hangzhou University is investigating the characteristics of personnel decision making in Chinese enterprises. The preliminary results show that there is a single pattern of personnel decision procedures across enterprises with a certain degree of autonomy. The personnel decisions are largely carried out in the form of serial processing according to certain regulations of personnel management. Some strategies for decision support have been proposed to improve the quality of personnel decisions, e.g. structuring personnel and job information (Wang & Wang, 1989).

Organizational Decision Making and Participation

Organizational decision making and participation has been a very active area in I/O psychology in China, especially since scientific and democratic procedures for organizational decision making became a major interest in economic and management reform in 1986 (Wan, 1986). Research showed that participation was a very important factor in determining both morale and decision effectiveness in Chinese enterprises (e.g. Wang, 1984; Chen, 1989). I/O psychologists in Beijing and Hangzhou were interested in the competence and skill utilization of managers and supervisors in organizational decision making. In one of the field studies examining decision-making styles between top managers (level 1 in the organizations) and their immediate subordinates (level 2 managers) (Wang, 1989a), managers reported that participative decision making had very positive effects upon management effectiveness. Average ratings of participative decisions made by Chinese managers was generally higher than similar ratings reported in studies from abroad. It was interesting to note that Chinese managers believed that participative decision making could actually speed up the decision-making process in the sense that team decision making would be more accurate, less prone to error and be more effective.

Since 1987, I/O psychologists at Hangzhou University and researchers from the Tavistock Institute of Human Relations in London have been conducting a large-scale study on organizational decision making, sponsored by the British Council, using some instruments developed from previous studies (Heller &

Wilpert, 1980; IDE Research Group, 1981). Ten Chinese companies are being compared with 10 British companies, half of the firms being manufacturing enterprises and half service organizations, in terms of decision-making patterns for different types of decisions. Preliminary results reveal different patterns and strategies of organizational decision making, depending upon the kinds of ownerships and management systems.

Wang (1990b) conducted a series of field studies looking at cognitive processes and strategies in decision making concerning computer system development in Chinese enterprises. In one of the field experiments, managers were asked to make decisions on what actions they should take in introducing management information systems (MIS). Verbal protocols and information search techniques were used in the experiment. Wang found that the cognitive strategies managers used in decision making were affected by the types of decision information structures, e.g. whether using a dimensional structure in which decision information was arranged according to several key dimensions or a causal structure in which decision formation was organized on the basis of causal relationships among variables. When decision-support information was provided, managers modified their decision behaviors and used more comprehensive cognitive strategies, which reduced decision biases and improved decision performance. More recently, some experiments have been carried out to elicit the knowledge structure from experts on organizational decision making and to develop training programs for management decision skills.

Organizational Development and Technological Innovations

In recent years the ideas and methods of organization development (OD) have become more and more popular in Chinese management reform. Chen (1989) reviewed the current practice of OD in China including flexible working time, management by objectives (MBO) and participative management. He believed that the quality of workers and managers is the ultimate determinant for organizational progress and that training and education becomes a major task in Chinese organizations.

Xu et al. (1985) conducted an organization development program in several enterprises using a modified PM scale of leadership behavior assessment. Assessment and diagnosis were made regarding eight aspects of management: work motivation, job satisfaction, welfare, mental health, team work, meeting efficiency, communication and performance norms. Some action plans were then proposed and implemented to improve management performance. It was shown that the results of leadership assessment could be effectively used as feedback information for managers to improve their work efficiency. Among those enterprises involved in the organization development program, management became more effective and productivity increased. Leadership behavior assessment was apparently an important tool for organization development.

One major approach to organization development and technological innovations in Chinese industries is action research. Action research as an OD technique has two critical features:

1. Close collaboration between OD specialists (often I/O psychologists) and enterprise personnel (managers, staffs and workers);
2. Accurate pre-action organizational assessment, feedback and evaluation (Chen, 1984; Huse & Cummings, 1989).

In an action research project on MIS development in 16 enterprises, an assessment and diagnostic instrument was developed on the basis of the theory of human–computer interface hierarchy (Wang, 1988a, 1989b). The theory views computing skill or expertise, system link or networking and participation as three facets of an interface hierarchy among people, computer systems and organizations. The characteristics of the key facets determine the degree of 'interface uncertainty' which affects the performance of technological innovations. Therefore, in action research, special attention was paid to the diagnosis and action plans of these key facets and related characteristics. Three major strategies were formulated for technological innovation (MIS development):

1. Skill strategy, focusing upon the improvement of skill, knowledge and expertise on computer system development;
2. System strategy, emphasizing reforms of organizational structure and communication networks;
3. Participation strategy, encouraging participative management styles, joint planning and user involvement.

This action research resulted in an optimization of the interface facets (computing expertise, system networking and participation), higher performance and better organizational climate (Wang, 1990a).

Job design is another area of organization development which has received some attention. Zhong (1989) conducted a field experiment on job design in a TV factory. An assembly-line production system was reorganized into a teamwork system. The results of this study indicated that under the new work system, both product quality and job satisfaction were improved. The study used the job characteristics model (Hackman & Oldham, 1980) as the framework. It was found that in the Chinese industrial context there were significant differences between assembly-line and nonassembly-line work in such job characteristics as task identity, task autonomy, skill variety and task feedback, but not in task significance. Workers in different jobs experienced a similar degree of task significance to the organization and society. It seems that the perception of job characteristics is not only based on the task itself but also dependent upon the value system and the social context. The collectivist nature of Chinese society and organizations may affect the relationship between job characteristics and important outcomes such as productivity.

In the last five years, more and more Sino-foreign joint-venture companies have been established in China. By the end of 1989 about 12 000 such joint ventures have been put into operation. Therefore, the selection, training, performance appraisal, decision making and organizational culture for the joint ventures have become interesting and promising areas of I/O psychology in China. Currently, several research projects are going on in these joint ventures. It is expected that the results from joint venture studies will have important implications for the development of Chinese I/O psychology and for the Chinese economic reform program.

CONCLUSION

Chinese Approach of Industrial and Organizational Psychology

Industrial and organizational psychology in China has been developing very rapidly since 1978 when China adopted the open door policy and launched its economic reforms. A Chinese approach to I/O psychology has emerged from recent research and applications in Chinese industrial organizations. It has several important characteristics. The first characteristic of the Chinese approach to I/O psychology is its special attention to the Chinese social and cultural context in their research and practice. Efforts have been made to develop some Chinese models in I/O psychology, especially in areas such as work motivation, attribution, team effectiveness, organizational decision making and organization development. The second characteristic of the Chinese approach is the close link of I/O psychology research with economic reform activities in various organizations. Most of Chinese I/O psychology studies were in fact carried out in actual organizational settings, testing theories and solving practical management issues. The third characteristic of the Chinese approach is its emphasis upon joint efforts and collaboration between academics and practitioners. Many research projects are in fact planned and implemented under such joint efforts. There is also close collaboration between I/O psychologists and related governmental departments (e.g. bureaus of mechanical industry and oil industry) in research and applications of I/O psychology. This Chinese approach to I/O psychology has been quite effective in developing and applying I/O psychological principles in Chinese work situations.

New Directions

Industrial and organizational psychology in China is moving toward a higher level of research and application. A number of new trends have appeared recently in Chinese I/O psychology.

Theoretical development in I/O psychology

More attention is now paid to developing Chinese theories and models of I/O psychology. After a decade of research and practice, the system of Chinese I/O psychology has now been largely formed. Several Chinese models of leadership behavior have been proposed (e.g. Lin, Chen and Wang, 1987; Xu et al., 1985; Wu, 1986), as well as models of attribution (Wang, 1986, 1988a), team effectiveness (e.g. Chen, 1987; Lu, 1987), decision making (e.g. Chen, 1983; Wang, 1989a, 1990b), human–computer interface hierarchy theory (Wang, 1989b) and organization development (e.g. Chen, 1984; Wang, 1990a). More research is needed to link Chinese ancient thinking on work and management to current practice and theoretical development in Chinese I/O psychology. It is expected that more systematic theories of I/O psychology will be developed from Chinese research and practice.

Holistic approach for industrial psychology

With the development of I/O psychology in China, there has been a greater need for joint research by I/O psychologists and engineering psychologists in areas such as human–computer–organization interaction, job design, technological innovation, decision support systems, occupational stress and technical training. Chen (1988b) used the concept of macro-ergonomics (including I/O psychology and human factors) and proposed it as a broader framework for a holistic approach in Chinese industrial psychology. Many Chinese I/O psychologists are integrating useful principles from various branches of applied psychology in their research and applications.

Cross-cultural perspective

With the development of academic contacts and collaborations between Chinese I/O psychologists and colleagues abroad, more and more people adopt a cross-cultural perspective in I/O psychology research in China. It is especially useful as Sino-foreign joint ventures become an important part of the economic reform program in China. In recent years, several international joint research projects in I/O psychology have been carried out. A number of Sino-foreign joint training centers of management are playing an active role in personnel training and education, including the senior management training program in Dalian sponsored jointly by China and the United States and the

China–European Community Management Institute in Beijing. Through cross-cultural research and international comparison, one can often obtain a much better understanding of the organizational behavior in his/her own country and formulate more effective strategies for enhancing organizational performance and improving the quality of working life.

In general, great progress has been achieved in I/O psychology in the recent decade. Chinese I/O psychologists are putting their shoulders to the wheel to increase research in and applications of I/O psychology to the new economic reform and socialist modernizations.

ACKNOWLEDGEMENT

I would like to express my great appreciation to the Council for International Exchange of Scholars, USA, for the support of a Fulbright Scholarship (1990) at Old Dominion University, Norfolk, where this chapter was written. I especially wish to thank Donald D. Davis for his encouragement, help and valuable comments on earlier drafts. I would also like to express my appreciation to the Fok Ying-Tung Education Foundation at Chinese State Education Commission for the support of the National Excellent Young Teacher Award (1989).

Correspondence address
Professor Zhong-Ming Wang, Department of Psychology, Hangzhou University, Hangzhou 310028, Zhejiang, People's Republic of China.

REFERENCES

Chao, R. C. *et al.* (1966) Signal displays of central control room at power stations. *Acta Psychologica Sinica*, (Chinese), **1**, 27–58.

Chen, L. (Li) *et al.* (1959) Some psychological issues on training textile workers. *Acta Psychologica Sinica*, (Chinese), **1**, 42–49.

Chen, L. (Li) (1983) Essentials of Industrial Psychology (Chinese), Hangzhou: Zhejiang People's Press.

Chen, L. (Li) (1984) Action research. *Psychology Abroad* (Chinese), **3**, 2–5.

Chen, L. (Li) (1987) Recent research on organizational psychology in China. Paper presented at the Sixth Annual Conference of Chinese Psychology Society, September, Hangzhou.

Chen, L. (Li) (1988a) *Psychology of Industrial Management* (Chinese), Shanghai People's Press.

Chen, L. (Li) (1988b) Macro-ergonomics in industrial modernization. *Chinese Journal of Applied Psychology*, **3** (1), 1–4.

Chen, L. (Li) (1989) Organization development in China: Chinese version. *Chinese Journal of Applied Psychology*, **4** (1), 1–5.

China Daily Business Weekly (1988) The Law of the People's Republic of China on Industrial Enterprises Owned by the Whole People. Sunday, 15 May.

Hackman, J. R., & Oldham, G. P. (1980) *Work Redesign*. Reading Mass: Addison-Wesley.

Heller, F. A., & Wilpert, B. (1980) *Competence and Power in Managerial Decision Making*. New York: Wiley.

Huse, E. F. & Cummings, T. G. (1989) *Organization Development and Change* (3rd edn). St. Paul, MN: West Publishing.

IDE Research Group (1981) *Industrial Democracy in Europe* Oxford: Clarendon Press.

Jin, P. T. (1983) Work motivation and productivity as influenced by group participative decision making, group cohesiveness and task interdependence. Unpublished master's thesis, Hangzhou University, China.

Li, C. G., Song X. H., & Li J. (1989) *An Introduction to Chinese Ancient Civil Service Systems* (Chinese). Labour and Personnel Press.

Liang, K. G. (1986) Factors influencing work motivation and satisfaction among enterprise managers and directors. Unpublished master's thesis, Hangzhou University, China.

Lin W. Q., Chen L. (Long), & Wang D. (1987) The construction of the CPM Scale for leadership behavior assessment, *Acta Psychologica Sinica* (Chinese), **19**(2), 199–207.

Lu, M. (1987) The criteria and characteristics of excellent work groups, Unpublished master's thesis, Hangzhou University, China.

Lu, S. Z., Wu L. L., Zheng, Q. Q., & Wang, Z. M. (1985) *Managerial Psychology* (Chinese). Zhejiang Educational Press.

Misumi, J. (1985) *The Behavioral Science of Leadership*. Ann Arbor: University of Michigan Press.

Misumi, J., & Peterson, M. F. (1985) The performance and maintenance theory (PM) of leadership: Review of a Japanese research program. *Administrative Science Quarterly*, **30**, 198–223.

Wan, L. (1986) An important topic in political system reform: democratic and scientific decision making. *People's Daily* (Chinese), 15 August, Beijing.

Wang, G. (1984) The necessity and feasibility of participative management in Chinese companies. Unpublished master's thesis, Hangzhou University, China.

Wang, Z. M. (1986) Worker's attribution and its effects on performance under different job responsibility systems. *Chinese Journal of Applied Psychology*, **1**, (2), 6–10.

Wang, Z. M. (1988a) *Work and Personnel Psychology*. (Chinese), Zhejiang Educational Press.

Wang, Z. M. (1988b) The effects of responsibility system change and group attributional training on performance: A quasi-experiment in Chinese factory. *Chinese Journal of Applied Psychology*, **3** (3), 7–14.

Wang, Z. M., & Wang, Y. B. (1989) Some characteristics and strategies of personnel decisions in Chinese enterprises, *Chinese Journal of Applied Psychology*, **4**(3), 8–14.

Wang, Z. M. (1989a) Participation and skill utilization in organizational decision making in Chinese enterprises. In B. J. Fallon, H. P. Pfister and J. Brebner (eds), *Advances in Industrial Organizational Psychology*, pp. 19–26, Amsterdam: Elsevier.

Wang, Z. M. (1989b) Human–computer interface hierarchy model and strategies in systems development. *Ergonomics*, special issue on cognitive ergonomics, **32** (11), 1391–1400.

Wang, Z. M. (1990a) Action research and OD strategies in Chinese enterprises. *Organization Development Journal*, Spring: 66–70.

Wang, Z. M. (1990b) Information structures and cognitive strategies in decision making on systems development. *Ergonomics*, special issue on ergonomics in China, **33** (7), 907–923.

Wu, L. L. (1986) A job analysis of management cadres in enterprises, *Chinese Journal of Applied Psychology*, **1**, (3), 12–16.

Wu, X. L. (1987) Group goal-directed behaviors in Chinese enterprise management. Unpublished master's thesis, Hangzhou University, China.

Xu, L. C. (1987) Recent development in organizational psychology in China, In Bass, B. (ed.), *Advances in Organizational Psychology: An International Review*, pp. 242–251. Sage.

Xu, L. C., & Chen L. (Long) (1988) Managerial Psychology (Chinese), *People's Daily Press*.

Xu, L. C., Chen L. (Long), Wang D., & Xue A. Y. (1985) The role of psychology in enterprise management. *Acta Psychologica Sinica* (Chinese). **17** (4), 339–345.

Xu, L. C., & Wang, Z. M. (1990) New development in organizational psychology in China, *International Journal of Applied Psychology* (in press).

Xu, X. D. (1986) Effects of production quota increase on workers' performance. *Information on Psychological Sciences* (Chinese), No. 2, 36–42.

Yang, X. S. (1983) Behavioural Sciences (Chinese), Shanghai: Enterprise Management Press.

Yu, W. Z. (1985) Measurement of group social psychological climate and team management in enterprises. *Information on Psychological Science* (Chinese), No. 4, 15–21.

Zhong, J. A. (1989) Perception of job characteristics and satisfaction among assembly-line workers. *Chinese Journal of Applied Psychology*, **4** (2), 14–21.

Chapter 2

MEDIATED COMMUNICATION AND NEW ORGANIZATIONAL FORMS

J. H. Erik Andriessen
University of Technology
Delft
The Netherlands

INTRODUCTION: ONLY VARIETY CAN BEAT VARIETY

Many organizations have to cope with major changes. General societal and economic developments increasingly require international orientation, geographical distribution, a shorter 'time to market', increased flexibility of the production process and of the work-force because of the dynamics of the product market. These developments have resulted in sometimes dramatic changes in organizational structure and functioning, reflected in phenomena such as 'just in time' logistics, decentralization of decision-making and 'externalization of labour'.

This later phenomenon is particularly reflected in 'buy or make' decisions and subcontracting, which has increased sharply in the past few years (FAST, 1988, p. 90). Another important development is the shift in employment from manufacturing industry to service industry. In Europe employment in manufacturing industry has decreased to 33% of total employment, in the USA to 28% (FAST, 1988). Employment in the service sectors, both private and public, is growing, which means that the number of 'information workers' or 'knowledge workers' (Reese, 1988), i.e. professional, managerial and clerical personnel, is rising at the cost of blue-collar workers. Information exchange and communication between individuals are therefore becoming even more essential to organizations. They are the vehicles for transactions, coordination and control.

Managers and professionals play a central role in these processes. A large part of their task has always consisted of communication activities, preferably face to face (Mintzberg, 1973; Bair, 1987; Krcmar, 1989). The developments

International Review of Industrial and Organizational Psychology 1991 Volume 6
Edited by C. L. Cooper and I. T. Robertson © 1991 John Wiley & Sons Ltd.

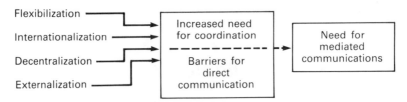

Figure 1   Barriers and needs for communication

mentioned above imply more barriers, however, to direct data exchange and face-to-face communication, while at the same time a growing need for information exchange, coordination and cooperation is becoming visible (see Figure 1).

The question is to what extent new media and mediated communication play or can play a role in organizations facing external turbulence and internal differentiation. The old adage 'organizational differentiation requires organizational coordination' implies that new forms of coordination have to be developed. New forms can for instance be found in new organizational structures and processes such as project teams. Coordination is, however, also increasingly sought via technical means, i.e. via information and telecommunication technology. In this field two developments can be distinguished (see next section): electronic exchange of administrative data, and electronic communication between people. Firms in the electronics and telecommunication sector and also academic institutions have been among the leaders in building large networks for electronic mail. Such networks are now being introduced more and more in other organizations and integrated with information systems, with distributed data processing and with electronic data interchange between firms. At the same time groups of managers and professionals are beginning to use electronic means to support small-scale meetings.

The research evidence presented in this chapter will show that the real issue is not what is technically feasible but what is organizationally desirable and possible. Technological deterministic theory might induce researchers to study the direct impact of the new technologies on human behaviour and organizational functioning. In this section, however, the view is held that the implications of mediated communication are a function of the human, (inter)organizational and 'political' forces that shape the situation.

Basic to this issue is the question of what the role and functions of communication in organizations are and to what extent these can be supported by electronic means. Communication can in the first instance be viewed as the exchange of data between two sources via an encoding and decoding process and a channel. Encoding, decoding and channel distortion (noise) can cause the communication to fail. Redundancy can to some extent neutralize noise. This view is useful for more or less technical analysis of simple information exchange processes. However, a distinction should be made between data exchange processes, information exchange and human communication. 'Raw' text, figures and images are data. Information exists where meaning is discerned in a pattern of data (Farace, Monge, & Russell, 1977). Human communication concerns the exchange of information between people in a social context, and thereby the exchange of meaning. This implies that two fundamental aspects of interpersonal communication have to be distinguished,—information concerning the actual content of a message, and information concerning the meaning, the interpretation of the message. The way in which something is said and the context in which a message is given are important for the interpretation of that message. These are termed the 'content' and the 'relation' aspects (also called 'metacommunication', Watzlawick, Beavin, & Jackson, 1967). This relational aspect is to a large degree based on non-verbal communication signals (cf. Burgoon, et al., 1984), on the existing social rules for speech utterances (Littlejohn, 1989, p. 116), and on the social (i.e. organizational) setting. The work group often forms the most direct context. Organization-wide structures, rules and processes, however, also determine to a large extent the communication structures and processes (Farace, Monge, & Russell, 1977; O'Reilly & Pondy, 1979).

The focus here will be mainly on electronically mediated and supported communication, not on office or production automation *per se*. The elements of office automation (document creation, data or image storage and retrieval, data analysis (MIS, DSS) and expert systems) or of production automation (CNC machines, CAD, CAM, etc.) will hardly be touched upon. Central to this discussion is the exchange of data, information and meaning between people in organizations, particularly managers, professionals, and office workers.

The subject of this chapter impinges on diverse fields of knowledge. Researchers and scientific circuits from widely divergent disciplines are involved: Organizational communication as such is studied, on the one hand, by organization scientists and, on the other, by communication scientists. Apart from organizational communication in general, one can distinguish at least three other relevant research traditions, i.e. the mainly social science oriented fields of computer mediated communication (CMC) on the one hand and telework on the other, and the computer science oriented field of computer supported cooperative work (CSCW).

Due to the lack of integration between these research areas and disciplines, the subject of mediated communication in the organizational context is highly fragmented. The present chapter is an attempt at integration of these fragments.

The chapter is structured as follows. In the next section the development of technical systems for mediated communication is presented, followed by a section on organizational applications such as those indicated by the term 'telework'.

Following this the next section reviews studies concerning the functioning and effects of these applications, after which the conditions for successful functioning are discussed. In the penultimate section the many fragments are brought together and confronted with (inter)organizational theory. The chapter ends with recommendations for research and design.

SYSTEMS FOR COMMUNICATION SUPPORT

In the previous section terms such as 'information and communication (IC) technology', 'communication' and 'media' have been used more or less interchangeably. When analysing the potential impact and implications of certain technologies a more precise specification and definition is needed. For this chapter it is relevant to distinguish between three levels of technology, namely the basic elements and infrastructures of IC technology, technical applications and organizational applications (see also Roe, 1991).

Information and Telecommunication Technology

In a certain sense telecommunication has a very old tradition. Indian smoke signals, the African drum, and the use of carrier-pigeons are the best-known examples. Radio, television, and the telephone are perfectly normal means of telecommunication. The telephone in particular has a substantial impact on organizational functioning, although this has received only minor attention (Sola Pool, 1977, 1988; Claisse & Rowe, 1987).

During the past two or three decades, new technical developments in the fields of miniaturization, data processing, data storage and data transport, not only for text and figures but recently also for images, have brought a whole range of new applications for communication. Future developments will probably even increase the rate of change in this area. Of particular relevance would seem to be the future standardization and improvement of telecommunication infrastructures and networks (the Integrated Services Digital Network, ISDN, and later the Broadband ISDN), which can process integrated text, voice and image information. The political issues raised by ISDN for the European Community are discussed by Weltevreden (1991) and the possible negative aspects of these developments by Kubicek (Kubicek & Fischer, 1988; Kubicek, 1991).

The result of this integration is often indicated by the term *telematics*. This term was used for the first time by two French authors, Nora & Minc (1980), to describe and predict the societal applications of these integrated technologies. The term 'teleinformatics' is also used.

A systematic discussion of the developments concerning the basic elements of IC technology is beyond the scope of this chapter.

Technical Applications and Services

Of particular relevance for mediated communication are technical applications such as databases and sophisticated data retrieval systems (e.g. hypertext), systems for the exchange of information (e.g. electronic mail), video networks, and software for the structuring of group activities (decision systems, brainstorming modules, etc.), and the services based on these applications.

Organizational Applications

The technical applications and services are used for certain organizational functions and activities, such as telework, small group meetings, the exchange of administrative data and interpersonal coordination over large distances. The specific forms these organizational applications will take will be termed 'work arrangements'. In this section the technical applications to mediate communications and some indications concerning their occurrence are presented. In the next section some organizational applications known under the umbrella term 'telework' are discussed.

The *functions of organizational information exchange* can be divided into six categories. In Figure 2 they are related to three kinds of communication (based on Bordewijk & van Kaam, 1982; Hacker & Milano, 1988; Bair, 1989; Roe, 1991; see Figure 2). For each of these kinds of communication, technical support systems have been developed.

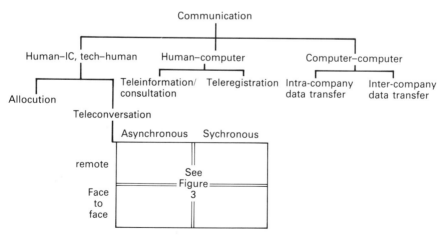

Figure 2 Types of mediated communication

1. Systems to support human to human communication: (a) unilateral information distribution to an audience, called 'allocution', e.g. radio broadcasting; (b) bilateral exchange of information: *teleconversation* systems, with the function of coordination, and cooperation in organizations.
2. Human–computer communication. This can take two forms, depending on who takes the initiative: (a) *information/consultation* systems: information systems make available large databases; consultation systems do not only provide general information but can also give personalized 'advice'; a mortgage system, for instance, may actually contain a model for the calculation of a particular mortgage; (b) *registration* systems whereby central databases gather information from human or from non-human sources: tele-ordering, automated polling, but also monitoring air pollution.
3. Computer–computer communication: electronic exchange of standardized administrative data beween computers, for internal data transfer or for transactions between organizations. The latter is often called electronic data interchange (EDI).

The differences between these systems are absolutely essential. The issue is confused, however, partly because all these systems are sometimes subsumed under the terms 'information systems' or 'office information', and partly because the separate functions are combined more and more in integrated services.

Nevertheless this chapter is focused mainly on systems for human–human communication. This means that consultation, information, registration, and transaction systems will receive less attention than conversation and allocution systems.

An enormously rapid increase can be observed in the use of transactions between firms through EDI-type systems for the electronic exchange of standardized data concerning products (see e.g. Hansen & Hill, 1989). Doing away with the repeated filling in and filing of more or less the same forms means a great improvement in efficiency. Although developments in this field are potentially very relevant for the discussion of organizational forms, social science research on this topic is still very scarce.

The category of conversation systems contains many widely divergent systems. They can be categorized in terms of three dimensions (based on Johansen, 1988, and Bair, 1989; see Figure 3).

The first two dimensions are related to the problem of how to communicate with other persons who are in a remote place and/or who cannot (and need not) be consulted at the same time. The solution is found in communication systems which allow for communication 'at a distance' (instead of face to face) and/or communication 'distributed in time' or 'asynchronous' instead of 'real time' communication. Asynchronous communication implies that messages are stored, and forwarded when it suits the addressee. These two dimensions are comparable with Lievrouw & Finn's (1988) dimensions of 'involvement' and 'temporality'.

The third dimension is that of 'allowed structure'. It refers to the extent to which a communication system allows for (or imposes) structure to an interaction. Broadcasting information is a rather unstructured activity; coordinating work activities sometimes asks for interaction structures such as a calendar system hooked to the electronic mail system (e-mail). Close cooperation is in certain systems supported by even more structured 'communication modules' such as voting systems (see 'cooperation systems' below). The more complex the interaction the more structure is sometimes required (Bair, 1989). Structured systems are often provided with sophisticated databases in which the results of the interaction are systematically stored.

The third dimension is reflected in the figures between brackets, which signify the following:

(1) = mainly for widespread information distribution;
(2) = can be used for coordination and mutual adjustment;
(3) = can be used for structured group cooperation.

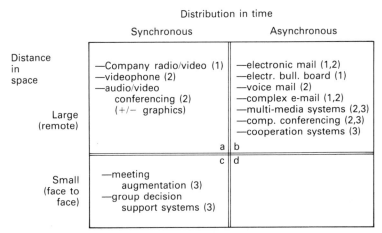

NB 1. = Mainly for widespread information distribution;
    2. = Can be used for coordination and mutual adjustment;
    3. = Can be used for structured group cooperation.

The examples in the figure are not exhaustive

Figure 3 Computer supported 'conversation' systems

Widespread use is made of the relatively simple 'electronic message systems' such as electronic mail, i.e. systems for transmitting short messages to everyone who is on the network. Other systems mentioned in cell b are much more complex. These systems support and structure cooperation and decision-making processes of people who are involved in a common task. The systems in Figure 3 are often called 'computer mediated communication systems'. Strictly speaking, however, this term is not correct. Firstly, some (older) audio and video systems do not involve computers, secondly, 'meeting augmentation' systems and group decision support systems (GDSSs) (cell c) do not mediate but only support communication, and thirdly the term 'communication systems' can also apply to human computer and computer–computer systems (see Figure 2). We therefore prefer to call the total range of systems in Figure 3 'computer supported conversation systems' (CSC systems). Another widely used term for more or less the same media is 'groupware' (Johansen, 1988).

In view of their role in organizational processes it appears to be fruitful to present the systems clustered into three categories:

1. Audio/video systems;
2. Electronic message system (EMS), i.e. the relatively simple systems for electronic mail, voice mail and multi-media systems (see Figure 3, cell b);
3. Cooperation supporting systems, i.e. the complex systems in Figure 3, cells c and b.

The various systems are, however, not mutually exclusive. Increasingly, CSC systems are combining features of various cells. The complex multi-media systems of the future will be able to communicate both in real time and asynchronously, both augmenting a face-to-face meeting as well as supporting distributed groups, possibly combining graphic screens and video, and in all cases making available the relevant databases (see e.g. Kündig, 1988).

The nature and use of the various systems presented in Figure 3 will now be discussed.

Audio/video systems

Telephone. Although communication by telephone is the most common form of mediated communication, very little research on the use and implication of this medium in organizations is being done. Strangely enough, parallel to the recent growth of so many new forms of mediated communication the interest in the telephone is also increasing (see e.g. Sola Pool, 1988; Rutter, 1987; Claisse & Rowe, 1987).

Company radio/video. Company radio as a means for distributing information about a firm has existed for a long time. There is, however, no literature concerning its use or effects.

Company video has actually two faces. Some companies are currently sending videotapes to all their establishments for the purpose of distributing information about the company and in that way building corporate identity (Werther, 1988). The second meaning of the term 'company video', or 'business television', applies to an in-company television network allowing the dissemination of common information from a central location to multiple sites simultaneously. Ruchinskas, Svenning & Steinfield (1990) report on a large company where business television was used 'for informing distributors, dealers, or field offices of new product lines, providing regular company updates, motivating a nationally or internationally dispersed sales force.'

Videophone; audio and video conferencing. Videophone and video conferencing are two applications of video technology in organizations. Videophone refers to a replacement for the normal telephone for bilateral communication. Videophone applications have met with very little success because the technical and financial demands are very high and the advantage over telephone connections negligible. A recent experiment involving multi media support for distributed but cooperating groups even showed that most participants preferred to use the videophone network only in exceptional cases because they did not want to be watched all the time (Smith, Zigurs & Pacanowsky, 1990).

Audio/video conferencing implies a geographically distributed meeting connected by telephone or through video channels. Audio conferencing services have been offered for many years. They are used to a certain extent but not widely. The reason is believed to lie in the fact that the rules for successfully conducting a telephone conference are very strict, and because of poor audio quality due to bandwidth limitation (Romahn & Mühlbach, 1988).

According to a survey conducted in The Netherlands among users of telephone conferences (PTT, 1987), time-saving is the main reason for making use of this medium, which apparently is useful only for quite short meetings (on average 30–45 minutes) of a small group of people (average six people).

The more sophisticated video systems provide the facility of seeing all, or at least several, participants on the screen at once, and also of adding text and graphic information. This last feature makes video conferencing a real computer-supported system. In the USA video conferencing was already operational in the 1970s. According to a survey by Dutton, Fulk, and Steinfield (1982), AT & T had facilities in 12 cities, used by hundreds of firms, although only a few reported regular use. Top managers and marketing professionals, in particular, used the facility, mainly for interorganizational exchange of information and opinions, and for group decision-making. Highly interpersonal activities such as conflict resolution, negotiation, and persuasion were seldom carried on via video conferencing (see also Short, Williams, & Christie, 1976; Wellens, 1986).

A number of national postal and telecommunication services in Europe have also carried out experiments in this field. Ruchinskas, Svenning, & Steinfield (in press) report on a study showing that some firms make very intensive use of their in-company video system, e.g. for 'staff meetings, project/program reviews, design meetings, problem solving, crisis intervention, interviewing, negotiating and training'. Video conferencing has, however, met with rather meagre success, partly because it is very expensive. Recently interest seems to be growing again (Gale, 1989) probably because the availability of ISDN will reduce telecommunication costs substantially. Moreover, advances in video compressing technology have greatly reduced the amount of bandwidth required to transmit full motion video, and the development of high-powered high resolution personal computers makes desktop video conferencing possible. Systems based on desktop facilities, called 'multipoint videoconferencing', are being developed (Rohmahn & Mühlbach, 1988).

Electronic message systems

Electronic mail and distribution list.   Basic to quite a few applications is the electronic mail system, connecting people who have a personal computer (PC) which is linked to a network. A network can be limited to a small local area network of a few PCs or be as extensive as Bitnet, a global network connecting, in particular, researchers at universities. This is an asynchronous system based on the principle of storing a message in the electronic postbox of the addressee and forwarding it whenever he is ready to receive it. Electronic mail systems are almost always provided with a distribution list facility which implies that one can send a message at the same time to all those who are on such a list. This facility has allowed e-mail systems to evolve into a medium for 'broadcasting', i.e. for the distribution of information (Steinfield & Fulk, 1988; Rice & Steinfield, 1991).

Electronic mail systems are widely used, not only by academics but also in companies. Most of their reported use is for general information exchange, the asking of questions and problem solving.

Pocock (1987) describes the situation at a company where the system is used by managers to send around letters and notes accompanied by the request for colleagues to add comments and paragraphs. In some multinational companies the number of users runs into the tens of thousands (Skyrme, 1989). By 1987, over 1.3 million commercial mailboxes were being used in the USA to exchange 14 million messages per month (Rice et al., 1990). Until now voice mail has not had the enthusiastic reception afforded to electronic mail. According to Finn (personal communication) e-mail is widely accepted because it is perceived to be a (faster) substitute for normal letters, while voice mail is perceived as a slower version of the normal synchronous telephone contact.

Complex e-mail and multi-media systems. Originally e-mail systems were quite simple. Gradually they are becoming more complex through the addition of various features. Two of these sophisticated e-mail systems are described below. Even more complex systems are presented under the headings 'computer conferencing' and 'cooperation systems'.

1. It is a quite common experience for people using e-mail to feel flooded with large quantities of 'junk mail', resulting in 'information overload' (see e.g. Denning, 1982; Hiltz & Turoff, 1985). A solution is to develop intelligent e-mail systems which include features for filtering and ordering messages (e.g. Malone *et al.*, 1987).
2. A second way in which e-mail systems become more complex is through the addition of media for voice and images (see e.g. Postel *et al.*, 1988).

Multi-media systems for office communication include, for instance, features for adding handwritten and spoken comments to documents and storing them digitally. Another example of multi-media systems is the digital image network in and between hospitals which radiologists and physicians use for access to and communication concerning patient images and other patient data (Andriessen, 1990).

Voice messaging. Voice messaging is a computer-aided telephone system capable of storing and forwarding digitized spoken messages. It is comparable to e-mail, with the difference that it is accessible via a normal telephone, and that the messages are voice based instead of text based. It can act as a telephone answering service (called 'voice answering'), but according to Stewart (1986) its real strength emerges when it is used for 'closed-community' messaging, meaning that it serves as an electronic messaging system among a group of users (called 'voice messaging', Rice & Steinfield, 1991). Users may record and send messages asynchronously to another user's mailbox. Other common features are: saving, deleting or redirecting messages, confirmation of delivery and the use of distribution lists and message notification to the addressee (Stewart, 1986; Rice & Shook, 1988). According to a review by Rice & Shook (1990), the first major commercial voice messaging system was installed in 1980. By early 1985 nine of the top 30 Fortune 500 companies were using voice message systems, and the market is expected to have trebled by 1990.

Cooperation supporting systems

Computer conferencing. When e-mail messages are not (or not only) sent to specific addressees but remain stored centrally and are accessible to all network users, the term 'electronic bulletin board' is used. This feature is developed one step further in 'computer conferencing' (CC), in which specified groups of network users participate in electronic discussions on certain topics. Unlike e-mail, messages are not directed to and filed by individuals but are stored in a collective space, according to topic or other filing categories. Conferences can in principle last indefinitely. Whereas e-mail is in principle a 'one to many' analogue of physical mail and telephony, CC is a 'many to many' analogue to face-to-face meetings.

The pioneers of CC systems have been Turoff and Hiltz at the New Jersey Institute of Technology, where they developed the early but already quite sophisticated system called EIES (Hiltz & Turoff, 1978). EIES includes various features which are discussed below.

According to Johansen (1988), CC has been technically possible since about 1970, but few organizations have really taken advantage of its full potential. It has proved very difficult to get people used to CC as a general-purpose medium of communication. Commercial systems are available, but only some private in-house systems are completely successful. Skyrme (1989) reports on the very widespread use of the VAX-NOTES system by the Digital Equipment Corporation. The system is used, among other things, for discussing proposals, co-authoring reports, for brainstorming and for opinion surveys within the company.

An interesting example of a conferencing system, alongside sophisticated EDI-type data exchange is to be found within the Colruyt Company (Taillieu, 1990).

The Colruyt Company

The Colruyt organization is a concern consisting of 17 companies and is developed from a chain of supermarkets in Belgium. The head of the organization, J. Colruyt, has invested heavily during the past 20 years in information technology. Daily data concerning prices, the buying behaviour of customers and sales are exchanged between the stores and head office. The company is linked to suppliers by means of an electronic ordering system.

These systems are the tools of a company characterized by almost aggressive market strategies and tactics and internally by a very cohesive and egalitarian culture. The corporate message is clear: to sell high-quality brands at the lowest possible price, with the target being a 1% profit on sales. The policy used to achieve this includes the following elements:

—basic facilities only in the supermarkets;
—maximum use of automation and information technology;
—a minimum of mainly full-time, all-round personnel, well paid, trained and willing to work hard;
—staff fully informed on company policy at all times to involve them permanently in trying to improve the organization and to beat the competition.

Separate from its logistic systems, Colruyt introduced in the mid-1970s the interactive system for information distribution (ISIV), an e-mail system which is used intensively throughout the organization. Every year more than 120 000 messages are exchanged. These have a standardized heading and are all filed systematically via keywords (to be given by the sender). Employees who are interested in a specific topic register their interest, thus constituting a 'network'. Examples of the topics are: heating, software, hierarchy etc. The number of networks so far totals about 900, all the messages of which are still on file. In order to counter the tendency to waste paper, money and time, every message shows its cost of production and distribution. Messages are printed every night by two central laser printers. They are collected and sorted automatically. Everyone receives a copy of his/her own messages, of messages directed to him/her, messages sent by subordinates, and information about the networks of which he or she is a member. Outsiders (suppliers, clients, etc.) can also be members of networks. In total about 10–15% of the messages are confidential.

People are encouraged to use this system because this is considered to be the only way in which information can be used efficiently, feedback and mutual adjustment between departments guaranteed, and maximum flexibility achieved.

Group decision support systems. Store-and-forward computer systems support asynchronous communication as distinct from synchronous (real-time) communication. However, 'real-time' meetings, both at the same place and over distances are also increasingly supported by computers. When face-to-face meetings are supported by 'electronic blackboards' (central screen connected to a personal computer), and other relatively simple devices, we are dealing with 'meeting augmentation'. When information systems are added for task-oriented activities such as planning or decision-making, the term 'group decision support systems' is used. This type of meeting support system is used by groups of managers, for example, to decide—in one or several real-time meetings—on the yearly budget, or by a group of researchers to find a solution to a certain problem.

According to Huber (1984), the need for such systems is a consequence of the clash of two important forces: (1) the environmentally imposed demand for more information sharing in organizations, and (2) resistance to the allocation of more managerial and professional time to attendance at meetings. Kraemer & King (1986) concluded on the basis of a survey, however, that these systems have met with limited success, partly because the systems themselves were not sufficiently highly developed.

A GDSS proper is limited to the above-mentioned task-oriented activities. Recent years have, however, seen a 'merging' with systems which are less oriented to decision-making and more to group communication activities. This field is sometimes called computer supported cooperative work (CSCW) (see e.g. Greif, 1988; Dennis *et al.*, 1988). The main functions of these systems are (Turoff, Hiltz & Bahgat, 1989):

—Providing structure for communication protocols and human roles that are part of the group process;
—Supporting the collection, organization, filtering, formatting, feedback and retrieval of any and all material (text, data, graphics) generated or required by the group to support its deliberations;
—Integration and utilization of sophisticated decision aids in support of the group process (e.g. structural modelling, games and simulations, statistical analysis and forecasting, etc.).

Turoff, Hiltz, and Bahgat (1989) argue that there is no good reason to restrict the above-mentioned functions to real-time meetings. In fact, they consider the success achieved with real-time GDSSs to be quite limited. They make a plea for the development of asynchronous GDSSs, and therefore add a fourth function:

—Providing alternative communication channels for the group. This is the process of allowing a group to work more efficiently and/or more effectively with text, structured data and graphics without regard to the limitations of synchronous meetings.

One of the first of such systems was developed for the US government to support decision-making during national emergencies. For over a decade it was used in some 20 or more federal crisis situations such as commodity shortages and major strikes (Hiltz & Turoff, 1978; Turoff, Hiltz & Bahgat 1989).

Some argue that GDSSs are particularly useful when large groups of people (tens or even hundreds) are involved. For small groups, improvements in output are sometimes negligible. Since it is very difficult to structure the communication of large groups, it can be very fruitful to support this with computer systems. Particularly for complex issues, there is difficulty in creating a common interpretation and image. Groupware programs can help with this (Robinson, 1988).

Desanctis and Gallupe (1988) distinguish three levels of GDSS. Level 1 includes relatively simple communication-supporting features for message transmission and receipt, agenda and calendar setting, brainstorming and voting. Level 2 GDSSs provide decision modelling and group decision techniques such as planning models, budget allocation models, delphi techniques, etc. Level 3 GDSSs are characterized by machine-induced group communication patterns. This last category in particular has recently received much attention, considering the contributions to the conferences on CSCW (Peterson, 1986; ACM, 1988; Proceedings, 1989). Wilson (1988) presents four traditions in this area:

1. Systems which have grown out of the e-mail tradition. At the end of the 1970s Hiltz and Turoff (1978) had already developed the EIES system, while Palme in Sweden constructed the COM system (Palme, 1988). Recently much more complex but also more structuring systems have been developed (e.g. Santo, 1988; Young, 1988).
2. Systems in the office automation tradition, which add features to office procedures in order to support group communication.
3. Systems based on speech act theory, a theory concerning the rules which govern interpersonal communication.
4. The above-mentioned synchronous Group Decision Support Systems.

This whole category of electronic meeting and cooperation systems is of very recent origin. The literature deals almost exclusively with the formal possibilities. In practice, empirical data on the implications hardly exists. The few results in this area are discussed in the section on Effects (p. 37).

Relevant characteristics

Every medium has its advantages and disadvantages, even face-to-face contact, which is sometimes considered the ideal form of communication. The advantage of a normal meeting is its large 'bandwidth', i.e. all kinds of verbal and non-verbal signals can be used to interpret the content of the utterances. However, it requires the physical attendance of several people at the same time, and the information generated (the spoken words) are difficult to register systematically and to process.

The characteristics which make electronic message systems attractive are the following: (1) *asynchronicity*; (2) the *distributionlist* facility; (3) *systematic storage potential*; (4) *processing facilities*. Rice (1987a; see also Rice & Steinfield 1991) presents four sets of variables to describe and compare all kinds of communication media:

1. *Constraints*: the extent to which the user (a) can identify the sender; (b)

must know the other communicator, and his/her address; (c) must be temporally or geographically proximate; (d) has access to the medium for initiating the process; (e) is able to store the message; (f) can retrief the content at a later time; (g) can reprocess the content of the message.

2. *Bandwidth*: the extent to which the medium allows the representation of different communication modes such as text, auditory and visual signals, gestures, and other non-verbal signals.

3. *Interaction*: the extent to which the medium allows (a) quickness of response; (b) the ability to terminate the communication; (c) the exchange of roles; (d) communicating at the same time.

4. *Network factors*: the extent to which the medium involves (a) different communication patterns (one-to-one, one-to-many or many-to-many); (b) distortion: does the pattern of communication inherently delay communications, or overload certain users? (c) different communication roles: e.g. gatekeepers, liaisons; (d) critical mass: are multiple other interacting users necessary for the system to have value?

In order to be able to characterize cooperation systems sufficiently the following aspects have to be added:

5. The extent to which the system structures the interaction;
6. Degree of member control over the system.

TELEWORK AND COMPUTER SUPPORTED COMMUNICATION

Organization members have been able to use electronic systems to exchange both administrative data and free messages over long distances and distributed in time. This exchange of data and information has played a major role in various new working arrangements. For some of these forms the terms 'telework' or 'distance working' have been used.

Telework has been defined as follows (Olson, 1988, p. 77). 'Organizational work performed outside of the normal organizational confines of space and time, augmented by computer and communications technology.' It is often associated with simple administrative office work, such as word processing or data entry, that is performed at home at a personal computer. The output is then sent to the office either on a diskette or electronically via a telephone connection. However, such clerical homework is only one form of telework, although still the most frequent.

In the 1960s and 1970s various authors and reports already argued that in the 1990s a large proportion of the working population would in one way or another participate in telework (cited in Korte, 1988). These predictions were based on two assumptions, the first of which was correct, the other incorrect. The first assumption held that the new information and communication technology would make possible all kinds of flexible work arrangements. The second assumption, based on a 'technological determinism' perspective, held that what could be done technologically would always be applied. The reality turned out to be very different. According to surveys in 1987, West Germany and the UK have a few thousand teleworkers, France and Italy less than 1000, and the USA approximately 10 000 (Korte, 1988). Comparing studies over the past decade, there appears to be a slow but steady increase in the number of teleworkers.

These figures, however, pertain to a narrow definition of teleworkers, i.e. people who perform a well-defined task (typing, programming, etc.) at home, using information and telecommunication technology. Olson's definition, however, also includes people in managerial, technical, sales or other professional occupations who take work home or who visit customers, conferences and other places far from their headquarters.

Moreover, there appear to be quite a few homeworkers who do not make use of information and communication technology. According to a national survey in the USA in 1982, 30% of office workers systematically took work home (Kraut, 1987b). Other surveys (Kraut, 1987a; Olson, 1988) reveal that up to half of the employed professionals work regularly from home. The time spent working at home appears, however, to be independent of the time people spend working in the office (Olson, 1989). Another survey revealed that of large groups of homeworkers 23–45% had no computer at all (Olson, 1989). According to a large-scale research project in four major European countries (Korte, 1988), about 25% of the employees whose work is suitable for being performed as more or less regular electronic homework are interested in this type of work arrangement.

The above findings indicate two things. Firstly, the potential for telework—in terms of technical support, interest amongst employees and already existing habits of taking work home—appears to be quite strong, while at the same time teleworkers other than the professional, en route or now and then at home with his (portable) PC, are very hard to find in actual practice. The main reason for this discrepancy, and for the failure for earlier predictions to be borne out, appears to be organizational inertia and managerial resistance (see next section).

Secondly, the term 'telework', although quite clear at first sight, appears to be used in a number of very different ways. The enthusiasm with which telework is discussed in journals and at conferences (see e.g. Korte, Robinson, & Steinle, 1988) suggests that it might be identified as a separate phenomenon.

On closer scrutiny there are, however, grave doubts about the usefulness of the concept. This can be made clear when one considers the various forms of telework that have been distinguished (e.g. Korte, Robinson, & Steinle, 1988; FAST, 1988):

Homeworking: 'Paid employment undertaken by a person working entirely or for the most part at home, with visits to the site of the employer or client' (FAST, 1988). Homeworkers can be divided rather clearly into administrative workers—mainly women—who perform simple word-processing or data-processing activities, and professionals, such as programmers. The first kind of homework is more widespread than the second. There are, however, various companies which employ homeworking programmers. Examples of other professional homeworkers are hard to find, except one, a company called F International (Shirley, 1988).

F International

This organization is a computer systems and software company in the UK. It has about 1100 'employees' of whom about 250 are employed mainly part-time and about 850 are freelance. The freelance employees are contracted for flexible hours on specific projects. There is a very small company headquarters with a few office-based staff, and 11 small offices distributed over a large area. Practically all 1100 employees are, however, full teleworkers. The majority of the people are in computing and telecommunications. However, all the other organizational functions of administration and support, together with the work of managers and secretaries, are also largely executed at home. The homeworkers often have very sophisticated office communication technology, including fax machines, e-mail and teletex, at their disposal.

The main reason for the development of this organizational formula was the lack of availability of a skilled workforce. By contracting home-based professionals (predominantly female) who could work whenever it suited them, F International could build up a very flexible organization. Even when people move to a remote city they can keep working for the company.

According to a survey, many employees do not generally look to the company for social stimulus. This may be explained by the fact that over half of the homeworkers are mothers with children under school age. This does not imply, however, that they spend all their time at home. Quite regularly they complement the electronic communication with colleagues by visits to one of the offices, or by visiting customers.

The advantages of the low overhead costs required for office accommodation, etc. is offset by other costs, particularly those of communication equipment and training. Both workers and managers receive intensive and repeated training in handling the particular aspects of cooperation at a distance.

A *satellite office* is an office of an enterprise located at or near the place where groups of employees live. The office is therefore not a functional unit but a workplace for all kinds of employees, who are connected to their own department by means of telecommunication facilities. In Germany one example houses mainly programmers, not only from the parent organization but also from other companies (FAST, 1988).

A *community hall/neighbourhood office/shared facility* is a work centre, equipped with various electronic facilities, used by a number of people who are unable to afford such facilities at home. The centres also offer additional opportunities such as training schemes and conference suites (FAST, 1988). Some examples can be found in Scandinavian countries where inhabitants of remote villages can be linked to their companies or to other places through this communal facility. The users can be self-employed or employees of distant companies.

Subcontracting. The general trend towards subcontracting activities that were previously carried out within a company has been expanded by Xerox into a special networking project. In this project former employees are trained and helped to set up their own companies. Xerox then contracts part of its services out to these companies. A large part of these services is taken up by programming, but there are also networking companies for market research, business planning, financial work, tax advice, safety, and security (Judkins, 1988).

A *distributed business system* comprises a number of separately located units or even separate enterprises involved in different stages of the production of an end product or service, linked together by information technology within a total production, service, or distribution system.

Mobile work pertains to sales representatives, service engineers or consultants, for example, who work in more than one place and communicate with head office by the use of portable communication facilities.

Particularly in this last case, the difference with normal employees who occasionally communicate with their office while attending a conference or a meeting is becoming very small. Basically this is the reason why the concept of 'telework' is a very confusing and hardly usable one. Teleworkers were originally a neatly distinguishable group of people: clerical workers or programmers working full time at home, while their work and contact with their organization is supported by computer and communications technology. However, both technological and organizational developments have blurred the boundaries with other work arrangements.

In the context of this chapter work arrangements can basically be distinguished along four dimensions (see also Jackson, 1990):

1. The level of telematic support;
2. Geo-spatial relationships: extent to which work is performed outside organizational premises;

3. Nature of task and level of expertise required; e.g. professional vs simple clerical;
4. Contractual relationship; full employment, semi-permanent contracts, completely freelance.

For simplicity, the last three dimensions are taken together and termed 'organizational binding', in order to visualize the various work arrangements discussed in this chapter (see Figure 4).

From Figure 4 it becomes clear that work arrangements can no longer be classified as either 'telework' or 'normal' (see also Olson, 1988). Some writers nevertheless make a plea for retaining the concept. 'Despite its lack of precision, the word telework has acquired a potent symbolic value. . . . The idea of the teleworker has become a representation of what the future of work might be' (Huws, 1988).

Three parties can be distinguished which can be involved in the setting up of telework, namely organizations, individuals and the government. Each can have its own reasons to support the development of such work arrangements (Olson, 1989; Mehlmann, 1988; Kraut, 1987a) (see Table 1).

Figure 4   Work arrangements supported by telematics

Table 1—Reasons for Developing and Accepting Telework Arrangements

1. Reasons for organisations	
For simple clerical work	Reduction of overheads
	Reduction of wages
	Flexibility of labour supply
For professional work	To attract and retain scarce expertise
	Production improvement
	Reduction of travel costs
2. Reasons for individuals	
Employment despite family constraints or handicap	
Need for flexible working hours	
Need for autonomy and independence	
Reduction of traffic problems	
3. Reasons for government	
Reduction of traffic problems	
Economic support for remote areas	
Increase in employment.	

EFFECTS OF MEDIATED COMMUNICATION

At first sight it might appear inconsequential to discuss effects when a contingency framework has been propagated in the first section. If there is no such thing as technological determinism, what is the value of statements about the effects of certain technologies? The answer is threefold. Firstly, the effects of a certain technology depend in principle on the situation, but situations are often quite comparable. The explanation for this remarkable claim is found in the fact that the choice of a technology is also to a considerable extent determined by the situation. To be more precise, the effect of certain CSC systems depends on the culture and style of the organization within which they are applied. However, it is often only organizations with a certain type of culture that make use of such systems (see next section). This implies that research concerning these systems is to some extent carried out in comparable settings, and the effects appear to be consistent.

Secondly, one may study the effects of technological applications on the users, on small-scale interactions between a few people, on larger subsystems of the organization or on the entire organization and/or its relations with the environment. The larger the system on which the technology is supposed to have effects the more contingent factors play a role. The impact of large technological systems on individuals and small groups can often by established quite clearly, while the impact on organizational structure may be very ambiguous.

Thirdly, the discussion is often not really about the effects of a technical application, but about a certain organizational configuration or work arrangement in which a technical application is embedded. Of interest is not, for example, the meaning of the technical system *per se* through which homeworkers can send their data to their department head, but the implication of work arrangements such as homeworking, including its technical, social and financial aspects.

For the presentation of research concerning the effects of new media in organizations, a heuristic model is used which is inspired by the conceptual framework of O'Reilly & Pondy (1979) (see Figure 5).

In the previous decade several reviews have dealt with the impact of electronic message systems (EMSs) on communication, interpersonal interaction, group and organizational processes (e.g. Hiltz & Turoff, 1978; Kiesler, Siegel & McGuire, 1984; Steinfield, 1986; Wellens, 1986; Culnan & Markus, 1987). The findings of these reviews, combined with more recent empirical evidence, will be summarized here.

The Impact on Communication Structure

The main findings are presented in Table 2. Summarizing the quite substantial and quite consistent evidence, one can come to the following conclusion: there is to a certain extent a substitution effect; more important, however, is the finding that the introduction of EMSs generally results in the growth of new communication channels and an increase in the amount of information exchange. This means that message systems increase connectivity and interaction. Connectivity refers to the structure of existing communication channels; high connectivity implies high potential for contact; interaction refers to the frequency of use of the communication channels. However, EMSs

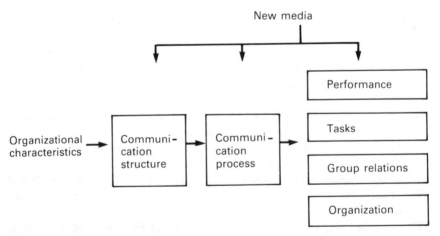

Figure 5   Heuristic schema for categorizing the impacts of new media

Table 2—Impact of Electronic Message Systems on Communication Structure

---

Reductions in telephone calls and letters (Rice, 1987a)
Speeding up the exchange of information (Hiltz & Turoff, 1978)
Exchange of new information (Sproull & Kiesler, 1986)
Many more people receive information than through the traditional channels (broadcasting function, Rice & Steinfield, 1991)
Expanded horizontal and diagonal contacts (Foster & Flynn, 1984; Köhler, 1987; Rogard, 1991; Rice *et al.*, 1990)
Easier to reach people by e-mail and voice messaging than through normal channels (Rice & Steinfield, 1991)
Senior personnel easier to communicate with since there is less screening by their secretaries for electronic messages than for letters and face-to-face meetings (Rice & Steinfield, 1991)
Less waiting time for colleagues and customers (Rice & Steinfield, 1991; Köhler, 1987)
Better coordination by supervisors of employees who are often out of the office (Rice & Steinfield, 1991)
Within existing groups the 'network connectedness' increases to some extent, after which it stabilizes (Rice & Barnett, 1985)
Interorganizational communication is enhanced, which is conducive for the transfer of innovations (Rice, 1987a, p. 84)

---

have not been reported to reduce travel or meetings, and physical proximity appears still to be the most important factor in establishing collaborative relationships (Bair, 1987, 1989).

Impact on the Communication Process

The interesting question is whether the nature and content of communication changes when it is mediated electronically. On the one hand, this is to be expected because of the lack of certain cues such as non-verbal signals. On the other, there appear to be ways of compensating to some extent for the absence of certain cues. The major results of relevant studies in this field are summarized in Table 3. The implications of these findings are discussed later (see 'impact on group relations').

Impact on Communication Outcomes

Impact on performance

The impact of office automation in general is well documented (e.g. Rice & Bair, 1984). A decreased turn-round time in document preparation and scheduling is repeatedly found, which implies time saved both for knowledge workers/professionals and for secretaries/typists. The result is often greater productivity. These effects are partly due to word processing and other stand-

Table 3—Impact of Electronic Message Systems on the Communication Process

---

Because of the lack of cues EMSs tend to be used more for information exchange tasks than for tasks requiring intensive interpersonal contact such as conflict resolution and bargaining (see reviews mentioned above)

The communication process becomes more informal than in comparable face-to-face contacts (Köhler, 1987; Foster & Flynn, 1984)

Quality of communication (for information exchange) is rated to be better (Aydin, 1989); videoconferencing is seen as more pleasant and friendly than audioconferencing, more effective for forming impressions of others and for complex information exchange, but as effective as face-to-face for simple exchange of information (Wellens, 1986). No significant direct effect was found on output quality, or time to completion

There are typographic ways to convey surrogates for non-verbal behaviour i.e. certain symbols to represent laughing, anger, etc. (e.g. Blackman & Clevenger, 1990)

Despite decreased bandwidth of EMSs, socio-emotional communication (social chats, etc.) appear to be widely used (Rice & Love, 1987; Hiltz & Johnson, 1989). There are even cases of very intimate exchanges, particularly with strangers, because one feels free and unthreatened (Hiltz & Turoff, 1978). The concept of 'electronic emotion' has been used (Rice & Love, 1987). Rice (1987a, p. 78) suggests that EMSs may actually increase the emotional content of the message itself because of the filtering of non-verbal cues

In both experimental and real-world situations, extreme emotional behaviour was found, called 'flaming' (Kiesler Siegel & McGuire 1984; Siegel *et al.*, 1986)

Communication is sometimes more task oriented (Hiltz & Turoff, 1978; Hiltz, Johnson & Turoff, 1986)

Under certain circumstances, the use of EMS can easily lead to information overload (Hiltz & Turoff, 1985; Schneider, 1987; Baird & Borer, 1987; Rice *et al.*, 1990; Köhler, 1990)

---

alone applications. However, the facilities for sending documents to and from remote places, the improved exchanges of documents and comments can also contribute substantially to increases in efficiency and effectiveness (e.g. Sullivan & Rayburn, 1990). A direct productivity increase through the use of computer systems for human-to-human communication is, however, more difficult to discover.

On the basis of a large-scale survey in the USA and Sweden, Hiltz (1988) concludes that there is a clear increase in productivity of work groups through the use of EMSs. For simple e-mail systems a direct but relatively small increase, and for more complex conferencing systems a substantial increase was found, but only after quite a long learning time. The efficiency gains mentioned earlier can be held responsible. Hiltz and Turoff (1978) also argue that people read more effectively than they listen. In other studies, however, there appeared to be much less evidence of productivity increase through EM systems (e.g. Eveland & Bikson, 1988). Apparently the impact on productivity depends on situational aspects such as the type of task.

Impact on tasks

Again, task changes have been observed as a result of the introduction of office automation in general. Task redistribution is a common phenomenon, but the direction depends on other factors. Sometimes a task enrichment and a blurring of boundaries between functions takes place, e.g. when professionals start producing their own documents. Sometimes a polarization takes place in which clerical tasks become even more routine and only a few professionals handle the exceptional cases (Kraut, 1987a). Often, however, this polarization is rather the effect of automatization and not of the implementation of EM systems.

The impacts in this respect are not yet very clearly documented. There are, however, indications that they can result in task redistribution. The most consistent finding is that professionals and managers report the addition of tasks such as text writing and graphics production, while secretaries become coordinators in an electronic network. The actual effect appears, however, to depend on the method of implementing the system (Baitsch & Grote, 1990).

Impact on group relations

Electronic media can have a substantial effect on the formation of groups. Organizational and geographical boundaries, which are traditionally very important, are overcome (Rice, 1984; Kling, 1987), and new groups are formed (Sproull & Kiesler, 1986; Finholt & Sproull, 1987).

It is consistently found that in 'electronic groups' status differences play a much less dominant role than in normal groups. The result is a lower barrier to communicating with others and more opportunity for creative and more equal participation by all group members (Siegel *et al.*, 1986; Eveland & Bikson, 1988, Hiltz, Turoff & Johnson, 1984). Influence thus appears to be based more on competence than on formal position (Foster & Flynn, 1984). The reason for this phenomenon is found in the absence of social constraints, i.e. precisely because the relationship is less personal people feel more free to speak out (Hiltz & Turoff, 1978).

The other side of this picture is that it is more difficult to achieve consensus and cooperation than in normal groups (Kiesler, Siegel & McGuire, 1984; Steinfield, 1986; Sproull & Kiesler, 1986; Hiltz, Johnson & Turoff, 1986). In certain tasks which require disciplined cooperation the lack of sufficient feedback of social norms and structure can result in rather chaotic functioning and the 'flaming' which has already been mentioned. It is, moreover, quite easy to misunderstand certain messages (Steinfield, 1990).

These findings point to the strong but also to the weak sides of these media. To exchange information freely, and in that way stimulate the growth of creative ideas, is their strong point. However, effective decision-making can be impaired by the lack of social structure, clear role patterns and leadership.

There appear to be two ways to solve this problem. One is to introduce rules and roles in the group, i.e. to appoint a leader and agree on certain procedures (see e.g. Baird & Bohrer, 1987). Both in experiments (Hiltz, Turoff & Johnson, 1984) and in a real-life setting of a design team (Fafchamps, Reynolds & Kuchinsky, 1989), it has been shown that computer conferences with a human leader are more effective in decision-making than groups without such a leader.

The other way is to build these rules and procedures into the system. That is exactly what GDSS and CSCW systems do. Research on the functioning and effects of GDSSs is still very scarce, particularly research on real-life use of these systems in organizations. The first studies indicate that as far as group processes are concerned GDSSs have the intended effects of equal and active participation, efficiency and effectiveness of decision-making (Hiltz, Johnson & Turoff, 1986; Zigurs, Poole, & Desanctis, 1988; Watson, Desanctis, & Poole, 1988; Dennis et al., 1988).

The results of a large experimental study by Watson, Desanctis & Poole (1988) suggest, however, that this type of outcome is found mainly in the case of planning and decision-making tasks. In tasks concerning the resolving of conflicts of personal preferences the effectiveness of the GDSS was much less. In fact 'GDSSs do not directly determine conflict behaviour or outcomes. Rather, group use of the technology mediates its impact' (Poole, Holmes, & Desanctis, 1989, p. 30). Moreover the GDSS appeared to induce procedure-oriented discussions, rather than issue-oriented ones.

Impact on organizational aspects

The impact on organizations of information systems in general is quite well researched (e.g. Swanson, 1987). However, the role of communications systems in this context is less clear. On the basis of an extensive research project, Rockart & Short (1989) synthesize various findings and theories, arguing that the most important role of information technology is to manage organizational interdependence, i.e. to serve as a mechanism for horizontal and vertical integration. They distinguish several organizational contexts in which this integration is particularly important:

— Value chain integration: computer-aided design, manufacturing and customer service to integrate, mainly through information systems, the product development chain, product delivery chain, and customer service chain;
— Functional integration of comparable (but often geographically distributed) departments through centralized information systems and standard data definitions;
— Planning and control through the use of a central executive support system.

On top of these coordinating information systems Rockart & Short (1989) note the growth of systems for 'team support', i.e. CSC systems. Today it appears to be feasible for team members 'to coordinate asynchronously (across time zones) and geographically (across remote locations) more easily than ever before'.

Access to large databases can provide employees with resources which may make them much more autonomous than before. On the other hand, management information systems can provide management with powerful tools to control the behaviour of employees. Various reviewers of the literature attempt to define the direction in which the introduction of information systems actually changes the locus of control (e.g. Peiro & Prieto, 1991, Moens & Valenduc, 1988; Swanson, 1987; Steinfield, 1986). Their conclusion is often in fact that no simple conclusion can be stated: both centralization and decentralization trends can be found in the literature reviewed. An important reason for this seeming contradiction is the fact that the actual effect depends on a complex of interacting factors, i.e. on the organizational setting (see next section). Another reason, however, may be found in not distinguishing between different systems (Andriessen, 1990). The implementation of new teleconsultation/information systems (see Figure 2) often tends to result in management having more control over the activities of workers (Björn-Andersen, Eason, & Robey, 1986). Andriessen (1990) however, comparing two X-ray image networks in hospitals, argues that the addition of human-to-human communication systems may to some extent neutralize the forces of rivalries and enhance cooperative behaviour.

Impact of Telework

In a previous section (pp. 32–37) several types of teleworking arrangements were distinguished. The two most clear-cut kinds were as follows:

1. The clerical homeworkers, mainly women, on a freelance basis and therefore with a fairly weak legal position;
2. The professional homeworkers (mainly programmers), employed full time, often carefully selected.

The implications of these two work settings (see e.g. Olson, 1988; Mehlmann, 1988) for the individuals and for the organization are rather different (see Table 4).

As Mehlmann (1988) puts it very succinctly, Table 4 'illustrates very clearly just why the predicted revolution is so long in coming. There is an inherent conflict of interest between employer and worker. Those forms of remote work which are profitable for the employer . . . carry the most disadvantages for

Table 4—Effects of Clerical and Professional Homeworking

Clerical homeworking
Effects for individual

Positive	Employment despite family constraints
	Flexible working hours
Negative	Social isolation
	Few chances for development/promotion
	Stress through combination of work and children
	Piece-rate payment
	Low job security

Effects for organization

Positive	Lower wage and social costs
	Lower housing costs
	Easier to cope with seasonal rushes

Professional homeworking
(e.g. programmers)
Effects for individual

Positive	Flexible working hours
	More time for home and family
	More autonomy
	Lower travel costs
	Less disturbance while working
	Chance to retain job despite moving
Negative	Need for personal discipline
	Feeling of being neglected (if full time at home)
	Work spills over into free time

Effects for organization

Positive	Ability to recruit and retain scarce staff
	Higher productivity
Negative	Selection, training and support costs
	Hard to supervise
	Need for improved planning and output specification

---

the employee—partly, but not principally, due to current legislation.' Moreover, those forms which are attractive for employees are considered difficult to organize and manage by the employer. Only in special cases will organizations be interested in developing telework to a large extent, i.e. when the labour and product markets force the organization to change its strategy radically. There are only a few examples of organizations which have done this, such as the above-mentioned Xerox (Judkins, 1988) and F International (Shirley, 1988).

CONDITIONS

In the previous sections it has been emphasized that in principle one cannot discuss the impacts of new media in themselves, because they depend on the nature of the context. The context has several elements and dimensions which will now be presented in this section. Theories concerning conditions are sometimes divided into three groups: theories about technical, individual and organizational factors (Markus, 1983; Hiltz, 1988; Latrille, 1989). These categorizations, however, have a more or less static nature. They do not sufficiently take into account the developmental aspect of the implementation of new systems. Others put more emphasis on the introduction process of new media as an important condition alongside technical, individual and organizational factors (e.g. Bikson, 1987; and Judkins, 1988, in relation to telework).

In this section the theories concerning the reasons for non-utilization or under-utilization, and the conditions for successful implementation and effects of new media, are therefore categorized according to a model which includes both the situational and the developmental aspects. According to diffusion and adoption theories (e.g. Rogers, 1983) a new technology is developed, a process of diffusion takes place, other organizations adopt the innovation and adapt it to their own situation in a more or less planned design and implementation process and finally the innovation is used operationally by members of the organization. Characteristics of the technology itself, of the users, of the organizational setting or of the implementation process (each by itself or in interaction) can be responsible for the use, the success or other effects of the new technology. The theories concerning determinants of success of, or resistance to, new technologies, and particularly information and communication technology (Bjorn-Andersen & Kjaergaart, 1987) can be categorized according to this schema. Figure 6 represents a heuristic model portraying the relevant variables.

Characteristics of CSC Systems

Social presence

A widely used argument, supported by various theories, holds that the effect of new media depends on the type of signals and information they can convey. Certain researchers, having a background in interpersonal communication, used in this context concepts such as 'interpersonal immediacy' (Mehrabian, 1971, mentioned in Wellens, 1986), 'formality' (Morley & Stephenson, 1969) or 'social presence' (Short, Williams & Christie, 1976). Others, referring to mass communication theories about media and channel characteristics, used terms such as 'bandwidth', 'information richness' (Daft & Lengel, 1984, 1986) or 'channel capacity' (Fulk & Steinfield, 1989).

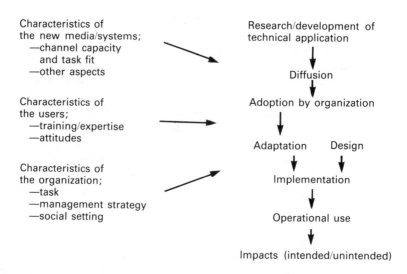

Figure 6 Heuristic model of conditions for successful use and effects of new media

Common to most of these 'media characteristics' theories are two central arguments. The first holds that media can be ordered along a dimension of experienced psychological 'nearness' of the person with whom one communicates. As one moves from the informationally rich face-to-face situation to the informationally sparse written bulletins or memos, the number and types of sensory channels available for information exchange are reduced. Two-way video is similar to face-to-face situations, telephone communication comes next while e-mail is similar to communication by memo.

Secondly, these theories argue that media use is, or at least should be, matched to the task at hand: tasks such as simple information exchange are best supported by information sparse media, because less distant media are unnecessarily rich and therefore inefficient. For tasks involving complex interpersonal communication such as bargaining or interpersonal relations, information-rich channels such as face to face or video conferencing are better suited.

Several studies have tested the media match theories (e.g. Rice & Williams, 1984; Steinfield & Fulk, 1986, 1987; Trevino, Lengel, & Daft, 1987; Thomas & Trevino, 1989, Fulk & Ryu, 1990; Schmitz & Fulk, 1990). To a certain extent those theories were supported which showed the relevance of these factors. However, the support was often rather limited. The reasons appear to be twofold. First of all researchers did not always distinguish adequately between the objective 'channel capacity' and the subjective 'social presence':

1. 'Channel capacity' (or cuelessness, bandwidth, etc.) refers to the number

and types of sensory channels available for information exchange, the possibility of using natural language and of direct feedback, and other more or less objective characteristics of the medium.

2. 'Social presence' (or media richness, interpersonal immediacy, etc.) refers to the experienced psychological nearness of the person with whom one communicates.

It appears that the two do not correlate completely. The rating of the 'social presence' of certain media such as e-mail therefore varies substantially between users (Fulk & Ryu, 1990) depending for example on the experience the user has with the medium (Short *et al.*, 1976).

The second reason for limited support of the media characteristics theories can be found in the importance of other variables, notably, on the one hand, space and time aspects of the situation (see next paragraph), and on the other the social context (see below).

Relative advantage

According to adoption and diffusion theories (Rogers, 1983) a major determinant of adoption of an innovation is the expected and/or perceived relative advantage over other comparable means. This finding is also corroborated in the case of CSC systems. An important predictor of attitudes towards video conferencing and EMS and towards their effectiveness is the expectation as to usefulness (Svenning & Ruchinskas, 1984; Rutchinskas, Svenning, & Steinfield, in press; Hiltz, 1988).

Other characteristics

Empirical studies have shown that the following characteristics are often necessary conditions for the successful use of e-mail and voice mail:

— User-friendliness (Culnan, 1985). Particularly when compared to what such systems really should be able to present and accomplish (see e.g. Kündig, 1988), present systems are still far from perfect.
— Geographical distance (Steinfield & Fulk, 1986; Trevino, Lengel, & Daft, 1987)
— Accessibility of PCs or terminals (Culnan, 1985; Rice & Shook, 1988).
— Critical mass of users (Culnan, 1985; Markus, 1987; Rice & Shook, 1988; Rice *et al.*, 1990). This amounts to the idea that communication media will only be used if a certain minimum number of relevant users is involved.
— Lack of urgency. When contact is urgent, the telephone is preferred to e-mail (Steinfield & Fulk, 1986; Trevino, Lengel, & Daft, 1987).

The above conditions apply particularly to electronic message systems. According to an analysis by Robinson (1989), the following characteristics of complex systems such as computer conferencing or group decision support systems are crucial for successful use:

— Equality, in terms of who benefits from, and who does the work in, the application. Examples are electronic calendar or project management systems. Most of them fail because of a 'disparity between those who will benefit (e.g. the project leaders) and those who must do the work' (e.g. team members or secretaries).
— Mutuality, i.e. participants should be able to change their input in the light of views and feelings expressed by others. 'Bad systems freeze viewpoints.'
— New competence, i.e. complex systems are only attractive if they add new possibilities to existing communication and decision procedures instead of only enhancing existing abilities.
— Double level language: some systems contain only a set of formal procedures to structure the group interaction. Besides this 'formal level', being the structure for the primary task, a second channel ('cultural level') should be present to talk about the formalized procedures in the case of ambiguities, questions, comments, etc.

Individual Characteristics

Expertise

The requirement of user-friendliness should not exclude the requirement of adequate training in using new media. Köhler (1991) distinguishes three kinds of expertise needed in the case of complex communication systems:

1. Software literacy and software economics: how to use the media and how to do it efficiently;
2. Communicative competence, to adopt techniques for gaining feedback and correct interpretations;
3. Organization knowledge for successfully taking the initiative in a CSC system and to develop adequate networks within and across organizations.

Particularly when full-time professionals are involved, teleworking appears to require intensive training not only by the teleworker but also by his organization-based manager and co-worker or secretarial staff (Heilmann, 1988; Judkins, 1988; Shirley, 1988).

Attitudes and motivation

The attention to media characteristics and expertise is to a large extent based on the assumption that media use is governed by a more or less rational choice of the channel that best fits the task at hand. However, organizational communication and information gathering appears to be a highly social and symbolic activity (Feldman & March, 1981). People systematically gather more information than they use, but continue to ask for more. Because of certain attitudes, preferences or style, they often do not match the communication channel to the task required (Thomas & Trevino, 1989). Blenker (1986) concludes that managers need a 'communicative rationality' instead of an information-processing rationality for new media to be used successfully. In the next subsection the importance of the social setting for the formation of preferences and attitudes towards new media is discussed.

Personality

There are some indications that certain personality structures thrive when using the rather impersonal electronic message systems (Finholt & Sproull, 1987, Huff, Sproull & Kiesler, 1988). In particular, introverted people or persons with slow reaction patterns seem to find themselves at home with asynchronous message systems. For certain forms of telework a strong need for independence appears to be required (Heilman, 1988; Judkins, 1988; Shirley, 1988).

Organizational Characteristics

Social setting

Fulk *et al.*, 1987 and Fulk, 1989 have adapted the 'social information processing theory' (Salancik & Pfeffer, 1978) to media use in organizations. They developed the 'social influence theory of communication technology use' to account for the consistent finding that the use of new media often depended less on the characteristics of the media than on the attitude, norms, and behaviour of the people one works with (see also Anderson & Meyer, 1989). The theory was supported by various studies (e.g. Trevino, Lengel, & Daft, 1987; Steinfield, Boahua, & Lin, 1988; Fulk & Ruy, 1990; Schmitz & Fulk, 1990). Even in groups which can easily meet face to face a message system will be a real relief when people do not like each other but have to cooperate (Markus, 1989). The results of a study by Markus and Forman (1989) point to the importance of the role of the leader in this respect. Aydin & Rice (1989) showed that attitudes towards the use of media were determined more by the 'social world' of the department and the function of the users than by the media characteristics.

Management strategy

The introduction of new information systems is often an occasion for shifts in power and control from lower-level managers or professionals to higher-level managers (e.g. Markus, 1983) or to other professionals (Aydin & Rice, 1989; Andriessen, 1990). The explanation is found in the inverse relationship between the information available and the delegation of decision-making. The better the information the less delegation, not because information itself causes centralization but because central authorities prefer to exercise control, and are only 'forced' to delegate when they encounter difficulty in getting or handling the necessary information adequately (Buckland 1989).

The question remains to what extent the same holds true for systems for mediated communication. Any change in organizational structures or technology, particularly information and communication technology, potentially challenges power relationships, and is therefore a political process (Markus, 1983; Bannon, Björn-Andersen, & Due Thomsen, 1988; Bansler, 1989). CSC systems in their communication function are meant to support lateral information exchange, and cooperation in problem solving. There are indications that bureaucratic hierarchical relations are to a certain extent challenged by these characteristics.

Carley (1984) describes a situation in a university where central management tried to block the open use of an e-mail system by prescribing exactly which employees were allowed access to which distribution lists. The users, however, developed their own distribution lists and again communicated widely with each other. Management then changed the system in such a way that they could monitor the communication activities of the employees permanently.

Ciborra & Lanzara (1991) tell the story of a large computer company in which the design process came to a standstill again and again. An electronic mail system was then installed which gave the designers the opportunity to consult colleagues. Management had also prescribed a much stricter method for systems development and project management, to overcome the design problems. The e-mail system appeared to be very effective for the communication process between designers and therefore for the design processes. The management disapproved, however, of the uncontrolled communication going on between designers from all kinds of departments, because these bypassed the prescribed steps in the system design procedures. Actually the management was blind to the positive effects of the e-mail system. The strict use of the systems development method was therefore enforced.

Zuboff (1988) also presents a case in which the use of a computer conferencing system was curtailed by management. In the company the system was at first generally appreciated because of its facilitation of the flow of information. However, when it appeared that the system was also used for social chat—which improved morale according to the users—the management began to feel it was losing control. In their eyes too much non-functional information about the organization and its members became public.

This lack of penetration of new technological potentialities is also found in other contexts. In his review of the development of information technology for managerial decision-making, Koopman (1989) concludes that 'despite optimistic predictions, the impact of technology on decision-making has been limited because managers have been reluctant to involve themselves with it'. The literature concerning telework comes to more or less the same conclusions. In an earlier section it was revealed that telework is much less widespread than was expected 20 or even 10 years ago. According to various studies (Korte, 1988; Olson, 1987, 1988; Gordon, 1988; Klein & Fröschle, 1988) the main reason is to be found in the attitude of management *vis-à-vis* telework. In a four-country survey in Europe among (4000) organizational decision-makers only a small proportion (3–18%, except for Italy, 43%) showed interest in telework, and then only for tasks such as typing and word processing, data entry and amendment and computer programming. The central objections of management are the lack of visible control over their employees, the need for formalizing supervision and for standardizing output criteria.

In contrast with these examples there appear to be cases in which e-mail and conferencing systems are widely and rather unrestrictedly used, with considerable success. The story of the Colruyt Company (see p. 28) is an example of such an organization. The reason for the successful introduction is to be found in the management strategy of maximum openness and personal networking. The restrictions are not brought about by formal rules but by the general culture of the company, i.e. self-discipline and social control.

Various other examples show the same phenomenon happening in large computer firms (Finholt & Sproull, 1987; Skyrme, 1989) and in certain French industries (Craipeau, 1991; Cambra, 1987).

These findings indicate that the real benefits of CSC systems can only be reaped in (parts of) organizations with cultures and structures characterized by debureaucratization and 'networking', and by 'organizational learning' (Köhler, 1991). This also implies that telematics will spread rapidly only if it is implemented as a flexible tool for management purposes (Moens & Valenduc, 1987). It is improbable that CSC systems will have any far-reaching effect when management is opposed to wide usage.

Design and Introduction

Design

Often the various stages of the research and adoption chain do not take place in the same organization. The first two stages in Figure 6 are largely managed by the organization(s) that develop a new product or system. The next two stages—adoption and adaptation—apply particularly to organizations that introduce systems which have already been developed and marketed. Some commercial message systems belong to this category. Other types of information and communication systems have to be tailor-made for the organization that will use them operationally. In that case a system is designed and developed in the organization itself (more or less on the basis of existing examples). However, unless a participative approach is followed, communication technologies are the outcome of how management and designers assess the process of human communication (Acker, 1989).

The problem with the design of CSC systems appears to be the fact that technically oriented systems designers view communication more in terms of data exchange and task-related machine communication than in terms of human communication (Boland, 1987; Hacker & Monge, 1988; Hacker & Milano, 1988, Denning, 1989; Qvortrup, 1991). This means, in terms of data transport, (maximizing) connectivity and optimizing sender–receiver channels (which implies that the social setting is viewed mainly as a possible source of disturbance, i.e. as noise) rather than in terms of relationships, interactivity, meaning formation in a social context, and organizational effects. Organizational science-oriented scholars, therefore, make a strong plea for participative design (e.g. Frese, 1987; Eason, 1987; Blackler, 1988; Bödker & Grönbaek, 1989; Baitsch & Grote, 1990).

Implementation strategies

The general theory concerning organizational change is also applicable to the implementation of new media. Central and powerful groups are often key elements for communication about, and acceptance of, innovations (Albrecht & Hall, 1989). For large-scale innovations such as important information systems or EDI systems, top-level attention is easily attracted. Nolan (1979) has, however, described the indirect way in which certain forms of 'lower profile' information technology such as personal computers penetrate a organization before it is 'perceived' by top management as a strategic element requiring a policy to be formulated. According to Turoff (1989), computer conferencing may be too *in*expensive to receive top-level attention. In the framework of a European Community research programme a general model for the implementation of information and communication applications in organizations has been developed (Ryan *et al.*, 1988).

NEW ORGANIZATIONAL FORMS AND MEDIATED SYSTEMS

The previous sections have illustrated the fact that there are developments in both the technical and organizational areas. More and more types of systems to mediate and support communications are being developed. More and more organizations are characterized by centrifugal forces, reflected in geographical distribution and externalization of labour. The question is to what extent these developments are related. In general, four perspectives on the role of technology in organizations can be distinguished:

1. *Technological determinism.* Technological changes are, according to this view, more or less forced upon organizations and have a direct and unambiguous effect of their own on the behaviour of people and the structure and functioning of the organization. Within this perspective an optimistic and a neutral view can be found. The optimistic view holds that the new communication technology will by itself result in free networking throughout the organization, thereby causing the hierarchical chains of traditional organizations to be shed. The neutral view holds that some technology will lead to more freedom and other technology to more control. It is clear from the evidence presented in the previous section that this perspective is hardly adequate. A few rather general implications of electronic message systems for communications have been mentioned, but even these are not unequivocal.

2. *Management tool perspective.* This perspective holds that technological changes are the expression of the existing structure and management philosophy of the organization. Bureaucratic mechanistic organizations will only introduce applications of information and communication technology which will strengthen the control orientation, while modern organic organizations will opt for applications which will enable creative networking. This is the perspective which lies behind the propagation of telecommunication in a strategic way to gain a 'competitive advantage'. Keen (1988): 'Telecommunications can be harnessed as a major new force for organizational design and redesign, and all large organizations need to exploit the opportunities it opens up.' But it is also the perspective of the labour process theorists, who consider modern management to be still basically Tayloristic and warn against the degrading and labour shedding which often accompanies the introduction of new technologies (see e.g. Knights & Wilmott, 1988).

   This view might to some extent apply in the case of the strategic choice of new large-scale technologies. However, systems such as e-mail and computer conferencing often penetrate organizations very gradually and only become a straegic issue after a certain time (see e.g. Nolan, 1979).

3. *Trigger perspective.* The idea of gradual penetration is more in agreement with the study by Aydin (1989), who notes that the introduction of a new technology can, sometimes unexpectedly, 'trigger' changes. She

concludes, however, that the direction of change depends after all on the organizational setting.

4. *Gradual change perspective.* This view combines to some extent elements of the previous views. Technological developments and organizational changes are both considered to be ongoing processes, which can interact with one other. Market forces determine to a large extent the way organizations change and the choice of technology that is necessary to support these changes. In agreement with the trigger perspective is the idea that some technologies penetrate some organizations to a certain extent without being strategically planned. This implies that certain technologies may have unforeseen consequences. If these consequences are strong enough they will become the object of strategic decision-making (see management tool perspective). However, if the effects are minor at the start, and the penetration slow, changes might occur which at a certain moment become almost irresistible.

The fourth perspective seems to be applicable to the introduction of certain new communication media. On the basis of the previous sections the following conclusions can be drawn. There is a widespread use of simple, free text, e-mail systems, often connected with computer conferencing systems. These systems sometimes substitute for traditional communication channels because they are faster than meetings, more informal than letters and are not subject to telephone lag. This means they increase the efficiency of existing communication. The same applies to video conferencing systems whose main function is to enable more or less formal meetings to be held across geographical distances. The video systems are, however, still too expensive to be very widespread.

Electronic mail and computer conferencing also increase the interactivity of people who are already in contact with one other, and foster the growth of new contacts and groups. Because a widespread exchange of information becomes possible where nothing existed before, the effectiveness of organizational communication is increased. Individuals and groups who are widely distributed geographically, and who work asynchronously, can now interact and coordinate their activities effectively. The examples presented in this chapter show that through this medium the necessary flexibility in organizational collaboration can be enhanced, despite space and time constraints. Moreover, partly because of the shift from manufacturing industry to service industry, a growing number of employees appear to become mobile and to work more or less regularly outside the confines of their organization.

However, because of the rather narrow bandwidth, and other factors such as accessibility and inexperience, the impact of electronic message systems is not (yet) revolutionary. In organizations where such systems are introduced, face-to-face meetings still appear to be necessary for activities which require intensive personal contact of a bargaining type. The same applies to various forms of telework. The phenomenon of full-time homeworkers, and of complete teleworking organizations such as F International, is still marginal. The more common form, with employees working a day at home now and then is frowned upon rather than considered a viable idea.

The main reason why the majority of present-day organizations, except for a few large corporations, have not yet introduced organization-wide communication systems, video conferencing or e-mail, let alone computer conferencing to support lateral communications inside and outside the organization, is, however, of a different nature. It requires a completely different, i.e. non-Tayloristic and non-bureaucratic, type of management philosophy. Such a new type of philosophy and strategic policy is not adequate for all (parts of) organizations, but even for those for which it is, old traditions die hard.

The potential for change in management philosophy and for the growth of new organizational forms is, however, quite substantial. *Firstly*, if systems for mediating communication are intensively used the fixed boundaries between departments disappear (Kling, 1987), the interaction between people from various levels and departments increases and hierarchical differences tend to be replaced by functional relations. Organizations in which these developments take place can be better characterized as 'networks' than 'pyramids'.

Allan and Hauptman (1987) have analysed the way in which the traditional tension between functional and product-oriented grouping can be alleviated through mediated communication systems. They focus on R & D staff members in organizations. These employees have two seemingly incompatible communication needs. On the one hand, they need communication with colleagues to stay up to date in the professional field. For this purpose functional groups of professionals are best suited. On the other hand, there is the need for communication with other organization members (marketing, production, sales, etc.) with an eye to coordination in the framework of new projects. For this purpose a project group organization is best suited. An organizational solution to this dilemma is the matrix organization. This type of organization appears, however, to be difficult to manage. Mediated communication systems such as computer conferencing, video conferencing, etc. allow the members of professional departments to keep in permanent contact with other organization members with whom they are cooperating on a certain project. The computer-supported cooperation of various professionals involved in industrial design as described by Morley (1991) proceeds more or less along these lines. *Secondly*, more and more organizations (such as the Colruyt Company, see p. 28) find themselves confronted by increasing environmental turbulence and complexity. In traditional bureaucratic organizations the integration necessary to coordinate horizontally and geographically differentiated activities is achieved by means of coordination mechanisms such as rules and procedures, central goal setting, standardization of tasks. The 'uncertainty' which remains is handled by hierarchical, vertical, communication. Lateral communication, crossing departmental boundaries is, at least formally, not necessary and not allowed. According to Galbraith (1977), information exchange is a fundamental characteristic of organizations, or rather organizations are information-processing organisms. Central to his theory is the concept of 'uncertainty reduction'. Changing environments and diversity and interdependence of tasks create uncertainty that has to be reduced. When the traditional coordination mechanisms (rule, hierarchy, etc.) cannot cope with the amount of information to be processed, uncertainty grows. Reduction of uncertainty can then in principle be achieved in two ways. On the one hand, there is reduction of the necessary information processing through the creation of slack resources, or through decreasing interdependence by making organizational subunits more independent (e.g. by changing a functional structure into a market-oriented structure). On the other hand, there is increase of the information-processing capacity through vertical information systems and/or through lateral communication systems. This can be realized by means of, for example, *ad hoc* task forces, project teams, liaison functions and matrix structures. The information systems often have, according to Galbraith, a centralizing effect because they provide higher echelons with systematic information about lower levels. The horizontal coordination mechanisms tend to have a decentralizing effect.

According to Keen (1987) coping effectively with external turbulence implies 'networking' processes, in which individuals, groups and departments have easy access to information bases, to each other and to the clients. Communication structures and processes in such circumstances have to be horizontal, boundary-spanning and short-lived. In such structures rapid information exchange and mutual adjustment between professionals can be realized. Communication of this type can only be realized when supported by new media.

Thirdly, more and more forms of 'externalization of work' are found. Externalization refers to the fact that certain organizational functions are redistributed both internally and externally (Huws, 1988). Within organizations branch departments are more and more performing functions which were previously executed at central headquarters. Other functions are subcontracted to freelance employees (e.g. clerical work to homeworkers), to newly constituted (often small) enterprises (e.g. Judkins, 1988), or to existing outside companies. These issues are part of more general changes in the boundaries between organizational functions, which are dealt with by the *transaction cost theory*.

The basic question in this theory is: Why are there firms and markets? Both are systems for the production and exchange of commodities, but for certain aspects or types of production process the first is chosen and for other aspects and types the second. The transaction cost theory, developed by Williamson (1975), views both systems as substitutes which can replace one another. The phenomenon of subcontracting services which were previously part of a company's in-house operations is an example of the replacement of a hierarchical organization of transactions by a market organization of those transactions. Ouchi (1979) has expanded the transaction cost theory to include three types of arrangement: markets, bureaucratic organizations, and clans. The theory explains the 'choice' between these arrangements on the basis of the balance between 'production costs' and 'coordination costs'. Production costs include the costs (financial and all others) of creating and distributing goods or services. Coordination costs include the costs of the information processing necessary to coordinate the activities of the people and machines involved in the production process (e.g. when determining the design, price, quantity, delivery schedule, etc. (Malone, Yates, & Benjamin, 1987, p. 485). The elements involved in the choice between the three arrangements are as follows (Ciborra, 1987, p. 259):

—When transactions are fairly well patterned and participants possess the relevant information, then the market is the most efficient means of division of labour and coordination of the exchange of goods or services. In the market the parties are autonomous and competition governs the interaction.
—When participants (and their expertise) are hard to find and/or when the product is complex, coordination costs in a market arrangement would be too high. In that case it is more efficient to bring the various steps in the production process together in a hierarchical organization, where management controls the transaction steps by specifying (standardizing) the work activities. Hierarchically organizing production activities implies large overhead costs, but this price has to be paid for the purpose of achieving complex ends.
—When services are extremely complex and transactions extremely ambiguous (e.g. because of frequent changes in requirements), the participants must trust each other and give up any attempt at a short-sighted calculation of the reciprocal costs and benefits accruing from the exchange. In this case the arrangement (a more informal one) of the group or clan is appropriate. The clan is a network where coordination is the central issue.

None of the three arrangements is to be found in pure form. In most cases a combination has developed, with one of the three dominating. Information and communications technology can support the processes required to coordinate the transactions. In general it is expected that it will reduce the costs of coordinating activities, and will therefore lead to an overall shift towards proportionately greater use of markets—rather than hierarchies—between organizations, and clans (networks) at several places within organizations to coordinate economic activities.

Huws (1988) gives as example of replacement of hierarchical coordination by market relations, the videotex terminals in travel agencies, which have enabled a great deal of information processing relating to the availability and booking of holidays to be transferred from the tour operators to travel agents. A recent report of the European Community (FAST, 1988, p. 93) even foresees that large firms could break down into small producing units integrated through telecommunications and through a network of financial relationships. The role of small firms might at the same time change from competitor to complement, living in symbiosis with the large organizations.

In previous sections several examples of clanlike networks of cooperating organization members supported by new media, were given.

IMPLICATIONS FOR RESEARCH AND DESIGN

Separate Research Circuits

The field of mediated communication systems is still a very young one. It is in fact an intersection of various subdisciplines of both computer science and social science. In both fields a large number of publications can be found. Specific research methods are also developed, such as the possibility of software monitoring of user behaviour (Monge & Capella, 1980; Rice & Borgman, 1983; Teubner & Vaske, 1988; Rice & Shook, 1988) and network analysis (Rice & Barnett, 1985). The total field of knowledge is, however, still rather fragmented, partly because of incomparability of concepts, methodology and research settings (Wellens, 1989).

In 1987 Steinfield & Fulk called for theory development because too many studies proceeded inductively. In this concluding section, however, a plea is made not for theory development but for theory integration. The problem is not one of too few theories but of too many fragmented theories, originating in different disciplines and often exclusively dealing with a single level (e.g. media characteristics, interpersonal or organizational) of this multi-level phenomenon. Some theories are quite similar but use different terms, partly because of the differing backgrounds of the researchers involved, and partly because of the lack of contact between the research circuits. In the first section three circuits were mentioned:

1. Research concerning Computer Mediated Communication (CMC), often based in communication science departments and strongly represented in the International Communication Association. Researchers into CMC originally analysed mainly the interactions of relatively large groups of professionals (often academics) using e-mail and computer conferences. Four well-known groups are those at the New Jersey Institute of Technology (Hiltz, Turoff and coworkers), those previously at the

Annenberg School of Communication, University of California (Rice, Steinfield, Fulk and coworkers), those at Carnegie Mellon University (Kiesler and coworkers) and Palme's group at Stockholm University.

2. Research concerning telework, its forms and effects. The majority of researchers in this field have a background in various social sciences. They can be found both in the USA and in Europe.

3. Research concerning Computer Supported Cooperative Work (CSCW), often rooted in computer science or cognitive psychology, although attempts are made to relate it to social and organization sciences (e.g. Bannon & Schmidt, 1989). CSCW researchers are particularly interested in developing systems for the support of structured interaction in comparatively small groups, such as management teams or groups of designers. Partly because of their disciplinary background, and partly because many systems are still in the design stage, the analysis of use in a real work situation is rarely carried out. Foci for exchanging information are the biannual CSCW conferences (see Peterson, 1986, and ACM, 1988, for the USA; and Proceedings, 1989 for Europe). In the context of European Community research programmes this field is now termed 'cooperation technology'.

The research subjects of the three circuits were originally quite separate. The differences are, however, becoming more and more blurred, because the types of systems are becoming integrated and applicable to all kinds of work arrangements. However, this integration of systems has not yet resulted in the integration of scientific circuits. Moreover, another relevant discipline and research circuit, i.e. work and organization psychology, is hardly involved in this area.

Research Questions

Despite the many studies already being carried out, the research agenda is still quite basic. How can cooperation across space and time be supported adequately by new media? How can systems for mediated communication contribute to effective organizational coping with changing environments and at the same time contribute to work arrangements adequate for human needs? How can organizational tasks and communication systems be designed jointly in such a way that all relevant criteria are met? The answers to questions such as these can only be found in cooperation between, on the one hand, design and evaluation-oriented social and organization scientists and, on the other, practical-minded systems designers.

Fundamental to these questions is a systematic analysis of organizational cooperation and communication in order to discover the functions, purposes and criteria relevant for the development of mediated communication systems (e.g. Bannon & Schmidt, 1989; Holand & Danielson, 1989; Schmidt, 1989; Poole & Desanctis, 1990). There are several good handbooks of organizational communication (e.g. Farace, Monge, & Russel, 1977; Wofford, 1977; Jablin et al., 1987; Goldhaber & Barnett, 1988). However, knowledge in this area has not yet been transferred sufficiently to the problem of mediated communication.

Ethical Issues

Every new technology, and particularly information and communication technology, is attended by changes in resources and therefore in relations between people. Several authors have warned that the choice of certain applications of these technologies is very strategic because it can result in a threat to privacy and security (Kubicek, 1988, 1991) and increased social stratification both within organizations and in society in general. If policy-makers are not alert there may be a growing 'class' of computer illiterates, and a sharp difference between information haves and have nots, in society but also, for example, in research communities (Ashmore, 1989). Greater differences in position, security and influence are noted in various studies of clerical homeworkers (Korte, Robinson & Steinle, 1988). Indications have also been found within organizations, however, of growing differences in network connections between 'knowledge workers' (professionals) and 'knowledge processors' (typists and secretarial personnel) (Reese, 1988). This is the more crucial since access to information and communication networks is becoming increasingly important. It will not be long before a person's status is largely dependent on his or her capacities for acquiring and selecting information resources and maintaining networks through the new media (Rice, 1987b).

It is the task of responsible researchers to contribute to the development of people, organizations and systems which counter these tendencies. Carrying out technology assessment studies (e.g. Bullinger & Kornwachs, 1987) is one of the ways.

ACKNOWLEDGEMENT

I wish to express my gratitude to Klaas ten Have and Johannes van Veen for their comments on an earlier draft.

Correspondence address
Department of Work and Organizational Psychology, University of Technology, Kanaalweg 26, 2628 EH Delft, The Netherlands

REFERENCES

Acker, S. (1989) Designing communication systems to human systems: values and assumptions of 'socially open architecture'. In J. A. Anderson (ed.), *Communication Yearbook 12*, Newbury Park, CA: Sage.

ACM (1988) *Proceedings of the Second Conference on Computer Supported Cooperative Work*. Baltimore: ACM Press.

Albrecht, T. L., & Hall, B. (1989) Relational and content differences between élites and outsiders in innovation networks. Paper for ICA Annual Convention, San Francisco, May.

Allen, T. J., & Hauptman, O. (1987) The influence of communication technologies on organizational structure. *Communications Research*, **14**(5), 575–587.

Anderson, J. A., & Meyer, T. P. (1989) *Mediated Communication. A Social Action Perspective*. University of Utah/University of Wisconsin.

Andriessen, J. H. Erik (1990) Computer supported consultation or conversation. The case of digital image networks in hospitals, *Proceedings of the International Conference "Computer, Man and Organisation II"*, Nivelles, Belgium: Free University of Brussels.

Ashmore, T. M. (1989) Assessing electronic information: a question of ethics. Paper for ICA Annual Convention. San Francisco, May.

Aydin C. E. (1989) Occupational adaptation to computerized medical information systems. *Journal of Health and Social Behavior* **30**(2) 163–179.

Aydin, C., & Rice, R. E. (1989) Social worlds, implementation, and individual differences: predicting attitudes toward a medical information system. Paper submitted to Technology and Innovation Management Division of Academy of Management Annual Conference, Washington, DC, August.

Bair, J. H. (1987) Users needs for office systems solutions. In R. E. Kraut (ed.) *Technology and the Transformation of White-collar Work*. Hillsdale, NJ: Erlbaum.

Bair, J. H. (1989) Supporting cooperative work with computers: addressing meeting mania. In *Proceedings of 34th IEEE Computer Society International Conference—COMPCON*. San Francisco, Spring.

Baird, P. M., & Borer, B. (1987) An experiment in computer conferencing using a local area network. *The Electronic Library*, **5**(3) 162–169.

Baitsch, Ch., & Grote, G. (1990) Strategies for implementing an office communication system: influences on the system's use and its organizational effects. *Proceedings of the International Conference "Computer, Man, and Organisation II"*, Nivelles: Free University of Brussels, May.

Bannon, L., Björn-Andersen, N., & Due-Thomsen, B. (1988) Computer support for cooperative work: an appraisal and critique. In H. J. Bullinger (ed.), *Information Technology for Organisational Systems*, Elsevier, EEC: Brussels–Luxembourg.

Bannon, L. J., & Schmidt, K. (1989) CSCW: Four characters in search of a context. *Proceedings of the First European Conference on CSCW—EC CSCW 89*, London.

Bansler, J. (1989) Systems development research in Scandinavia: three theoretical schools. *Scandinavian Journal of Information Systems*, **1**, 3–20.

Bikson, T. K. (1987) Understanding the implementation of office technology. In R. E. Kraut, *Technology and the Transformation of White-collar Work*. London: Erlbaum.

Björn-Andersen, N., & Kjaergaart, D., (1987) Choices en route to the office of tomorrow. In R. E. Kraut (ed.), *Technology and the Transformation of White-collar Work*. London: Erlbaum.

Björn-Andersen, N., Eason, K. & Robey, D. (1986) *Managing Computer Input. An International Study*. Norwood, NY: Ablex.

Blackler, F. (1988) Information technologies and organizations: lessons from the 1980s and issues for the 1990s. *Journal of Occupational Psychology*, **61**, 113–127.

Blackman, B. I., & Clevenger, T. (1990) On line computer messaging: surrogates for nonverbal behavior. Paper for ICA Annual Convention Dublin, June.

Blenker, P. (1986) On the implications of information technology for managerial rationality. Paper for EIASM Workshop. Brussels, 15–16 September.

Blomberg, J. L. (1987) Social interaction and office communication: effects on user evaluation of new technologies. In R. E. Kraut (ed.), *Technology and the Transformation of White-collar Work*. London: Erlbaum.

Bödker, S., & K. Grönbaek (1989) Cooperative prototyping experiments: users and designers envision a dental case record system. *Proceedings of First European Conference on CSCW*. London, September.

Boland, R. J. (1987) The information of information systems. In R. J. Boland & R. A. Hirschheim, (eds), *Critical Issues in Information Systems Research*. London: Wiley.

Bordewijk, J. L., & Kaam, B. van (1982) *Allocutie, Enkele gedachten over communicatie-vrijheid in een bekabeld land*. Baarn: Bosch & Keuning.

Buckland, M. K. (1989) Information handling, organizational structure, and power. *Journal of the American Society for Information Science*, **40**(5), 329–333.

Bullinger, H. J., & Kornwachs, K. (1987) Technology assessment concerning impacts of information systems. In H. J. Bullinger & B. Shackel (eds), *Human Computer Interaction–INTERACT'87*, Amsterdam: Elsevier, pp. 787–792.

Burgoon, J. K., Buller, D. B., Hale, J. L., & de Turck, M. A. (1984) Relational messages associated with nonverbal behaviors. *Human Communication Research*, **10**, 351–378.

Cambra, G. (1987) The implementation of a French textual teleconferencing prototype and experiments in IT uses. In L. Qvortrup (ed.), *Social Experiments with Information Technology*. Dordrecht: Reidel.

Carley, K. (1984) Electronic mail as managerial tool. Internal paper, Carnegie-Mellon University.

Ciborra, C. U. (1987) Research agenda for a transaction costs approach to information systems. In R. J. Boland & R. A. Hirschheim, *Critical Issues in Information Systems Research*. London: Wiley.

Ciborra, C. U., & Lanzara, G. F. (1991) Designing networks in action, formative contexts and post-modern systems development. In J. H. Erik Andriessen & R. A. Roe (eds), *Telematics and Work* (in press).

Claisse, G., & Rowe, F. (1987) The telephone in question: questions on communication. *Computer Networks and ISDN Systems*, **14**, 207–219.

Craipeau, S. (1991) The new modes of organization of work and the professions of regulation. In J. H. Erik Andriessen & R. A. Roe (eds), *Telematics and Work* (in press).

Culnan, M. J. (1985) The dimensions of perceived accessibility to information: implications for the delivery of information systems and services. *Journal of the American Society of Information Systems*, **36**(5), 302–308.

Culnan, M. J., & Markus, M. L. (1987) Information technologies. In F. M. Jablin, L. L. Putnam, K. H. Roberts, and L. W. Porter (eds), *Handbook of Organizational Communication*. Newbury Park, CA: Sage.

Daft, R. D., & Lengel, R. H. (1984) Information richness: a new approach to managerial behavior and organizational design. In B. Staw & L. L. Cummings (eds), *Research in Organizational Behavior*, Vol.6. Greenwich, CT: JAI Press, pp. 191–233.

Daft, R. L., & Lengel, R. H. (1986) Organizational information requirements, media richness and structural design. *Management Science*, **32**(5), 554–571.

Denning, P. (1982) Electronic junk, *Communications of the ACM*, **25**, 163–165.

Dennis, A. R., Georg, J. F., Jessup, L. M., Nunamaker, J. F., & Vogel, D. R. (1988) Information technology to support electronic meetings. *MIS Quarterly*, **12** (December), 591–613.

Desanctis, G., & Gallupe R. B. (1987) A foundation for the study of group decision support systems. *Management Science*, **33**(5), 589–609.

Dutton, W., Fulk, J., & Steinfield, C. (1982) Utilization of videoconferencing. *Telecommunications Policy*, **6**, 164–178.

Eason, K. D. (1987) Methods of planning the electronic workplace. *Behaviour and Information on Technology*, **6**(3), 229–238.

Eveland, J. D., & Bikson, T. K. (1988) Work group structures and computer support: a field experiment. *ACM Transactions on Office Information Systems*, **6**(4), 354–379.

Fafchamp, D., Reynolds, D., & Kuchinsky, A. (1989) The dynamics of small group decision making over the E-mail channel. *Proceedings of the First European Conference on CSCW*, London, September.

Farace, R. V., Monge, P. R., & Russel, H. M. (1977) *Communicating and Organizing*. Reading, Mass: Addison-Wesley.

FAST (1988) *The FAST II Programme. Results and Recommendations. Volume 2. Prospects for Human Work, Industrial & Organisational Strategies.* Brussels: Commission of the European Communities.

Feldman, M. S., & March, J. G. (1981) Information in organizations signal and symbol. *Administrative Science Quarterly*, **26**, 171–186.

Finholt, T., & Sproull, L. (1987) Electronic groups at work. Research paper, Carnegie Mellon Univeristy.

Foster, L. W., & Flynn, D. M. (1984) Management information technology: its effect on organizational form and function. *MIS Quarterly*, **3**, 229–236.

Frese, M. (1987) Human computer interaction in the office. *International Review of Industrial and Organizational Psychology*. Chichester: Wiley.

Fulk, J. (1989) Rational and social influences on communication media use. Paper for ICA Annual Convention, San Francisco, May.

Fulk, J., & Ryu, D. (1990) Perceiving electronic mail systems: a partial test of social information processing model of communication media in organizations, Paper for ICA Annual Convention, Dublin, June.

Fulk, J. & Steinfield, C. W. (1990) Context and communication: task requisites and electronic media use in a high technology organization. *Organization Science* (in press).

Fulk, J., Steinfield, C. W., Schmitz, J., & Power, J. G. (1987) A social information processing model of media use in organizations. *Communications Research*, **14**(5) 529–552.

Galbraith, J. R. (1977) *Organization Design*. Reading, Mass., Addison-Wesley.

Gale, S. (1989). Adding audio and video to an office environment. *Proceedings of the First European Conference on CSCW*, London.

Goldhaber, G. M., & Barnett, G. A. (1988) *Handbook of Organizational Communication*. Norwood, N. J., Ablex.

Gordon, G. E. (1988) The dilemma of telework: technology vs. tradition. In W. B. Korte, S. Robinson, & W. J. Steinle (eds), *Telework: Present Situation and Future Development of a New Form of Work Organization*. Amsterdam: North-Holland.

Greif, I. (ed.) (1988) *Computer Supported Cooperative Work. A Book of Readings*. San Mateo CA: Morgan Kaufmann.

Hacker, K. L., & Milano, R. (1988) Fundamental communication issues in the design of computer-mediated communication (CMC) systems. Paper presented to the International Communication Association Annual Convention, New Orleans, May.

Hacker, K., & Monge, L. (1988) Toward a communication-information model: a theoretical perspective for the design of computer-mediated communication systems. In A. O. Moscardini & E. H. Robson (eds), *Mathematical Modelling for Information Technology*. Chichester, England: Ellis Horwood, pp. 198–211.

Hansen, J. V., and Hill, N. C. (1989) Control and audit of electronic data interchange. *MIS Quarterly*, **8**, 403–413.

Heilmann, W. (1988) The organizational development of teleprogramming. In W. B. Korte, S. Robinson, & W. J. Steinte (eds), *Telework: Present Situation and Future Development of a New Form of Work Organization*. Amsterdam: North-Holland.

Hiltz, S. R. (1988) Productivity enhancement from computer-mediated communication: a systems contingency approach. *Communications of the ACM*, **31**(12), 438–1454.

Hiltz, S. R., & Johnson, K. (1989) Measuring acceptance of computer mediated communication systems. *Journal of the American Society for Information Science*, **40**, 386–397.

Hiltz, S. R. & Turoff, M. (1978) *The Network Nation: Human Communication Via Computer*. Reading, MA: Addison-Wesley.

Hiltz, S. R. & Turoff, M. (1985) Structuring computer-mediated communication systems to avoid information overload. *Communications of the ACM*, **28**, 680–689.

Hiltz, S. R., Turoff, M., & Johnson, K. (1984) Group decision support systems: a field experiment. Paper for ICA Annual Convention, San Francisco, May.

Hiltz, S. R., Johnson, K., & Turoff, M. (1986) Experiments in group decision making, communication process and outcome in face-to-face versus computerized conferences. *Human Communications Research*, **113**(2) 225–252.

Holand, U. & Danielsen, T. (1989) The psychology of cooperation—comsequences of descriptions. The power of creative dialogues. *Proceedings of First European Conference of CSCW*. London, September.

Huber, G. P. (1984) Issues in the design of group decision support systems. *MIS Quarterly*, September.

Huff, C., Sproull, L., & Kiesler, S. (1988) Computer communication and organizational commitment: tracing the relationship in a city government. Research paper, Carnegie Mellon University.

Huws, U. (1988) Remote possibilities: some difficulties in the analysis and quantification of telework in the UK. In W. B. Korte, S. Robinson & W. J. Steinle (eds), *Telework: Present Situation and Future Development of a New Form of Work Organization*, Amsterdam: North-Holland.

Jablin, F. M., Putnam, L. L., Roberts, K. H., & Porter, L. W. (1987) (eds) *Handbook of Organizational Communication, an Interdisciplinary Perspective*. London/Beverly Hills: Sage.

Jackson, P. (1990) Teleworking. Paper for the International Conference Computer Man and Organisation II, Nivelles: Free University of Brussels, May.

Johansen, R. (1988) *Groupware: Computer Support for Business Teams*. New York: The Free Press.

Judkins, P. E. (1988) Towards new patterns of work. In W. B. Korte, S. Robinson, & W. J. Steinle (eds), *Telework: Present Situation and Future Development of a New Form of Work Organization*, Amsterdam: North-Holland.

Keen, P. (1988) *Competing in Time: Using Telecommunication for Competitive Advantage*. Cambridge, MA: Ballinger.

Keen, P. G. W. (1987) Telecommunications and organizational choice. *Communications Research*, **14**(5), 588–606.

Kiesler, S., Siegel, J., & McGuire, T. W. (1984) Social psychological aspects of computer-mediated communication. *American Psychologist*, **39**(10), 1123–1134.

Klein, B., & Fröschle, H. P. (1988) Decentralization via teletex. Organizational and technical impact. In W. B. Korte, S. Robinson & W. J. Steinle (eds), *Telework: Present Situation and Future Development of a New Form of Work Organization.* Amsterdam: North-Holland.

Kling, R. (1987) Defining the boundaries of computing across complex organizations. In R. J. Boland and R. A. Hirschheim (eds), *Critical Issues in Information Systems Research.* London, Wiley.

Knights, D., & Wilmott, H. (eds) (1988) *New Technology and the Labour Process.* Basingstoke: Macmillan Press.

Köhler, H. (1987) Research on the use of computer based message systems in organizations—the Swedish IDAK project. In H.-J. Bullinger, & B. Shackel, (eds), *Human–Computer Interaction INTERACT '87.* Amsterdam: North-Holland.

Köhler, H. (1990) Introduction of municipal computer conferencing in Sweden. Paper for International Conference Computer Man and Organization II, Nivelles: Free University of Brussels, May.

Köhler, H. (1991) Potentials of computer conferencing, methodological contributions to the development of good computer support for human communication at work. In: J. H. Erik Andriessen and R. Roe (eds), *Telematics and Work* (in press).

Koopman, P. L. (1989) New information technology and organizational decision making. Paper for workshop on Current Issues in Organizational Studies at NIAS, The Netherlands, November.

Korte, W. B. (1988) Telework-potential, inception, operation and likely future situation. In W. B. Korte, S. Robinson & W. J. Steinle (eds), *Telework: Present Situation and Future Developments of a New Form of Work Organization.* Amsterdam: North-Holland.

Korte, W. B., Robinson, S., & Steinle, W. J. (eds) (1988) *Telework: Present Situation and Future Development of a New Form of Work Organization.* Amsterdam: North-Holland.

Kraemer, K. L., & King, J. L. (1986) Computer-based systems for cooperative work and group decisionmaking: Status of use and problems in development. In D. Peterson, *Proceedings of the Conference on Computer Supported Cooperative Work,* Austin, TX.

Kraut, R. E. (1987a) Predicting the use of technology: the case of telework. In R. E. Kraut (ed.), *Technology and the Transformation of White-collar Work,* Hillsdale, NJ: Lawrence Erlbaum.

Kraut, R. E. (ed.) (1987b) *Technology and the Transformation of White-collar Work.* Hillsdale, NJ: Lawrence Erlbaum.

Krcmar, H. (1989) Considerations for a framework for CATeam research, *Proceedings of the first European Conference on Computer Supported Cooperative Work.* London.

Kubicek, H. (1991) Different options for the development of telecommunication infrastructures. In J. H. Erik Andriessen & R. Roe (eds), *Telematics and Work* (in press).

Kubicek, H., & Fischer, U. (1988) (Tele-)Homework in the Federal Republic of Germany: historical background and future perspectives from a worker's perspective. In W. B. Korte, S. Robinson, & W. J. Steinle (eds), *Telework: Present Situation and Future Development of a New Form of Work Organization.* Amsterdam: North-Holland.

Kündig, Ä. T. (1988) Future computer and communication supported working environments. In R. Speth (ed.) *Research into Networks and Distributed Applications.* EEC, Brussels: North-Holland.

Latrille, J. (1987) Socio-technical aspects of electronic mail implementation. *Computer networks and ISDN Systems,* **14**, 83–290.

Lengel, R., & Daft, R. (1988) *The Selection of Communication Media as an Executive Skill.* Academy of Management Executive, p. 225–232.

Lievrouw, L. A., & Finn, A. T. (1988) Identifying the common dimensions of communication: the communication systems model. Paper presented to the International Communication Association, New Orleans, May.

Littlejohn, S. W. (1989), *Theories of Human Communication*. Belmont CA: Wadsworth.

Malone, T., Yates, J., & Benjamin, R. I. (1987) Electronic markets and electronic hierarchies. *Communications of the ACM*, 30(6), 484–497.

Malone, T. W., Grant, K. R., Turbak, F. A., Brobst, S. A., & Cohen, M. D. (1987) Intelligent information sharing systems. *Communications of the ACM*, 30(5), 390–402.

Markus, M. L. (1983) Power, politics and MIS implementation. *Communication of the ACM*, 26, 430–444.

Markus, M. L. (1987) Toward a 'critical mass' theory of interactive media: universal access, interdependence and diffusion. *Communications Research*, 14(5), 491–511.

Markus, M. L. (1989) Asynchronous tools in small face-to-face groups. Information Systems Working Paper 3-90, J. E. Anderson Graduate School of Management, UCLA.

Markus, M. L. & Forman, J. (1989) A social analysis of group technology use. *Information Systems Working Paper*, 2-90, School of Management, UCLA.

Mehlmann, M. (1988) Social aspects of telework: facts, hopes, fears, ideas. In W. B. Korte, S. Robinson, & W. J. Steinle (eds), *Telework: Present Situation and Future Development of a New Form of Work Organization*. Amsterdam: North-Holland.

Minzberg, H. (1973) *The Nature of Managerial Work*. New York: Harper & Row. Reissued in 1980, Englewood Cliffs, NJ: Prentice-Hall.

Moens, L., & Valenduc, G. (1987) Assessment of impacts of telematics onto industrial structures. *Computer Networks & ISDN Systems*, 14(2–5), 245–249.

Monge, P., & Capella, J. A. (eds) (1980) *Multivariate Techniques in Human Communication Research*. New York: Academic Press.

Morley, I. E. (1991) Computer supported cooperative work (CSCW) and engineering product design. In J. H. Erik Andriessen and R. Roe (eds), *Telematics and Work* (in press).

Morley, I. E., & Stephenson, G. M. (1969) Interpersonal and interparty exchange: a laboratory simulation of an industrial negotiation at the plant-level. *British Journal of Psychology*, 60, 543–545.

Nolan, R. L. (1979) Managing the crisis in dataprocessing. *Harvard Business Review*, March–April.

Nora, S., & Minc, A. (1980) *The Computerization of Society* (translated from French, 1978). Cambridge, MA: MIT Press.

O'Reilly, C. A., & Pondy, L. R. (1979) Organizational communication. In S. Kerr (ed), *Organizational Behavior*. Columbus, OH: Grid.

Olson, M. (1987) Telework: practical experience and future prospects. In R. E. Kraut (ed.), *Technology and the Transformation of White-collar Work*. London: Erlbaum.

Olson, M. (1988) Organizational barriers to telework. In W. B. Korte, S. Robinson & W. J. Steinle (eds), *Telework: Present Situation and Future Development of a New Form of Work Organization*. Amsterdam: North-Holland.

Olson, M. H. (1989) Work at home for computer professionals: current attitudes and future prospects, *ACM Transactions on Office Information Systems*, 7(4), 317–338.

Ouchi, W. G. (1979) A conceptual framework for the design of organisational control mechanisms, *Management Science*, September, 833–848.

Palme, J. (1988) Extending message handling to computer conferencing. In *Computer Communication Technologies for the 90's, Proceedings*. North-Holland, pp. 44–49.

Peiro, J. M., & Prieto, F. (1991) Telematics and organizational processes. In J. H. Erik Andriessen & R. A. Roe (eds), *Telematics and Work* (in press).

Peterson, D. (ed.) (1986) *(CSCW '86) Proceedings of the Conference on Computer-Supported Cooperative Work*, Austin, TX.

Pocock, R. A. (1987) Communicating in the global office. *Computer Networks and ISDN Systems*, **14**, 251–258.

Poole, M. S. & Desanctis (1990) Understanding the use of group decision support systems: the theory of adaptive structuration. In J. Fulk & C. W. Steinfield (eds), *Organizations and Communication Technology*, Newbury Park CA: Sage.

Poole, M. S., Holmes, M. & Desanctis, G. (1989) *Conflict Management in a Computer Supported Meeting Environment*. University of Minnesota, Department of Speech Communication. MS-42-88.

Postel, Jonathan B., Finn, G. G., Katz, A. R. & Reynolds, J. K. (1988) An experimental multimedia mail system. *ACM Transactions on Office Information Systems*, **6**(1), 63–81.

Proceedings of the First European Conference on Computer supported cooperative work (1989), London, September.

PTT (1987), *Onderzoek onder de gebruikers van de dienst telefonisch vergaderen*. Den Haag: PTT.

Qvortrup, L. (1991) The analysis and change of computerized organizations: structured analysis versus pragmatic interactionism. In J. H. Andriessen & R. A. Roe (eds), *Telematics and Work* (in press).

Reese, S. D. (1988) New communication technologies and the information worker: the influence of occupation. *Journal of Communication*, **38**(2), 59–70.

Rice, R. E. (1984) Mediated group communication. In R. Rice and associates, *The New Media*. Beverly Hills: Sage.

Rice, R. E. (1987a) Computer-mediated communication and organizational innovation. *Journal of Communication*, **37**(4), 65–94.

Rice, R. E. (1987b) New patterns of social structure in an information society. In J. E. Schement and L. A. Lievrouw (eds), *Competing Visions Complex Realities: Social Aspects of the Information Society*. Norwood, NJ: Ablex.

Rice, R. E., & Bair, J. H. (1984) New organizational media and productivity. In R. Rice and associates, *The New Media*. Beverly Hills: Sage.

Rice, R. E., & Barnett, G. A. (1985) Group communication networking in an information environment: applying metric multidimensional scaling. In M. McLaughlin (ed.), *Communication Yearbook 9*. Beverly Hills: Sage, pp. 315–338.

Rice, R. E., & Borgman, C. L. (1983) The use of computer-monitored data in information science and communication research. *Journal of the American Society of information Science*, **34**(4), 247–256.

Rice, R. E., & Love, G. (1987) Electronic Emotion. *Communication Research*, **14**(1), 85–108.

Rice, R. E., & Shook, D. E. (1988) Access to, usage of, and outcomes from an electronic messaging system. *ACM Transactions on Office Information Systems*, **6**(3), 255–276.

Rice, R. E. & Shook, D. E. (1990) Voice messaging, coordination and communication. In J. Galegher, R. Kraut & C. Egido (eds), *Intellectual Technology: Social and Technological Foundations of Cooperative Work*. Hillsdale, NJ: Erlbaum.

Rice, R. E., & Steinfield, C. (1991) New forms of organizational communication via electronic mail and voice messaging. In J. H. Erik Andriessen & R. A. Roe (eds), *Telematics and Work* (in press).

Rice, R. E., & Williams, F. (1984) Theories old and new: the study of new media. In R. Rice and associates, *The New Media*. Beverly Hills: Sage.

Rice, R. E., Grant, A., Schmitz, J., & Torobin, J. (1990) A network approach to predicting the adoption and outcomes of electronic messaging. *Social Networks*, March.

Robinson, M. (1988) Computer assisted meetings: modelling and mirroring in organizational systems. In H. J. Bullinger, E. N. Protonotarios, D. Bouwhuis, & F. Reim (eds), *Increased Competitiveness*, Brussels–Luxemburg: Elsevier.

Robinson, M. (1989) Double level languages and cooperative working. *Proceedings of Conference 'Support, Society and Culture'*, University of Amsterdam, March.

Rockart, J. F., & Short, J. E. (1989) IT in the 1990s: managing organizational interdependence. *Sloan Management Review*, Winter, 7–17.

Roe, R. A. (1991) Reflections on telematics and work. In J. H. Erik Andriessen & R. A. Roe (eds), *Telematics and Work* (in press).

Rogard, V. (1991) Implementation of electronic mail in the banking sector: a strategical issue. In J. H. Erik Andriessen & R. A. Roe (eds), *Telematics and Work* (in press).

Rogers, E. M. (1983) *Diffusion of Innovations*. New York: The Free Press.

Romahn, C., & Mühlbach, L. (1988) Multipoint teleconferencing: empirical studies with different variate. Paper for International Symposium Human Factors in Telecommunication, The Hague.

Ruchinskas, J., Svenning, L., & Steinfield, C. (1990) Video comes to organizational communications. The case of ARCO vision. In B. Sypher (ed.), *Case Studies in Organizational Communication*, New York: Guilford.

Rutter, D. R. (1987) *Communication by Telephone*. Oxford: Pergamon Press.

Ryan, G. M., Wynne, R., Cullen, K., Ronayne, T., Dolphin, C., Korte, W. B., & Robinson, S. (1988) Concepts, methodology and guidelines for understanding and managing it uptake processes in user organisations. *Commission of European Communities, Proceedings of the 5th Annual ESPRIT Conference*. Brussels, November.

Salancik, G. R., & Pfeffer, J. (1978) A social information processing approach to job attitudes and task design. *Administrative Science Quarterly*, 22, 427–456.

Santo, H. (1988) AMIGO: advanced messaging in groups—interim report. *Computer Networks and ISDN Systems*, 15, 55–60.

Schmidt, K. (1989) Cooperative work. A conceptual framework. In J. Rasmussen, J. Leplat & B. Brehmer (eds), *Modelling Distributed Decision Making*, New York: Wiley.

Schmitz, J. & Fulk, J. (1990) The role of organizational colleagues in media selection. *Annual Convention of the International Communication Association*, Dublin, Ireland.

Schneider, S. C. (1987) Information overload: causes and consequences. *Human Systems Management*, 7, 143–153.

Shirley, S. (1988) Telework in the UK. In W. B. Korte, S. Robinson & W. J. Steinle (eds), *Telework: Present Situation and Future Development of a New Form of Work Organization*. Amsterdam: North-Holland.

Short, J., Williams, E., & Christie, B. (1976) *The Social Psychology of Telecommunications*. London: Wiley.

Siegel, J., Dubrowski, V., Kiesler, S., & McGuire, T. W. (1986) Group processes in computer-mediated communication. *Organizational Behavior and Human Decision Processes*, 37, 157–187.

Skyrme, D. J. (1989) *Computer Conferencing at Digital*, Reading, UK: DEC.

Smith, T. H., Zigurs, I. & Pacanowsky, M. (1990) *Multimedia Communication Support for Distributed Groups: An Exploratory Field Study*. University of Colorado, College of Business and Administration, Faculty Working Paper series.

Sola Pool, I. de (1988) *Forecasting The Telephone. A Retrospective Technology Assessment*. Norwood, NY: Ablex.

Sola Pool, I. de (ed.) (1977) *The Social Impact of the Telephone*. Cambridge MA: MIT Press.

Sproull, L. S., & Kiesler, S. (1986) Reducing social context cues: electronic mail in organizational communication. *Management Science*, **32**(11), 1492–1512.

Steinfield, C. W. (1985) Computer-mediated communication in an organizational setting: Explaining task-related and socioemotional uses. In M. McLaughlin (ed.), *Communication Yearbook 9*. Beverly Hills: Sage.

Steinfield, C. W. (1986) Computer-mediated communication systems. In M. Williams (Ed.), *Annual Review of Information Science and Technology*, Vol. 21. White Plains, NY, Knowledge Industry Publications, pp. 167–202.

Steinfield, C. W. (1988) A preliminary test of a social information processing model of media use in organizations. Paper for ICA Annual Convention, San Francisco.

Steinfield, C. W. (1990) Computer-mediated communications in the organization. Using electronic mail at Xerox. In B. D. Sypher (ed.), *Case studies in Organizational Communication*. New York: Guilford.

Steinfield, C. W., & Fulk, J. (1986) Information processing in organizations and media choice. Paper for the International Association Communication Annual Convention.

Steinfield, C. W., & Fulk, J. (1987) On the role of theory in research on information technologies in organizations, an introduction to the special issue. *Communication Research*, **14**(5), 479–490.

Steinfield, C. W., & Fulk, J. (1988) Computer-mediated communication systems as mass communication media. Paper for Telecommunication Policy Research Conference, Arlie House, VA.

Steinfield, C. W., Boahua Jin, & Lin Lin Ku (1988) A preliminary test of a social information processing model of media use in organizations. Paper for the ICA Annual Conference, New Orleans.

Stewart, C. M. (1986) Voice messaging: guidelines for implementation. Paper for Office System Research Association Annual Conference, Houston, TX.

Svenning, L. L., & Ruchinskas, J. E. (1984) Organizational teleconferencing. In R. E. Rice and associates, *The New Media: Communication, Research and Technology*. Beverly Hills, CA: Sage.

Sullivan, S., & Rayburn. J. D. (1990) The impact of electronic mail on the legislative process in the Florida House of Representatives, Paper for the ICA Annual Convention, Dublin, June.

Swanson, E. B. (1987) Information systems in organization theory: a review. In R. J. Boland & R. A. Hirschheim (eds), *Critical Issues in Information Systems Research*. New York: Wiley.

Taillieu, T. (1990) The impact of an integrated information network in a Belgian supermarket chain. *Proceedings of International Conference 'Computer, Man and Organization II'*, Brussels: Free University, May.

Tavakolian, H. (1989) Linking the information technology structure with organizational competitive strategy: a survey. *MIS Quarterly*, September, 309–317.

Teubner, A. L., & Vaske, J. J. (1988) Monitoring computers users' behavior in office environments. *Behavior and Information Technology*, **7**, 67–78.

Thomas, J. B. & Trevino, L. K. (1989) The strategic implications of media mismatch: coping with uncertainty and equivocality. Paper for ICA Conference, San Francisco, May.

Trevino, L., Lengel, R. & Daft, R. (1987) Media symbolism, media richness and media choice in organizations. A symbolic interactionist perspective. *Communications Research*, **14**(5), 553–574.

Turoff, M. (1989) The anatomy of a technological innovation: computer mediated communication. *Journal of Technological Forecasting and Social Change*, **36**, 107–132.

Turoff, M., Hiltz, S. R., & Bahgat, A. N. F. (1989) Distributed group decision support systems and computer mediated communication systems. *MIS Quarterly*.

Watson, R. T., Desanctis, G., & Poole, M. S. (1988) Using a GDSS to facilitate group consensus: some intended and unintended consequence. *MIS Quarterly*, September, 463–478.

Watzlawick, P., Beavin, J., & Jackson, D. (1967) *Pragmatics of Human Communications: A Study of Interactional Patterns, Pathologies and Paradoxes*. New York: Norton.

Wellens, A. R. (1986) Use of a psychological distancing model to assess differences in telecommunication media. In L. Parker and C. Olgen (eds), *Teleconferencing and Electronic Media* (5). Madison: Center for Interactive Programs.

Weltevreden, P. S. (1991) The strategy of the European Community. In J. H. Erik Andriessen & R. A. Roe (eds) *Telematics and Work* (in press).

Werther, W. B. Jr. (1988) Corporate video applications. *LODJ*, No.9, 4.

Williamson, O. E. (1975) *Markets and Hierarchies: Analysis and Antitrust Implications*. New York: Free Press.

Wilson, P. (1988) Key research in computer supported cooperative work (CSCW). In R. Speth (ed.), *Research on Networks and Distributed Applications*. EEC, Brussels: Elsevier.

Wofford, J. L. (1977) *Organizational Communication*. New York: McGraw-Hill.

Young, R. E. (1988) Interim report on the cosmos project. *Report No. 45.5*. London: Queen Mary College.

Zigurs, I., Poole, M. S., & Desanctis, G. L. (1988) A study of influence in computer-mediated group decision making. *MIS Quarterly*, December, 625–644.

Zuboff, S. (1988) *In the Age of the Smart Machine. The Future of Work and Power*. New York: Basic Books.

Chapter 3

PERFORMANCE MEASUREMENT: A MULTI-DISCIPLINE VIEW

Daniel R. Ilgen and Jeffrey Schneider
Department of Psychology
Michigan State University
USA

Performance measurement plays a number of important roles in organizations. The ones most familiar to the readers of this volume are those that guide personnel decisions or provide counsel and guidance to employees. Both of these functions are central to human resource management. In the case of human resource management, the performance of interest is that of employees on clusters of tasks typically labeled jobs. Performance measurement procedures are guided by information gained from job analyses, and the measured performance is typically mapped onto individual employees. Although the measurement process may involve any combination of objective outcomes of employees' job behaviors or subjective evaluations of employee performance, for a large number of jobs, the primary measure is a subjective rating, a performance appraisal.

Human resource management concerns for the measurement of performance are by no means the only ones in organizations. Performance measurement plays a major role in at least two other domains. One of these is the human factors focus on the design and evaluation of human and machine subsystems. Of interest to the human factors specialist is the performance of the subsystem, with particular attention paid to the human being as part of that system. Human performance is measured with reference to the total system and to the capacity of the human, himself or herself. Thus, for example, interest would not only be in the number of units an individual produces but also in that number as a function of the individual's total capacity to produce such units over a known time period.

A third area in which performance measurement is central is that of production control and operations management. The performance of interest

International Review of Industrial and Organizational Psychology 1991 Volume 6
Edited by C. L. Cooper and I. T. Robertson © 1991 John Wiley & Sons Ltd.

in these cases is that of the total production system or some identifiable subunit of it. Although employees frequently are imbedded in these systems and influence the systems' performance, unlike human resource management and human factors, human beings are not necessarily a part of the targeted systems. Furthermore, even when they are a component, the performance measurements that are taken on the systems may not isolate human contributions.

Although performance measurement plays a major role in all three of the above domains, there is surprisingly little overlap among the performance measurement literature generated within any one of them. This state of affairs is unfortunate. It is unfortunate because the parochial concerns within each domain tend to focus too narrowly on the types of performance measurement issues that are typically addressed within any particular domain. For example, each domain tends to focus at one level of analysis, paying little attention to the implications of multi-level issues that have been raised by others (e.g. Roberts, Hulin, & Rousseau, 1978; Rousseau, 1985). Performance measurement from the human resource management perspective addresses performance only at the individual level. For human factors, performance measurement deals with subsystems limited primarily to the individual–technical system interaction, and operations management focuses on larger systems up to and including the entire organization. Since any one of the levels of analysis is, in some ways, dependent on the other, the isolation within levels represented by the three domains leads to overlook contributions that each could make to the other.

The orientation of the present chapter is toward the measurement of performance for purposes traditionally of interest in the area of human resource management. Yet, it is our belief that both human factors and operations management approaches to performance measurement have potential for contributing performance measurement in the human resource management domain. Therefore, we shall discuss major issues related to performance measurement in each of the three domains. We will then suggest potential contributions to performance measurement provided by an understanding of the work on performance measurement in human factors and operations management. However, before presenting performance measurement from within each domain, we shall briefly develop a common framework for the definition of performance and performance measurement.

PERFORMANCE, PERFORMANCE MEASUREMENT, AND PERFORMANCE EVALUATION: A POINT OF VIEW

Interdependent Processes

At first glance, performance, performance measurement, and performance evaluation are straightforward, relatively independent outcomes or processes that can be combined in serial fashion to provide a summary evaluation of the person or unit for whom or which performance is of interest. Performance is what the person or system does. Performance measurement is the quantification of what was done, and performance evaluation is the attachment of a judgment of the value or quality of the quantified performance measurement. In actuality, the three constructs are far more complex and interdependent than this description implies, and yet the complexitities and interdependencies are frequently overlooked. As a result, in our opinion, naive and unrealistic statements are often made about the distinctiveness of the three and the ability of any one of them, particularly performance measurements and performance evaluations, to successfully capture the variables for which they were designed to address. At the same time, while recognizing the pitfalls of oversimplification, we also recognize the errors of making the problem of measuring performance too convoluted by getting overly involved in the complexies. Therefore, we will simply mention some of the interconnections among the three.

Performance is typically defined as the execution of some action or the manner of reacting to some stimuli. Yet, regardless of the person or system for which performance is of interest, not all actions or reactions constitute performance. A necessary condition for performance is the identification of the *domain* of activities or outcomes that constitute performance. It is also necessary to identify the levels of the actions or reactions that will reflect an ordering of performance along some scale from good to bad within any particular dimension. Thus, the performance of any system or person exists in some space defined by content dimensions and levels of activity along these dimensions. The space is defined by a judgment process. In the case of human resource management, this process is called a job analysis, and the prescribed levels on the dimensions are referred to as performance standards. Put another way, to define performance, it is first necessary to determine a performance space comprised of descriptive dimensions with two or more levels in which performance will take place and be measured.

Performance measurement results when actors (used here to refer both to persons and systems) act or react in the defined performance space. Performance measurement, by definition occurs either during or after the performance has occurred. It involves mapping actions or reactions onto a measurement scale that, by previous design, contains dimensions and levels of those dimensions that have been defined to constitute the performance space. The result is a score or a set of scores indicating what actions have taken place. Finally, the measure is associated with some person or system; it must be referenced to someone or something.

Performance evaluation is the result of a comparison process whereby the measured performance is compared to the standards for performance. Often the evaluation is seen as something that occurs after measurement. However, just as frequently, measurement immediately implies evaluation. Consider, for example, the case in which the performance dimension has only two levels, such as might be the case for an employee's attendance on a particular day. In this case, the initial definition of performance identifies attendance as an important dimension, and, as soon as attendance is measured and an employee is found to be either present or absent, the evaluation is immediately implied from the measurement.

The above discussion of performance, performance measurement, and performance evaluation was meant to lay out the essential factors in any performance measurement system. We contend that all performance measurement explicitly involves two processes and either implicitly or explicitly involves a third. The first process is a descriptive one in which the nature of the performance domain is described. The second is a measurement and mapping process that measures the performance and maps it onto (i.e. attributes it to) a performer. The third process is that of evaluation. At times, performance measurement is discussed as if it is only concerned with the second of these three processes.

However, it is not possible to do the second if there does not exist a description of the domain of performance that is to be measured. Furthermore, that description is not carried out in a vacuum. Any descriptive process must take into account issues of measurement related to whether or not particular dimensions are measurable. Therefore, performance measurement is interdependent with performance description. Finally, although sometimes it is argued that evaluation may come after description and measurement, we would argue the evaluation is involved in the nature of the dimensions that are measured in a performance measurement system as well as the units of measurement that are used within the dimensions. All performance measurement systems assess performance on those dimensions of performance that are believed to be important for effective performance. The identification of a dimension as 'important' is an evaluation. Next, on the dimension, whatever is used to measure the amount or degree to which that dimension is present or absent contains evaluation. The evaluation may be explicit, as is the case when judgments are made regarding the level of performance along a dimension in units such as percentages of standard where the standard is indexed to 'good' performance. It is implicit when the measurement process simply counts the presence or absence of particular behaviors or outcomes, but these outcomes have been chosen on some a priori basis of their importance or relevance for good performance.

In conclusion, we see performance measurement as a function of the interaction of three interrelated processes, none of which is free from subjectivity. This perspective provides the backdrop against which we review performance measurement. The view may seem so intuitively obvious. We contend that it is not. Frequently discussions of performance measurement ignore necessary interdependencies and give the impression of independence that we do not feel is justified. There is also a tendency among advocates of some performance measurement systems to see their systems as objective and others as not. From our point of view, all performance measurement systems rely upon subjective judgments somewhere in the measurement process. Likewise, there is the tendency to view performance as different from performance measurement where the former is objective and the latter is not. Such statements occur within human resource management, human factors, and operations management. They also appear when measurement systems attributed to one domain are compared to the other. For example, there is a tendency to view performance measurement done by operations management systems as more objective than those systems found in the human resource management (HRM) domain. Our point is that all measurement of performance depend upon subjective judgments to some degree; thus, dealing with subjectivity is an issue of making tradeoffs, an issue that is often ignored in discussions of performance measurement.

Performance Measurement Issues

In our discussion of performance measurement within HRM, human factors, and operations management, we shall address five key elements of the performance measurement process. We first assume that all performance measurement systems are constructed to serve some *purpose*. It is possible that the outputs from the measurement system may be used for purposes that differ from those for which the system was originally designed, but, even in this case, the use is also made for some purpose. Next, we shall assume that the measured performance is to be attributed to (associated with) some *source*. In the HRM area, the source to which performance is associated is typically an employee. The third ingredient of performance measurement is that of *performance criteria*. It will be argued that to measure performance requires that decisions be made regarding what it is that will constitute performance. Next, we shall address the *criteria for performance measures*. These are the criteria against which the quality of the measure is judged; they are different from the performance criteria that are used to define the nature of the measurement. Finally, the actual *methods* of measuring performance will be addressed. The discussion of methods at one level is simply descriptions of how performance is measured, but these descriptions must be put in context by considering the extent to which they address the first five issues mentioned above.

PERFORMANCE MEASUREMENT IN HUMAN RESOURCE MANAGEMENT

Purpose

Performance measurement in HRM is designed to accomplish one or both of two primary purposes. One of these is to generate information about employees that can be used by supervisors and other persons in the organization to make personnel decisions regarding the employees, and the other is to provide feedback to the employees about performance (Bernardin & Beatty, 1984; Latham & Wexley, 1981). There are a wide variety of personnel decisions to which such information can be put, such as decisions regarding promotions, raises, who to send for training and many others. With respect to employee feedback the uses can be classified into those that are aimed at aiding the person to learn about how the job should be done and those concerned with motivating the person to perform well. Frequently, the same performance measurement system is used to accomplish both purposes aimed at organizational personnel decision making and those related to the individual employee's learning and motivation. Unfortunately, in spite of the desire for parsimony and a unitary system, the combination of all purposes into one system does not work very well.

Recent interest at the purposes of performance measurement in HRM has focused on how performance ratings are affected by the rater's knowledge of the purpose of the ratings. Almost all performance measurement in the HRM domain involves performance ratings. These ratings depend upon human judgment, and there is reasonable evidence that awareness of the purpose to which ratings are to be put affects the ratings that are produced by raters. These effects are independent of the actual performance of the person being rated. Zedeck & Cascio (1982) varied methods of rater training and the purpose of ratings and found that the purpose had a greater effect on the accuracy of ratings than did the methods of training that they employed. Explanations for purpose effects are both motivational (Kane, 1980) and cognitive (Ilgen & Feldman, 1983). Kane (1980) argued that conditions in work settings often motivate people to bias ratings in a particular direction. Consistent with this interpretation is the data of Farh & Werbel (1986) that found self-ratings of students were more lenient when the ratings were to be used as part of the students' grade in a course than when they were not. Less obvious but still consistent with a motivational interpretation, is the purpose effects found with police rookies (Bernardin, Orban, & Carlyle, 1981) and college students (McIntyre, Smith, & Hassett, 1984). In the former case, when rateers believed their ratings of rookie police officers would be used for administrative decisions, the ratings were more lenient than when they were to be used as private feedback for personal information and self-improvement. Likewise, evaluations of graduate teaching assistants that were either to be used to judge the accuracy of the raters or to be given as feedback to the teaching assistants produced ratings that differed somewhat although the size of the difference was not very large (McIntyre, Smith, & Hassett, 1984).

From a cognitive standpoint, rating purpose is believed to frame the decision-making task, and framing effects have been shown to affect ratings. Such cognitive effects may explain the interactions between purpose and gender observed by Dobbins, Cardy, & Truxillo (1986; 1988). In the 1988 study, those with traditional stereotypic views of women and work rated the performance of women less accurately when ratings were to be used for administrative purposes than for experimental purposes. The authors suggested that the combination of the cues from the stereotypes and the traditional work-related cues inherent in the description of administrative purposes may have framed the performance judgment task in ways that affected the judgment.

Regardless of the way in which rating purpose impacts on ratings, the important conclusion regarding performance measurements in the HRM domain is that the purposes to which they are put are likely to impact the rating itself because of the heavy reliance upon human judgment in the measurement process. We would agree with Latham (1986) that training is likely to modify this effect; however, we are less convinced than he that the effect will go away or be so much affected by training as not to be a concern. In our opinion, regardless of training, the purpose under which performance ratings are gathered is likely to have some influence on the rating. Training may decrease the extent to which the purpose will bias ratings for a number of uses of performance appraisals that are relatively consistent with the purpose for which the data were gathered. However, if the purposes under which the ratings were made are inconsistent with the purposes to which the ratings are to be applied, a great deal of caution is needed regarding the latter use of the ratings. The inconsistent purpose effect is most likely to be a problem when personal records containing performance ratings obtained for one purpose are later accessed and used for another purpose (Ilgen, Barnes-Farrell, & McKellin, 1990).

Source

Almost without exception, measures of performance in the HRM domain are mapped back onto the individual. This is the case, regardless of whether the measure is used for administrative purposes, employee learning, or employee motivation.

The one exception to the above is team performance. In the last few years there has been an increasing interest in organizing work around work teams. There has been a great deal of debate about the value of individual performance appraisals in settings where teamwork and cooperation are necessary (see, e.g., descriptions of Deming's beliefs, in Moss & Moen, 1989), but most of these issues have not been addressed empirically. Given the increased interest in organizing work around teams, the issue of the level at which performance should be measured and to whom it should be attributed is an important one which deserves considerable attention in the near future. The work of Pritchard and his colleagues (Pritchard et al., 1989) regarding productivity measurement is a step in the right direction. This work will be discussed under HRM measures.

Performance Criteria

Performance criteria in HRM are referenced to the job and developed for the persons who hold the job. These criteria differ in the way that they are established or developed and in the types of standards against which performance is measured. With respect to criterion development, performance standards are either established a priori for the job and applied to all those who hold a job with the same description in an organization, or they are generated for a particular person in his or her job. In the former case, the combination of a job analysis and the setting of job standards can be used to establish expectations and descriptions of jobs that include the behaviors expected of people in the job and quantity and quality standards for those who hold those positions. This procedure is used when there are a number of persons who hold the same job. The individualized approach to job standard setting typically involves some form of management by objectives (MBO) where job incumbents working directly with their supervisors develop a set of objectives and goals for a given period of time that describe what will be done and the outcomes that will be produced during that time period. These goals and objectives then become the standards against which performance is measured.

A final class of performance standards is that of a relative comparison of employees' performance. This relative comparison may be in comparison to others in the work group or some other defined reference group. In this case, performance is rated by another on some scale that asks the rater to judge the person's performance relative to the group. Verbal anchors such as 'outstanding' or 'above average' are presented to the rater and, when done well, these anchors are described in sufficient detail for all raters using the scale to have similar perceptions about the meaning of the anchors. For example, if an anchor of 'outstanding' were used, it might be described to mean those conditions when the person met all performance goals and accomplished all tasks with a level of quality that would be found only by those who were in the top 5% of those in the job. The combination of the verbal descriptions along with training on the use of the scales helps to standardize the set of raters by creating a common frame of reference for the rating. Nevertheless, the rating is still a relative judgement and does not provide an absolute standard for the performance measure. Many of the performance measures in HRM use performance criteria that are of this form.

Performance Measurement Criteria

Thorndike, in 1949, described four criteria for performance measures: validity, reliability, freedom from bias, and practicality. The inclusion of validity and reliability in the list of criteria implies that the standards for performance measures are similar to those of the tests. The measures are, in a sense, analogs of tests where the construct being measured by the test is job performance. This perspective on performance measures is maintained in the most recent principles for personnel selection procedures published by the Society of Industrial and Organizational Psychology (SIOP, 1987). Freedom from bias most frequently originates from two relatively independent mechanisms. The first of these is that of rater bias. In this case, those who use the rating may systematically rate the performance of particular individuals either higher or lower across a number of dimensions than is justifiable from the ratees' performance. These biases are most frequently suspected when there exist systematic mean differences in elevation or depression of mean ratings for identifiable subgroups of employees, such as women or minorities. Finally, the concern for practicality as a measurement criterion is obvious. Ironically, in spite of its obvious importance, very little attention is given to the discussion of issues of practicality in the literature.

Although there has been little disagreement in the four criteria for performance measurement over the last 40 years, there are disagreements in the relative importance of some of them. In particular, the issue of whether or not performance measures should be considered analogous to tests and, therefore, be carefully scrutinized with respect to their reliability and validity in the psychometric sense has been debated. The debate arises, in our opinion, because of the tension between the difficulty of establishing the validity of performance measures and the criterion of practicality. Since jobs do not often possess objective standards against which to compare performance measures, inferences about validity must be indirect. The psychometric or test-analog focus on performance measures recognizes this, but argues that this difficulty does not decrease the need to attempt to validate the measure (SIOP, 1987). Certainly, construct validation would allow for developing some inferences about the measure's validity. In the United States, those concerned about the practicality of validation have looked to the reactions of the courts in attempting to decide how much validity seems to be needed. In an early decision responding to performance appraisals, *Brito* v. *Zia Co.* (1973), it was ruled that performance appraisals should be considered as tests and subject to the same standards as expressed in the Uniform Guidelines on Employee Selection

Procedures (1978). However, subsequent court decisions tended to respond to the practices surrounding the use of performance measures such as the availability of the appeals systems, the extent to which performance measures were reviewed by the employees being rated and a superior of the rater, etc. than to the validity of the measures (Barrett & Kernan, 1987; Field & Holley, 1982; Werner, 1990). Barrett & Kernan (1987) went so far as to conclude that, if one looked only at the actions of the courts, professional validity issues were not of crucial importance for the design of performance appraisals that would be viewed as acceptable by the legal system.

Since the Barrett & Kernan (1987) review, a US Supreme Court Decision (*Watson* v. *Fort Worth Bank and Trust*, 1988) has interpreted performance measures much more in line with the test analogue than was the case of the decisions reviewed by Barrett & Kernan (1987). Therefore, it is premature to conclude the performance appraisals will not be subject to more stringent scrutiny regarding their validity. It is too early to tell the impact of the *Watson* v. *Fort Worth Bank and Trust* at this time, but it is reasonable to expect that it will nudge practices in the United States more in the direction of paying attention to the validity criterion.

Measures

Both objective and subjective performance measures can be used for HRM purposes, although subjective measures based on raters' judgments are far more common. This preference is due, in part, to weaknesses in objective measures, the most serious of which are contamination by factors not under the control of the individuals whose performance is being measured and the tendency for objective measures to be simple countable outputs that often do not capture the major performance issues in the job (Landy & Farr, 1983). In addition, there are a large number of jobs for which objective performance measures are not readily available. Although subjective measures are hardly free of contamination and can be implemented in ways that create the counting mentality, they are more easily adapted to most jobs so are not as restricted with respect to the pool of jobs to which they apply. For these and other reaons, subjective measures remain overwhelming methods of choice for assessing performance for HRM purposes. For that reason, we shall limit our attention to subjective performance appraisal measures.

An extensive literature exists on performance appraisals, and this literature continues to grow. Performance appraisal options and issues are well documented in a number of recent books on the topic (see for example, Berk, 1986; Bernardin & Beatty, 1984; DeVries *et al.*, 1986; Landy & Farr, 1983; Latham & Wexley, 1981; Landy, Zedeck, & Cleveland, 1983, as well as the review chapter by Latham (1986) in the first volume of the *International Review of Industrial and Organizational Psychology* series).

Since the Latham (1986) review, no new measurement procedures have been introduced. Therefore, most of the conclusions about the nature of performance measures reached in the earlier reviews still hold and we will not repeat them here. One possible exception to this involves appraisals that focus on employee behaviors. Virtually all discussions of performance appraisals in the recent past argue for the use of appraisals that require the rating of behaviors rather than rating personal traits. The underlying assumption of this work is that behaviors are more objective and observable and require fewer inferences on the part of the rater. The work on performance accuracy leads to questioning of this assumption (Feldman, 1981; Nathan & Lord, 1983; Pulakos, 1986). It is argued that appraising the performance of another is a social perception and judgment process for the rater. These perceptions are influenced by general impressions that distort memory and recall in line with impressions such that descriptions of behaviors may not reflect actual behaviors observed, but reconstructions of what the rater believes occurred based upon the general impressions. Borman (1987) found that regardless of what should be done, raters rate others on the basis of impressions that are trait-like rather than on the basis of behaviors. Presenting the raters with appraisals that require ratings of behaviors rather than traits is not likely to remove the influence of trait-like general impressions, or are the ratings of behaviors necessarily accurate reflections of the behaviors that occurred because the recall of the behaviors by the rater will have been 'filtered through' the trait-like beliefs held by the rater. Therefore, at this point in time, the evidence from the literature on performance accuracy calls into question the assumption that behaviors are somehow better representations of employees' actual performance than other measures (Ilgen et al., in press). At the same time, this does not mean that some of the other advantages of behaviorally focused appraisals, such as those associated with performance improvement discussions, do not favor behavioral scales.

PERFORMANCE MEASUREMENT IN HUMAN FACTORS

Purpose

Human factors are devoted to achieving performance efficiency of a system consisting of human and machine components. Optimal performance efficiency is viewed as a function of exploiting a system's capacity while at the same time being sensitive to a system's capacity limits, beyond which errors occur too frequently to be tolerated. Measurement is applied to understand a system's capacity, and capacity is both a function of human capacity and machine capacity. Thus, measurement is applied to both the human and machine components of a system to understand system capacity and capacity limits.

Two interventions are commonly used to achieve the purpose of increasing system capacity and efficiency: (1) distribution of tasks to human or machine, and (2) changes in system components. First, since some tasks are better performed by the human and some better by the machine, given their respective capacities and capacity limits, tasks need to be optimally delegated to human and machine components. Kantowitz & Sorkin (1983) use a four-level classification system to illustrate how task responsibilities are distributed in different human–machine systems (see Figure 1).

Second, efficiency can be increased by changing human and machine components. For example, a machine can be redesigned to locate a lever within the human's reach if the human has difficulty reaching a lever. Adding a co-pilot to help the pilot is an example of how the human component of a system can be changed to increase efficiency and reduce error. Both interventions follow from measurement of the capacity of a system and its components.

Source

Performance in the human factors domain is focused on two sources, human beings and machines. Figure 2 depicts the features of human and machine system components that are commonly the focus of measurement. We will emphasize the measurement of person elements in the system since our focus is human performance measurement. These person elements include human perceptual, information processing, and motor capacities. It should be noted that the measurement of human perceptual, information processing, and motor capacities occurs at multiple levels. At the system level (human–machine), the output of the system as a whole can be measured, and *inferences* about human capacities drawn. Measurements are also taken at the subcomponent (subhuman)

Task	Human contribution	Machine contribution
Level 1 Human using shovel	Power, control, info. processing	
Level 2 Human welding	Control, info. processing	Power
Level 3 Manufacturing in automized plant	Control	Info. processing, power
Level 4 Piloting a jet	Monitoring	Info. processing, control, power

Figure 1 Distribution of tasks among human and machine components (from Kantowitz & Sorkin, 1983, reproduced by permission)

level and aggregated to understand the capacity of the human components. For example, human capacity for lifting may be understood by aggregating measures of arm strength and stamina.

Performance Criteria

The overarching performance criterion in human factors is performance efficiency. As stated earlier, optimal performance is a function of both exploiting a system's capacity and minimizing errors. As such, *capacity* and *errors* are common criteria for measurement in human factors. *Human capacity* is often measured with particular emphasis on *capacity limits*. If a human is pushed beyond these limits for any given capacity, the probability of error increases sharply. *Human error* tends to be measured at the system level or component level. Occurrences of error are often taken to indicate that the system or the human component in the system has been pushed beyond capacity limits. Thus, inferences about human capacity limits are drawn when an error occurs.

The structure for the remainder of the human factors section follows from our explanation of the purpose, source, and performance criteria. In the methods section that follows, we will first explore how human capacities including perceptual, information processing, and motor capacities are measured within human factors. Second, the measurement of human error and how it is used to draw inferences about human performance capacity will be examined. Prior to examining methods and in keeping with the overall structure of this chapter, we will review the criteria used in judging the efficacy of human factors measurement technique.

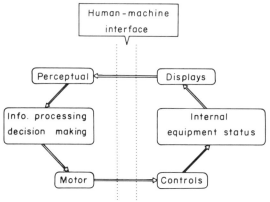

Figure 2 Human and machine capacities measured in human factors (adapted from Meister, 1971)

Criteria for Measurement

Many of the criteria for judging the efficacy of measures in human factors are correlates of classical reliability theory criteria. Criteria are used to estimate the accuracy of measurement and consistency of measurement. A third criterion is application oriented and attempts to estimate the ease or generalizability of applying the measures. This criterion is particularly associated with physiological measures.

Accuracy of measurement

In keeping with the classical definition, *validity* is an index of the extent to which the 'true' value of a phenomenon is represented by the value produced through measurement. True scores, however, are as much hypothetical constructs in the human factors domain as in any other. As Meister (1986) raises in his discussion of the limits of validity for evaluating human factor measures, comparing different methods on the basis of their validity becomes academic since true scores are not available. *Efficiency* of measurement represents a criteria that is more readily attainable. Efficiency is an index of agreement between predicted and actual levels of performance. An index of efficiency is calculated based on the degree of correspondence between the predictions made prior to the operation of a system with post-operational measures (Meister, 1986). Two indices of accuracy are used almost exclusively to measure mental workload. *Sensitivity* refers to the capability of discriminating between different levels of mental workload. For example, some measures may be capable of fine distinctions between levels when measuring in the low to moderate range, yet may be quite insensitive to distinctions between levels in the moderate to high range (Kramer, in press). Wierwille (1988) adds a temporal notion to sensitivity by including how quickly a measurement technique responds to sudden changes in human performance. The latter addition is particularly important since a measurement technique that is not appropriately sensitive may not detect changes that actually occur. *Diagnosticity*, also associated with physiological measures of mental workload, refers to the capability to discriminate among the various sensory, perceptual, cognitive, and psychomotor aspects of human performance (Lysaught *et al.*, 1989). This is particularly important since workload as a human capacity is considered to be multi-dimensional. A highly diagnostic measure is needed when the goal is to discriminate among types of capacity used (i.e. deciding whether task performance will be most efficient when information is provided by a visual versus an auditory signal).

Consistency of measurement

Consistency, particularly associated with subjective measures, refers to the degree to which a measure is resistant to bias due to subjective elements involved in using the method (i.e. are there inter-individual differences when different people use the same measurement technique in different situations?). Consistency can also refer to the stability of subject performance across measurements (Meister, 1986). *Reliability* is defined by the classical test theory definition and can be estimated by comparing results from two or more measurements based on similar experimental procedures, conditions, and samples. Kramer (in press) suggests that formulae traditionally associated with estimates of reliability (e.g. split half, test-retest, etc.) are appropriate even though they have not commonly been used.

Application oriented criteria

Intrusiveness refers to the ability to measure without interfering with task performance. This is particularly important for physiological measures that can potentially restrict the movement of workers. *Generality of application*, a category developed by Kramer (in press) in his review, considers the extent to which artifacts in local administration exist; measures are conducive to laboratory, simulator, field experiment, or operational applications; applications for multiple purposes such as training, system development, and personnel selection are possible; and measures can be applied in on-line or off-line contexts.

Measures

The measures of human performance most frequently of interest in human factors work can be divided into those that focus on human capacities and those that concentrate on human errors. The former is concerned with expressing performance in terms of some known conditions about the limits of human performance. The latter is less concerned about the ranges or limits of performance and more concerned with the frequency of inappropriate performance.

Estimates of human capacities

Human capacity measures are frequently applied to measures of *perceptual* and *motor performance*. Audition and vision are most common among human factor measurements of human sensory/perceptual capacity. Identifying thresholds within which a sound or visual stimuli can be perceived is important for understanding people's ability to perform tasks demanding their perceptual skills. Measurement of strenth and stamina, reaction time, and anthropometry (measurements of the dimensions of the human body) are also common measurement pursuits within human factors. However, these have limited applicability for our purpose of discovering performance measures that may be useful for HRM practices. Therefore, such measures will not be pursued in depth.

The study of humans as *information processors* represents a large sector of research within human factors covering topics such as attention, memory, and decision making. We feel that the advances made in pursuing the measurement of *mental workload* are most pertinent to the purpose of this chapter, and thus, we will focus exclusively on this topic in the paragraphs that follow.

Mental workload and its measurement rests on the view that humans possess a finite pool of cognitive/attentional resources that can be devoted to task performance at any given time (Wickens, 1984). The demands on cognitive/attentional resources increase as the difficulty of a task increases or as additional tasks are added. The human operator is able to allocate resources in accordance with increasing task difficulty until a point where resource limits are reached. Performance begins to decline beyond this point. Mental workload, then, is defined as the costs, in terms of the allocation of cognitive/attentional resources, associated with performance of different tasks (Kramer, in press). Early in its conceptualization, researchers hoped to represent the mental workload associated with a task with a single index. The pursuit of a single index of mental workload resulted in a large, inconsistent, and confusing body of data (Derrick, 1988). These findings led to a number of researchers to view mental workload as a multidimensional construct requiring several measurement approaches to be integrated at some theoretical level (Sanders, 1979; Moray et al., 1979). The methods of measurement can be classified into three categories: (a) physiological, (b) objective, and (c) subjective.

The rationale for using *physiological methods* is based on the reasoning that physiological measures of activation or arousal are associated with increased activity in the nervous system. Increased nervous system activity is equated with an increase in the load on the operator. Common physiological measurements include: (a) cardiovascular system—heart rate, blood pressure, etc.; (b) respiratory system—respiration rate, oxygen consumption, etc.; (c) nervous system—brain activity, muscle tension, pupil size; and (d) biochemistry—catecholamine (Meister, 1986). Kramer (in press) summarizes physiological measures in two categories: central nervous system (CNS) measures including electroencephalographic activity (EEG), event-related brain potentials (ERP), magnetic activity of the brain (MEG), measures of brain metabolism such as positron emission tomography (PET), and measures of electroculographic activity (EOG); and peripheral nervous system (PNS) measures including the functions of the autonomic nervous system (ANS) such as cardiovascular activity, measures of pupil diameter, respiratory measures, and electrodermal measures.

We will review a few examples of physiological measures to provide a flavor of how they are used. For a more exhaustive review, see Kramer (in press).

1. *Electroencephalograph (EEG)*. The EEG has a long history of use in workload measurement dating back to 1929. EEG recordings are commonly taken from the scalp, and the units of measurement span a range of frequency bands including delta (0–2 Hz), theta (4–7 Hz), alpha (8–13 Hz), beta (14–25 Hz) and also vary by amplitude. EEG measurements seem applicable and valid in both simulator and operational environments (Natani & Gomer, 1981; Sterman *et al.*, 1987) and generalize to a variety of subjects (Beatty & O'Hanlon, 1979).

2. *Event-related brain potentials (ERP)*. The ERPs are transient series of voltage oscillations in the brain recorded in the scalp in response to a discrete event. Unlike EEG which is measured in frequencies, ERPs are measured in time units such as number of milliseconds between stimuli and response (Kramer, in press). The intrusiveness of ERP measurement depends on the technique used. For example, some techniques requiring an overt response to the presentation of an auditory or visual stimulus may be quite intrusive. Techniques have been developed to eliminate the additional processing demands placed on the operator by the measurement technique (Bauer, Goldstein, & Stern, 1987). ERP measurement has been primarily successful in the laboratory. A number of questions about on-line applications of ERP measurement remain unanswered including those related to a poor signal-to-noise ratio in single trials and whether or not ERPs can provide information on workload in real time.

3. *Cardiac activity* Measures of cardiac activity include the electrocardiogram (EKG), blood pressure, and blood volume measures; the electrocardiogram seems to show the most promise for measuring workload (Kramer, in press). EKGs measure electrical impulses generated by pacemaker cells in the heart by placing two electrodes on the body. Units of measurement include both time and frequency. Heart rate is the easiest to obtain among the EKG measures, yet research exploring the relationship between heart rate and workload has resulted in mixed findings (Casali & Wierwille, 1983; Hicks & Wierwille, 1979). Kramer suggests that an EKG is a relatively nonintrusive measure of mental workload since: (a) recordings can be taken in the absence of discrete stimuli and responses; (b) a large signal-to-noise ratio exists; and (c) measurements can be taken without interfering with performance.

Three fundamental criticisms have been raised against physiological measures of workload by Meister (1986). First, he questions the validity of the measures. The evidence supporting a relationship between physiological and other workload indices is not strong, and the meaning of these relationships when they do occur is frequently difficult to interpret. Second, the measures themselves are highly sensitive to contaminating conditions according to Meister. Third, he argues that the measures are intrusive and/or impractical. Physiological measures can restrict or interfere with the operator's task performance, and restrictions imposed by the job—task demands, safety considerations, etc.—can often limit the number and kind of physiological measures used at one time. Kramer (in press) lists a number of other disadvantages including cost, difficulty in scoring and interpreting physiological data, and the potential confound of noise.

The second of three classes of measures of mental workload has been labeled *objective* measures (Sanders, 1979; Moray *et al.*, 1979). Task performance is frequently used to infer the amount of workload, both mental and physical. From a task-focused framework, workload is defined as the cost of performing one task in terms of the capacity to perform additional tasks, given that two tasks overlap in their resource demands (Kramer, in press). Stated another way, workload is 'the difference between the information-processing capacity available to the operator and the capacity required for criterion task performance at any given time' (Derrick, 1988, p. 96). Task measures are typically divided into primary and secondary task measures. In primary task performance measurement, task difficulty for a single task is manipulated and performance variations are assumed to reflect changes in workload. In secondary or comparative task performance measurement, the person is first presented with a single task and then a second task is added, or performance is compared across two different tasks and changes in performance are recorded. A performance decrement on the primary task, once the second task is added, is assumed to be the result of an increase in load. An index of effort is then constructed such that effort is scaled inversely with the size of the performance decrement. The synthetic multiple task approach is a variation on the secondary task approach where people perform multiple tasks individually and then simultaneously; the same kinds of conclusions are drawn from changes in task performance.

Task performance methods have revealed a great deal about the multidimensionality of workload. For example, Wickens (1984) has discovered three dimensions of operator workload using task performance measures: (a) stages of processing—encoding, central processing, and responding; (b) codes of processing—verbal and spatial; and (c) modalities of input—visual and auditory. Wickens proposes that if any two tasks demand common resources on any of the dimensions, performance decrements will result. In particular, time sharing will be less efficient, and changes in difficulty of one task will be likely to influence performance of the other task. Empirical research has supported the predicted relationships when tasks draw from intra-vs interdimensional resources. Supporting the independence of the stages of processing dimension, Wickens & Kessel (1980) found that performance on a tracking task (responding) was disrupted by performance on another tracking task (responding), but not by a mental arithmetic task (central processing). Regarding the modalities dimension, Triesman & Davies (1973) and Rollins & Hendricks (1980) found that performance on various detection tasks was better in cross-modal conditions than when stimuli were either both visual or both auditory. Research by McLeod (1986), Wickens (1980), and Wickens, Sandry, & Vidulich (1983) supported the hypotheses regarding the codes of processing. Each study confirmed that time sharing among tasks is more efficient when verbal tracking tasks employ vocal rather than verbal/manual response mechanisms.

Task-based measurement has advantages in that it has high face validity and it is amenable to quantitative/empirical testing. Task measures present a number of challenges, however. First, conclusions based on the task performance are based on the limited resource model, namely that individuals have a finite pool of resources which can be devoted to one task or distributed among tasks with associated costs in performance. If this model does not hold, then the conclusions from this method are not valid (Meister, 1986). Second, this procedure has a great deal of utility in the lab where task performance and introduction of new tasks can be highly controlled (Meister, 1986). However, there are some practical restrictions in applying the method. For example, secondary task measures cannot be used in cases where the performance decrement introduced into the primary task by adding the secondary task result in danger to the operator (i.e. when the primary task is flying an airplane) (Wickens, 1984). Third, it is often difficult to cross-calibrate (scale) diverse measures across tasks (Wickens, 1984). Within a particular task, changes in performance may be reasonable estimates of differing levels of workload responses, but the metric for change may be very dependent on the task. Scaling the change in units based on performance prior to introduction of other tasks provides a comparison across tasks only if the original tasks in the set of interest have been compared. As a result, most secondary task workload measures have been used for comparisons within tasks. Fourth, it may not be reasonable in all cases to assume that the manipulation of task demands results in increased workload. This can be assumed if the operator invests the resources necessary to achieve the best possible performance in every condition, but cannot be assumed if the operator is at all lax in focusing resources on the task across conditions.

A final set of measures of workload is comprised of *subjective* measures (Sanders, 1979; Moray *et al.*, 1979). Subjective measures of workload are applied to gain access to the subjects' perceptions of the level of load they are facing in task performance. Rating scales, questionnaires, and interviews are used to collect opinions about workload. While these methods may not have the empirical or quantitative appeal of physiological or objective measures of workload, it is often argued that subjective measures are most appropriate since individuals are likely to work in accordance with their feelings regardless of what physiological or behavioral performance measures suggest (Moray *et al.* 1979). An assumption of the subjective workload assessment is that people are aware of, and can introspectively evaluate, changes in their workload and that this assumption holds regarding general impressions of the difficulty of ongoing experiences. Yet, people are not accustomed to quantifying or verbalizing these experiences and, in fact, may not readily recall them (Hart & Staveland, 1988). Some subjective measures are considered below.

1. *NASA Task Load Index.* The *NASA Task Load Index* (Human Performance Research Group, 1987) system is one example of a subjective measure of mental workload. An overall index of mental workload is produced based on ratings of a specific task on six factors of workload: mental demands, physical demands, temporal demands, own performance, effort, and frustration. A two-part response is required. First, respondents are presented with the 15 possible pairwise comparisons of the six scales and select the member of each pair that contributes more to the workload of that task. Next, the respondents rate each of the six factors on a 20-interval scale ranging from high to low. The six factor weights are multiplied by the factor ratings and summed to arrive at an overall mental workload index. The measure is completely adapted to a computer which makes ratings in operational settings possible. Videotape replay or computer regeneration of the operator's performance can also prompt the memory of the subject for rating purposes (Human Performance Research Group, 1987). Research also suggests that no detrimental effects result when ratings are given retrospectively with visual mnemonic devices (Hart *et al.*, 1986; Haworth, Bivens, & Shively, 1986).

2. *Decision tree rating scales.* Lysaught *et al.* (1989) list the Cooper–Harper scale and the Bedford scale examples of subjective mental workload rating scales which use decision tree methodologies. Subjects first work through a series of yes/no questions such as 'is the aircraft controllable', and 'is adequate performance attainable with tolerable workload', and are eventually channeled into comparisons of two to three options which lead to a final rating of work load (Lysaught *et al.*, 1989, pp. 86–89).

3. *Subjective workload assessment technique (SWAT).* Subjects using SWAT evaluate workload on three dimensions—time load, mental effort, and psychological stress—each of which is operationally defined at three levels (Lysaught *et al.*, 1989). In phase one, subjects sort 27 cards that contain all possible combinations of the three dimensions and three levels. An interval scale ranging from 1 (no workload) to 100 (maximum workload)

is constructed from the card rankings using conjoint scaling procedures (Krantz & Tversky, 1971). In phase two, subjects assign a level (1, 2, or 3) to each of the three dimensions. These ratings are translated into a numerical value on the 0–100 interval scale of workload.

Subjective measures of mental workload have been evaluated both internally, comparing different measures to each other, and externally, comparing subjective measures to other types of measures. For example, studies comparing different rating formats suggest that highly similar results are obtained when using different rating formats for the same task, and frequently the same rank order for task difficulty is found even in studies using two or more different techniques (Lysaught et al., 1989). When comparing subjective measures with performance measures, high correlations have been found during early and middle stages of overload (Lysaught et al., 1989). Usually higher subjective ratings of workload correspond to poorer performance, yet there is evidence that respondents rate workload higher in a task that they perform better (Yeh & Wickens, 1988). The latter is problematic since opposite conclusions may be drawn depending on whether subjective or task-based measures are used. The advantages of subjective measures as a group include ease of implementation, nonintrusiveness, low cost, face validity, sensitivity to workload variations, and the wide variety of available techniques (O'Donnell & Eggemeier, 1986). Among the disadvantages, subjective ratings of workload are confounded with task performance.

Measurement of human error

A commonly used method of measuring performance of human–machine systems is counting/estimating errors. An error is conceptualized as the discrepancy between actual and desired performance (Meister, 1986). Reliability is an estimate of a system's capacity to operate without error (mathematically, reliability = 1 − probability of an error occurring). Error/reliability can be estimated for both the human and machine components of a system, although our interest here is primarily on human error.

Human error is not necessarily a result of conscious human failure, but may result from task demands that violate the tolerance limits of individuals. A typical intervention aimed at assessing error is to change the nature of the human–machine interface so that human capacity limits are not violated. The basic unit of human reliability is the human error probability (HEP) which equals the number of errors divided by the number of opportunities for error. Human reliability then equals 1 − HEP (Kantowitz & Sorkin, 1983). It is worth noting that the human factors' approach to work is that of the experimental design rather than individual differences. As a result, variance across individuals is not seen as a function of individual differences but rather as a function of random error. This view of performance errors differs from the HRM perspective which attributes error to individual differences in skill and uses error to evaluate a person's job performance.

Numerous classifications for human errors have been proposed (see Fleishman & Quaintance, 1984). Human errors can be described in terms of

1. The nature of the error (omission, commission, extraneous act, sequential, time) (Swain & Guttman, 1980 cited in Kantowitz & Sorkin, 1983);
2. Mission stage during which error occurs (take-off, landing, etc.);
3. Behavioral function associated with error (decision making, tracking, etc.);
4. The procedure/procedural step during which the error was made;
5. Equipment associated with the error;
6. Presumed cause of error (motivation, fatigue, overload) (Meister, 1986).

One technique for modeling complex tasks to estimate human error is the reliability tree (Dhillon, 1986, p. 17). Most tasks can be broken down into a series of subtasks and the links between these subtasks can be described as series, parallel, or series–parallel, a combination of both. These terms are used in accordance with traditional engineering uses of these terms. These subtasks and links are used to compose a reliability tree, a flow chart representing the performance of the whole task. The probability of error can be estimated by estimating the error associated with each subtask and combining all subtasks into a total error probability for the whole task. Mathematical rules specify how to combine subtask probabilities that are linked in series, parallel, or series–parallel sequences.

The estimation of human error is both a descriptive and a predictive science. In order to describe a system that is currently operating, the actual number of errors made during operation can be counted. In system development, estimations of error occurrence are used to produce the best possible system before the system becomes operational. The following methods are used.

1. *Manual collection*. In this method, human observer records task performance/error according to a specified protocol for task performance (i.e. step-by-step checklist). A number of variations in this procedure are possible. The observer may focus solely on the task or may record environmental stimuli (noise, temperature, etc.) that are presumed to affect the task. Observers may draw conclusions about cause and effect, or may stick with recording of observables only and making no inferences about performance. Observations may be taken continuously, or on a periodic sampling basis. The high cost of this method is obvious, and given that the observer is capable of error in observation, the procedure can be unreliable (Meister, 1986).

2. *Automatic collection.* Instruments can be developed to record performance automatically. This procedure reduces some of the reliability and intrusiveness problems involved in manual collection. Some examples of automatic collection techniques include video or audio recorders for recording events; and light or sound meters or accelerometers (vibration effects). Systems that become increasingly computerized become highly amenable to automatic data collection. Subroutines can be created to record all operator inputs and their timing in relation to machine activity (Meister, 1986).

Automatic data collection is often thought to be much more 'objective' and, therefore, more valid than other measurement methods. Vreuls & Obermayer (1985) note that the technical capability for automatic collection (i.e. training simulators) may not necessarily increase effectiveness of performance measurement. Some of the problems are due to the fact that performance measurement depends on well-defined behavioral requirements and cognitive activities that make up performance. Yet, we have not been effective at breaking down complex tasks like team performance and decision making into measurable segments. Automatic collection only offers increased recording accuracy, it does not guarantee that the performance data collected is better or more reflective of total task performance than the data gained measured through other methods.

3. *Self report.* Errors can be verbally reported (i.e. to a supervisor) or recorded by the subject. However, for errors, there is one serious problem; self-report measures often suffer from problems of honesty in reporting. Not too surprisingly, job incumbents are often reluctant to report or admit to making errors. Questionnaires or other methods that preserve anonymity tend to work better (Meister, 1986).

4. *Experimental studies.* Controlled experiments can be used to determine the probability of human error associated with a task. This is particularly useful for predictive purposes, but also can be quite costly.

5. *Expert judgment.* Expert judgments are commonly used during the system development phase for predicting the amount of error that is likely to occur during the operation of a system development phase. This is practically more feasible and less costly than other methods, particularly when the number that need to be judged is not too large.

Contributions of HF to Performance Measurement in HRM

The work on performance measurement conducted within the HF domain can contribute to performance management in HRM in a number of ways. The most fundamental of these is to provide a different perspective on human performance. Firmly anchoring performance in either the person or the person–task system is one such perspective difference. A great deal of attention is paid to scaling performance measures, in particular scaling them in terms of capacity or of efficiency. In the former case, tasks are assessed as to their demands—physical, cognitive, and emotional— and then judgments are made as to the demands these tasks place on the physical, cognitive, and emotional abilities that individuals drawn from the population of people likely to be placed on the tasks are likely to possess. By measuring the performance of people on the tasks by means discussed earlier, inferences regarding capacities in task performance or ability units can be drawn. Typically, capacity is based on norms established using sample data where a particular individual's capacity is based on a comparison of his or her performance to standards developed on a group that serves as a norm group. It is also possible to use multiple samples of the individual's own performance, and then the capacity index can be based on his or her own performance. For efficiency, systems or individuals are measured with respect to the extent to which observed performance matches predicted performance.

In contrast, HRM measures pay less attention to scaling, and performance measures are rarely scaled in capacity or efficiency units. Like HF, performance measurement in HRM begins with the task, typically tasks clustered into jobs. On the basis of a job analysis, job dimensions are defined. In most cases, the dimensions serve to identify a set of behaviors or outcomes targeted to the particular dimension, and unanchored performance judgments serve as the performance measure. Such measures are usually scaled in neither a task nor an individual system, although the alternatives for scoring performance imply an interpersonal comparison scale (e.g. below average, average, above average), or a frequency of occurrence scale (e.g. seldom, frequently). An exception to the attention to scaling of performance measures for HRM purposes was the work that was done with behavioral anchored rating scales (BARS) (Smith & Kendall, 1963). Although BARS scales were initially believed to possess better psychometric properties than other scales, this no longer appears to be the case (Schwab, Heneman, & DeCotis, 1975). It is likely that the involvement of the users of the scales in their development, the use of critical behaviors as descriptive anchors, and other conditions, may have contributed to their superiority rather than the scaling properties of the measures. In any event, the measures were never scaled in units of capacity or efficiency.

Capacity or efficiency (particularly capacity) measures may be useful in HRM when performance is assessed to aid the development or evaluation of training programs or when it is to be used for feedback for individuals for learning their jobs. Most recently, training research has focused on organizational needs analysis (Ford & Wroten, 1984; Goldstein, 1990; Ostroff & Ford, 1989). We would suggest that performance measures expressed in units of human capacities along particular dimensions should be quite valuable for assessing the future training needs of an organization. Such units are also consistent with recent work in the area of motivation (Kanfer, 1990; Naylor, Pritchard, & Ilgen, 1980) and skill acquisition (Ackerman, 1987; 1988; 1989; Kanfer & Ackerman, 1989) that blurs the distinction between motivation and abilities by treating performance as a resource allocation task. From this perspective, allocation of time and effort to behaviors is viewed as a result of the demand that tasks place on individuals' cognitive resources. Capacity measures should be useful for assessing performance in terms of cognitive resources.

The HF perspective on the nature of errors is another relatively fundamental difference between it and HRM performance measure, and one from which the latter has something to gain. Although from the HF perspective, it is recognized that human errors are made by people, the responsibility for the errors is often attributed to characteristics of the person–machine system, and, in particular, the machine portion of the system. Errors are viewed in terms of their probability of occurrence over trials, and there is an attempt to determine the base rate for errors in the system (discussed earlier as HEP). Furthermore, efforts are made to describe and model errors in a system as was mentioned regarding the calculation of error-performance trees. Performance as measured for HRM purposes is more likely to attribute errors to the individual himself or herself and to hold the person responsible for the error. Part of this tendency is no doubt due to the fact that human performance is measured almost exclusively to make judgments about individual performance, and the performance is mapped onto the person (i.e. goes into the personnel record of a particular person). Part is also due to the use of human judgment to rate performance. Fundamental attribution errors in the judgment of others leads to the tendency to attribute the poor performance of others being observed to the person more than to the task (Feldman, 1981). Regardless of the cause, more attention to the base-rates of errors and to an expanded set of potential causes of errors would be useful for many functions served by performance measures for HRM functions. At a more specific level, the particular error measures discussed earlier may provide ways to begin to break out of the narrow view that currently exists.

Finally, the concept of mental workload may be useful for thinking about performance measurement in HRM, particularly performance measurement for assessing training needs, competencies, and performance measurement for purpose of job design. Since the 1960s, good performance measurement from a HRM perspective has stressed the need to move to measures of job behaviors from the measurement of the outcomes produced on the jobs (Latham, 1986). However, in the recent past jobs are moving more and more to jobs that require monitoring machines or interacting with technology through a computer terminal. The result is that the jobs demand more performance along dimensions that are less observable to an outsider. Thus, thinking about such behaviors from the standpoint of mental effort and looking to multiple measures from the three sets described earlier (physiological, objective, and subjective) may provide a way to assess performance on jobs where observations of behavior does not provide much information.

PERFORMANCE MEASUREMENT IN OPERATIONS CONTROL

The elements that make up this section of the review are not neatly packaged within a single discipline. At the job-task analysis level, we draw from industrial engineering (IE). These data are aggregated to the operation or organization level of analysis. At the organizational level, we also draw from management information systems (MIS). Summing across these multiple levels, provides the potential to develop a powerful performance measurement system for setting performance standards and collecting data regarding performance against these standards.

Purpose

Much like human factors, the goal of operation control is efficiency. Industrial engineering is the building block of production control since IE techniques are used to establish production procedures and standards. Procedures define the 'best' way to manufacture a product, and standards circumscribe the performance expectations, both quantity and quality, for performance units ranging from one person performing a job to multiple machine technologies performing multiple production tasks. The results of task analysis and standards setting have many applications including estimating labor costs associated with a particular process or plant, bidding for contracts, pricing products, forecasting, and designing flow shop configuration (Starr, 1989). Standards may also serve as the basis for a wage incentive plan (Barnes, 1980).

The purpose of MIS is to support management decision making. Decision support systems, a close relative of MIS, are used to gather data related to specific problems. Marketing, manufacturing, and financial data represent the typical categories of information that are compiled in MIS (McLeod, 1986). The human resource application of MIS, human resource information systems (HRIS), is used for strategic personnel planning and keeping a data base on employees. Performance appraisal data are often kept in HRIS.

Source

Industrial engineering is focused at the task/job level. Expert observers first break down whole jobs into their basic task performance elements, and then observe and record the performance of each element. This breakdown of tasks is often achieved with flow charts, diagrams, still photos and motion pictures. Quantitative performance standards are set. Descriptive statistics are employed to arrive at performance values for the 'average' worker, and fluctuations around the standards are attributed to error not necessarily individual differences. These job level data are also commonly aggregated to higher levels of analysis such as the plant, functional area, or the entire organization.

Management information systems are content free in that there are no a priori specifications about what data should be collected and stored. The content is provided by subject-matter experts in such areas as marketing, finance, and human resources. Thus, unlike HRM and HF, the source of a measured system in MIS is not as readily definable. There is, however, within the discipline of MIS, one important distinction, and that is between data and information (McLeod, 1986). Data are the raw, unorganized, uninterpretable forms of information. They are transformed by the specialist and become information that is organized, meaningful, interpretable, and useful. For performance measurement within production control, we recognize that a great deal of data is collected and is, can, or should be transformed into usable performance measurement information.

Criteria

Fein (1986) includes the following in his discussion of criteria for measurement in industrial engineering. *Accuracy* refers to the degree of agreement between a measured value and its true value. Again, as in other areas, it is not possible to obtain accuracy because of the hypothetical nature of the concept of true score, and as Fein suggests, accuracy has no meaning within work measurement. Even though work measurement analysts over time develop a level of confidence of the 'accuracy' of particular values obtained through measurement, Fein notes that these judgments of 'accuracy' are ultimately subjective. *Precision* represents a more practical index by which measurement methods can be judged. Precision represents the level of agreement between repeated, independent, applications of same measurement process under the same conditions. *Reliability*, closely associated with precision, is represented by a reliability index calculated on the basis of the size and representativeness of the sample.

MIS offers criteria of a different nature than those previously reviewed. MIS criteria correspond to qualities regarding the storage of data, and not necessarily to the accuracy or precision of the data itself. McLeod (1986) lists five qualities. *Reduced redundancy* refers to the extent to which data is stored as economically as possible without threatening safety. *Recovery from failure* refers to the extent to which a system can withstand failures ranging from human errors to natural disasters. *Accessibility* indexes the extent to which data are easily assessable to multiple users. *Security* is an estimate of how well the system is insulated from sabotage and maintains appropriate levels of confidentiality of the information. Accessibility and security are often at odds with each other since making data more easily accessible to multiple users also makes data more susceptible to security threats. *Independence* refers to the extent to which programs are properly insulated from logical or organizational changes in other parts of the data base.

Methods

IE methods of work measurement

Recording methods vary widely. Repetitive, short cycle tasks are frequently timed with a stopwatch, and statistical averages are computed across observations and subjects (commonly called the time study method). Nonrepetitive or long cycle tasks such as those done by office workers, researchers, skill trade workers, or professionals are not conducive to time study so observers tend to record behaviors according to nominal categories (Barnes, 1980).

The data collected through observation is then translated into standards for the job. Standards are the key units of measurement for a job. Performance is typically indexed with respect to the standard with the expected level of performance set at 100% of standard, the expected level of performance a task holder could be expected to maintain when doing a job at a normal pace over an eight-hour day. Early time studies were quite primitive; time studies were based on many cycles performed by one individual who was supposed to be representative of the 'average' worker. IEs developed a technique called 'leveling' to adjust the observed value according to the extent to which the person represented an average worker. Another correction in the adjusted time was made for rest and delay. The final figure after both corrections, the standard time, has the potential for containing a number of errors. Increasingly sophisticated statistical methods of sampling have been adopted to reduce the errors in estimating standards. Current practice often involves use of synthetic time standards. Lists of generic tasks with estimated standards are summed to create standards for whole tasks.

Other performance measures

A number of other performance measures are used in production control, but these measures do not differ significantly from the methods discussed earlier under HFs. The measures cluster into three sets. *Production control* measures assess the number and quality of units produced to track and record units as they flow through the production system. *Automatic data collection* measures function similarly and often unobtrusively keeping track of outputs from specific systems as part of the normal workflow process. Finally, for the human subsystems, *physiological measures* can measure workload and signal needs to modify task designs and workload requirements when the physiological data are judged to be problematic. Since each of these measurement procedures were discussed earlier, they will not be repeated here.

Contributions of MIS to Performance Measurement in HRM

Since an overriding difference between performance measurement for MIS purposes in comparison to those of HRM is that of the level at which performance is measured, the contributions of MIS to HRM are most likely to be those of orientation toward performance measurement rather than direct transfer. However, this does not mean that some of the measurement practices in MIS could not be incorporated into HRM if they were adapted to fit the individual orientation demanded by the purpose for which measures are used in HRM.

Two orientations toward performance in MIS may contribute to HRM. The first of these is that of modeling performance. To develop MISs, a great deal of attention is placed on developing a model for the performance of that system. These models are often mathematical models adapted to the demands of the particular situation based on the flow and interdependences of the components of that system. The models then serve to guide the development of performance measures and as the basis against which feedback about the adequacy of the system's performance is judged. There are a number of advantages of such models. For example, they provide a structure for understanding the performance of the system, a way to monitor the performance of the system, and a means of constructing feedback that is meaningful within the system that is developed. When performance deviations arise between that predicted by the model and the actual performance of the system, ways can be sought either to try to affect the performance of the units in the system or to modify the model itself if there is reason to believe that it is inadequate for the situation. Although these models are developed for systems at the level of the work unit, plant, division or above, there is no inherent reason that models could not be developed for individuals' performance. The development of such models could be useful for better understanding the performance of individuals and for designing jobs and training systems.

A second general focus of MIS toward performance measurement is that of paying close attention to performance standards. Standards are developed for systems in which performance is measured either directly through the measurement and evaluation of the system in operation or synthetically by breaking down the system into components and then using guidelines developed from other jobs or systems that imply standards for the new one. Regardless of the technique used, the development and use of standards is considered an integral part of performance measurement in MIS.

Performance standards are also important in HRM. However, standard development often tends to get separated from the development of performance measures. For example, the development of rating scales and the training of raters to do ratings is often treated somewhat independently of the task of putting the rating into practice such as by using the rating in an MBO system or tying pay to performance through the use of performance appraisals. The latter practices raise the issue of performance standards, but they are often considered after the measure is constructed. It is not uncommon for articles on performance measurement totally to ignore performance standards presumably because the setting of standards is assumed to be separate (or at least separable) from the measurement task. A greater emphasis on the performance standards as an integral part of performance measurement should be useful for developing useful HRM performance measurement systems.

Two criteria of MIS performance measurement, but rarely considered when developing HRM measures, are accessibility and security. HRM persons normally consider these outside the domain of performance measurement and the responsibility of those who use the performance data generated by the measurement procedure. That is to say, accessibility and security are normally addressed after the system has been designed. In MIS these are considered as the measurement system is developed because they influence what information is measured, the nature of the units that are constructed in the measurement system, and how the information is stored and coded.

We would contend that the more inclusive view of accessibility and security taken in the MIS case would be very useful for HRM for at least two reasons. First, because a large proportion of the HRM performance measures are subjective ratings, these ratings are affected by the raters' beliefs and expectations about what will be done with the ratings. The fact that the purpose of a rating affects the ratings is an indication of the effects of such beliefs and expectations (e.g. Zedeck & Cascio, 1982). Beliefs and expectations about who is to have access to the ratings, and the degree to which they are secure, should affect the ratings that are provided by a rater for many of the same reasons as does the purpose affect them. Regardless of the reason, it seems likely that knowledge of the accessibility and security of the data will affect the nature of the performance data that are collected.

A second reason for greater HRM interest in accessibility and security of performance rating data is related to the growing interest in employee career issues. The focus on careers shifts some of the responsibility for employee placement and development from the organization to the employee (Hall, 1986). Employees are encouraged to learn more about their capabilities, job performance, and interests and to be more actively involved in managing their own careers. Part of being able to aid employees to do this is being able to allow them some access to data concerning their own performance and that of others with work experience and qualifications similar to their own. To do this, it may be advisable to develop data bases from performance data that are accessible to a wider group of persons than is typically the case with personnel records while, at the same time, protecting the individual rights to privacy of the employee through aggregate data and other means. To the extent that HRM becomes more interested in developing support systems for a career program, we would predict that issues of accessibility and security will become more important considerations for performance measurement in HRM. Looking to MIS performance measurement may provide useful cues on how to manage this task.

Finally, the practice of imbedding performance measures in the natural flow of the system as practiced in MIS deserves more attention in HRM. When performance measurement systems are developed for the whole system, efforts are made to develop measures of performance for subcomponents that can be obtained in the normal operation of the system. These are primarily outcome measures such as counting the number of units processed during a given time period. The measures are never assumed to capture the total performance of the system, but they are believed to represent part of what is meant by performance. Furthermore, they are designed to assess performance unobtrusively, without interrupting the normal production process.

Performance measurement for HRM purposes pays less attention to continuous performance measurement. Part of this may be due to the fact that performance units generated as part of normal task performance tend to be outcomes of task performance, and outcomes have not been very well received as measures of individuals' performance (Latham, 1986). The suggestion that appraisers keep diaries of individuals' interim performance to be used for later performance ratings (Bernardin & Walters, 1977; DeNisi, Robbins, & Cafferty, 1989) is an exception to the general practice. However, diary keeping requires a conscious effort on the part of the rater and is obtrusive in that it is not entirely part of the natural routine. The search for more opportunities to gather intermediate information without being overly obtrusive may be valuable for HRM and a closer look at MIS practices worthwhile.

CONCLUSIONS

In spite of recent criticisms to the contrary (e.g. Demming, cited in Moss & Moen, 1989), the measurement of employee has and is likely to continue to play a major role in organizations. In an excellent review of performance measurement in HRM, Latham (1986) urged a return to the basic elements of sound appraisals based on well carried out job analyses, sound scale construction, well trained raters, and well maintained and managed performance appraisal systems. He concluded that following the basic guidelines for good appraisals was firmly supported in the literature and that such practices offered not only the best that could be done within the performance measurement domain. He suggested that, although there was no reason to abandon the study of rating scales or the rating process, the real need was in studying the supportive structures in the organizational context in which performance measurement systems are imbedded.

Since Latham's (1986) review, little has changed to change that position (see, for example, Murphy & Cleveland (1990) for a more recent review and extensive interpretation). One possible exception is the developing dilemma concerning the use of behavioral dimensions for performance ratings. In spite of the continued insistence on focusing on such dimensions for performance evaluations, research on the rating process indicates that, regardless of what those who develop the measures feel raters should do, raters think about and rate traits rather than specific behaviors. For example, when supervisors were asked to describe the way that they think about performance, their list of dimensions included initiative and hard work, maturity and responsibility, organization, technical proficiency, and assertive and supportive leadership (Borman, 1987). These look much more like traits than behaviors. These results are very consistent with the person perception work that is most closely related to the performance appraisal process where the implication is also that the behavioral measures are less likely to represent reports of observed behaviors than reconstructions of general trait-like impressions (DeNisi, Cafferty, & Meglino, 1984; Feldman, 1981; Ilgen & Feldman, 1983; Nathan & Lord, 1983). Although the process work does raise questions about the behavior ratings that are obtained from performance measures using perform-ance appraisals, it does not provide any answers. No one, to our knowledge, is suggesting that appraisals return to trait measures. Therefore, the advice of Latham (1986) to do well that which has been recommended in the past, still remains the best alternative available within the performance measurement domain of HRM.

In spite of the fact that the old standard techniques and practices appear to be the best that we have to offer within the HRM performance measurement domain, there still remains a great deal of dissatisfaction with performance appraisals (Murphy & Cleveland, 1990). To address that dissatisfaction, the recent tack taken by those in HRM concerned with the problems is to look more closely at the context within which appraisals occur. Latham (1986) concluded with this type of recommendation when he suggested that attention be directed at providing support for raters so that they will be able to accomplish the rating task. Longenecker and his colleagues (Longenecker, 1989; Longenecker & Gioia, 1988; Longenecker, Gioia, & Sims, 1987) have vividly illustrated that performance appraisals, used as performance measurements, are frequently driven by the political culture rather than the actual performance of the persons being rated. More broadly speaking, others have suggested that the social context (Ilgen, Barnes-Farrell, & McKellen, in press) or the culture in which the ratings are conducted (Murphy & Cleveland, 1990) deserves more attention after the basics of performance appraisal systems have been addressed. Padgett (1988) showed that the social context becomes mapped into ratings through the beliefs and expectations of the raters. In all these cases, suggestions for improving performance measurement for HRM purposes have focused on the broader organizational environment in which the measurement takes place.

In this chapter we have suggested one overlooked source of information regarding the development and conduct of measures of human performance in organizations is the literature and practices in other disciplines that have been concerned about performance in organizations. In particular, both human factors and MIS specialists have been actively involved in the measurement of performance in organizations, but the work in these areas is, for the most part, ignored. Although we readily admit that a number of the specific measurement techniques do not translate directly into the HRM domain, we also suggest that some of them may be able to be adapted to fit HRM needs. Such fitting may become more important as jobs in organizations become more heavily loaded with information processing activities involving the monitoring instrument panels and interfacing with information systems through computer terminals. These types of activities are less easily measured through interpersonal observations of peoples' behavior, but it is easier to imbed performance traces into the natural flow of work activities.

Beyond the specific measurement procedures, performance measurement in HF and MIS have general orientations toward performance measurement that differ somewhat from the orientation of HRM in ways that we have suggested could expand the way the performance is viewed in HRM. One example of this is the treatment of performance errors as a system level problem. To adopt such a perspective may provide a way of reducing the attributional biases that creep into performance ratings. Another example of possible inroads is to attempt to build models of the human performance system and then fit the performance measures to the models. Here again, specific techniques are not readily available for simple borrowing. However, searching for models may provide ways of capturing the situational or contextual variables that have been overlooked up to this time, and bring them into the performance measurement process. Thus, the other disciplines may not only be a domain in which we can expand beyond the 'basics' of performance measurement in HRM; they may also provide a way to integrate calls for supportive systems, contexts, and culture into the performance measurement systems developed for HRM purposes.

Correspondence address
Department of Psychology, Psychology Research Building, Michigan State University, East Lansing, Michigan 48824, USA

REFERENCES

Ackerman, P. L. (1987) Individual differences in skill learning: An integration of psychometric and information processing perspectives. *Psychological Bulletin*, **102**, 3–27.

Ackerman, P. L. (1988) Determinants of individual differences during skill acquisitions: Cognitive abilities and information processing. *Journal of Experimental Psychology: General*, **117**, 288–313.

Ackerman, P. L. (1989) Individual differences in skill acquisition. In P. L. Ackerman, R. J. Sternberg, & R. Glaser (eds), *Learning and Individual Differences: Advances in Theory and Research*. New York: Freeman, pp. 165–217.

Barnes, R. M. (1980) *Motion and time study design and measurement of work*. New York: Wiley.

Barrett, G. V., & Kernan, M. C. (1987) Performance appraisal and terminations: A review of court decisions since *Brito* v. *Zia* with implications for personnel practices. *Personnel Psychology*, **40**, 489–503.

Bauer, L., Goldstein, R., & Stern, J. (1987) Effects of information processing demands on physiological response patterns. *Human Factors*, **29**, 213–234.

Beatty, J., & O'Hanlon, J. (1979) Operant control of posterior theta rhythms and vigilance performance: Repeated treatments and transfer of training. In N. Birbaumer & K. Kimmel (eds), *Biofeedback and Self Regulation*. Hillsdale, NJ: Erlbaum.

Berk, R. A. (1986) *Performance Assessment: Methods and Applications*. Baltimore, MD: Johns Hopkins University Press.

Bernardin, H. J., & Beatty, R. W. (1984) *Performance Appraisal: Assessing Behavior at Work*. Boston: Kent Publishing Company.

Bernardin, H. J., Orban, J. A., & Carlyle, J. J. (1981). *Performance Appraisal as a Function of Trust in Appraiser and Rater Individual Differences*. Proceedings of the 41st annual meetings of the Academy of Management, pp. 311–315.

Bernardin, H. J., & Walters, C. S. (1977) The effects of rater training and diary keeping on psychometric error in ratings. *Journal of Applied Psychology*, **62**, 64–69.

Borman, W. C. (1987) Personal constructs, performance schemata, and 'Folk Theories' of subordinate effectiveness: Explorations in an army officer sample. *Organizational Behavior and Human Decision Processes*, **40**, 307–322.

Brito v. *Zia Co.* (1973) 478 F.2d 1200 (10th. Cir. 1973).

Casali, J., & Wierwille, W. (1983) A comparison of rating scale, secondary task, physiological, and primary task workload estimation techniques in a simulated flight task emphasizing communications load. *Human Factors*, **25**, 623–642.

DeNisi, A. S., Cafferty, T. P., & Meglino, B. M. (1984) A cognitive model of the performance appraisal process: A model and research propositions. *Organizational Behavior and Human Performance*, 33, 360–396.

DeNisi, A. S., Robbins, T., & Cafferty, T. P. (1989) Organization of information used for performance appraisals: Role of diary keeping. *Journal of Applied Psychology*, 74, 124–129.

Derrick, W. L. (1988) Dimensions of operator workload. *Human Factors*, 30, 95–110.

DeVries, D. L., Morrison, A. M., Shullman, S. L., & Gerlach, M. L. (1986) *Performance Appraisal on the Line*. Greenboro, NC: Center for Creative Leadership.

Dhillon, B. S. (1986) *Human Reliability with Human Factors*. New York: Pergamon Press.

Dobbins, G. H., Cardy, R. I., & Truxillo, D. M. (1986) The effects of ratee race and purpose of appraisal on the accuracy of performance evaluations. *Basic and Applied Social Psychology*, 7, 225–241.

Dobbins, G. H., Cardy, R. I., & Truxillo, D. M. (1988) The effects of purpose of appraisal and individual differences in stereotypes of women on sex differences in performance ratings: A laboratory and field study. *Journal of Applied Psychology*, 73, 551–558.

Farh, J. L., & Werbel, J. D. (1986) Effects of purpose of the appraisal and expectation of validation on self-appraisal leniency. *Journal of Applied Psychology*, 71, 527–529.

Fein, M. (1986) How 'reliability,' 'precision,' and 'accuracy' refer to use of work measurement data. In R. L. Shell (ed.), *Work Measurement: Principles and Practice*. Atlanta, GA: Industrial Engineering and Management Press.

Feldman, J. M. (1981) Beyond attribution theory: Cognitive processes in performance appraisal. *Journal of Applied Psychology*, 66, 127–148.

Field, H. S., & Holley, W. H. (1982) The relationship of performance appraisal system characteristics to verdicts in selected employment discrimination cases. *Academy of Management Journal*, 25, 392–406.

Fleishman, E. A., & Quaintance, M. K. (1984) *Taxonomies of Human Performance*. New York: Academic Press.

Ford, J. K., & Wroten, S. P. (1984) Introducing new models for conducting training evaluation and for linking training evaluation to program design. *Personnel Psychology*, 37, 651–665.

Goldstein, I. L. (1990) *Training and Development in Organizations*. San Francisco: Jossey-Bass.

Hall, D. T. (1986) *Career Development in Organizations*. San Francisco: Jossey-Bass.

Hart, S. G., Shively, R. J., Vidulich, M. A., & Miller, R. C. (1986) The effects of stimulus modality and task integrity: predicting dual-task performance and workload from single-task levels. In *Twenty First Annual Conference on Manual Control*. Washington, DC: NASA Conference Publication 2428, pp. 5.1–5.18.

Hart, S. G., & Staveland, L. E. (1988) Development of NASA–TLX (Task Load Index): Results of empirical and theoretical research. In P. Hancock & N. Meshkati (eds), *Human Mental Workload*. Amsterdam: Elsevier.

Haworth, L. A., Bivens, C. C., & Shively, R. J. (1986) An investigation of single-piloted advanced cockpit and control configurations for map-of-the-earth helicopter combat mission task. *Proceedings of the 1986 Meeting of the American Helicopter Society*. Washington, DC, pp. 657–672.

Hicks, T., & Wierwille, W. W. (1979) Comparison of five mental workload assessment procedures in moving base driving simulator. *Human Factors*, 21, 129–144.

Human Performance Research Group (1987) *NASA Task Load Index*. Moffet Field, CA: NASA Ames Research Center, V. 1.0.

Ilgen, D. R., Barnes-Farrell, J. L., & McKellen, D. B. (in press) Performance appraisal accuracy. *Organizational Behavior and Human Decision Processes.*

Ilgen, D. R., & Feldman, J. (1983) Performance appraisal: A process approach. In B. M. Staw & L. L. Cummings (eds), *Research in Organizational Behavior*, vol. 5. Greenwich, CT: JAI Press, pp. 141–198.

Kane, J. (1980) Alternative approaches to the control of systematic error in performance appraisals. Paper presented at the 1st annual Scientist-Practitioner Conference in Industrial/Organizational Psychology, Old Dominion University, Norfolk, VA.

Kanfer, R. (1990) Motivation theory and industrial/organizational psychology. In M. D. Dunnette (ed.), *Handbook of Industrial and Organizational Psychology*, vol. 1. Palo Alto, CA: Consulting Psychologists Press.

Kanfer, R., & Ackerman, P. L. (1989) Motivation and cognitive abilities: An integrative/aptitude-treatment interaction approach to skill acquisition. *Journal of Applied Psychology*, **74**, 657–690.

Kantowitz, B. H., & Sorkin, R. (1983) *Human Factors: Understanding People-system Relationships*. New York: Wiley.

Kramer, A. F. (in press) Physiological metrics of mental workload: A review of recent progress. In D. Damos (ed.), *Multiple Task Performance*. Taylor & Francis.

Krantz, D., & Tversky, A. (1971) Conjoint-measurement analysis of composition rules in psychology. *Psychological Review*, **78**, 151–169.

Landy, F. J., & Farr, J. (1983) *Performance Appraisal*. Englewood Cliffs, NJ: Prentice-Hall.

Landy, F. J., Zedeck, S., & Cleveland, J. (1983) *Performance Measurement and Theory*. Hillsdale, NJ: Erlbaum.

Latham, G. L. (1986) Job performance and appraisal. In C. L. Cooper and I. Robinson (eds) *Review of Industrial and Organizational Psychology*, vol 1. Chichester, England: Wiley.

Latham, G. L., & Wexley, K. N. (1981) *Increasing Performance Through Performance Appraisal*, 2nd edn. Reading, MA: Addison-Wesley.

Longenecker, C. O. (1989) Truth or consequences: Politics and performance appraisals. *Business Horizons*, **6**, 1–7.

Longenecker, C. O., & Gioia, D. A. (1988) Neglected at the top: Executives talk about executive appraisals. *Sloan Management Review*, **29**(2), 41–47.

Longenecker, C. O., Gioia, D. A., & Sims, H. P. (1987) Behind the mask: The politics of employee appraisal. *Academy of Management Executive*, **1**, 183–197.

Lysaught, R. J., Hill, S. G., Dick, A. O., Plamondon, B. D., Linton, P. M., Wierwille, W. W., Zaklad, A. L., Bittner, A. C., Jr, & Wherry, R. J. (1989) *Operator Workload: Comprehensive Review and Evaluation of Operator Workload Methodologies* (Analytics Tech. Rep. 2075-3). Alexandria, VA: US Army Research Institute for Behavioral and Social Sciences.

McIntyre, R. M., Smith, D. E., & Hassett, C. E. (1984) Accuracy of performance ratings as affected by rater training and perceived purpose of rating. *Journal of Applied Psychology*, **69**, 147–156.

McLeod, R., Jr (1986) *Management Information Systems*. Chicago: SRA.

Meister, D. (1971) *Human Factors: Theory and Practice*. New York: Wiley.

Meister, D. (1986) *Human Factors: Testing and Evaluation*. Amsterdam: Elsevier.

Moray, N., Johannsen, G., Pew, R., Rassmussen, J., Sanders, A., & Wickens, C. (1979) Final report of the experimental psychology group. In N. Moray (ed.), *Mental Workload: Its Theory and Measurement*. New York: Plenum, pp. 101–114.

Moss, S. M., & Moen, R. D. (1989) Appraise your performance appraisal process: the performance appraisal system: Deming's deadly disease. *Quarterly Progress*, **22**(11), 58–66.

Murphy, K. R., & Cleveland, J. M. (1990) *Performance Appraisal: An Organizational Perspective*. Boston, MA: Allyn & Bacon.

Natani, K., & Gomer, F. (1981) *Electrodermal Activity and Operator Workload: A Comparison of Changes in the Electroencephalogram and in Event-related Potentials* (Tech. Rep. MDC E 2427). McDonnell-Douglas Corporation.

Nathan, B. R., & Lord, R. G. (1983) Cognitive categorization and dimensional schemata: a process approach to the study of halo in performance ratings. *Journal of Applied Psychology*, **68**, 102–114.

Naylor, J. C., Pritchard, R. L., & Ilgen, D. R. (1980) *A Theory of Behavior in Organizations*. New York: Academic Press.

O'Donnell, R. D., & Eggemeier, F. T. (1986) Workload assessment methodology. In K. R. Boff, L. Kaufman, & J. Thomas (eds), *Handbook of Perception and Human Performance: Cognitive Processes and Human Performance*. New York: Wiley.

Ostroff, C., & Ford, J. K. (1989) Assessing training needs: Critical levels of analysis. In I. L. Goldstein (ed.), *Training and Development in Organizations*. San Francisco: Jossey-Bass.

Padgett, M. Y. (1988) Performance Rating in Context: Motivational factors in performance appraisals. Unpublished dissertation. East Lansing: Michigan State University, Department of Management.

Pritchard, R. D., Jones, S. D., Roth, P. L., Stuebing, K. K., & Ekeberg, S. E. (1989) Effect of group feedback, goal setting, and incentives on organizational productivity. *Journal of Applied Psychology, Monograph*, **73**, 337–358.

Pulakos, E. D. (1986) The development of training programs to increase accuracy with different rating tasks. *Organizational Behavior and Human Decision Processes*, **38**, 76–91.

Rollins, R. A., & Hendricks, R. (1980) Processing works presented simultaneously to eye and ear. *Journal of Experimental Psychology*, **6**, 99–109.

Roberts, K. H., Hulin, C. L., & Rousseau, D. M. (1978) *Developing an Interdisciplinary Science of Organizations*. San Francisco, CA: Jossey-Bass.

Rousseau, D. M. (1985) Issues of level in organizational research: Multi-level and cross-level perspectives. In L. L. Cummings & B. M. Staw (eds), *Research in Organizational Behavior* vol. 7. Greenwich, CT: JAI Press, pp. 1–38.

Sanders, A. F. (1979) Some remarks on mental load. In N. Moray (ed.), *Mental Workload: Its Theory and Measurement*. New York: Plenum, pp. 41–78.

Schwab, D. P., Heneman, H. G., III, & DeCotis, T. (1975) Behaviorally anchored rating scales: A review of the literature. *Personnel Psychology*, **28**, 549–562.

Smith, P. C., & Kendall, L. M. (1963) Retranslation of expectations: An approach to the construction of unambiguous anchors for rating scales. *Journal of Applied Psychology*, **47**, 149–155.

Society of Industrial and Organizational Psychology (SIOP) (1987) *Principles for the Validation and Use of Personnel Selection Procedures* (3rd edn). College Park, MD.

Starr, M. K. (1989) *Managing Production and Operations*. Englewood Cliffs, NJ: Prentice-Hall.

Sterman, B., Shummer, G., Duschenko, T., & Smith, J. (1987) Electroencephalographic correlates of pilot performance simulation and in-flight studies. In K. Jessen (ed.), *Electrical and Magnetic Activity of the Central Nervous System: Research and Clinical Applications in Aerospace Medicine*. France: NATO AGARD.

Thorndike, R. L. (1949) *Personnel Testing*. New York: Wiley.

Triesman, A., & Davies, A. (1973) Divided attention to eye and ear. In S. Kornblum (ed.), *Attention and Performance IV*. New York: Academic Press.

Uniform Guidelines on Employee Selection Procedures (1978) *Federal Register*, **43**, 38290–38315.

Vreuls, D., & Obermayer, R. W. (1985) Human-system performance measurement in training simulators. *Human Factors*, **27**, 241–250.

Watson v. *Fort Worth Bank and Trust* (1988) *108 Supreme Court Reporter*, pp. 2778–2797.

Werner, J. M. (1990) Predicting W. S. Courts of Appeals decisions involving performance appraisal: How well did Field and Holley (1982) hold up in the 1980s? Paper presented at the 50th annual meeting of the Academy of Management. San Francisco, CA.

Wickens, C. D. (1980) The structure of attentional resources. In R. Nickerson & R. Pew (eds), *Attention and Performance* VII. Englewood Cliffs, NJ: Prentice-Hall, pp. 239–275.

Wickens, C. D. (1984) *Engineering Psychology and Human Performance.* Columbus, OH: Charles E. Merrill.

Wickens, C. D., & Kessel, C. (1980) The processing resource demands of failure detection in dynamic systems. *Journal of Experimental Psychology: Human Perception and Performance*, **6**, 564–577.

Wickens, C. D., Sandry, D., & Vidulich, M. (1983) Compatibility and resource competition between modalities of input, central processing, and output: testing a model of complex task performance. *Human Factors*, **25**, 227–248.

Wierwille, W. W. (1988) Important remaining issues in mental workload estimation. In P. Hancock & N. Meshkati (eds), *Human Mental Workload.* Amsterdam: Elsevier.

Yeh, Y-Y., & Wickens, C. D. (1988) Dissociation of performance and subjective measures of workload. *Human Factors*, **30**, 111–120.

Zedeck, S., & Cascio, W. (1982) Performance decision as a function of purpose of rating and training. *Journal of Applied Psychology*, **67**, 752–758.

Chapter 4

ERGONOMICS: TRENDS AND INFLUENCES

E. D. Megaw
School of Manufacturing and Mechanical Engineering
University of Birmingham
UK

INTRODUCTION

Despite its gender bias, the definition of ergonomics given by Murrell (1965, p. xiii), still remains one of the more satisfactory:

Ergonomics has been defined as the scientific study of the relationship between man and his working environment. In this sense, the term environment is taken to cover not only the ambient environment in which he may work but also his tools and materials, his methods of work and the organization of his work, either as an individual or within a working group. All these are related to the nature of the man himself: to his abilities, capacities and limitations.

The term 'ergonomics' has been rivalled by the extensive use, particularly in America, of the terms human factors and human factors engineering. In analysing definitions obtained from 74 references, Licht, Polzella, & Boff (1989) found that where comparisons were made between two or all three terms, ergonomics, human factors and human factors engineering, some authors considered them distinct while others considered them equivalent. They went on to analyse the definitions of the three terms in respect of three components: the category of classification (the predicate complement of the definition), the subject domain, and the objectives. The most popular category of classification was 'the application of human data to design'. While 'discipline' was occasionally used as a category, 'profession' was used very rarely. However, there were some differences in relation to the three subject terms. For example, many definitions of ergonomics were classified as the 'study of humans at work' while this was never the case for definitions of human factors engineering. If the definitions are considered in terms of domain, ergonomics-based definitions in particular showed a strong preference for 'human performance capacity'. Other popular domains were 'general behavioural science' and 'biology, physiology and medicine'. Finally, if one considers objectives, the three most popular were to change the 'human–machine system' or the 'equipment' or the 'environment'. Only some ergonomics-based definitions emphasize a change to 'jobs or tasks'.

It has always been appreciated, in terms of its domain, that ergonomics is essentially multi- or interdisciplinary and this has led to difficulties in describing what is and what is not ergonomics. To appreciate the breadth of ergonomics, it is worth listing the titles of the review papers which have appeared in the three volumes of the *International Reviews of Ergonomics* (Oborne, 1987, 1988, 1989). These are shown in Table 1. Apart from illustrating the diversity of topics that can be viewed as ergonomics, these reviews relieve me of the task of giving a general overview of the subject. In fact, I have chosen to limit this chapter to three issues. In the first place, I will discuss the key influences and trends in ergonomics. I will then take two much researched areas, the use of colour in displays and the measurement of mental workload, to illustrate some of the problems that arise in the practice of ergonomics. In the final section, I will briefly consider some issues of methodology.

INFLUENCES AND TRENDS

There is little doubt that recent developments in ergonomics in industrialized countries have been driven by the introduction of new technology and in particular of computers into our lives. This is reflected in the comparatively recent arrival of five journals: *Behaviour and Information Technology* beginning in 1982, *Human–Computer Interaction* in 1985, *Computers in Human Behavior* in 1985, and *Interacting with Computers* and *International Journal of Human–Computer Interaction* in 1989. A further major but related impetus for ergonomics has been the occurrence of numerous major accidents beginning with Three Mile Island in 1979 and continuing with Bhopal in 1984, Chernobyl and the Space Shuttle disasters in 1986 and Zeebrugge in 1987. Interspersed with these, there have been, among others, the all too familiar aviation accidents. In all these incidents what is commonly termed *human* error has attracted the attention of both the public and system designers. What is not disputed is that the lack of application of ergonomics contributed to the underlying causes of all these incidents (Hornick, 1987). Moreover, as Meshkati (1989b) points out in discussing the Bhopal incident which led to the deaths of over 3500 and the permanent injuries to over 200 000 inhabitants, each incident should not be considered as unique as there were clear similarities

Table 1—Review Articles Appearing in the Three Volumes of the *International Reviews in Ergonomics* (Oborne, 1987, 1988, 1989)

Title (page numbers)	*Author*
Volume 1, 1987	
In praise of ergonomics—a personal perspective (1–20)	Branton, P.
The role of colour in visual displays (21–42)	Davidoff, J.
The ergonomics of tools (43–75)	Freivalds, A.
Third world ergonomics (77–118)	Kogi, K. & Sen, R. N.
Current research and applications of ergonomics in mining (119–134)	Leamon, T. B.
VTOL control and display design: principles and methods (135–158)	Roscoe, S. N.
Nonverbal behaviour at the human–computer interface (159–172)	Sheehy, N. P. & Chapman, A. J.
Ergonomics aspects of neck and upper limb disorders (173–200)	Wallace, M. & Buckle, P.
The pathophysiology of hypothermia (201–218)	Mekjavic, I. B. & Bligh, J.
Volume 2, 1988	
'Words, words, words' revisited (1–30)	Chapanis, A.
Human–computer interface standards: origins, organizations and comment (31–54)	Abernethy, C.
Lighting and visual performance (55–84)	Boyce, P.
Cost–benefit analysis of ergonomic and work design changes (85–104)	Corlett, E. N.
Commercial diving and diving performance (105–122)	Leach, J. & Morris, P.
Mental workload since 1979 (123–150)	Moray, N.
Human factors in robot design and robotics (151–176)	Parsons, H. M.
Accident proneness: a review of the concept (177–206)	Porter, S.
Visual accommodation: mediated control and performance (207–232)	Randle, R.
Ergonomics aspects of gloves: design and use (233–250)	Riley, M. & Cochran, D.
The ergonomics of automatic speech recognition interfaces (251–290)	Hapeshi K. & Jones, D.
Volume 3, 1989	
Human factors in the design of coins (1–14)	Bruce, V.
A review of human-centred manufacturing technology and a framework for its design and evaluation (15–47)	Clegg, C. & Symon, G.
Reading and understanding (49–63)	Colley, A. M.
Traffic signs (65–86)	Dewar, R.
Environmental conditions and health in offices (87–110)	Hedge, A.
Human factors implications of shiftwork (111–128)	Monk, T. H.
Icon design for the user interface (129–154)	Rogers, Y.
Perceptual and motor skills of divers under water (155–181)	Ross, H. E.
Occupational stress in the offshore oil and gas industry (183–215)	Sutherland, V. J. & Cooper, C. L.
Cumulative trauma disorders (217–272)	Ayoub, M. A. & Wittels, N. E.

between the incidents in respect of the lack of application of ergonomics.

While it is gratifying to know that the Three Mile Island disaster and subsequent incidents, along with issues concerning the introduction of new technology, have resulted in an appreciation of the importance of considering ergonomics factors, some might argue that these areas have received attention to the exclusion of others. Certainly, if one looks at the employment of ergonomists in Britain, one cannot fail to notice the virtual absence of professional ergonomists working at the shopfloor level in manufacturing industry, whether employed by management or trade unions. This is despite the general concern and interest in topics such as musculoskeletal disorders, manual materials handling, posture, and seating which have featured prominently in recent volumes of the journals *Ergonomics* (see Volume 30 (1987), issue 2; Volume 31 (1988), issues 1 and 9; Volume 32 (1989), issues 1, 3, 5 and 8) and *International Journal of Industrial Ergonomics* (see Volume 2 (1987), issues 3 and 4; Volume 3 (1988), issues 1 and 3; Volume 5 (1990), issue 1). General health at work is given wide coverage by, for example, the *Scandinavian Journal of Work, Environment and Health*.

Other recent influences include the employment of ergonomists as expert witnesses not only in the context of public inquiries such as the Sizewell 'B' inquiry in Britain (e.g. Ergonomics Society, 1983) but also in the context of insurance claims relating to industrial injuries. The influence of the military on ergonomics continues and the mandatory adoption of MANPRINT by the US military is particularly significant. One of the main objectives of the MANPRINT programme is to integrate human factors engineering, system safety, health hazard assessment, and manpower, personnel, and training throughout the design process (Malone *et al.*, 1988). While there is a good deal of other legislation in force around the world relevant to ergonomics, for example in relation to product safety and working conditions, this has so far failed to have as significant an impact as many ergonomists had hoped. On the other hand, standards and guidelines are becoming more visible and, hopefully, their influence will become increasingly effective. As an example of the many available standards and guidelines, Walters, Schroeder & Burgy (1989) have classified 36 major documents which are pertinent to the design of nuclear power plants.

A general point worth making is that the responsibility of introducing and applying ergonomics very often lies with people who have not received a full course of training in ergonomics but who may have completed an ergonomics option while undergoing a course, for example in psychology, computer science or industrial engineering. Alternatively, they may have attended some kind of short course while in employment.

To put some of these trends into perspective, I have prepared at the end of this chapter a list of books that have been published from 1986 onwards. They have been classified according to major topic groupings. Many of the books were written or edited by people who would not consider themselves primarily to be ergonomists but to be cognitive or occupational psychologists, systems designers, reliability engineers, or computer scientists. This in itself reflects a significant trend. I have excluded those books which are little more than reprints of conference proceedings. Some books may not appear because they have been referred to in the text and, therefore, are listed with the references.

The Three Mile Island Incident

To get a better understanding of the background to some of the major growth areas in ergonomics, it is worth describing in some detail the events which took place at the Three Mile Island (TM1) Unit 2 nuclear plant near Harrisburg, Pennsylvania, on 29 March 1979. Readers may like to refer to the illustration of Unit 2 shown in Figure 1 while following this section. More detailed accounts of the incident are given by Perrow (1984) and Rubinstein & Mason (1979).

The accident began in the cooling system. The primary cooling system circulates water around the core of the reactor under high pressure and at a high temperature. This water passes to the steam generator where heat is exchanged with water in the secondary cooling system, which is also under pressure, in order to prevent the core in the reactor from overheating and to provide the steam in the secondary system which drives the turbines to produce electricity. The water in the secondary system is not radioactive but must be kept very pure to prevent damaging the turbines. The purpose of the 'polisher' is to remove the impurities from the secondary water.

As in the case of what appears to be a majority of major accidents, the TMI accident started during the night shift, at 4.00 a.m. officially. Although there is some confusion over the precise details surrounding the first of a series of hardware failures, there is no disagreement that they arose from problems occurring in the purification plant. Operators had been working on these problems for some 11 hours before the accident began and during the course of this work, according to the account given by Perrow (1984), some moisture leaked out of the polisher system and entered the instrument air system of the plant. Somehow this interrupted the air pressure controlling the valves on some of the pumps and signalled them to close, albeit unnecessarily, so that at 4.00 a.m. the condensate pumps tripped (closed down automatically) and one second later the main feedwater pumps tripped. Thus the flow of cold water to the steam generator ceased. When this occurred, the turbines shut down automatically. To keep the core cool and prevent the primary cooling water from overheating, the emergency water pumps came on automatically to pass water from an emergency tank through the secondary cooling system.

This is when the second major failure occurred. The pipes in the emergency system were blocked because valves had been accidentally left in the closed

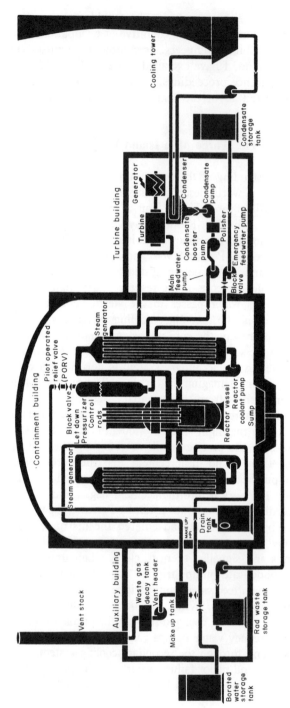

Figure 1 Diagram of part of the Three Mile Island nuclear power plant (reproduced by permission from Adams, 1989)

position following maintenance work carried out two days previously. There were two indicators on the control panel which did indicate that the valves were shut rather than open, but one was obscured by a repair tag hanging from the switch above it. In fact, it took operators a further eight minutes to realize they were blocked. Without any circulation of the secondary water supply, the temperature and pressure in the reactor vessel rose until the reactor tripped (SCRAMed). This is a process whereby the nuclear chain reaction is stopped by lowering graphite control rods into the core. However, the decaying radioactive material still produces a considerable amount of heat which should be drawn off over a few days by the action of the cooling systems. With the secondary cooling systems inactive, other automatic safety devices came into operation. The first of these was the activation of the pilot-operated relief valve (the PORV). This relieves the pressure by channelling the primary reactor coolant from the core through a large vessel called the pressurizer and out via the drain pipe ('the hot leg') into a drain tank and then, if necessary, a sump. The valve must only be opened for a short period of time because if the pressure falls by too much, the water can flash into steam, restrict the flow of coolant and cause hot spots which, if near the uranium rods, can start them fissioning again.

We now come to the third and fourth major failures. The PORV failed to close automatically, and to make things worse a recently installed indicator to display the state of the PORV control panel also failed and indicated to the operators that the valve had in fact closed. Therefore, the operators, convinced the PORV was closed, waited for the reactor pressure to rise again after its rapid drop when the valve was opened. The reason for the indicator to show an incorrect state was probably a faulty solenoid.

It should be emphasised that all the events that have been described so far took only 14 seconds. The PORV would remain open for 2 hours and 20 minutes when a new shift supervisor discovered it, partly as a result of taking a 'fresh' look at the problem or partly by luck. In the meantime, with the radioactive coolant passing into the drain tank and the pressure in the reactor dropping but the temperature remaining high, there was a danger of steam developing, blocking the flow of coolant. At this stage, one of two emergency reactor coolant pumps started up automatically. A second one was started manually a short time later (41 seconds into the incident). Although the operators gained the impression that things had stabilized, they had not, so that two minutes into the incident, a high-pressure injection (HPI) system was automatically switched on which forced water directly on to the core. It was at this stage that the key operator error was made. After two minutes of operation of the HPI system, an operator manually overrode the automatic safety system and reduced the water supply. This would eventually cause the core to be uncovered and melt, and radiation to be released into the atmosphere.

Although it is not entirely clear why the HPI was turned off, it appears that the operators were confused by the information displayed on two dials, one indicating that pressure was still falling in the reactor and the other that the pressure was dangerously high in the pressurizer. Normally, they both move up and down together as they reflect the states of closely related parts of the cooling system of the plant. In the absence of the knowledge that that PORV was stuck open and the feedwater pipes blocked, the operators clearly had difficulties interpreting the evidence. They came to the conclusion that the core was already flooded as a result of the action of the HPI and that water was being sent up to the pressurizer, thus increasing the pressure there. By this action, the operators thought they were preventing an imminent Loss of Coolant Accident (LOCA), possibly due to a cracked pipe, but in fact they were already experiencing a LOCA and, moreover, were making matters worse.

One could spend a lot of time conjecturing why the operators came to the inappropriate diagnosis. The Kemeny Commission (Kemeny, 1979) into the TMI accident was highly critical of the operators' actions and claimed that there were two indications that a LOCA was under way and in particular that the PORV was stuck open. Operators should have monitored the temperature in the pipes leading from the PORV to the drain tank. An abnormally high reading would have indicated a loss of coolant. The operators did, in fact, note high readings, but concluded this was due to valve leakage, a fault they were aware of before the accident. Secondly, they could have monitored the pressure in the drain tank. So high was the pressure in the drain tank that in addition to the relief valve opening, the tank 'blew' and coolant flowed into the sump and the radioactive waste storage tanks. However, the drain tank pressure indicator was mounted on the back of one of the primary control panels at a height of 7 feet.

It is important to note that fairly long into the incident, operators were still unaware that the reactor was suffering from a LOCA to the extent that at 74 and 100 minutes they manually turned off the emergency reactor coolant pumps. One of the reasons for turning off the pumps was the vibrations which could be felt in the control room. These actions probably determined the fate of the reactor because by then all coolant circulation had stopped. It was only after it was discovered that the PORV valve was stuck open some 2 hours and 20 minutes into the incident that operators made any real progress into controlling the core. After $13\frac{1}{2}$ hours, the operators managed to get one of the reactor coolant pumps to start, and from then on it was a comparatively easy task to stabilize conditions.

The lay person must be surprised to learn that such a potentially dangerous system as a nuclear power plant can contain hardware components with such low reliability. To some extent, this is safeguarded by the inclusion of numerous back-up systems and automatic safety devices. What was also worrying to hear from the subsequent inquiries was that the manufacturers of the TMI plant could not agree on the extent to which the various failures contributed to the final accident. That is to say, they were themselves uncertain as to how the plant would respond in various unfamiliar circumstances.

While poor display and control design along with poor internal communications and problems with shift work and maintenance procedures all contributed to the accident, the key issue was the inability of the operators to correctly diagnose the failures in the plant partly because of time pressure but also because of them following inappropriate procedures. There was no agreement among the operators as to what was the appropriate strategy to follow at various stages during the incident. Often operators followed procedures without taking into account all the available information, possibly as a result of insufficient training.

A popular framework to discuss operator behaviour in this kind of task has been provided by Rasmussen (1983, 1986) where he described three levels of control of human actions as skill-based, rule-based and knowledge-based behaviours. Skilled-based behaviour is analogous to skilled psychomotor performance which proceeds with little or no conscious attention or control. Rule-based behaviour is controlled by stored rules or procedures which are executed when particular signs in the environment are recognized by an operator. The procedures reflect established sequences of behaviour which have led to successful goal attainment on previous occasions. In unfamiliar situations, operators have to revert to problem-solving activity where alternative procedures are evaluated on the basis of their knowledge of the system they are controlling. In this case, information is perceived as symbols. The boundary between rule-based and knowledge-based behaviours is fuzzy, but it is usually the case with the former that goals do not have to be explicitly formulated while with the latter they do. In discussing the behaviour of the operators in the TMI incident, Rasmussen (1986) illustrates the difficulty the operators had in shifting from rule-based to knowledge-based behaviour by making reference to the testimony of two operators given to the US Congress, Oversight Hearings (1979 pp. 138, 139):

Mr Frederick: Let me make a statement about the indications. All you can say about them is that they are designed to provide indications for whatever anticipated casualties you might have. If you go out of bounds of an anticipated casualty, if you go beyond what the designers think might happen, then the indications are insufficient and they may lead you to make wrong inferences. In other words, what you are seeing on the gauge, like what I saw on the high pressurizer level, I thought it was due to excess inventory [coolant]. In other words, I was interpreting the gauge based on the emergency procedure, where the emergency procedure is based on the design casualties. So the indications are then based upon my interpretation. Hardly any of the measurements that we have are direct indications of what is going on in the system. They are all implied measurements.

and

> Mr Faust: What maybe you should try to understand here is that we are trying to gain the proper procedure to go at it. We were into possibilities of several procedures, not just one, to cover what was happening. It had not been written, in fact. So we are trying to determine which procedure to go by.

How information is interpreted is, as Rasmussen (1986) points out, dependent on the context in which it is perceived. In the TMI incident, what was clear was that the operators were continually interpreting the information on the basis that the POVR was closed and that there was excess coolant rather than a severe loss of coolant. Most of the procedures they followed arose from that assumption. It is tempting to argue, though there is no direct evidence for it, that operators were overlooking critical information as a result of making such an assumption and in effect were operating very much in a top-down mode. Returning to Rasmussen's taxonomy of levels of control of human actions (Rasmussen, 1986), when operators experience an unfamiliar situation they should display knowledge-based behaviour whereby troubleshooting or problem solving is achieved by reference to some kind of mental or conceptual model which represents the internal structure of the system with which they are interacting.

Mental models

The notion of mental models has been popularized by Toffler (1970) but has been around in psychology for a considerable time before, as reflected in the ideas developed by Craik (1943, p. 61) when he wrote:

> If the organism carries a 'small-scale model' of external reality and of its possible actions within its head, it is able to try out various alternatives, conclude which is the best of them, react to future situations before they arise, utilize the knowledge of past events in dealing with the present and the future, and in every way to react in a much fuller, safer, and more competent manner to the emergencies which face it.

A precise definition of the term 'mental model' has been difficult to establish partly because the term is used interchangeably with other terms such as metaphors (Bayman & Mayer, 1984), analogous models (Gentner & Gentner, 1983) and a user's conceptual model (Moran, 1981). However, by considering a selection of definitions of mental models and related concepts one can immediately appreciate their relevance to ergonomics. Young (1981, p. 51):

> The notion of a user's 'conceptual model' is a rather hazy one, but central to it is the assumption that the user will adopt some more or less definitive representation or metaphor which guides his actions and helps him interpret the device's behaviour. Such a model, when appropriate, can be helpful or perhaps even necessary for dealing with the device, but when inappropriate or inadequate can lead to misconceptions and errors.

Kieras & Bovair (1984, p. 255):

> By 'mental model' is meant some kind of understanding of how a device works in terms of its internal structure and processes . . . this type of mental model will be termed a device model to distinguish it from any other senses of the term mental model, such as that used by Johnson-Laird (1980).

Halasz & Moran (1983, p. 212):

> . . . we take a mental model to be a cognitive representation of the system's internal mechanics, i.e. its component parts and their behaviors — what Young (1983) calls a 'surrogate model'.

Rouse & Morris (1986, p. 351):

> Mental models are mechanisms whereby humans are able to generate descriptions of system purpose and form, explanations of systems functioning and observed system states, and predictions of future systems states. It is important to emphasise that this definition does not differentiate between knowledge that is simply retrieved and knowledge that involves some kind of calculation. Thus mental models are not necessarily computational models.

A particularly amusing introduction to mental models can be found in Norman (1988) where the author muses on the psychology of everyday things. Despite its title, but in keeping with its contents, the book is concerned with design very much from an ergonomics perspective. Based on his ideas developed in an earlier paper (Norman, 1986), he discusses the problems we encounter with everyday objects as a result of a mismatch between three conceptual models. The design model represents the designer's conceptual model, while the user's model is the mental model developed through interaction with the system. The user's model may also reflect a model developed during special training or through previous interaction with a different but related system (i.e. an analogous system). Finally, there is what Norman terms the system image which reflects the physical structure of the system (i.e. the interface characteristics), including documentation, instructions and labels. It is hoped that the design model matches the user's model. However, the designer does not communicate directly with the user but through the system image. Therefore, if the system image does not make the system model transparent and consistent, the user could end up with an inappropriate model. Norman (1988) provides a very good example of an inappropriate system image resulting from poor control design coupled with misleading instructions for controlling the temperatures of the freezer and fresh food compartments of a fridge. The system image leads one to believe there are two thermostats, one in each compartment, while in fact there is only one thermostat in the fridge.

Lindgaard (1987) and Wilson & Rutherford (1989) have provided useful discussions on the use of mental models in ergonomics. Examples of their application to human–computer interaction can be found in Ackermann & Tauber (1990) and to text representation in Garnham (1987).

Training

While it might seem obvious that the provision of suitable training, rather than the reliance on trial and error behaviour, might encourage the development of appropriate mental models, this approach does have its problems. In many studies which have systematically compared different types of training, such as procedural versus conceptual (Kieras & Bovair, 1984), results have often been confounded by the fact that conceptual training has usually involved longer training time. Furthermore, particularly when concerned with complex systems, it is difficult to ascertain whether or not the user has learned the correct model. Very minor discrepancies might lead to serious errors in performance. In circumstances where some kind of simulation is used for training, this could occur if the simulation fidelity is low (Plott, Wachtel & Laughery, 1988).

However, there can be no doubt that training plays a central role in the safe operation of complex systems and this was emphasized at a meeting of the International Safety Advisory Group (INSAG, 1986) following the Chernobyl incident where recommendations were made for greater attention to be given to training, with special emphasis on the need for operators to acquire a good understanding of the reactor and its operations, and for the use of simulators giving a realistic representation of severe accident sequences. This recommendation did not go unheeded and in the following year a large symposium on training of nuclear reactor personnel was held in Florida (Committee on the Safety of Nuclear Installations, 1987). The importance of the topic is reflected in several other publications (e.g. Johnson, 1987; Marshall & Baker, 1989; Janssens *et al.*, 1989).

Decision support systems

Another approach to improving operator performance in complex cognitive tasks has involved rethinking the allocation of function within the design process (Madni, 1988). This is reflected in much of the current interest in decision support systems (Roth, Bennett & Woods, 1987; Cats-Baril, 1988; Zachary, 1988) not only for the nuclear industry but for space technology (Mitchell, 1988), advanced manufacturing systems (Ammons, Govindaraj & Mitchell, 1988; Sharit & Elhence, 1990) and medicine (Richards, 1988). While it is assumed that decision support systems should reduce the workload of operators, there is a potential problem in that operators, particularly those acting primarily as supervisors, may not trust automatic control systems (Muir, 1987; Muir & Moray, 1989). To some extent this distrust might be overcome by ensuring that the support system is adaptive so it performs only those tasks that the operator overlooks for some reason or other (Rouse, 1988). Alternatively, tasks could be reallocated to the decision support system if the operator becomes temporarily overloaded (Hancock & Chignell, 1987; Kamoun, Debernard & Millot, 1989).

What I have attempted to demonstrate in this section is how the events at TMI have stimulated the involvement of ergonomists into understanding human cognitive processes so as to improve training and redesign jobs by introducing decision aids. In effect, the TMI incident has been one of the most important events in the evolution of cognitive ergonomics. To gain an insight into how cognitive ergonomics has developed since then, readers are referred to a recent collection of papers edited by Barber and Laws (1989) on cognitive ergonomics and to the *Proceedings of the Second European Meeting on Cognitive Science Approaches to Process Control* (Commission of the European Communities, 1989).

PROBLEMS OF ERGONOMICS IN PRACTICE

It is somewhat paradoxical that many nuclear power plants currently in service appear old-fashioned with a visible absence of contemporary technology. This is a direct result of the long development cycle, often in excess of 10 years, but is in strong contrast with many other working environments such as the modern office where the new technology is so much in evidence. This is the context in which it is often said that ergonomics is driven by the technology rather than being an intricate component of the design cycle. In reality, the same could be said for nuclear plant technology. However, the shorter development cycle, with new computer hardware and software continually emerging and products soon becoming obsolete, has reinforced the picture of ergonomics acting very much in a retroactive manner.

One of the main reasons for ergonomics having to act in this manner is the lack of suitable sources of information for designers and others who have no formal education in ergonomics but who nevertheless are responsible for making critical decisions relating to ergonomics factors. Few, if any, of the currently available ergonomics data bases, whether or not they are computerized, facilitate access to relevant ergonomics information (Megaw, 1990) and the same can be said of many of the collections of guidelines and standards, many of which are referenced in this chapter. A more serious problem is that there are considerable gaps in our knowledge, often making the application of research findings a dangerous process. Two examples of this will now be discussed.

The Role of Colour in Displays

In some circumstances, colour coding in electronic displays can be very beneficial. For example, there is no disagreement that colour greatly enhances searching maps (Taylor, 1984) and that it can aid the comprehension of computer programs presented on a VDU screen (van Laar, 1989). In addition, subjects often report greater satisfaction with coloured displays than with achromatic ones even in tasks where performance is not significantly improved (Greenstein & Fleming, 1984). On the other hand, Krebs & Wolf (1979) have demonstrated that the indiscriminate use of colour can severely reduce performance. An example of the inconsistent benefits of the use of colour is provided by the results of Hoadley (1990) who showed that while the introduction of colour improved the speed at which subjects could extract information from pie charts and bar graphs, it tended to have the opposite effect for line graphs. At the same time, while colour facilitated the speed of information extraction with tabular presentation, it did this at a cost of decreased accuracy.

The disadvantages and limitations with the use of colour (Narborough-Hall, 1985) are considerable. Some of these result from the characteristics of the human visual system. For example, coloured text and graphics, particularly if pure colours are involved, are sometimes reported to 'float' in space with reds appearing closer and blues more distant. This effect is referred to as chromastereopsis and is a result of chromatic aberration in the eye. Often, these apparent depth effects will not have any serious repercussions, but if the displays are being used to present three-dimensional information, then perception of depth will be confounded by these effects (McLain, 1989). In many applications display space is at a premium, so that there is a tendency to reduce symbol size to a minimum. However, the visual system is unable to distinguish the colours of very small objects (Carter, 1989). If large displays are used, account should be taken of the relative sensitivity of peripheral vision to different pure colours. In general, the eye is more sensitive to spatial variation in luminance than to spatial variation in colour. Hence, to achieve legibility of text or graphics, there is a need to ensure good luminance contrast with the background, particularly if blues are involved. One should also not forget that at least 8% of the male and 0.4% of the female population have defective colour vision, in some cases severely limiting their ability to discriminate certain colours and this must be taken into account when designing computer graphics (Meyer & Greenberg, 1988). Further problems can arise because the colour appearance of an object is affected by factors such as the colour and brightness of surrounding coloured objects and surfaces (Jacobsen, 1986).

Problems can also be encountered with the display itself, where changes in the colour of text or graphics frequently occur as the brightness and contrast settings are altered. Turning to the question of colour coding, there is a strong tendency to group information of identical or similar colour. While this can significantly speed up information search (Christ, 1975), important differences in information may be overlooked. For example, it is traditional with mimic displays in the chemical and nuclear industries to use red to code both high-priority alarms and stopped instruments such as a closed valve or pump shut-off (Thompson et al., 1989). Clearly, this could be confusing. Additionally, the indiscriminate use of colour may increase the perceived clutter of a display. There is also the question of population stereotypes. In a study comparing the associations for colour between Chinese and US subjects, Courtney (1986) found that in general the US subjects were more consistent in their choice of colours. For example, US subjects showed a 100% association between the concept of 'stop' and the colour red, while for the Chinese subjects only 49% chose red.

Results of this kind should lead one to be extremely wary when consulting many of those publications which have made recommendations on the use of colour in displays (Long, 1984; Murch, 1984; Smith & Mosier, 1986; National Aeronautics and Space Administration, 1989; US Department of Defense, 1989). To be on the safe side, it is often recommended that graphics should be designed on the assumption that the display will be achromatic and that colour should then only be introduced to enhance whatever other form of coding is used (Foley & Grimes, 1988). An alternative approach is to use colour only when certain conditions prevail. Gertman and Blackman (1987) evaluated displays where the entire display was green provided all nuclear plant conditions were acceptable, but if any parameter approached a critical value, that parameter located on the display turned yellow and if it exceeded the value it turned red.

Colour is just one of the many factors to consider in display design. Others include display complexity and clutter (Morrison et al., 1988; Sylla, Drury & Babu, 1988; Tullis, 1988), design of windows (Billingsley, 1988; Myers, 1988), methods of linking display pages (Morrison & Duncan, 1988) and, for some applications, the use of three-dimensional graphics (Zenyuh et al., 1988). Again, it is difficult to give designers universal guidelines on these factors except to remind them not to be too hasty in adopting new display technologies. To take just one example, Ellis, McGreevy & Hitchcock (1987) found that experienced pilots were able to take appropriate avoidance action quicker with a perspective display than a conventional plan-view display. However, these results may not be transferable to air traffic control tasks where experienced operators are unlikely to represent their task primarily in a visual–spatial mode, but rely heavily on verbal codes.

Measurement of Mental Workload

It has always been one of the ambitions of ergonomists to measure mental workload partly as a response to one of the main criticisms of the approaches of work study and Taylorism which concentrate only on directly observable aspects of behaviour, and partly as a response to the relatively successful development of methods and techniques to measure physical workload (Rodahl, 1989). In addition, workload assessment has now become mandatory for several military applications in America (Military Specification MIL-H-46855B). However, progress in developing reliable and valid measures of mental workload has been slow and partially disappointing. This might have been predicted from the conclusions reached at an early NATO symposium on mental workload in 1977 (Moray, 1979). Not only was a consensus not reached on a definition of mental workload but many contributors were unable to provide a definition in the first place. This is how one group of contributors began their report:

> The origin of the concept of 'mental workload' is in the ordinary everyday experience of human beings who perform tasks which are not necessarily physically demanding but which are experienced as exhausting and stressful. . . . On the other hand the concept is at present very ill-defined with several probably distinct meanings. There is at present no satisfactory theory of 'mental workload'. Indeed a case can be made for dropping the term 'mental' in contrast to 'physical', and substituting some neutral term such as 'human operator workload' (Johanssen et al., 1979, p. 101).

If one turns to the opening paper by Jex (1988) in a collection of papers on mental workload published some 10 years later (Hancock and Meshkati, 1988) there is an immediate feeling of *deja vu*: 'Unfortunately, like the terms, happiness, love, and fatigue, the term mental workload is a primitive construct which "everybody knows", but hardly anybody can define in precise, operationally useful terms' (Jex, 1988 p. 8).

In the context of general models of occupational stress (Cooper, 1986; Fletcher, 1988; Sutherland & Cooper, 1989), workload whether physical or mental, has been classified as one of the many intrinsic job factors. Another intrinsic factor is time pressure which ergonomists tend to see as one of the contributors to mental workload, thus reflecting its multifaceted nature. As with the general models of occupational stress there has been a tendency for ergonomists to modify the engineering- or stimulus-based definition of stress to living systems (Steinberg & Ritzmann, 1990) where load reflects an objective measure of the stress or stressors and strain reflects the cost of the load to an individual. Because there are numerous mediating factors affecting the relationship between stress and strain, it is not difficult to see that there is some confusion as to whether ergonomists are primarily interested in measuring workload *per se* or strain. Many researchers have side-stepped the implications of this by saying that our understanding of mental workload can only be appreciated by examining the relationship between objective measures of load, measures of strain and, to make things more complex, measures of task performance. However, to make sense of such relationships, we require a sufficient understanding or model of the complex underlying cognitive processes. We do not have this at the moment, but there have been some important developments which have had implications for our understanding of mental workload and for improving task design. These are discussed shortly.

Essentially, three classees of empirical methods have been developed over the years to measure operator strain: secondary task methods, subjective methods and physiological methods. In comparing the relative merits of these different groups of methods, certain evaluation criteria have been identified by Sheridan & Stassen (1979) and subsequently modified by Wickens (1984):

Sensitivity. The measure should reflect changes in task difficulty or resource demand.

Diagnosticity. The measure should indicate the causes of the variation in workload.

Selectivity. The measure should differentiate mental workload from other factors such as physical demands and emotional stress.

Obtrusiveness. The recording of the measure should not disrupt performance on the task being assessed, particularly where this can have an effect on safety.

Reliability and bandwidth. Apart from normal considerations of reliability, the measure should allow fluctuations in workload with time to be identified, where appropriate.

Secondary task techniques

It is the secondary task-based methods which rely heavily on models of information processing or cognitive functioning. Underlying the early application of these methods were the assumptions that operators have a fixed information-processing capacity and that normally most tasks can be adequately performed without requiring this total capacity, leaving some spare capacity. Hence, in order to evaluate the total demands of a particular task it is suggested that subjects perform an additional concurrent or secondary task so that the total processing capacity is used. Two variants of the secondary task method were developed which were characterized by whether subjects were instructed to give priority to the primary task (subsidiary technique) or to the secondary task (loading technique). With the subsidiary technique (see Brown & Poulton, 1961), the demands of the primary task were assessed in terms of the relative decrement in secondary task performance, ideally secondary task performance being inversely proportional to the demands of the primary task. With the loading technique (see Schouten, Kalsbeek & Leopold, 1962), it was assessed in terms of the relative decrement in the performance of the primary task itself.

It soon became obvious that trying to quantify workload demands by these techniques could be misleading because of the assumptions underlying the model of processing capacity. This can be appreciated by considering a number of key findings. While it has always been realized that one can perform two tasks simultaneously provided one of them has become highly automatized through learning (e.g. walking), there are also examples where it can be shown that people are capable of performing two demanding tasks simultaneously. Allport, Antonis & Reynolds (1972) had proficient pianists sight-read some piano music at the same time as shadowing (shadowing is a technique whereby subjects repeat aloud verbal material presented to either one or both ears). Results showed little if any decrement or interference to either task when compared with single task performance. Similarly, Shaffer (1975) reported that a highly skilled typist could type as quickly and as accurately when shadowing as when not.

There is now considerable evidence that many cognitive tasks do not require processing resources in so far that increase in task difficulty does not affect performance. According to Schneider & Shiffrin (1977), such tasks involve automatic processing without stressing the capacity limitations of the system and without necessarily demanding attention, while other tasks require so-called controlled processing which require processing and are capacity limited and usually proceed in a serial fashion. A similar distinction is found in Treisman and Gelade's feature integration theory of attention (Treisman & Gelade, 1980) where certain processes can take place in parallel and hence do not require focused attention, while others take place serially and do require attention. A further distinction is made by Norman & Bobrow (1975) between performance that is resource limited and data limited. Data-limited tasks are those where performance is limited by the quality of the data so that allocating more attention (effort or processing resources) will not cause an improvement in performance. For example, performance on a simple visual search task can be limited by the conspicuity of the target so that no significant improvements in performance will be gained if the subject puts more effort into performing the task. Similarly, it is likely that as operators become more skilled from practice and training (Wickens, 1989a; Bainbridge, 1989) performance will become less resource limited.

A slightly different approach to modelling attention was taken by Kahneman (1973) who emphasized the point that physiological measures of arousal vary while subjects perform a task in response to momentary changes in the task demands and that, therefore, arousal and effort are usually not determined before a task is performed but depend on the load at any instant of time. According to the model of Kahneman, processing capacity is not fixed but varies as a function of the processing demands. To illustrate this, Kahneman asks readers to compare two situations, one where they are given a simple task but where the consequences of poor performance may have serious repercussions, and a second where they are given a difficult task but with no such repercussions. Kahneman makes the point that no matter how severe the repercussions, one feels one is unable to work as hard on the simple task as on the more difficult one. This implies that the allocation of processing capacity should be considered as a dynamic process controlled by feedback from task demands.

Given these findings, it is not difficult to appreciate the problems in trying to quantify mental workload by means of the secondary task method. On the other hand, there have been considerable benefits from our better understanding of attentional and processing resources. On the assumption that people are able to allocate their processing resources while performing tasks concurrently, Norman & Bobrow (1975) have shown how performing operating characteristics can be plotted to illustrate the relative performance levels of two tasks performed concurrently as resources are allocated in different proportions to them and depending on the extent performance on the tasks is data limited or resource limited. More recently Strayer & Kramer (1990) have used performing operating characteristics to identify the attentional requirements of memory tasks involving either automatic or controlled processing. Extending their use to more practical tasks could yield promising results.

A criticism of Kahneman's model of attention stems from its assumption that there is essentially a single undifferentiated pool of resources. However, the degree of interference between two concurrently performed tasks is a function of the similarity between the mental processes underlying the two tasks. We have already seen examples where there is no interference between two demanding tasks (Allport, Antonis & Reynolds, 1972; Shaffer, 1975). Therefore, Wickens (1984) has proposed a multiple-resource theory. In its simplest form, resources are divided between three dichotomous dimensions: early versus late stage processes, auditory versus visual information encoding and spatial versus verbal processing codes. The implications of this model are considerable and are not confined to the quantification of mental workload but more significantly can be extended to the design of complex tasks where operators are often in effect performing several tasks concurrently.

The most obvious advantage of the secondary task techniques is that they have a high face validity in that they reflect more or less the amount of residual attention or processing capacity available when performing a task. On the other hand, the loading task technique can only be used in situations where a decrease in primary task performance will not lead to serious consequences. The same argument applies to the subsidiary task method, in this case as a result of possible interference between primary and secondary performance. Of course, the interference effect can be considered as a useful diagnostic for inferring the factors contributing to the workload of the primary task and, therefore, can play a part in task design.

Subjective techniques

These have become increasingly popular since the successful use of the Cooper–Harper rating scale to assess aircraft handling qualities (Cooper & Harper, 1969). However, apart from being restricted to aviation tasks, the scale does not reflect the multidimensional nature of workload. As a result of these limitations, there have been several recent attempts to develop multidimensional scaling techniques to quantify workload. The most well known of these are NASA–TLX (Task Load Index) and SWAT (Subjective Workload Assessment Technique). The NASA–TLX is not confined to mental workload evaluation and in the latest version (Hart & Staveland, 1988) there are six scales on which subjects are asked to rate a particular task: mental demand, physical demand, temporal demand, performance achievement, effort and frustration level. In addition to rating a task in relation to each of these six dimensions, subjects are required to weight the importance of the dimensions using a paired comparisons technique. The resulting workload scores can then take a value ranging from 1 to 100. SWAT requires subjects to rate a task on three dimensions: time load, mental effort load and psychological stress load. Subjects are restricted to only three levels for each dimension equivalent to low, medium and high, and descriptors are provided for these levels in relation to each of the three dimensions. However, before subjects rate a particular task, they are required to develop a workload scale. This is achieved by getting them to rank all 27 possible combinations of dimension and level from the lowest to the highest demand. For this purpose, subjects are required to imagine tasks with which they are familiar and comply with the various combinations of levels and dimensions. Once the rankings have been obtained, they are subjected to a conjoint measurement procedure which in effect weights the importance the subjects attach to the three dimensions and produces an interval scale of mental workload. A full description of the technique is given by Reid & Nygren (1988). It is difficult to come down in favour of one or other of the two techniques. Clearly, the strength of SWAT is in providing an interval scale. On the other hand, it is limited by restricting the scaling of each dimension to just three values.

The main advantage of subjective techniques arises from their unobtrusiveness and their ease of derivation. However, doubts linger as to how well self-reports of workload accurately reflect processing demands. Wickens (1989b) has warned against using subjective measures in the context of system design in preference to performance measures. Although better performance is usually correlated with lower levels of reported workload, there are examples where performance and subjective workload measures dissociate (Yeh & Wickens, 1988).

Physiological techniques

A whole host of physiological measures have been proposed which it is claimed somehow reflect the demands of a task and the operator's strain. Somehow these measures are considered to reflect the expenditure of physiological effort and more specifically the state of physiological activation or arousal. However, as Wilson & O'Donnell (1988) point out, no single measure has been found to consistently reflect differences in demands of a variety of tasks. From what has already been said about the multidimensionality of workload and resources, one can appreciate that an increase in mental workload may not result in a general increase in activation or arousal. In this context, considerable evidence has accumulated suggesting that the evoked brain potentials may be a useful indicator of perceptual and cognitive load but not of motor or response load (Wilson & O'Donnell, 1988; Doherty, 1989). McCloskey (1987) reported that while task event-related brain potentials were able to differentiate the demands imposed by a spatial task, heart rate and heart-rate variability did not, although they did show changes with time-on-task suggesting they reflected changes in levels of general arousal.

Another physiological measure that has received favour recently is adrenal secretion as reflected by measures of catecholamines and corticosteroids. Frankenhaeuser & Johansson (1986) have shown that levels of adrenaline correlate with the perceived effort required to perform a task, while levels of cortisol reflect perceived stress or distress. Thus they found that when they compared adrenal activity of operators performing either a monotonous or demanding process control task, the levels of adrenaline secretion were greater for the demanding job but the levels of cortisol excretion were higher for the monotonous task, indicating a higher level of stress was associated with performing the monotonous task despite the lower task demands. This suggests that the general model of stress at work as described by Sutherland & Cooper (1989) should acknowledge that work underload as well as work overload can constitute an intrinsic job stressor, thus reflecting the much quoted hypothetical inverted U-shaped relationship between workload and performance (e.g. Grandjean, 1988, p. 193).

Multiple measures

Numerous studies have used multiple measures of mental workload (e.g. Weber *et al.*, 1980; Wierwille, Rahimi & Casali, 1985). Not surprisingly, a very low correlation was found between the measures. Weber *et al.* investigated the workload underlying various conditions of repetitive work. Of the several measures used, only neck muscle tension, heart-rate variability, and subjective measures discriminated between the conditions of repetitive work. Mean heart rate, critical fusion frequency, integrated EEG, catecholamine excretion rate, and primary task performance were insensitive to the conditions. In the study of Wierwille, Rahimi & Casali a flight simulator was used and the task demands were varied by altering the difficulty of navigational problems while maintaining an appropriate flight path. Measures that were sensitive to changes in the primary task demands included subjective measures, one of the two secondary task measures, two out of the five primary task performance measures. None of the five physiological measures was sensitive to the different loads. This dissociation between the various measures can only be understood when a more coherent predictive model of mental workload has been established.

Selecting the most appropriate technique from the many alternatives remains a delicate problem. Harris, Hill & Lysaght (1989) have developed an expert system to aid the selection process; however, in most cases, one cannot do much better than adopt rough guidelines like those suggested by Wickens (1984, p. 328) where he concludes that:

> If workload is intended to predict performance margins or the 'residual attention' available to cope with failures in critical operational environments, it seems wiser to use secondary- or primary-task measures to guide the choice of systems, despite the fact that the chosen system may demonstrate higher subjective or physiological ratings of difficulty. If, on the other hand, the issue is one of consumer usability, of setting of work-rest schedules, or of job satisfaction and variations in performance are relatively less critical, then greater weight should be provided to the subjective measures (and perhaps to their physiological counterparts).

METHODOLOGY

In order for ergonomics to be perceived other than as a collection of related scientific disciplines, it must promote its own methodology related to its aims. While ergonomics employs many of techniques employed by other sciences and technologies such as physiological recording, measures of task performance, simulation and modelling, questionnaires and surveys, observation techniques, interviews, protocol analysis and so on, it is task analysis which is very much the basis of the ergonomist's tool kit. This is not to the exclusion of other methods as task analysis tends to incorporate whatever other methods or techniques are considered appropriate at the time. It has long been recognized that in order to devise training programmes or design equipment it is necessary to gain insight in to how people perform jobs. The earliest methods for observing human activity can be seen in the techniques employed by work study. However, these techniques were limited to the observation of physical actions and took little or no account of underlying mental operations. Although Crossman (1956) was able to improve on the work study techniques by allowing for the inclusion of mental operations, it was the work of Miller (1962) and the subsequent developments by Annett & Duncan (1967) which are most often associated with the origins of task analysis. As reviewed by Stammers, Carey & Astley (1990), the initial concern of those developing task analysis techniques was with the way to represent the information collected, while more recently the emphasis has moved towards techniques for obtaining data and in particular going beyond simple observational techniques. While there remains disagreement over a definition of task analysis and consequently what does and what does not constitute task analysis, there is little doubt over its aims. As stated by Drury (1983, p. 19):

> The purpose of Task Analysis, and its related technique of Function Analysis, is to make a step-by-step comparison of the demands an operation makes on an operator with the capabilities of the operator. This analysis is identical whether it is to be used to design the equipment, the procedure, the training system or the selection requirements. How it is implemented will differ greatly in each case but the basic information remains common.

This definition highlights the objective of ergonomics to ensure that tasks are neither overdemanding or underdemanding. In this sense, task analysis can be considered as an alternative to the empirical methods described in the previous section for evaluating mental workload (Hill et al., 1987). The definition of task is conveniently left vague, but generally reflects a unit of activity within a work situation, and can refer among other things to actions, procedures, rules, processes, goals, state transitions. Additionally, a task can be described at a number of levels so that at the finest level a task may reflect a simple physical or cognitive action in which case it may be termed an 'operation'. In general, task analysis can be broken down into three stages; data collection involving the collection and documentation of source data using whatever data-collection techniques are appropriate (e.g. interviews, observation, questionnaires, film and video, verbal protocol, etc.); task description whereby a description document is produced, again a variety of methods are used from diagrammatic and tabular methods to textual representation and simulation; and analysis whereby the analyst obtains the required information.

A selection of task analysis methods and their relevant application areas are shown in Table 2. The methods do not reflect the data-collection techniques but more the description and analysis techniques. Many of the references given in Table 2 refer to key papers. They clearly demonstrate that task analysis has made significant developments from its earlier applications to non-automated tasks, where it tended to concentrate on sequences of task actions, to knowledge-based tasks. When it comes to knowledge-based tasks, Walsh (1989) has stressed that no task analysis method is appropriate for all applications. A majority of the methods appear better suited to single activities such as text editing or operating a calculator, but less well suited to investigating all the various activities that are performed in a large environment such as an office (i.e. a distinction can be made between micro and macro methods, Harris & Brightman, 1985). Other distinctions between suitability of methods can be made in relation to whether tasks are structured or unstructured or whether they are better suited to system development (HTA and TAKD) or to system evaluation (TAG). TAG has been developed from the ideas introduced by Moran (1981) in his paper on Command Language Grammar (CLG). CLG refers to a method of representing the task description in a textual form obeying grammatical rules. TAG allows designers to analyse the relation between the computation someone is trying to perform with a device such as a calculator and what that person has to do in order to execute the computation. This is referred to as Task/Action Mapping and marks a significant extension of traditional concepts of stimulus-response compatibility used in the context of psychomotor tasks to cognitive tasks (Proctor & Reeve, 1990). In general, the more complex and inconsistent the mapping, the more complex need be the user's mental model and the greater the mental workload involved in performing the task.

A FINAL THOUGHT

It is easy to get the impression from reading this chapter that most people spend most of their time controlling nuclear power plants or interacting with computer systems! It should not be forgotten that approximately 75% of the world's population live in so-called developing countries and that between 80 and 90% of those people work in agriculture. This has led to a considerable interest in the role of ergonomics in developing countries not only in respect of the kinds of task performed in such countries (Sen, 1984; Kogi & Sen, 1987; Wisner, 1985, 1989) but also in relation to technology transfer (Shahnavaz, 1989; Meshkati, 1989a, 1989b; Chavalitsakulchai & Shahnavaz, 1990). While the ergonomics improvements introduced by Manuaba (1985) and illustrated in Figure 2 might seem trivial to those of us living in industrialized countries, we should do well not to forget that within manufacturing industry in industrialized countries there is still a need for the application of what is often termed knobs-and-dials ergonomics or, as it is sometimes referred to in a derogatory manner, common sense.

Correspondence address
Ergonomics Information Analysis Centre, School of Manufacturing and Mechanical Engineering, University of Birmingham, Birmingham B15 2TT, UK

Figure 2 A traditional (a) and newly designed (b) workstation in Bali, Indonesia (photographs reproduced by permission of A. Manuaba)

Table 2—Task Analysis Techniques and Their Applications

Technique	Application area	Author(s)
Abilities requirements	Personnel selection	Fleishman & Quaintance (1984)
ATOM	Software design	Walsh (1989)
CHI/TA	Interface design and evaluation	Phillips *et al.* (1988)
ConTA	Office and clerical work	Dunckel (1989)
CTA	Complex cognitive control tasks	Hollnagel, Pederson & Rasmussen (1981)
	Learning of human–computer dialogues	Barnard (1987)
	Interface design and evaluation	Carey & Whalley (1989)
	Intelligent tutoring systems	Means & Gott (1988)
	Knowledge base organization	Redding (1989)
EVTA	Workload assessment	Shaffer, Hendy & White (1988)
FAST	Allocation of function	Williams (1988)
	Operating procedure design	
GOMS	Interface design and evaluation	Card, Moran & Newell (1983)
	Complex cognitive control tasks	
HTA	Interface design and evaluation	Annett *et al.* (1971)
	Training	Shepherd (1989) and
		Shepherd & Hinde (1989)
	Office work	Sebillotte (1988)

JPC	Interface design and evaluation Communications links	Tainsh (1985)
Link analysis	Interface design evaluation Workspace design Workload assessment	Chapanis (1959)
OSTA	Socio-technical systems	Eason (1988)
PAQ	Personnel selection Task performance evaluation	McCormick (1976)
Performance taxonomy	Task performance evaluation	Berliner, Angel & Shearer (1964)
Tabular	Training Process plant design	Miller (1962) Kirwan & Reed (1989)
TAG	Interface design and evaluation Knowledge elicitation Text editing	Payne (1985, 1989)
TAKD	Interface design and evaluation Training	Johnson, Diaper & Long (1985) Diaper & Johnson (1989)

Note: ATOM = Analysis for Task Object Modelling; CHI/TA = Computer–Human Interface/Task Analysis; ConTA = Contrastive Task Analysis; CTA = Cognitive Task Analysis; EVTA = Empirically Validated Task Analysis; FAST = Functional Analysis Systematic Technique; GOMS = Goals, Operators, Methods and Selection; HTA = Hierarchical Task Analysis; JPC = Job Performance Charts; OSTA = Open Systems Task Analysis; PAQ = Position Analysis Questionnaire; TAG = Task Action Grammar; TAKD = Task Analysis for Knowledge Description.

REFERENCES

Ackermann, D. & Tauber, M. J. (eds) (1990) *Mental Models and Human–computer Interaction*, vol. 1. Amsterdam: Elsevier.

Adams, J. A. (1989) *Human Factors Engineering*. New York: Macmillan.

Allport, D. A., Antonis, B., & Reynolds, P. (1972) On the division of attention: A disproof of the single channel hypothesis. *Quarterly Journal of Experimental Psychology*, **24**, 225–235.

Ammons, J. C., Govindaraj, T., & Mitchell, C. M. (1988) Decision models for aiding FMS scheduling and control. *IEEE Transactions on Systems, Man and Cybernetics*, **18**, 744–756.

Annett, J. & Duncan, K. D. (1967) Task analysis and training design. *Occupational Psychology*, **41**, 211–221.

Annett, J., Duncan, K. D., Stammers, R. B., & Gray, M. J. (1971) *Task Analysis*. London: HMSO, 23 pp.

Bainbridge, L. (1989) Development of skill, reduction of workload. In L. Bainbridge & S. A. Ruiz Quintanilla (eds), *Developing Skills with Information Technology*. Chichester: Wiley, pp. 87–116.

Barber, P. J. & Laws, J. V. (eds) (1989) A special issue on cognitive ergonomics. *Ergonomics*, **32**, (11).

Barnard, P. J. (1987) Cognitive resources and the learning of human–computer dialogs. In J. M. Carroll (ed.), *Interfacing Thought: Cognitive Aspects of Human–computer Interaction*. Cambridge, MA: MIT Press, pp. 113–158.

Bayman, P. & Mayer, R. E. (1984) Instructional manipulation of users' mental models for electronic calculators. *International Journal of Man–Machine Studies*, **20**, 189–190.

Berliner, D. C., Angell, D., & Shearer, J. (1964) Behaviors, measures and instruments for performance evaluation in simulated environments. In *Proceedings of the Symposium and Workshop on the Quantification of Human Performance*. Albuquerque: University of New Mexico, pp. 277–296.

Billingsley, P. A. (1988) Taking panes: issues in the design of windowing systems. In M. Helander (ed.), *Handbook of Human–Computer Interaction*. Amsterdam: North-Holland, pp. 413–436.

Brown, I. D. & Poulton, E. C. (1961) Measuring the spare 'mental capacity' of car drivers by a subsidiary task. *Ergonomics*, **4**, 35–40.

Card, S. K., Moran, T. P., & Newell, A. (1983) *The Psychology of Human–Computer Interaction*. Hillsdale, NJ: Erlbaum.

Carey, M. & Whalley, S. (1989) Cognitive task analysis techniques in the design and evaluation of complex technological systems. In P. Comer (ed.), *11th Advances in Reliability Technology Symposium*. London: Elsevier Applied Science, pp. 11–26.

Carter, R. (1989) Calculate (don't guess) the effect of symbol size on usefulness of color. In *Proceedings of the Human Factors Society 33rd Annual Meeting*. Santa Monica, California: Human Factors Society, pp. 1368–1372.

Cats-Baril, W. L. (1988) Designing decision support systems for human error reduction: the need to address information distortion. In B. A. Sayers (ed.), *Human Factors and Decision Making: Their Influence on Safety and Reliability*. London: Elsevier Applied Science, pp. 256–269.

Chapanis, A. (1959) *Research Techniques in Human Engineering*, Baltimore: Johns Hopkins University Press.

Chavalitsakulchai, P. & Shahnavaz, H. (1990) Woman workers and technological change in industrially developing countries from an ergonomic perspective. Lulea University of Technology, Research Report, TULEA-1990:01.

Christ, R. E. (1975) Review and analysis of color coding research for visual displays. *Human Factors*, **17**, 542–570.

Commission of the European Communities (1989) *Proceedings of Second European Meeting on Cognitive Approaches to Process Control*. Ispra: CEC–JRC.

Committee on the Safety of Nuclear Installations (1987) *Proceedings of the CSNI Specialist Meeting on Training of Nuclear Reactor Personnel*. NUREG/CP-0089, CSNI Report No. 138. Washington, DC: US Government Printing Office.

Cooper, C. L. (1986) Job distress: recent research and the emerging role of the clinical occupational psychologist. *Bulletin of the British Psychological Society*, **39**, 325–331.

Cooper, G. E. & Harper, R. P. (1969) The use of pilot ratings in the evaluation of aircraft handling qualities. NASA Ames Technical Report, NASA TN-D-5153. Moffett Field, California: NASA Ames Research Center.

Courtney, A. J. (1986) Chinese population stereotypes: colour associations. *Human Factors*, **28**, 97–99.

Craik, K. (1943) *The Nature of Explanation*. Cambridge: Cambridge University Press.

Crossman, E. R. F. W. (1956) Perceptual activity in manual work. *Research*, **9**, 42–49.

Diaper, D. & Johnson, P. (1989) Task analysis for knowledge descriptions: theory and application in training. In J. Long & A. Whitefield (eds), *Cognitive Ergonomics and Human–Computer Interaction*. Cambridge: Cambridge University Press, pp. 191–224.

Doherty, P. C. (1989) Investigation of the mental workload requirements of five tests from the criterion task set using performance measures and the P3 component of the EEG event related potential. In E. D. Megaw (ed.), *Contemporary Ergonomics 1989, Proceedings of the 1989 Annual Conference of the Ergonomics Society*. London: Taylor and Francis, pp. 502–507.

Drury, C. G. (1983) Task analysis methods in industry. *Applied Ergonomics*, **14**, 19–28.

Dunckel, H. (1989) Contrastive task analysis. In K. Landau & W. Rohmert (eds), *Recent Developments in Job Analysis*. London: Taylor and Francis, pp. 125–136.

Eason, K. (1988) *Information Technology and Organisational Change*. London: Taylor and Francis, 247 pp.

Ellis, S. R., McGreevy, M. W. & Hitchcock, R. J. (1987) Perspective traffic display format and airline pilot traffic avoidance. *Human Factors*, **29**, 371–382.

Ergonomics Society (1983) *Sizewell 'B' Public Inquiry: Proofs of Evidence Presented by the Society, ES P1-4*. The University of Loughborough: The Ergonomics Society.

Fleishman, E. A. & Quaintance, M. K. (1984) *Taxonomies of Human Performance*. New York: Academic Press.

Fletcher, B. (1988) The epidemiology of occupational stress. In C. L. Cooper & R. Payne (eds), *Causes, Coping and Consequences of Stress at Work*. Chichester: Wiley, pp. 3–50.

Foley, J. D. & Grimes, J. (1988) Using color in computer graphics. *IEEE Computer Graphics & Applications*, **8**, 25–27.

Frankenhaeuser, M. & Johansson, G. (1986) Stress at work: psychobiological and psychosocial aspects. *Applied Psychology: An International Review*, **35**, 287–299.

Garnham, A. (1987) *Mental Models as Representations of Discourse and Text*. Chichester: Ellis Horwood.

Gentner, D. & Gentner, D. R. (1983) Flowing waters or teeming crowds: mental models of electricity. In D. Gentner & A. F. Stevens (eds), *Mental Models*. Hillsdale, NJ: Erlbaum, pp. 99–129.

Gertman, D. I. & Blackman, H. S. (1987) Application of multidimensional rating techniques to CRT-generated display formats. *Perceptual and Motor Skills*, **65**, 731–739.

Grandjean, E. (1988) *Fitting the Task to the Man* (4th edn). London: Taylor and Francis.

Greenstein, J. J. & Fleming, R. A. (1984) The use of colour in command control electronics status boards. In C. P. Gibson (ed), *Proceedings of the NATO Workshop on Colour Coded vs Monochrome Electronics Displays*. London: HMSO, pp. 5.1–5.10.

Halasz, F. G. & Moran, T. P. (1983) Mental models and problem solving in using a calculator. In *Proceedings of CHI '83 Human Factors in Computing Systems*. New York: ACM, pp. 212–216.

Hancock, P. A. & Chignell, M. H. (1987) Adaptive control in human–machine systems. In P. A. Hancock (ed.), *Human Factors Psychology*. Amsterdam: North-Holland, pp. 305–345.

Hancock, P. A. & Meshkati, N. (eds) (1988) *Human Mental Workload*. Amsterdam: North-Holland.

Harris, R. M., Hill, S. G., & Lysaght, R. J. (1989) OWLKNEST; an expert system to provide operator workload guidance. In *Proceedings of the Human Factors Society 33rd Annual Meeting*. Santa Monica, California: Human Factors Society, pp. 1486–1490.

Harris, S. E. & Brightman, H. J. (1985) Design implications of a task-driven approach to unstructured cognitive tasks in office work. *ACM Transactions on Office Information Systems*, **3**, 292–306.

Hart, S. A. & Staveland, L. E. (1988) Development of NASA-TLX (Task Load Index): results of empirical and theoretical research. In P. A. Hancock & N. Meshkati (eds), *Human Mental Workload*. Amsterdam: North-Holland, pp. 139–183.

Hill, S. G., Plamondon, B. D., Wierwille, W. W., Lysaght, R. J., Dick, A. O., & Bittner, A. C. (1987) Analytical techniques for the assessment of operator workload. In *Proceedings of the Human Factors Society 31st Annual Meeting*. Santa Monica, California: Human Factors Society, pp. 368–372.

Hoadley, E. D. (1990) Investigating the effects of color. *Communications of the ACM*, **33**, 120–139.

Hollnagel, E., Pederson, O., & Rasmussen, J. (1981) *Notes on Human Performance Analysis*. Report No. Riso-M-2285, Roskilde, Denmark: Riso National Laboratory.

Hornick, R. J. (1987) Dreams—design and destiny. *Human Factors*, **29**, 111–121.

INSAG (1986) Summary report on the post-accident review meeting on the Chernobyl accident. *Safety Series No. 75, INSAG.1*. Vienna: International Atomic Energy Agency.

Jacobsen, A. R. (1986) The effect of background luminance on color recognition. *Color Research and Application*, **11**, 263–269.

Janssens, L., Grotenhuis, H., Michiels, H., & Verhaegen, P. (1989) Social organizational determinants of safety in nuclear power plants: operator training in the management of unforeseen events. *Journal of Occupational Accidents*, **11**, 121–129.

Jex, H. R. (1988) Measuring mental workload: problems, progress and promises. In P. A. Hancock & N. Meshkati (eds), *Human Mental Workload*. Amsterdam: North-Holland, pp. 5–39.

Johanssen, G., Moray, N., Pew, R., Rasmussen, J., Sanders, A., & Wickens, C. (1979) Final report of experimental psychology group. In N. Moray (ed), *Mental Workload: Its Theory and Measurement*. New York: Plenum Press, pp. 101–114.

Johnson, P., Diaper, D., & Long, J. (1985) Tasks, skills and knowledge: task analysis for knowledge based descriptions. In B. Shackel (ed), *Human–Computer Interaction — INTERACT '84*. Amsterdam: North-Holland, pp. 449–503.

Johnson, W. B. (1987) Development and evaluation of simulation-oriented computer-based instruction for diagnostic training. In W. B. Rouse (ed), *Advances in Man–Machine Systems Research*, vol. 3. Greenwich, Connecticut: JAI Press, pp. 99–127.

Johnson-Laird, P. N. (1980) Mental models in cognitive science. *Cognitive Science*, **4**, 71–115.

Kahneman, D. (1973) *Attention and Effort*. Englewood Cliffs, NJ: Prentice-Hall.

Kamoun, A., Debernard, S., & Millot, P. (1989) Comparison between two dynamic task allocations. In *Proceedings of the Second European Meeting on Cognitive Science Approaches to Process Control*. Commission of the European Communities, pp. 349–359.

Kemeny, J. G. (1979) *Report of the President's Commission on the Accident at Three Mile Island*. Washington, DC: US Government Printing Office.

Kieras, D. E. & Bovair, S. (1984) The role of a mental model in learning to operate a device. *Cognitive Science*, **8**, 255–273.

Kirwan, B. & Reed, J. (1989) A task analytical approach for the derivation and justification of ergonomics improvements in the detailed design phase. In E. D. Megaw (ed.), *Contemporary Ergonomics 1989, Proceedings of the 1989 Annual Conference of the Ergonomics Society*. London: Taylor and Francis, pp. 36–43.

Kogi, K. & Sen, R. N. (1987) Third world ergonomics. In D. J. Oborne (ed.), *International Reviews of Ergonomics*, vol. 1. London: Taylor and Francis, pp. 77–118.

Krebs, M. & Wolf, J. (1979) Design principles for the use of color in displays. In *Proceedings of the Society for Information Display*, vol 20, pp. 10–15.

van Laar, D. (1989) Evaluating a colour coding programming support tool. In A. Sutcliffe & L. Macaulay (eds), *People and Computers V*. Cambridge: Cambridge University Press, pp. 217–230.

Licht, D. M., Polzella, D. J., & Boff, K. R. (1989) *Human Factors, Ergonomics and Human Factors Engineering: An Analysis of Definitions*. Publication from the Crew System Ergonomics Information Analysis Centre, CSERIAC-89-1.

Lindgaard, G. (1987) Who needs what information about computer systems: some notes on mental models, metaphors and expertise. Telecom Australia Research Laboratories, Branch Paper No. 126, Clayton, Victoria.

Long, T. (1984) Human factors principles for the design of computer colour graphics displays. *British Telecom Technology Journal*, **2**, 5–14.

McCloskey, K. (1987) Evaluating a spatial task: behavioral, subjective, and physiological correlates. In *Proceedings of the Human Factors Society 31st Annual Meeting*. Santa Monica, California: Human Factors Society, pp. 774–778.

McCormick, E. J. (1976) Job and task analysis. In M. D. Dunnette (ed.), *Handbook of Industrial and Organizational Psychology*. Chicago: Rand McNally, pp. 651–696.

McLain, M. S. (1989) Hue and disparity in advanced stereoscopic aircraft displays. In *Proceedings of the Human Factors Society 33rd Annual Meeting*. Santa Monica, California: Human Factors Society, pp. 1422–1426.

Madni, A. M. (1988) HUMANE: a designer's assistant for modelling function allocation options. In W. Karwowski, H. R. Parsaei & M. R. Wilhelm (eds), *Ergonomics of Hybrid Automated Systems I*. Amsterdam: Elsevier, pp. 291–302.

Malone, T. B., Perse, R. M., Heasly, C. C., & Kilpatrick, M. (1988) MANPRINT in the program initiation phase of system acquisition. In *Proceedings of the Human Factors Society 32nd Annual Meeting*. Santa Monica, California: Human Factors Society, pp. 1108–1112.

Manuaba, A. (1985) Ergonomics in the rural sector. In *Proceedings of the International Symposium on Ergonomics in Developing Countries, Jakarta*. Geneva: International Labour Office, pp. 405–415.

Marshall, E. & Baker, S. (1989) Training operators to use advanced display systems for process control. In L. Bainbridge & S. A. Ruiz Quintanilla (eds), *Developing Skills with Information Technology*. Chichester: Wiley, pp. 217–226.

Means, B. & Gott, S. P. (1988) Cognitive task analysis as a basis for tutor development: articulating abstract knowledge representations. In J. Psotka, L. D. Massey & S. A. Mutter (eds), *Intelligent Tutoring Systems: Lessons Learned*. Hillsdale, NJ: Erlbaum, pp. 35–57.

Megaw, E. D. (1990) The future role of ergonomics databases. *Ergonomics*, **33**, 469–476.

Meshkati, N. (1989a) Technology transfer to developing countries: a tripartite micro- and macroergonomic analysis of human-organization-technology interfaces. *International Journal of Industrial Ergonomics*, **4**, 101–115.

Meshkati, N. (1989b) An etiological investigation of micro- and macroergonomics factors in the Bhopal disaster: lessons for industries in both industrialized and developing countries. *International Journal of Industrial Ergonomics*, **4**, 161–175.

Meyer, G. W. & Greenberg, D. P. (1988) Color-defective vision and computer graphics displays. *IEEE Computer Graphics & Applications*, **8**, 28–40.

Miller, R. B. (1962) Task description and analysis. In R. M. Gange (ed.), *Psychological Principles in System Design*. New York: Holt, Rinehart and Winston, pp. 187–228.

Mitchell, T. M. (1988) AI systems in the space station. In T. B. Sheridan, D. S. Kruser & S. Deutsch (eds), *Proceedings of the Symposium on Human Factors in Automated and Robotic Space Systems*. Washington, DC: National Research Council, pp. 91–112.

Moran, T. P. (1981) The command language grammar: a representation for the user interface of interactive computing systems. *International Journal of Man–Machine Studies*, **15**, 3–50.

Moray, N. (ed.) (1979) *Mental Workload: Its Theory and Measurement*. New York: Plenum Press.

Morrison, D. L. & Duncan, K. D. (1988) The effect of scrolling hierarchically paged displays and ability on fault diagnosis performance. *Ergonomics*, **31**, 889–904.

Morrison, G. R., ross, S. M., O'Dell, J. K. & Schultz, C. W. (1988) Adapting text presentations to media attributes: getting more out of less in CBI. *Computers in Human Behavior*, **4**, 65–75.

Muir, B. M. (1987) Trust between humans and machines, and the design of decision aids. *International Journal of Man–Machine Studies*, **27**, 527–539.

Muir, B. M. & Moray, N. (1989) Operators' trust in and use of automatic controllers. In *Proceedings of the Annual Conference of the Human Factors Association of Canada*. Mississauga, Ontario: Human Factors Association of Canada, pp. 163–166.

Murch, G. M. (1984) Physiological principles for the effective use of color. *IEEE Computer Graphics & Applications*, **4**, 49–54.

Murrell, K. F. M. (1965) *Ergonomics*. London: Chapman and Hall.

Myers, B. A. (1988) A taxonomy of window manager user interfaces. *IEEE Computer Graphics & Applications*, **8**, 65–84.

Narborough-Hall, C. S. (1985) Recommendations for applying colour coding to air traffic control displays. *Displays Technology and Applications*, **6**, 131–137.

National Aeronautics and Space Administration (1989) *Man–Systems Integration Standards: NASA-STD-3000*, 2 vols. Houston, Texas: NASA, Lyndon B. Johnson Center.

Norman, D. A. (1986) Cognitive engineering. In D. A. Norman & S. W. Drapers (eds), *User Centered System Design*. Hillsdale, NJ: Erlbaum, pp. 31–61.

Norman, D. A. (1988) *The Psychology of Everyday Things*. New York: Basic Books.

Norman, D. & Bobrow, D. (1975) On data-limited and resource-limited processing. *Journal of Cognitive Psychology*, **7**, 44–60.

Oborne, D. J. (ed.) (1987) *International Reviews of Ergonomics: Current Trends in Human*

Factors Research and Practice, vol. 1. London: Taylor and Francis.

Oborne, D. J. (ed.) (1988) *International Reviews of Ergonomics: Current Trends in Human Factors Research and Practice*, vol. 2. London: Taylor and Francis.

Oborne, D. J. (ed.) (1989) *International Reviews of Ergonomics: Current Trends in Human Factors Research and Practice*, vol. 3. London: Taylor and Francis.

Payne, S. J. (1985) Task-action grammars. In B. Shackel (ed.), *Human–Computer Interaction—INTERACT '84*. Amsterdam: North-Holland, pp. 527–532.

Payne, S. J. (1989) A notation for reasoning about learning. In J. Long & A. Whitefield (eds), *Cognitive Ergonomics and Human–Computer Interaction*. Cambridge: Cambridge University Press, pp. 134–165.

Perrow, C. (1984) *Normal Accidents: Living with High-risk Technologies*. New York: Basic Books.

Phillips, M. D., Bashinski, H. S., Ammerman, H. L., & Fligg, C. M. (1988) A task analytic approach to dialogue design. In M. Helander (ed.), *Handbook of Human–Computer Interaction*. Amsterdam: North-Holland, pp. 835–857.

Plott, C., Wachtel, J., & Laughery, K. R. (1988) Operational assessment of simulator fidelity in the nuclear industry. In *Proceedings of the Human Factors Society 32nd Annual Meeting*. Santa Monica, California: Human Factors Society, pp. 705–709.

Proctor, R. W. & Reeve, T. G. (eds), (1990) *Stimulus-Response Compatibility: An Integrated Perspective*. Amsterdam: Elsevier.

Rasmussen, J. (1983) Skills, rules, knowledge: signals, signs, and symbols and other distinctions in human performance models. *IEEE Transactions of Systems, Man and Cybernetics*, **13**, 257–267.

Rasmussen, J. (1986) *Information Processing and Human–Machine Interaction*. Amsterdam: North-Holland.

Redding, R. E. (1989) Perspectives on cognitive task analysis: the state of the state of the art. In *Proceedings of the Human Factors Society 33rd Annual Meeting*. Santa Monica, California: Human Factors Society, pp. 1348–1352.

Reid, G. B. & Nygren, T. E. (1988) The subjective workload assessment technique: a scaling procedure for measuring mental workload. In P. A. Hancock & N. Meshkati (eds), *Human Mental Workload*. Amsterdam: North-Holland, pp. 185–218.

Richards, B. F. (1988) Intelligent job aids for professionals: lessons learned from medicine. *Performance Improvement Quarterly*, **1**, 19–32.

Rodahl, K. (1989) *The Physiology of Work*. London: Taylor and Francis.

Roth, E. M., Bennett, K. B., & Woods, D. D. (1987) Human interaction with an 'intelligent' machine. *International Journal of Man–Machine Studies*. **27**, 479–525.

Rouse, W. B. (1988) Adaptive aiding for human/computer control. *Human Factors*, **30**, 431–443.

Rouse, W. B. & Morris, N. M. (1986) On looking into the black box: prospects and limits in the search for mental models. *Psychological Bulletin*, **100**, 349–363.

Rubinstein, E. & Mason, A. F. (1979) The accident that shouldn't have happened: an anlaysis of Three Mile Island. *IEEE Spectrum*, **16**, 33–57.

Schneider, W. & Shiffrin, R. M. (1977) Controlled and automatic human information processing: I. Detection, search and attention. *Psychological Review*, **84**, 1–66.

Schouten, J. F., Kalsbeek, J. W. H., & Leopold, F. F. (1962) On the evaluation of perceptual and mental load. *Ergonomics*, **5**, 251–260.

Sebillotte, S. (1988) Hierarchical planning as method for task analysis: the example of office task analysis. *Behaviour and Information Technology*, **7**, 275–293.

Sen, R. N. (1984) Applications of ergonomics to industrially developing countries. *Ergonomics*, **27**, 1021–1032.

Shaffer, L. H. (1975) Multiple attention in continuous verbal tasks. In P. M. A.

Rabbitt & S. Dornic (eds), *Attention and Performance V*. London: Academic Press, pp. 157–167.

Shaffer, M. T., Hendy, K. C., & White, L. R. (1988) An empirically validated task analysis (EVTA) of low level army helicopter operations. In *Proceedings of the Human Factors Society 32nd Annual Meeting*. Santa Monica, California: Human Factors Society, pp. 178–183.

Shahnavaz, H. (1989) Ergonomics: an emerging concept in industrially developing countries. *International Journal of Industrial Ergonomics*, **4**, 91–100.

Sharit, J. & Elhence, S. (1990) Allocation of tool-replacement decision-making responsibility in flexible manufacturing systems. *International Journal of Industrial Ergonomics*, **5**, 29–46.

Shepherd, A. (1989) Analysis and training in information technology tasks. In D. Diaper (ed.), *Task Analysis for Human–Computer Interaction*. Chichester: Ellis Horwood, pp. 15–55.

Shepherd, A. & Hinde, C. J. (1989) Mimicking the training expert: a basis for automating training needs analysis. In L. Bainbridge & S. A. Ruiz Quintanilla (eds), *Developing Skills with Information Technology*. London: Taylor and Francis, pp. 153–175.

Sheridan, T. B. & Stassen, H. G. (1979) Definitions, models and measures of human workload. In N. Moray (ed.), *Mental Workload: Its Theory and Measurement*. New York: Plenum Press, pp. 219–233.

Smith, S. L. & Mosier, J. N. (1986) *Guidelines for Designing User Interface Software*, Report No. MTR 10090 ESD-TR-86-278. Bedford, MA: Mitre Corporation.

Stammers, R. B., Carey, M. S., & Astley, J. A. (1990) Task analysis. In J. R. Wilson & E. N. Corlett (eds), *Evaluation of Human Work: A Practical Ergonomics Methodology*. London: Taylor and Francis, pp. 134–160.

Steinberg, A. & Ritzmann, R. F. (1990) A living systems approach to understanding the concept of stress. *Behavioral Science*, **35**, 138–146.

Strayer, D. L. & Kramer, A. F. (1990) Attentional requirements of automatic and controlled processing. *Journal of Experimental Psychology: Learning, Memory, and Cognition*, **16**, 67–82.

Sutherland, V. J. & Cooper, C. L. (1989) Occupational stress in the offshore oil and gas industry. In D. J. Oborne (ed.), *International Reviews of Ergonomics*, vol. 3. London: Taylor and Francis, pp. 183–215.

Sylla, C., Drury, C. G., & Babu, A. J. G. (1988) A human factors design investigation of a computerized layout system of text-graphic technical material. *Human Factors*, **30**, 347–358.

Tainsh, M. A. (1985) Job process charts and man-computer interaction within naval command systems. *Ergonomics*, **28**, 555–565.

Taylor, R. M. (1984) Colour coding in information displays: heuristics, experience and evidence from cartography. In C. P. Gibson (ed.), *Proceedings of the NATO Workshop on Colour Coded vs Monochrome Electronics Displays*. London: HMSO, pp. 35.1–35.46.

Thompson, K., Kirwan, B., Whalley, S. P., & Megaw, E. D. (1989) The effect of colour interference and information density on user performance with mimic displays. In E. D. Megaw (ed.), *Contemporary Ergonomics 1989, Proceedings of the 1989 Annual Conference of the Ergonomics Society*. London: Taylor and Francis, pp. 180–187.

Toffler, A. (1970) *Future Shock*. London: Bodley Head.

Treisman, A. M. & Gelade, G. (1980) A feature-integration theory of attention. *Cognitive Psychology*, **12**, 97–136.

Tullis, T. S. (1988) Screen design. In M. Helander (ed.), *Handbook of Human–Computer Interaction*. Amsterdam: North-Holland, pp. 377–411.

US Congress, Oversight Hearings, Washington (1979) *Accident at the Three Mile Island*

Nuclear Power Plant, May 9–15, 1979. Washington, DC: US Government Printing Office.

US Department of Defense (1989) *Human Engineering Design Criteria for Military Systems, Equipment and Facilities: Military Standard MIL-STD-1472D*. Philadelphia: Naval Publications and Forms Center.

Walsh, P. (1989) Analysis for Task Object Modelling (ATOM): towards a method of integrating task analysis with Jackson System Development for user interface software design. In D. Diaper (ed.), *Task Analysis for Human–Computer Interaction*. Chichester: Ellis Horwood, pp. 186–209.

Walters, R. M., Schroeder, L. R., & Burgy, D. C. (1989) Developing human factors criteria for a new reactor plant. In *Proceedings of the Human Factors Society 33rd Annual Meeting*. Santa Monica, California: Human Factors Society, pp. 1114–1118.

Weber, A., Fussler, C., O'Hanlon, J. F., Gierer, R., & Grandjean, E. (1980) Psychophysiological effects of repetitive tasks. *Ergonomics*, **23**, 1033–1046.

Wickens, C. D. (1984) *Engineering Psychology and Human Performance*. Columbus, Ohio: Charles E. Merrill.

Wickens, C. D. (1989a) Attention and skilled performance. In D. H. Holding (ed.), *Human Skills* (2nd edn). Chichester: Wiley, pp. 71–105.

Wickens, C. D. (1989b) Models of multitask situation. In G. R. McMillan, D. Beevis, E. Salas, M. H. Strub, R. Sutton & L. van Breda (eds), *Applications of Human Performance Models to System Design*. New York: Plenum Press, pp. 259–273.

Wierwille, W. W., Rahimi, M., & Casali, J. G. (1985) Evaluation of 16 measures of mental workload using a simulated flight task emphasizing mediational activity. *Human Factors*, **27**, 489–502.

Williams, J. F. (1988) Human factors analysis of automation requirements: a methodology for allocating functions. In *Proceedings of the 10th Advances in Reliability Symposium*. Amsterdam: Elsevier, pp. 103–113.

Wilson, G. F. & O'Donnell, R. D. (1988) Measurement of operator workload with the neurophysiological workload test battery. In P. A. Hancock & N. Meshkati (eds), *Human Mental Workload*. Amsterdam: North-Holland, pp. 63–100.

Wilson, J. R. & Rutherford, A. (1989) Mental models: theory and application in human factors. *Human Factors*, **311**, 617–634.

Wisner, A. (1985) Ergonomics in industrially developing countries. *Ergonomics*, **28**, 1213–1224.

Wisner, A. (1989) Variety of physical characteristics in industrially developing countries—ergonomic consequences. *International Journal of Industrial Ergonomics*, **4**, 117–138.

Yeh, Y. Y. & Wickens, C. D. (1988) The dissociation between subjective workload and performance. *Human Factors*, **30**, 111–120.

Young, R. M. (1981) The machine inside the machine: users' models of pocket calculators. *International Journal of Man–Machine Studies*, **15**, 51–85.

Young, R. M. (1983) Surrogates and mappings: two kinds of conceptual models for interactive devices. In D. Gentner & A. F. Stevens (eds), *Mental Models*. Hillsdale, NJ: Erlbaum, pp. 267–297.

Zachary, W. W. (1988) Decision support systems: designing to extend the cognitive limits. In M. Helander (ed.), *Handbook of Human–Computer Interaction*. Amsterdam: North-Holland, pp. 997–1030.

Zenyuh, J. P., Reising, J. M., Walchli, S., & Biers, D. (1988) A comparison of a stereographic 3-D display versus 2-D display using an advanced air-to-air format. In *Proceedings of the Human Factors Society 32nd Annual Meeting*. Santa Monica, California: Human Factors Society, pp. 53–57.

BOOKS IN ERGONOMICS AND ERGONOMICS RELATED TOPICS

General Ergonomics

Boff, K. R. & Lincoln, J. E. (eds) (1988) *Engineering Data Compendium: Human Perception and Performance*, vols 1, 2 and 3 and *User's Guide*. Ohio: Harry G. Armstrong Aerospace Medical Research Laboratory.

Burgess, J. H. (1986) *Designing for Humans: The Human Factor in Engineering.* Princeton, NJ: Petrocelli Books.

Burgess, J. H. (1989) *Human Factors in Industrial Design: The Designer's Companion.* Blue Ridge Summit, Pennsylvania: TAB.

Fraser, T. M. (1989) *The Worker at Work: A Textbook Concerned with Men and Women in the Workplace.* London: Taylor and Francis.

Hancock, P. A. (ed.) (1987) *Human Factors Psychology.* Amsterdam: North-Holland.

Ivergard, T. (1989) *Handbook of Control Room Design and Ergonomics.* London: Taylor and Francis.

Kroemer, K. H. E., Kroemer, H. J., & Kroemer-Elbert, K. E. (1986) *Engineering Physiology: Physiological Bases of Human Factors/Ergonomics.* Amsterdam: Elsevier.

Nicholson, A. S. & Ridd, J. E. (eds) (1988) *Health, Safety and Ergonomics.* London: Butterworths.

Pheasant, S. (1986) *Bodyspace: Anthropometry, Ergonomics and Design.* London: Taylor and Francis.

Salvendy, G. (ed.) (1987) *Handbook of Human Factors.* New York: Wiley.

Singleton, W. T. (1989) *The Mind at Work: Psychological Ergonomics.* Cambridge: Cambridge University Press.

Woodson, W. E. (1987) *Human Factors Reference Guide for Electronics and Computer Professionals.* New York: McGraw-Hill.

Ergonomics Methodology

Evans, G. W., Karwowski, W., & Wilhelm, M. R. (eds) (1989) *Applications of Fuzzy Set Methodologies in Industrial Engineering.* Amsterdam: Elsevier.

Harrison, M. & Thimbleby, H. (eds) (1990) *Formal Methods in Human–Computer Interaction.* Cambridge: Cambridge University Press.

Karwowski, W. & Mital, A. (eds) (1986) *Applications of Fuzzy Set Theory in Human Factors.* Amsterdam: Elsevier.

Kirakowski, J. & Corbett, M. (1990) *Effective Methodology for the Study of HCI.* Amsterdam: North-Holland.

McMillan, G. R., Beevis, D., Salas, E., Strub, M. H., Sutton, R., & van Breda, L. (eds) (1988) *Applications of Human Performance Models to System Design.* New York: Plenum Press.

Meister, D. (1986) *Human Factors Testing and Evaluation.* Amsterdam: Elsevier.

Meister, D. (1989) *Conceptual Aspects of Human Factors.* Baltimore: Johns Hopkins University Press.

Ravden, S. & Johnson, G. J. (1989) *Evaluating Usability of Human–Computer Interfaces: A Practical Method.* Chichester: Ellis Horwood.

Rouse, W. B. & Boff, K. R. (eds) (1987) *System Design: Behavioral Perspectives on Designers, Tools, and Organizations.* New York: North-Holland.

Wilson, J. R. & Corlett, E. N. (eds) (1990) *Evaluation of Human Work: A Practical Ergonomics Methodology*. London: Taylor and Francis.

Ergonomics in Human–computer Interaction

Barker, P. (1989) *Basic Principles of Human–Computer Interaction Design*. London: Hutchinson.

Bolc, L. & Jarke, M. (eds) (1986) *Cooperative Interfaces to Information Systems*. Berlin: Springer-Verlag.

Booth, P. (1989) *An Introduction to Human–Computer Interaction*. Hove: Erlbaum.

Bosman, D. (ed.) (1989) *Display Engineering*. Amsterdam: North-Holland.

Brown, C. M. (1988) *Human–Computer Interface Design Guidelines*. Norwood, NJ: Ablex.

Brown, J. R. & Cunningham, S. (1989) *Programming the User Interface*. New York: Wiley.

Carey, J. M. (ed.) (1988) *Human Factors in Management Information Systems*. Norwood, NJ: Ablex.

Carroll, J. M. (ed.) (1987) *Interfacing Thought: Cognitive Aspects of Human–Computer Interaction*. Cambridge, MA: MIT Press.

Cleal, D. M. & Heaton, N. O. (eds) (1988) *Knowledge-Based Systems: Implications for Human–Computer Interfaces*. Chichester: Ellis Horwood.

Coates, R. B. & Vlaemink, I. (1987) *Man–Computer Interfaces*. Oxford: Blackwell Scientific Publications.

Durrett, H. J. (ed.) (1987) *Color and the Computer*. Orlando, FL: Academic Press.

Ehrich, R. W. & Williges, R. C. (eds) (1986) *Human–Computer Dialogue Design*. Amsterdam: Elsevier.

Fourcin, A. J., Harland, G., Barry, W., & Hazan, V. (eds) (1989) *Speech Input and Output Assessment: Multilingual Methods and Standards*. Chichester: Ellis Horwood.

Frese, M., Ulich, E., & Dzida, W. (eds) (1987) *Psychological Issues of Human–Computer Interaction in the Workplace*. Amsterdam: North-Holland.

Gardiner, M. M. & Christie, B. (eds) (1987) *Applying Cognitive Psychology to User–Interface Design*. Chichester: Wiley.

Guindon, R. (ed.) (1988) *Cognitive Science and Its Applications for Human–Computer Interaction*. Hillsdale, NJ: Erlbaum.

Hancock, P. A. & Chignell, M. H. (eds) (1989) *Intelligent Interfaces: Theory Research and Design*. Amsterdam: North-Holland.

Hartson, H. R. & Hix, D. (eds) (1988) *Advances in Human–Computer Interaction*, vol. 2. Norwood, NJ: Ablex.

Helander, M. (ed.) (1988) *Handbook of Human–Computer Interaction*. Amsterdam: North-Holland.

Hendler, J. A. (ed.) (1988) *Expert Systems: The User Interface*. Norwood, NJ: Ablex.

Horton, W. K. (1990) *Designing and Writing Online Documentation: Help Files to Hypertext*. New York: Wiley.

Kearsley, G. (1988) *Online Help Systems: Design and Implementation*. Norwood, NJ: Ablex.

Long, J. & Whitefield, A. (eds) (1989) *Cognitive Ergonomics and Human–Computer Interaction*. Cambridge: Cambridge University Press.

Myers, B. A. (1988) *Creating User Interfaces by Demonstration*. Boston, MA: Academic Press.

146   INTERNATIONAL REVIEW OF INDUSTRIAL AND ORGANIZATIONAL PSYCHOLOGY 1991

Nickerson, R. S. (1986) *Using Computers: The Human Factors of Information Systems*. Cambridge, MA: MIT Press.
Nielson, J. (ed.) (1990) *Coordinating User Interfaces for Consistency*. London: Academic Press.
Norman, D. A. & Draper, S. W. (eds) (1986) *User Centered Systems Design*. Hillsdale, NJ: Erlbaum.
Rivlin, C., Lewis, R. & Davies-Cooper, R. (eds) (1990) *Guidelines for Screen Design*. Oxford: Blackwell Scientific Publications.
Rubin, T. (1988) *User Interface Design for Computer Systems*. Chichester: Ellis Horwood.
Rutkowska, J. C. & Crook, C. (eds) (1987) *Computers, Cognition and Development: Issues for Psychology and Education*. Chichester: Wiley.
Sher, S. (ed.) (1988) *Input Devices*. Boston, MA: Academic Press.
Shneiderman, B. (1987) *Designing the User Interface: Strategies for Effective Human–Computer Interaction*. Reading, MA: Addison-Wesley.
Shorrock, B. (1988) *System Design and HCI—A Practical Handbook*. Wilmslow: Sigma Press.
Sutcliffe, A. (1988) *Human–Computer Interaction*. Basingstoke: Macmillan Education.
Veer, G. C. van de, Green, T. R. G., Hoc, J. M., & Murray, D. M. (eds) (1988) *Working with Computers: Theory versus Outcome*. London: Academic Press.
Waterworth, J. A. & Talbot, M. (eds) (1987) *Speech and Language-based Interaction with Machines: Towards the Conversational Computer*. Chichester: Ellis Horwood.
Winograd, T. & Flores, F. (1986) *Understanding Computers and Cognition: A New Foundation for Design*. Norwood, NJ: Ablex.

Impact of New Technology

Blackler, F. & Oborne, D. (eds) (1987) *Information Technology: Designing for the Future*. Leicester: British Psychological Society.
Boddy, D. & Buchanan, D. A. (1986) *Managing New Technology*. Oxford: Basil Blackwell.
Bradley, G. (1989) *Computers and the Psychosocial Work Environment*. London: Taylor and Francis.
Brotchie, J. F., Hall, P. & Newton, P. W. (eds) (1987) *The Spatial Impact of Technological Change*. London: Croom Helm.
Clegg, C., Warr, P., Green, T., Monk, A., Kemp, N., Allison, G. & Lansdale, M. (1988) *People and Computers: How to Evaluate Your Company's New Technology*. Chichester: Ellis Horwood.
Cooper, C. L. & Payne, R. (eds) (1988) *Causes, Coping and Consequences of Stress at Work*. Chichester: Wiley.
Dainoff, M. J. & Dainoff, M. H. (1987) *A Manager's Guide to Ergonomics in the Electronic Office*. Chichester: Wiley.
Danziger, J. N. & Kraemer, K. L. (1986) *People and Computers: The Impacts of Computing on End Users in Organizations*. New York: Columbia University Press.
Davidson, M. J. & Cooper, C. L. (eds) (1987) *Women and Information Technology*. Chichester: Wiley.
Dyer, H., & Morris, A. (1990) *Human Aspects of Library Automation*. Aldershot: Gower.
Eason, K. (1988) *Information Technology and Organisational Change*. London: Taylor and Francis.

Fallik, F. (1988) *Managing Organizational Change: Human Factors and Automation.* London: Taylor and Francis.

Gale, A. & Christie, B. (eds) (1987) *Psychophysiology and the Electronic Workplace.* Chichester: Wiley.

Grandjean, E. (1987) *Ergonomics in Computerized Offices.* London: Taylor and Francis.

Grief, I. (ed.) (1988) *Computer-supported Cooperative Work: A Book of Readings.* San Mateo, CA: Morgan Kaufmann.

Hurrell, J. J., Murphy, L. R., Sauter, S. L., & Cooper, C. L. (eds) (1988) *Occupational Stress: Issues and Developments in Research.* London: Taylor and Francis.

Leuder, R. (ed.) (1986) *The Ergonomics Payoff: Designing the Electronic Office.* Toronto: Holt, Rinehart and Winston.

McLoughlin, I. & Clark, J. (1988) *Technological Change at Work.* Milton Keynes: Open University Press.

Majchrzak, A. (1988) *The Human Side of Factory Automation.* San Francisco, CA: Jossey-Bass.

Majchrzak, A., Chang, T. C., Barfield, W., Eberts, R., & Salvendy, G. (1987) *Human Aspects of Computer-Aided Design.* London: Taylor and Francis.

Shotton, M. A. (1989) *Computer Addiction? A Study of Computer Dependency.* London: Taylor and Francis.

Wall, T. B., Clegg, C. W., & Kemp, N. J. (eds) (1987) *The Human Side of Advanced Manufacturing Technology.* Chichester: Wiley.

Warner, M., Wobbe, W., & Brodner, P. (eds) (1990) *New Technology and Manufacturing Management: Strategic Choices for Flexible Production Systems.* Chichester: Wiley.

Willcocks, L. and Mason, D. (1987) *Computerising Work: People, Systems Design and Workplace Relations.* London: Paradigm.

Williams, T. A. (1988) *Computers, Work and Health: A Socio-Technical Approach.* London: Taylor and Francis.

Environmental Ergonomics

Dupuis, H. & Zerlett, G. (1986) *The Effects of Whole-body Vibration.* Berlin: Springer-Verlag.

Griffin, M. J. (1990) *Handbook of Human Vibration.* London: Academic Press.

Haymes, E. M. & Wells, C. L. (1986) *Environment and Human Performance.* Champaign, IL: Human Kinetics Publishers.

Loeb, M. (1986) *Noise and Human Efficiency.* Chichester: Wiley.

Mekjavic, I. B., Banister, E. W., & Morrison, J. B. (eds) (1988) *Environmental Ergonomics: Sustaining Human Performance in Harsh Environments.* London: Taylor and Francis.

Rivolier, J., Goldsmith, R., Lugg, D. J., & Taylor, A. J. W. (eds) (1988) *Man in the Arctic.* London: Taylor and Francis.

Ruck, N. C. (ed.) (1989) *Building Design and Human Performance.* New York: Van Nostrand Reinhold.

Vischer, J. C. (1989) *Environmental Quality in Offices.* New York: Van Nostrand Reinhold.

Wasserman, D. E. (1987) *Human Aspects of Occupational Vibration.* Amsterdam: Elsevier.

Wineman, J. D. (ed.) (1986) *Behavioral Issues in Office Design.* New York: Van Nostrand Rheinhold.

Human Error and Decision Making in Complex Industrial Systems

Bereiter, S. R. & Miller, S. M. (1989) *Troubleshooting and Human Factors in Automated Manufacturing Systems*. Park Ridge, NJ: Noyes Data Corporation.

Dhillon, B. S. (1986) *Human Reliability with Human Factors*. New York: Pergamon Press.

Dhillon, B. S. (1987) *Reliability in Computer Systems Design*. Norwood, NJ: Ablex.

Dougherty, E. M. & Fragola, J. R. (1988) *Human Reliability Analysis. A Systems Engineering Approach with Nuclear Power Plant Applications*. New York: Wiley.

Goodstein, L. P., Anderson, H. B. & Olsen, S. E. (eds) (1988) *Tasks, Errors and Mental Models*. London: Taylor and Francis.

Hoyos, C. G. & Zimolong, B. (1988) *Occupational Safety and Accident Prevention: Behavioural Strategies and Methods*. Amsterdam: Elsevier.

Park, K. S. (1987) *Human Reliability: Analysis, Prediction, and Prevention of Human Errors*. Amsterdam: Elsevier.

Patrick, J. & Duncan, K. D. (eds) (1988) *Training, Human Decision Making and Control*. Amsterdam: North-Holland.

Rasmussen, J., Duncan, K. & Leplat, J. (eds) (1987) *New Technology and Human Error*. Chichester: Wiley.

Reilly, R. (ed.) (1987) *Communication Failure in Dialogue and Discourse: Detection and Repair Processes*. Amsterdam: North-Holland.

Singleton, W. T. & Hovden, J. (eds) (1987) *Risk and Decisions*. Chichester: Wiley.

Swain, A. D. (1989) *Comparative Evaluation of Methods for Human Reliability Analysis*. Cologne: Gesellschaft fur Reaktorsicherheit (GRS) mbH.

Aviation Ergonomics

Birch, N. (1988) *Passenger Protection Technology in Aircraft Accident Fires*. Aldershot: Gower.

Campbell, R. D. (1987) *Flight Safety in General Aviation*. London: Collins.

Committee on Airline Cabin Air Quality (1986) *The Airline Cabin Environment: Air Quality and Safety*. Washington, DC: National Academy Press.

Jensen, R. S. (ed.) (1989) *Aviation Psychology*. Aldershot: Gower.

Rolfe, J. M. & Staples, K. J. (eds) (1986) *Flight Simulation*. Cambridge: Cambridge University Press.

Wiener, E. L. & Nagel, D. C. (eds) (1988) *Human Factors in Aviation*. San Diego: Academic Press.

Posture, Musculoskeletal Disorders and Manual Materials Handling

American Conference of Governmental Hygienists (1987) *Ergonomics Interventions to Prevent Musculoskeletal Injuries in Industry*. Chelsea, MI: Lewis Publishers.

Ayoub, M. M. & Mital, A. (1989) *Manual Materials Handling*. London: Taylor and Francis.

Zacharkow, D. (1988) *Posture: Sitting, Standing, Chair Design and Exercise*. Springfield, IL: Charles C. Thomas.

Chapter 5

AGEING AND WORK

D. R. Davies
Human Factors Research Unit
Aston Business School
Aston University
UK
G. Matthews
Department of Psychology
University of Dundee
UK
C. S. K. Wong
Human Factors Research Unit
Aston Business School
Aston University
UK

INTRODUCTION

Research into occupational aspects of ageing, also known as industrial gerontology (Murrell, 1959), is concerned with 'the employment and retirement problems of middle-aged and older workers' (Sprague, 1970). As workers become older, they become more vulnerable to the vagaries of the labour market. Age-related employment problems begin to appear in the forties and by the mid-fifties they have worsened considerably (Casey, 1984). These problems have not changed appreciably since they were outlined by the Director-General of the International Labour Office in 1962 (International Labour Office, 1962). Middle-aged and older workers may face difficulties in adapting to new methods and techniques and, in certain jobs, in maintaining the pace and rhythm of work. They may be unable to gain access to training programmes. They run a greater risk of long-term unemployment. They may encounter age discrimination in various forms both while employed, and, if made redundant, when seeking re-employment. But since the 1960s early

International Review of Industrial and Organizational Psychology 1991 Volume 6
Edited by C. L. Cooper and I. T. Robertson © 1991 John Wiley & Sons Ltd.

retirement has become much more widespread, and numerous public and private early retirement schemes have been introduced in many industrialised countries, variously directed at employed, unemployed, and disabled older workers, with the definition of 'disability' sometimes being extended to include older workers' labour market prospects. In consequence, older workers, especially men in their late fifties and early sixties, are increasingly likely to have left the labour force (Mirkin, 1987). The employment and retirement problems of middle-aged and older workers can be seen against a background of rapid population ageing (Clark, 1984), rising elderly dependency ratios (the retired population expressed as a proportion of the economically active population), and increasing real values of social security benefits, which, in some industrialised countries, have risen at a faster rate than the income growth of the working population (Holtzmann, 1989).

We begin this chapter by outlining the position of the older worker in the labour market, in both industrialised and developing countries, and discuss some of the factors determining the labour force participation rates of older individuals. We next consider the effects of age discrimination in relation to employment. We then review studies concerned with the work performance (productivity, accident rates, and withdrawal behaviour) of middle-aged and older workers. The chapter concludes by surveying research on retirement, in particular the determinants of the retirement decision and of the adjustment to retirement.

AGE AND LABOUR FORCE PARTICIPATION

Over the past century the size of the labour force in most industrialised countries has increased, its average age has risen, and its composition has changed. In the Western industrial democracies in particular there has been a shift from a society in which the majority of the labour force was employed in agriculture and the extraction industries to one in which most people work in the service sector, with a sizeable but declining proportion of the labour force employed in manufacturing. This transition has been more marked and has taken place more rapidly in some countries than in others. But one consequence, common to all countries that have made the transition, has been a progressive reduction in the labour force participation rates of older men, beginning with those over 65 and moving gradually downwards to affect those in lower age groups. Belbin & Clarke (1971), for example, compared the percentages of men aged 65 and over employed in 21 agricultural countries, 30 semi-industrialised countries, and 21 industrialised countries in about 1950, and found that the average percentages declined from 71% for agricultural countries, to 61% for semi-industrialised countries to 38% for industrialised countries. By the mid-1960s the percentage for 14 agricultural countries had fallen to 57%, and for 17 industrial countries to 30%. Similarly, in a cross-national, longitudinal study of economic development and social policy variables influencing the labour force participation rates of men aged 65 and over, covering the period 1950–75, Pampel & Weiss (1983) found that the percentage of males in agricultural occupations had the largest and most consistent effect on the labour force participation of elderly men, with the level of public pension provision also playing a significant role. The process of economic development, involving modernisation, urbanisation, industrialisation and technological change, thus appears to be associated with reduced labour force participation rates in elderly male workers, as well as with somewhat complex changes in the labour force participation rates of women (see Pampel & Tanaka, 1986; Semyonov, 1980).

The reduction in the labour force participation rates for men aged 65 and over over the past 40 years or so (see Table 1) is associated with the social institutionalisation of retirement (see Atchley, 1982) through the establishment of mandatory retirement ages, linked to public pension schemes which prescribe the age of pension entitlement; in many industrialised countries this is 65 for men and 60 for women. But as Easterlin, Crimmins, & Ohanian (1984) pointed out, the rate of decline in labour force participation rates of American men aged 65 and over is much the same for the period 1890–1940 (when, following the Social Security Act of 1935, the US system of social security began to provide retirement income for eligible workers aged 65 and over) as for the period from 1941 to 1980. Over the long term, therefore, some factor other than mandatory retirement linked to pension entitlement must be responsible for the decline in elderly male participation rates. Easterlin, Crimmins, & Ohanian (1984) suggested that the decline is due primarily to reduced earnings opportunities, resulting from the fall in demand for agricultural workers, a decrease in self-employment, and the growth of large companies at the expense of smaller ones, all of which would tend to diminish the job prospects of men aged 65 and over.

In the United States and other industrialised countries the labour force participation rate for men aged 55–64 remained fairly stable from the 1890s to the late 1950s, when it began to decline, decreasing still further in the 1970s and 1980s. Easterlin, Crimmins, & Ohanian (1984) account for this decline in the United States in terms of new US government programmes, such as the initiation of disability coverage in 1957, and the establishment of an early retirement option under Social Security, with reduced benefits, in 1956 for women and in 1962 for men. In the 1950s and 1960s labour unions began to negotiate a number of early retirement schemes which enabled workers to retire on pension after a fixed period of service. In the 1970s and 1980s governments sought to cope with the problem of rising unemployment and employers attempted to rejuvenate their workforces by developing a variety of early retirement policies (see Mirkin, 1987, for a comprehensive international overview). The increased availability of government and employers' schemes designed to facilitate, if not encourage, early retirement is one of the principal determinants of the decline in participation rates of men aged 55–64 since the late 1950s, and particularly during the 1970s and 1980s. Another is poor

Table 1—Labour force participation rates for men aged 65 and over in 10 industrialised countries, 1950–1988/89

	1950	1960	1970	1980	1988	1989
Belgium	24.7	9.8[a]	—	8.8	—	—
Finland	56.7	39.7	19.0	17.0	9.7[f]	8.8[f]
France	38.0	30.5	15.1	6.0	4.7[a]	3.5
Germany	26.6	22.6	19.9	7.4	4.9	4.5
Italy	43.7[b]	23.6[c]	12.9	12.6	—	7.9
Japan	51.7	56.0	48.9	45.5	36.0	35.8
The Netherlands	35.5[d]	—	11.4	4.8	—	—
Sweden	36.1	27.1	19.2	14.2	—	—
United Kingdom	32.5	25.4	19.9	10.8	7.5[h]	—
United States	42.1	30.3	25.7	17.7[e]	15.9	16.0
Average	38.8	29.4	21.3	14.5	—	12.0[i]

[a]1961; [b]1951; [c]1961; [d]1947; [e]1981; [f]65–74 years old; [g]1987; [h]1986; [i]Simple arithmetic average of rates for 7 countries (incl. UK 1986).
Data from Davies & Sparrow (1985); Mirkin (1987); ILO *Year Book of Labour Statistics*, copyright © International Labour Organisation (1989–90).

health, a major cause of involuntary early withdrawal from the labour force (Chirikos & Nestel, 1981; Kingson, 1981a, 1981b; Parnes & Nestel, 1981). A third is the effect of long-term unemployment on older workers, which is discussed later. As might be expected, the fall in the participation rate for men aged 60–64 from 1960 to 1987 (an average reduction of about 28% for the 10 industrialised countries shown in Table 2) has been much greater than that for men aged 55–59 over the same period (an average reduction of about 12%; see Table 3). In most countries, men in the latter group do not yet qualify for public pension entitlements, and must rely on private pension arrangements if they are to retire early. But for 60–64-year-olds, the growth of pension coverage, together with increasingly attractive public and private pension schemes, has made early retirement a much more feasible proposition. Nevertheless, there is considerable variation across employment sectors in the extent of private pension provision and of worker participation in company pension schemes, and in the level of benefit provided on retirement (see O'Rand & MacLean, 1986).

In developing countries the labour force participation rates for older workers tend to be much higher than in industrialised countries (see Kinsella, 1988). Participation rates for men aged 65 and over, together with those for men aged 60–64 and for those aged 55–59, in a sample of developing countries are shown in Table 4. The discrepancies between the participation rates for workers in these age groups in industrialised and developing countries respectively are attributable to various factors. First, and most obviously,

Table 2—Labour force participation rates for men aged 60–64 in 10 industrialised countries, 1960–1988/89

	1960	1970	1980	1988	1989
Belgium	70.8[a]	—	40.1[b]	—	—
Finland	79.1	65.0	43.0	29.5	27.8
France	—	68.0	47.6	25.7[e]	23.1
Germany	—	74.9	44.2	34.5	34.2
Italy	53.6[a]	—	39.6	—	35.2
Japan	83.7[c]	—	—	71.1	71.4
The Netherlands	—	73.9[d]	50.1	26.8	24.5
Sweden	—	78.7[d]	69.0	—	62.9
United Kingdom	—	87.0	71.2	53.4[f]	—
United States	77.1	71.7	61.0	53.6	54.1
Average	72.9	74.2	51.7	—	43.0[g]

[a]1961; [b]1979; [c]1965; [d]1971; [e]1987; [f]1986; [g]Simple arithmetic average of rates for 9 countries (incl. UK 1986).
Data from Davies and Sparrow (1985); Mirkin (1987); ILO *Year Book of Labour Statistics*, copyright © International Labour Organisation (1989–90).

Table 3—Labour force participation rates for men aged 55–59 in 10 industrialised countries, 1960–1988/89

	1960	1970	1980	1988	1989
Belgium	85.1[a]	—	74.0[b]	—	—
Finland	90.4	76.6	67.6	59.1	59.7
France	82.4[c]	—	80.9	67.3[f]	70.2
Germany	88.7[a]	89.2	82.3	79.8	78.6
Italy	83.7[a]	81.0	74.8	—	67.8
Japan	91.2[d]	—	—	91.3	91.6
The Netherlands	—	86.9[e]	74.2	66.6	65.3
Sweden	—	90.9[e]	87.7	—	87.0
United Kingdom	—	93.1	90.1	80.3[g]	—
United States	88.9	89.5	81.9	78.9	78.8
Average	87.2	86.7	79.3	—	75.5[h]

[a]1961; [b]1979; [c]1968; [d]1965; [e]1971; [f]1987; [g]1986; [h]Simple arithmetic average of rates for 9 countries (incl. UK 1986).
Data from ILO *Year Book of Labour Statistics*, copyright © International Labour Organisation (1962, 1970, 1989–90); Mirkin (1987).

relatively small proportions of the labour forces of developing countries are in jobs where a mandatory retirement age has been established. Second, although most developing countries operate some form of publicly funded social security system, benefits are low and coverage is usually extremely limited (in many Asian countries, for instance, coverage is not extended to the agricultural sector, where older workers are typically concentrated). Moreover, very few workers belong to occupational or other private pension schemes. Third, large numbers of workers in developing countries are self-employed, especially in rural areas, and in the absence of adequate public or private pension provision are obliged to continue working for as long as they are able. Traditionally, elderly people in developing countries who have ceased to work have been cared for by their families, especially their adult children. But the level of family assistance to the elderly has declined in many developing countries, as a result of increased urbanisation and reduced fertility rates, so that a smaller number of adult children is available to provide economic and social support.

The labour force participation rates of women aged 55–59 over the period 1970–87 in a sample of advanced industrialised countries are shown in Table 5. It can be seen that the overall level of participation is lower than that for men in the same age range (see Table 3), but the average participation rate rose by about 4% for women from 1970 to 1987, while falling by about 12% for men. The small increase in participation rates for women aged 55–59 during the 1970s and 1980 may reflect the growing demand for women workers, particularly in expanding employment sectors, employers' greater willingness, in comparison with men, to substitute older women for younger, when the latter are in short supply, and the greater fragmentation of women's

Table 4—Labour force participation rates for men aged 55–59, 60–64, and 65 and over, in 10 developing countries

		55–59	60–64	65+
China	(1982)	83.0	63.7	30.1
Costa Rica	(1984)	83.0	69.6	38.9
Guatemala	(1981)	90.3	85.8	66.9
Indonesia	(1980)	84.6	76.7	53.4
Korea	(1980)	82.6	68.9	40.6
Mexico	(1980)	91.4	85.6	68.6
Morocco	(1982)	89.5	68.9	42.1
Peru	(1981)	94.9	88.5	63.2
Thailand	(1980)	84.4	67.8	39.3
Tunisia	(1984)	82.1	59.2	38.5
Average		86.6	73.5	48.2

Adapted from Kinsella (1988).

working lives which may encourage them to remain in the labour force for as long as possible in order to increase pension entitlements (DeViney & O'Rand, 1988; Easterlin, Crimmins, & Ohanian 1984; O'Rand & Henretta, 1982). The standard retirement age for women in industrialised countries ranges from 55 (e.g., in Italy) to 67 (e.g., in Denmark and Norway); in some countries, such as Austria, Belgium, Italy, and the United Kingdom, the standard retirement age is lower for women than for men, while many others, such as Denmark, Finland, France, Ireland, the Netherlands, Norway, Spain, Sweden, the Federal Republic of Germany, and the United States, it is the same for both men and women, typically either 65 or 67. Nevertheless, the labour force participation rates of women aged 60–64 in industrialised countries tend to be lower than those for women aged 55–59, and have been declining during the 1970s and 1980s (see Table 5), although the rate of decline has been slower than that for men aged 60–64 (see Mirkin, 1987). Participation rates for women aged 65 and over in most industrialised countries are negligible, as Table 5 also shows. In a cross-national longitudinal analysis of the determinants of female retirement in 93 nations at all levels of economic development over the period from 1960 to 1970, Pampel & Park (1986) concluded that economic development increases the probability of female retirement, because it is likely to be associated with more mature systems of public and private pension provision, greater sexual equality with respect to employment conditions, and smaller families. Economic development should thus lead to similar male and female retirement patterns. But even in advanced industrialised countries, such as the United States, women are over-represented in employment sectors where pension coverage is low, are generally less able to meet eligibility requirements relating to age and length of service, and are therefore significantly less likely to be covered by pension schemes than are men. Even when women are covered they are less likely to receive benefits, and the levels tend to be lower (O'Rand & Henretta, 1982; Quadagno, 1988).

Labour force participation rates for older women workers in developing countries (see Table 6) tend to be much lower than those for men (see Table 4), and appear to be declining, although participation rates for women aged between 25 and 44 are increasing (Kinsella, 1988). As in industrialised countries, women in developing countries have lower educational attainment levels than men, although the difference is more marked than in industrialised countries, and the level of attainment reached falls with age, older cohorts having lower attainment levels than younger ones. For example, in China in 1982, 39% of men aged 60 and over were literate, compared with less than 5% of women, while in Indonesia in 1980 13.5% of men aged 25–34 had completed a secondary-school education, compared to 6.7% of women in the same age range; for Indonesian men and women aged 55 and over the percentages were less than 2% and less than 1% respectively (see Kinsella, 1988).

156

Table 5—Labour force participation rates for women aged 55–59, 60–64, and 65+ in 10 industrialised countries 1970–1988/89

	55–59				60–64				65+			
	1970	1980	1988e	1989e	1970	1980	1988e	1989e	1970	1980	1988e	1989e
Belgium	21.3a	19.1b	—	—	—	6.4b	—	—	—	1.7c,d	—	—
Finland	56.1	57.0	55.5	58.6	35.9	27.4	22.6	22.1	4.4	6.0	3.9f	3.4f
France	43.5a	47.3	—	45.1	—	27.3	—	18.1	—	6.8d	—	1.7
Germany (FRG)	37.2	38.7	41.1	40.9	22.5c	13.0	11.1	11.2	10.7d	3.0	1.8	1.6
Italy	18.2	21.4	—	20.2	10.6	11.0	—	9.8	2.6	3.5	—	2.2
Japan	—	—	50.9	52.2	—	—	38.6	39.2	—	—	15.6	15.7
Netherlandsg	17.7c	18.2	24.0	24.0	11.9c	9.8	7.6	8.9	2.2c	0.9	—	—
Sweden	54.6c	68.8	—	78.5	34.5c	41.0	—	50.7	8.7c	3.7	—	—
United Kingdomh	50.9	53.6	51.5	—	28.8	22.4	18.8	—	6.3c,d	3.6d	2.7	—
United States	49.0	48.6	53.0	54.5	36.1	33.3	33.5	35.2	9.7	8.1	7.4	7.8
Average	38.7	41.4	—	46.2i	25.7	21.3	—	23.8i	6.4	4.1	—	5.0j

a1975; b1979; c1971; dData relate to 65–69-year-olds; eSource: Mirkin 1987; ILO *Year Book of Labour Statistics, 1989/90* (Chapter I, Table 1). Copyright © International Labour Organisation; fPersons 65–74 years old; gPersons 15–64 years old; h1986; iSimple arithmetic average of rates for 9 countries (incl. UK 1986); jSimple arithmetic average of rates for 7 countries (incl. UK 1986).

Occupational Age Structures

In industrialised countries, older workers tend to be concentrated in a fairly narrow range of occupations, and this concentration becomes more pronounced as age increases (Makeham, 1980). In the United States workers aged 65 and over are relatively concentrated in 'marginal' occupations, defined in terms of job security, the number of weeks worked per year, the rate of occupational growth or decline, and social status (Nelson, 1980). Older men are found in disproportionate numbers in the retail trade, in miscellaneous services, including many unskilled service occupations requiring relatively low levels of skill and training, and in declining industries such as mining, textiles, and the railways (Morrison, 1983; Sobel, 1970). Among professional workers, too, older people tend to cluster in occupations showing below-average rates of employment growth. Older workers are also more highly represented among the self-employed, who tend to work longer hours and to have lower earnings than their counterparts among wage and salary earners (Becker, 1984). Age-related occupational concentration is also apparent in developing countries, where, as noted earlier, the great majority of older men work in the agricultural sector, although, as Kinsella (1988) observes, in some developing countries significant numbers of older men are employed in manufacturing and in sales.

The concentration of older workers in a relatively narrow range of occupations is attributable to numerous economic, social, and cultural factors. In developing countries, for example, economic and technological changes have increased the range of occupations available, and younger workers, who generally have higher levels of educational attainment than do older workers, are increasingly moving into professional, clerical, manufacturing, and service sector jobs. At

Table 6—Labour force participation rates for women aged 55–59, 60–64, and 65+ in 10 developing countries

		55–59	60–64	65+
China	(1982)	32.9	16.9	4.7
Costa Rica	(1984)	11.6	6.9	3.1
Guatemala	(1981)	10.1	9.0	6.5
Indonesia	(1980)	40.8	32.9	19.0
Korea	(1980)	43.3	31.3	13.0
Mexico	(1980)	25.8	24.1	18.6
Morocco	(1982)	14.6	11.2	5.3
Peru	(1981)	23.6	23.4	12.5
Thailand	(1980)	59.1	43.1	19.0
Tunisia	(1984)	9.8	4.4	3.5
Average		27.2	20.3	10.5

Adapted from Kinsella (1988).

the same time, fewer younger workers are entering the agricultural sector. In consequence the proportion of the labour force engaged in agriculture rises sharply with age. Low levels of educational attainment and the lack of vocational training among older workers are likely to restrict the range of occupational choice and to lead to age-related occupational concentration, both in developing and industrialised countries. Employers' perceptions of the types of jobs to which older workers are best suited (usually low-level, low-skilled and generally low-paid jobs) also limit the employment opportunities available to older workers (Metcalf & Thompson, 1990). Perhaps more fundamentally, the concentration of older workers in particular jobs may reflect, at least in part, increasing difficulties in coping with job demands, resulting from the changes in performance capacity associated with the ageing process. For example, the sensory performance of older people, as indexed by absolute and difference sensory thresholds, is inferior to that of younger persons (Verrillo & Verrillo 1985). Ageing is also associated with declines both in levels of physical activity and in the capability for strenuous physical exertion (Stones & Kozma, 1985). There is also a marked tendency for the speed of behaviour to decrease with age (Salthouse, 1985). In industrialised countries the age structures of jobs within particular industries, and more generally the age structures of occupations, may thus be to some extent determined by task requirements which pose problems for older workers (Murrell & Griew, 1958; Welford, 1958). Older workers might be expected, for instance, to experience difficulties with jobs imposing relatively heavy perceptual demands, such as dial reading, the perception of small detail, and working to very fine tolerances. In a series of studies conducted in the light engineering industry in England during the 1950s, Murrell and his co-workers found that there were disproportionately fewer older workers performing jobs in which such demands were present (Griew & Tucker, 1958; Murrell & Tucker, 1960; Murrell, Griew & Tucker, 1957). Heavy physical work, at least in some jobs, may create greater difficulties for older workers than for younger ones and, as age increases, so do transfers to lighter work (Belbin, 1955; Powell, 1973; Richardson, 1953). Belbin (1953) showed that older workers tended not to be found in jobs involving time stress, where the tempo of work was maintained either by machine pacing or by time pressure resulting from a piece-rate pacing system; the decline in numbers began for men at around the age of 35, and for women even earlier, and became greater in older age groups. Barrett et al. (1977) also reported that older individuals tended to leave jobs placing a premium on speeded sensorimotor performance. More recent findings relating to the age structure of jobs in French industry, which essentially confirm those just described, are reviewed by Teiger (1989).

The age structure approach has been extended from jobs in particular industries to occupational categories in a series of studies by Smith (1969, 1973, 1974, 1975) using United Kingdom census data. Smith developed various methods for computing the age structure of occupations, and evaluated two hypotheses concerning the determinants of an occupation's age structure, one (hypothesis H) emphasising historical factors, and the other (hypothesis A) emphasising work difficulties. Smith compared the 1966 age structures predicted by the two hypotheses from the 1961 census data with the actual age structures derived from the 1966 census data and found that for just over 70% of the 188 occupations surveyed hypothesis A had superior predictive power. Although, as Makeham (1980, p. 22) has stated, 'age sensitive jobs cannot be identified simply by comparing occupational age structures', it nevertheless appears likely that different jobs make different demands on the skills and abilities of older workers, and that the nature of these demands is reflected in the age structures of certain occupations.

AGE DISCRIMINATION IN EMPLOYMENT

In this section we examine stereotypes of the older worker, together with various employment practices which may reflect the 'age discrimination' that older workers are often held to experience (see e.g. Palmore & Manton, 1973; Sheppard, 1970; Slater, 1972). It has frequently been suggested that the employment problems of older workers, especially older men, are largely attributable to age-related stereotypes held by employers and other employees (e.g., Stagner, 1971, 1985). Employers certainly seem to prefer to hire younger men, where possible, since younger employees are seen as more recently trained, more physically capable, and less expensive than are older ones (Pampel & Williamson, 1985). Stereotypes of older employees emphasise their inferior trainability, greater resistance to change, poorer potential for self development, and, perhaps most importantly, lower productivity (see Arvey, 1979, Cleveland & Landy, 1981; Rhodes, 1983; Stagner, 1985; Tuckman & Lorge, 1952) although older workers are regarded as more stable than younger workers (Rosen & Jerdee, 1976a). Rosen & Jerdee (1976b) used an in-basket simulation exercise to investigate business students' perceptions of decisions allegedly made by older and younger managers. In addition to being perceived as more resistant to change, older managers were viewed as significantly less promotable, less suitable for taking financial decisions involving risk, and less motivated to keep up to date. Some studies find that older workers receive lower ratings for interpersonal skills (e.g., Cleveland & Landy, 1981) while others report no age differences (Rosen & Jerdee, 1976a). In Rosen & Jerdee's (1976a) study, in which a group of realtors and business school students were surveyed, it was found that older workers were regarded as less fitted than were younger workers for highly demanding and challenging positions. They were also seen as being relatively inflexible and resistant to change, and as likely to perform less well in tasks requiring high levels of creativity, producitivity, and motivation.

Haefner (1977a) reported that sex, age (25 or 55) and level of competence (highly competent or barely competent, being defined in terms of education, recommendations, and aptitude scores) significantly influenced hypothetical hiring decisions for semi-skilled jobs made by a sample of 286 Illinois employers, although race was a non-significant factor. The employers indicated that they would prefer to hire highly competent males rather than highly competent females and highly competent younger workers than highly competent older ones. In a subsequent survey of employee attitudes in Illinois, Haefner (1977b) found that men preferred to work with younger rather than with older individuals, as did younger employees, while women and older workers expressed no age preference. In a study in which interviews concerning the employment and utilisation of older workers were conducted with senior personnel managers in 20 British companies, Metcalf & Thompson (1990) reported that older workers were regarded as unsuitable for jobs making heavy physical demands, for jobs involving time pressure, and for jobs requiring information technology skills.

Older workers report themselves or their peers as frequently encountering age discrimination when attempting to find a job (Kasschau, 1976, 1977; McAuley, 1977; Slater, 1972) and age-related hiring limits appear to be a major impediment to older workers seeking employment or re-employment (Jolly, Creigh, & Mingay, 1980; Slater, 1973). Jolly, Creigh, & Mingay (1980) surveyed some 16000 job vacancies in the United Kingdom, using national records from the Manpower Services Commission, and found that age-related hiring limits operated in over a quarter of cases, although there was considerable variation across occupations, the highest frequencies being found in the distributive trades and manufacturing industries. Of vacancies where age limits applied, 45% had an upper age limit of 30, rising to 65% with an upper age limit of 40. Jolly, Creigh, & Mingay also analysed the percentage of jobs open to individuals of different ages seeking professional employment, and found that 47% remained open to 45-year-old applicants, 24% to 50-year-olds, and only 2% to 60-year-olds. Metcalf & Thompson (1990) found that there was considerable variation in the use of age-related hiring limits in job advertisements both between and within the companies they investigated. Age limits were most likely to be employed in advertisements for management level jobs. In addition to explicit age limits in job advertisements, implicit age limits also appeared to influence recruitment for a wide range of jobs in different industries, particularly for jobs requiring a period of training. Companies attempted to ensure that they would receive a reasonable return on their investment in training and in consequence were reluctant to hire workers over the age of 50, even though it was acknowledged that older workers were less likely than were younger workers to leave the company once they had been trained. But older workers were thought to be less trainable, particularly with respect to information technology skills. In addition to the 'payback' from training, eligibility criteria for participation in occupational schemes may also adversely affect the recruitment of older workers (Metcalf & Thompson, 1990).

Some possible psychological factors underlying age-related hiring limits emerge from an ingenious study conducted by Craft *et al.* (1979). These investigators asked 304 master's level business administration students, the majority of whom had some supervisory experience in industry, to complete an 'employee assessment exercise', ostensibly to determine how quickly they were able to assess an employee on the basis of a list of six personal characteristics, including age. The students were divided into four groups, each of whom were presented with the same list of personal characteristics, with only the age varying, from 35–50 to 60–70. They were first asked to describe briefly their impression of the employee, drawing from a set of 28 adjectives, mostly concerned with job capability, performance, and potential activity level. Relatively few differences were found across groups, suggesting that age did not appear to be a critical variable affecting the perception of work-related characteristics. However, when the students were asked about their willingness to employ the different groups of workers, they were much less willing to hire the 60- and 70-year-olds than the 35- and, to a lesser extent, the 50-year-olds, largely on the grounds that the older workers were too old, and had only a short work life ahead of them. Thus although the four age groups were assessed as being essentially equally capable, the older groups were less likely to obtain employment.

Since the interview remains one of the most widely used selection instruments, a number of studies have attempted to examine how age stereotypes affect the judgements made by raters in simulated interview and decision-making settings. Many such studies have employed college students as raters, which may reduce their external validity, although differences between student and professional raters appear to be minimal (Bernstein, Hakel & Harlan, 1975). The results are mixed, some studies finding that older employees with similar qualifications to younger employees are less likely to be favourably evaluated (Avolio & Barrett, 1987; Britton & Thomas, 1973; Walsh & Connor, 1980) while others report that evaluations are unaffected by age (Connor *et al.* 1978; Locke-Connor & Walsh, 1980). Lee & Clemons (1985) found that employment decisions were more likely to favour older workers when no choice had to be made between a younger and an older worker, and when specific and detailed information relating to the older worker was supplied.

The results of surveys and opinion polls conducted in the United States indicate that between 60 and 90% of employers agree that age discrimination occurs (see, e.g., Stagner, 1985). Besides influencing hiring policies, age discrimination may also affect the earnings of older workers. For example, Quinn (1979) found that even when differences in education, vocational training, years of job experience, and health had been taken into account, older workers still had lower earnings than younger workers. Similarly, Wanner & McDonald (1983), in a 10-year longitudinal study of earnings trends in a cohort of full-time male workers aged 45–54 in 1966, when the study began, observed a slight decline in the real earnings of this group, compared to a 12.4% gain for the labour force as a whole, over the same period. This decline, which resulted from smaller and less frequent pay increases than those awarded to younger workers, occurred after productivity indicators, such as health, time on the job, occupational training, as well as other factors known to affect earnings levels, had been controlled for. It was concluded that the lower earnings of older workers were attributable to a combination of the older worker's perceived vulnerability in the labour market, and the stereotype of the older worker as being less productive. As Wanner & McDonald (1983) pointed out, however, various groups of older workers, such as those with well-defined career structures, or those in highly unionized employment sectors, are less likely to have experienced the earnings decline found in their study.

Although unemployment rates for workers aged 55 and over are generally lower than for workers in the age group 25–54 in most industrialised countries (Sorrentino, 1981), the duration of male unemployment rises with age and the long-term unemployed are more likely to be aged 55 and over, although there were marked increases in the proportion of long-term unemployed men aged 25 and under during the recessions of the mid-1970s and early 1980s. Age also appears to be an increasingly important criterion in the selection of employees for redundancy (Jolly, Creigh, & Mingay, 1980), and this tendency has been encouraged by the provisions of many early retirement schemes (Casey, 1984). Using the data from a 10% national survey of the unemployed in the United Kingdom, Daniel (1974) found that workers aged 55 and over were three times more likely to have been made redundant than were workers below the age of 25, and that the average duration of unemployment was 12 times greater for the older group. Similarly, in a survey of the long-term unemployed for the United Kingdom Manpower Services Commission, Colledge & Bartholemew (1980) found that redundancy was the reason most frequently given by workers aged 55 and over for leaving their previous jobs, and Axelbank (1972) noted that in the United States the over-45 age group constituted 76% of the long-term unemployed. In a study of over 2000 American workers who had lost their jobs due to plant closures or relocations Love & Torrence (1989) found that the median duration of unemployment for workers aged 55 and over was 27 weeks, while that for workers aged 45 and under was 13 weeks; moreover, those in the former group who were successful in obtaining re-employment earned on average about 16.5% less than did younger workers, even after other non-age characteristics had been accounted for. However, this earnings differential between older and younger workers was not apparent in workers who obtained re-employment on a full-time basis, suggesting that it was attributable to the lower earnings of those workers who secured part-time re-employment. Whether such workers would have preferred to obtain full-time jobs is unclear.

Older workers who become unemployed are much less likely to obtain new employment than are younger workers (Rones, 1983) and if they do find a job, they are likely to experience a sharp decline both in occupational status and in earnings (Parnes, Gagen & King, 1981). Unemployed older workers may 'downgrade' their skill levels in an attempt to secure re-employment (Daniel, 1974; Parnes & King, 1977), and are more likely to seek part-time rather than full-time employment and to spend less time looking for work (Rones, 1983). Some older workers, discouraged by their inability to find a job, may leave the labour force altogether, seeking early retirement as a 'refuge' from the rigours of the labour market (Bould, 1980; Walker, 1985). The unemployment of older workers can thus be masked by early retirement, and the extent to which retirement among some groups of older workers can be regarded as voluntary is difficult to determine (Laczko et al., 1988). Further, as Sheppard & Rix (1977, p. 6) observed, many people choose retirement 'not because they want literally to retire, but more because of their strong reluctance to stay in the same dissatisfying job. The difficulties the older workers may have in finding more satisfying kinds of employment may mean that early retirement is the only alternative.'

In 1967 the US Congress passed the Age Discrimination in Employment Act (ADEA), which was intended to prohibit the discrimination on grounds of chronological age alone with respect to hiring, firing, promotion, pay, or other aspects of employment (see Snyder & Barrett, 1988). The ADEA was originally intended to cover workers only between the ages of 40 and 65, the standard retirement age. In consequence the ADEA did not encourage employment beyond the age of 65, and patterns of retirement were little affected (Morrison, 1979). But in 1978 the ADEA was amended to include workers up to 70 years of age, and in a further amendment in 1984 mandatory retirement at any age for federal government employees was prohibited. The ADEA now covers all workers over the age of 40, although there are various exemptions (see Snyder & Barrett, 1988, for further details). Snyder & Barrett (1988) also provide a comprehensive discussion of the two main ways in which a plaintiff may establish a prima-facie case (disparate treatment or disparate impact) and of the four legitimate defences available to an employer (bona fide occupational qualifications, reasonable factors other than age, bona fide seniority systems/employee benefit plans, or good cause). Since the ADEA became law many workers have been successful in recovering lost pay, in gaining damages, and in winning reinstatement privileges and other benefits. There has also been a marked increase in the number of employment-related age discrimination complaints filed with state and federal government agencies, rising from 5000 in 1979 to over 19000 in 1982 (Faley, Kleiman, & Lengnick-Hall, 1984). However, in a survey of 272 ADEA cases concerning such personnel decisions as workforce reductions, termination, mandatory retirement, selection, promotion and demotion, constructive discharge, and benefits,

Snyder & Barrett (1988) found that employers won the great majority of cases in every category except that of mandatory retirement, where only 50% of 36 cases were decided in favour of the employer. Over all categories the employer won 65% of cases. Snyder & Barrett (1988) highlighted the assessment and appraisal of job performance as the critical issue in the majority of the ADEA cases they surveyed, and emphasised the potential contribution of psychological research to the development of valid job performance criteria for older workers (see also Kleiman & Durham, 1981).

AGE AND JOB PERFORMANCE

Laboratory studies of task performance have demonstrated age-related sensory deficits across a wide range of psychological functions, involving peripheral sensory and motor mechanisms, memory and information processing (Welford, 1985). Older people tend to be particularly disadvantaged when tasks are complex or demanding, as in multi-source monitoring (Thackray & Touchstone, 1981), dual-task performance (McDowd & Craik, 1988), and reaction-time tasks with incompatible stimulus-response mapping (Welford, 1977). There are two broad explanations for the sensitivity of complex tasks to age-related decrements. One possibility is that older people have a lower 'mental speed', and execute elementary information processes more slowly (Birren, Woods, & Williams, 1980). If so, the speed advantage of young people will be compounded on more complex tasks, which presumably require a greater number of elementary processes. Alternatively, increasing age may selectively impair specific components of complex task performance, such as central computational processing (Cerella, 1985), working memory (Charness, 1985), or attentional capacity (Ponds, Brouwer & van Wolffelaar, 1988).

From laboratory studies of ageing and task performance it would therefore be expected that older individuals would perform less well in situations requiring the utilisation of complex 'real world' skills. In some situations this appears to be the case. For example, older people tend to be slower at learning computer skills, such as word processing (Elias et al., 1987) and the use of spreadsheets (Gist, Rosen, & Schwoerer, 1988). However, not all skills show such differential effects of ageing (Salthouse, 1988). Salthouse suggests that age differences in skilled performance may operate at two different levels: the molecular level of the elementary component processes of skill, and the molar level of overall performance. There is ample evidence that when tested on the components of complex skills in isolation, older people generally perform worse than do younger people (Kausler, 1982; Salthouse & Somberg, 1982; Welford, 1985). Given the sizeable negative relationship between age and performance on what are held to be measures of basic cognitive processes (Salthouse, Kausler, & Saults, 1988), it would be reasonable to assume that older people would be less efficient at acquiring complex skills, since the presumed components of such skills are impaired by the ageing process. But it is possible that the relationship of the molecular components of a skill to the molar skill itself undergoes some alteration with age (Salthouse, 1988). If older and younger adults exhibit similar levels of molar skill proficiency, as they can do, this may result from compensation, wherby some component processes of the molar skill decline with age while others improve. Salthouse (1988) argues that the *compensation hypothesis* implies that adults of different ages should have different regression weights in multiple regression equations predicting molar performance from measures of molecular processes. The compensation hypothesis can be compared with the *compilation hypothesis*, which suggests that as a skill is acquired its components, like computer subroutines, become 'compiled' into an efficient operational form and are, in consequence, much less dependent upon the efficiency of molecular component processes. As a complex skill is acquired, therefore, the correlations between measures of component processes and overall proficiency should progressively approach zero for both young and old adults. The available evidence, from studies of the performance of older and younger adults at bridge (Charness, 1979, 1983), chess (Charness, 1981), and typing (Salthouse, 1984) has been interpreted as supporting the compensation hypothesis rather than the compilation hypothesis (Salthouse, 1988).

The extent of likely age differences in job performance should not be overstated, for several reasons. First, not all laboratory tasks show strong or consistent age differences. For instance, the accuracy of sustained attention is surprisingly resistant to age effects (Davies & Parasuraman, 1982; Giambra & Quilter, 1988). Second, age differences in performance can often be eliminated entirely by allowing older individuals to undergo more extensive practice, although it is unlikely that practice can compensate for all age differences (Charness, 1985). Third, age differences are considerably reduced if the task is a familiar one (Murrell & Griew, 1965), even for complex skills such as chess and bridge playing (Charness, 1985). Another aspect of task familiarity is that age differences in skill retention appear to be small (Salthouse, 1988). In other words, in occupational settings older workers may take longer to train (Belbin, 1958), but once trained, may perform at comparable levels to younger workers. Fourth, in the typical work environment, older people may be able to compensate for any cognitive deficits in order to maintain an acceptable level of performance; in many jobs this could be achieved most simply by spending a higher proportion of the available time on work activities. Older workers may compensate for declining cognitive abilities through greater job involvement (Rabinowitz & Hall, 1977) and greater organisational commitment (Arnold & Feldman, 1982). More subtly, older individuals may modify the way in which they process information to compensate for losses of cognitive efficiency. For instance, Salthouse (1984) suggests that older typists may maintain their level of performance, in spite of deteriorations in some of the elementary components of typing, by previewing more extensively the characters to be typed.

Methodological Difficulties

The assessment of age effects upon performance in occupational settings can encounter some quite considerable methodological difficulties (Griew, 1959; Smith, 1981; Welford, 1958). Some factors will tend to inflate the apparent efficiency of older workers, others will bias performance measures against the elderly, and yet other factors will simply decrease the reliability and comparability of performance measures across age groups. For example, the use of psychometrically unreliable performance indices will attenuate any age differences operating (see Cronbach, 1984). A variety of biases collectively described as selective attrition may arise from selection processes. On the one hand, less productive workers are likely to be transferred to other work, sacked, or persuaded to take early retirement (Welford, 1958; Welford & Speakman, 1950). If productivity decreases with age, then those more productive older workers remaining on the job will be unrepresentative of their age cohort, and any comparison of the productivity of different age groups will tend to favour older workers. Conversely, older workers with relatively good production records may be promoted to supervisory positions, leaving less productive older workers behind, so that any age group comparison will tend to favour younger workers. Furthermore, the most efficient younger workers may leave for jobs elsewhere, especially in industries where there is a high demand for labour. Selection biases may operate even for newly hired workers, because older individuals tend to perform more poorly on psychometric personnel aptitude tests (Avolio & Waldman, 1987). In general, therefore, age comparisons of job performance are most likely to be useful when turnover and internal transfer rates are low (Davies & Sparrow, 1985).

Even if methodological problems can be surmounted, and relatively bias-free age differences are observed, they may be difficult to interpret. In some occupational contexts, it may suffice simply to demonstrate the presence or absence of age differences. Frequently, however, the explanation of age differences will also be important, if, for example, counter-measures are to be devised to improve the performance of the older worker. Negative, non-artifactual relationships between age and performance cannot necessarily be attributed to age-related impairment of cognitive functioning. For example, physical fitness is positively associated with psychomotor speed, but negatively correlated with age (Spirduso, 1980). Thus age–performance correlations may be mediated in part by the declining physical fitness of the older worker. Associations between age and performance may also result from cohort effects, such as age differences in educational level (Avolio & Waldman, 1987). Moreover, when attempts are made to control for educational level across age groups, the sample of older people is likely to be less representative of its population than is the sample of younger people. Thus in studies which match older and younger people with respect to educational level, age differences tend to be smaller than in studies which do not (see, e.g. Green, 1969). Indeed, several studies concerned with ageing and cognitive performance have shown that educational level is a much better predictor of performance in memory and problem-solving situations than is age, and in some such studies which have statistically controlled for the effects of educational level, age effects have been found to be negligible or non-existent (Charness, 1985). Conversely, there are other factors which will favour the older worker. For example, older workers may benefit from having had more practice on the job than younger workers. Job tenure or seniority is typically highly correlated with age (Gordon, Cofer, & McCullough, 1986; Sparrow & Davies, 1988).

Age and Job Performance: Empirical Reviews

Job performance is typically assessed either by objective productivity or output measures, or by ratings, typically made by supervisors. We consider first summary reviews and meta-analyses of the relationship between age and these two types of performance measure. We then describe in more detail findings from studies of productivity and rating measures of performance.

The most comprehensive review of age and job performance is that of Rhodes (1983). She summarised the relationship between age and performance in a total of 34 samples, from a variety of occupations, and employing a variety of performance indices. Overall, the results were highly variable, comprising eight positive relationships between age and performance, nine negative relationships, eight inverted-U relationships, and nine studies showing no linear or curvilinear relationship. While age is related to performance more often than would be expected on a chance basis, there must be other moderating variables operating which influence the nature and direction of the age–performance association. These might include experience, training, type of work, and type of performance measure.

Two meta-analyses (McEvoy & Cascio, 1989; Waldman & Avolio, 1987) provide only limited insights into the nature of these moderating variables, and both meta-analyses have the following limitations. First, only a relatively small number of studies yield sufficient information to be included in a meta-analysis. Second, only linear age–performance relationships were analysed, although Rhodes's review suggests that inverted-U relationships are relatively common. Third, the only moderating variables investigated were type of performance measure (productivity or rating), and occupational type (professional or non-professional.) A summary of the two meta-analyses is given in Table 7.

Table 7 shows marked discrepancies between the results of the two meta-analyses. The Waldman & Avolio (1987) meta-analysis suggests that there is a small but appreciable positive relationship between age and productivity measures of job performance. The positive correlation was of similar magnitude in both professional ($r = 0.27$, $N = 1764$) and non-professional ($r = 0.26$, $N = 981$) groups. Supervisor ratings fail to reflect this trend, and may therefore be influenced by rater bias. Differing results for productivity and rating measures of job performance have also been obtained within individual studies. For instance, Motowidlo (1982) obtained both supervisory ratings and an objective measure, total dollar sales, for a sample of 128 salesmen working for industrial cleaning products companies. Age was found to be positively and significantly correlated with the objective measure, albeit modestly ($r = 0.23$, $p < 0.05$), but was unrelated to supervisory ratings. In contrast to Waldman & Avolio (1987), the meta-analysis conducted by McEvoy & Cascio (1989) indicated that age was essentially unrelated to job performance, irrespective of the type of performance measure and the type of occupation. Rating data are difficult to compare across the two meta-analyses, because McEvoy & Cascio (1989) included only three studies involving peer ratings, and so were unable to analyse these studies as a separate category.

Age and Job Performance: Production Records

The use of data derived from output or production records is probably the most satisfactory way of assessing relationships between age and job performance, provided that the methodological difficulties outlined earlier can be minimised or avoided. For skilled and semi-skilled manual and technical jobs, an inverted-U relationship between age and job performance is relatively common, with

Table 7—Mean correlations (r) between age and productivity and rating measures of performance reported in two meta-analyses

	Productivity measures		Rating measures					
			Supervisor		Peer		Non-supervisor[a]	
Study	N	r	N	r	N	r	N	r
Waldman & Avolio (1987)	2 745	0.27	3 660	−0.14	3622	0.10	—	—
McEvoy & Cascio (1989)	13 184	0.07	18 781	0.03	—	—	3227	−0.09

[a]Ratings by peers, subordinates, self, and outsiders.

performance peaking in the late thirties or early forties (Davies & Sparrow, 1985: Rhodes, 1983). Usually, the performance decline in older workers is fairly gradual, so that the productivity of workers in their fifties exceeds that of workers in their teens or twenties (Davies & Sparrow, 1985). For example, Clay (1956) investigated age differences in productivity at two British printing works, for 35 machine compositors, 100 hand compositors, and 14 proof-readers. Turnover rates were negligible and just over a third of the sample were aged 50 and over. Production records were obtained for three 13-week periods spread over three years. Clay found that peak performance occurred in the forties, and that the productivity of workers in their fifties declined by between 2% and 16% from the peak level, depending upon the particular works and the type of job performed. King (1956) also found that performance peaked in the late thirties or early forties in a sample of women knitwear workers. Because turnover rates were relatively high, King compared the performance of 'stayers' (those who remained) and 'leavers' (those who left). Since no evidence of selective attrition was observed, it was concluded that the performance decrements occurring in the forties and fifties were associated with losses of sensorimotor skill.

The US Department of Labor (1957; see also Greenberg, 1960) conducted a large-scale study of output records in a range of industries. Data from 15 companies in the men's footwear industry showed that performance peaked in the mid-thirties, and then steadily but gradually declined, reaching a level of 17% below peak performance in employees aged 65 and over. Similar results were obtained from 11 companies manufacturing household furniture, the decline from peak performance levels reaching 17% by age 64. Data for federal mail sorters indicated that performance peaked in the mid-twenties, although differences among age groups were small. More recently, Sparrow & Davies (1988) conducted a large-scale study of the job performance of 1308 service engineers, mostly aged between 26 and 55, employed by a multinational office equipment company. Turnover and internal transfer rates were low, and educational levels were similar across age cohorts. In addition to age, Sparrow & Davies (1988) also examined the effects of tenure, recency of training, and job complexity, indexed by the size of the machine to be serviced, and the range of functions of which it was capable. Two output measures were collected: quality of performance, assessed as the rate of machine performance between services, compared to the national average for machines of its type, and speed of performance, assessed by the time taken to service a machine. Surprisingly, although job complexity significantly affected both performance measures, in neither case did it interact significantly with age. Age and the quality of performance were curvilinearly related, with performance peaking in the mid-thirties and early forties. A somewhat complex interaction between age and training was also observed. The curvilinear relationship was most pronounced in engineers who had not been trained for five years or more, but was not found in engineers who had received no further training beyond induction. Speed of performance was affected more strongly by training and tenure than by age, although the youngest group were significantly faster than the other age groups. But for both performance measures, each main effect or interaction involving age accounted for less than 1% of the variance, whereas job complexity accounted for 23% of the variance in the speed of performance measure.

The curvilinear relationship between age and job performance is not confined to technical jobs. For example, a study of salespeople working in two large department stores showed that performance tended to improve with both age and experience, peaking in the early fifties (Kelleher & Quirk, 1973). Studies of publication output in research scientists have also consistently obtained a curvilinear relationship between age and productivity, although the average age at which performance peaks varies with the research domain (Cole, 1979; Simonton, 1988). In some disciplines, such as theoretical physics, the peak level of performance occurs relatively early, in the thirties or even the late twenties, and output declines quite sharply thereafter, falling to a level of about 25% of the maximum. In others, such as medicine, there is a more gradual rise to a later peak, in the late forties or early fifties, with a subsequent minimal decline in output. In yet other disciplines, such as psychology, output reaches a maximum in the early forties and then exhibits an appreciable, though moderate, decline (Horner, Rushton & Vernon, 1986). In contrast, a number of other studies have failed to find a curvilinear relationship between age and productivity. For instance, Heron & Chown (1960) and Salvendy (1972) obtained no effects of age on performance for workers in manufacturing jobs. Similarly, Gordon & Fitzgibbon (1982) observed no relationship between either age or seniority and performance in a sample of sewing-machine operators, following a change of job in a garment manufacturing plant. Eisenberg (1980), however, found a negative relationship between age and the piece-rate earnings of sewing-machine operators. He attributed this finding to the speeded nature of the work. In the same manufacturing plant, age was positively related to productivity for examiners and material handlers, whose jobs were more dependent on skill. Gordon, Cofer & McCullough (1986) examined trainability, rather than job performance, in a sample of 106 textile workers. Trainability was assessed by the time taken to train a worker to a performance criterion in a variety of jobs such as carving, weaving, and spinning, relative to standard training times. It was found that neither age nor seniority independently predicted trainability. In summary, the effects of occupation in moderating the age–productivity relationship are rather inconsistent, although there are indications that age effects may vary with the type of work performed.

Other studies suggest that positive correlations between age and job performance, as reported for example in the Waldman & Avolio (1986) meta-analysis, may sometimes be an artifact of individual differences in job experience. Schwab & Heneman (1977) found that both age and length of service correlated significantly and positively with productivity in a sample of 124 semi-skilled assemblers. However, when length of service was controlled for, no age differences in productivity emerged, although length of service predicted productivity independently of age. In this study, therefore, experience was a stronger predictor of job performance than was age. Very similar results were obtained by Giniger, Dispenzieri, & Eisenberg (1983) in a sample of 667 garment workers, both for jobs requiring speed and for those requiring skill. Kutscher & Walker (1960) also found that in a sample of 6000 office workers, age differences in performance disappeared when experience was controlled for.

Age and Job Performance: Performance Ratings

An alternative method for assessing job performance is through performance ratings, typically made by supervisors, although ratings are less satisfactory than objective measures. There tends to be unreliability across raters and across time, and ratings are notoriously susceptible to bias on the part of the rater (Cattell & Kline, 1977). Lifson (1953) showed that even experienced raters may disagree on rating the speed of simple factory-type jobs, although inter-rater agreement can be improved by training (Pursell, Dossett & Latham, 1980). Raters may be influenced by conscious or unconscious stereotypes of a ratee's characteristics, such as educational level, sex, or age. As mentioned earlier, several studies suggest that a negative stereotype of the older worker is common in industry. Since the stereotype includes beliefs about the productivity of older workers, it may affect ratings of job performance. But despite the possibility of negative stereotyping, several studies have obtained no significant differences in the job performance ratings given to older and younger workers. Examples include studies of women clerical workers (Arvey & Muscio, 1973), of skilled, unskilled and clerical workers in a large manufacturing company (Smith, 1953), and of Californian industrial workers (Crook & Heinstein, 1958), although Crook and Heinstein did find that men aged 60 and over received lower ratings than did younger men if they were treated as a separate group.

However, some studies of technical and managerial jobs have found age differences in performance ratings. Several studies of the performance of American air-traffic controllers reported that age was negatively related to pre-training aptitude test scores, to objective performance measures, and to performance ratings made by supervisors, crew chiefs, and peers (Cobb, Nelson, & Mathews, 1973; Trites & Cobb, 1962), although in some of these studies average inter-rater reliabilities were rather low, and the age of the rater sometimes affected the rating given. Dalton & Thompson (1971) and Price,

Thompson, & Dalton (1975) obtained ratings from managers concerning the job performance of a large sample of engineers employed by six large technological companies, three of which were in the aerospace industry. Rated performance rose with age initially, peaked in the mid-thirties, and declined thereafter, reaching a level of 75% of peak performance in the 55–65 age group. Price, Thompson, & Dalton (1975) emphasised the high degree of overlap between performance levels in different age groups. Ratings appeared to be biased by the difficulty of the job being performed, and by the differential assignment of younger engineers to more difficult jobs. Age tended to become a progressively stronger predictor of performance over the period of the study, from 1960 to 1968. Dalton & Thompson (1971) attributed this effect to an acceleration during the 1960s of the obsolescence of technical expertise.

Horner (1980) found age differences in the ratings given to 600 middle-level managers working in a large American public utility company. Managers over the age of 50 tended to be rated as less receptive to new ideas and as slower to acquire new skills, but were regarded as more technically competent. In a study of 79 line managers, designed to investigate the effects of age, length of service, and decision-making experience upon managerial decision making, Taylor (1975) employed a personnel decision simulation exercise from which several measures of decision-making performance could be derived. Age was associated with more accurate ratings of the value of items of information, but also with longer decision times, partly because older managers used more information in arriving at their decisions. Older managers were actually more flexible than younger ones. Age did not affect the accuracy of the final decision, but rather the strategy employed. Another simulation study, designed to assess the performance of plant managers in a large electrical company, found a negative relationship between age and rated performance (Meyer, 1970). Thus, as with productivity studies, studies of age differences in rated performance have yielded somewhat inconsistent results.

In summary, the relatively small number of studies that have investigated the relationship between age and job performance are somewhat limited in scope. Most of them are cross-sectional, thus potentially confounding age with cohort effects, involve low sample sizes and variables that may moderate the effects of age on job performance are rarely systematically examined. Only a small part of the occupational spectrum, mainly blue-collar and technical jobs, has received detailed scrutiny, and even here results are not always in agreement. Moreover, investigators have not always focused on the same level of occupational activity, some reporting data from large occupational groupings, such as office workers, other from workers in particular jobs, such as service engineers in the office equipment industry, and others still from people performing highly specific tasks, such as personnel decision-making exercises. Additionally, little control appears to have been exercised over task allocation within particular jobs, a potential source of confounding, particularly, perhaps, in performance rating studies. Overall, however, no clear evidence emerges of a universal age deficit in job performance, although older workers may be disadvantaged in particular kinds of jobs, for example those requiring physical strength, speeded reactions, or close attention to visual detail. The range of performance variation is considerable, probably more so among older than among younger workers, and in many cases older workers seem able to perform at least as well as, and sometimes better than, their younger colleagues.

AGE AND ACCIDENTS

Some researchers define an accident as a 'near miss' resulting from inappropriate behaviour which does not necessarily lead to injury (Hale & Hale, 1971). Others treat an accident in terms of injury (e.g. Dillingham, 1981a) or in terms of disability due to injury. Injuries requiring medical attention are regarded as more reliable indicators of accident behaviour than are self-reports of 'near miss' incidents. Hence, researchers often use data from compensation files (Mitchell, 1988) or surgery records (Boyle, 1980).

Studies examining accident frequency in relation to age have reported mixed results. The most common finding is that accident rates are lower in older workers compared with workers aged 24 and below (Kossoris, 1940; Chelius, 1979; Root, 1981) and equal to accident rates in prime-age workers of 25 to 44 years (Dillingham, 1981b). Others (Griew, 1958; Barrett et al., 1977) found that accident frequency increased with age. Yet others report inverted-U (Kossoris, 1948), U-shaped (Kossoris, 1940; Padley, 1947; Vernon, 1945) or non-significant age–accident relationships. These findings can perhaps be explained in terms of the different samples used, and the operations of a range of moderating variables, for example, exposure to risk, type of occupation, and type of industry. Different occupations have different ambient risk levels associated with them (Hale & Hale, 1972) and accident rates have been shown to vary by occupation (Dillingham, 1979). In a study conducted in New York, blue-collar work was found to account for 70% of all injuries and was estimated to be eight times riskier than white-collar employment, and more than twice as risky as market work (Dillingham, 1981a). Accident rates are generally lower in women than men because women tend to be employed in less hazardous occupations (Dillingham, 1981b). Older employees are also liable to incur more accidents in jobs that are normally occupied by younger workers (Griew, 1958). This effect occurred for those aged between 45 and 52 years rather than those over 52 years of age. Griew (1958) suggested that workers above the age of 52 were more likely to leave hazardous jobs since they were unable to meet the demands (see also Powell, 1973).

In their review of research on industrial accidents, Hale & Hale (1972) suggested that length of service and accident rates were negatively related, at least during the initial period in the job. Accident rates tend to be relatively high early in an individual's working life and, with increasing experience, fall to a plateau reached after varying periods of time depending upon job complexity (Van Zelst, 1954). However, as Hale & Hale (1972) pointed out, there are several different sorts of experience which could be relevant to accidents, and in a number of studies the relationship between experience, age, and accident rates has not been straightforward. For example, Van Zelst (1954) also found that older groups had lower accident rates than did younger groups, both when experience was equated across age groups and when the older group was less experienced. Additionally, Surry (1977) concluded that a lack of experience could be an important determinant of accidents among new recruits to a job, but after the initial period of employment, experience became a less important factor. Moreover, Boyle (1980) showed that, even when controls are applied for such factors as risk levels, age, and job experience, individual differences in accident rates remain. Hansen (1989) employed path analysis to test a causal model of accident rates in chemical industry workers. An accident risk measure, which was assessed as the safety responsibility inherent in each employee's job using the company's job rating scheme, was employed. The general finding that younger workers have higher accident rates than older and more experienced workers was not obtained. Age and experience were highly positively related. Age and job experience were also positively related to accident risk, which suggests that older, more experienced workers were more likely to assigned to jobs involving greater risk. Additionally, Hansen (1989) employed an accident consistency measure. Accident consistency was a composite measure of accident behaviour indexed by the number of accidents incurred by one individual plus the number of years the same individual incurred at least one accident and was intended to indicate how regularly or consistently a worker experienced accidents. For example, an employee who experiences one accident for each of four years is considered to be more at risk than another employee who has a clean record but experiences four accidents during one, seemingly atypical, year. There was a slight tendency for older workers to have higher accident consistency levels than younger workers, but when accident risk was controlled for this relationship became negligible. Furthermore, when both age and job experience were partialled out, the accident risk–accident consistency path coefficient increased. Moreover, when accident risk was removed, path coefficients revealed negligible relations between age and accident risk, and age and accident rates. Hansen pointed out that his findings only gave the impression that greater job experience was associated with more accidents. He concluded that it was a greater exposure to risk that caused accidents and that accident risk modified any relationship between age, job experience, and accident rates.

Older workers may experience lower incidences of injury but, on average, they lose more time per injury than do younger workers (Kossoris, 1940; Root, 1981; Dillingham, 1981b). Older employees may require a longer period to recover, and the severity of injury may increase with age. Kossoris (1948) observed a U-shaped relationship in the duration of disability across age groups. Stevens (1929) reported a non-significant relationship between injury from burns and scalds, and age. But for injuries, such as cuts and lacerations, bruises, fractures, sprains and hernias, the length of disability increased significantly with age. An injury is also more likely to result in permanent disability for older employees (Kossoris, 1940). However, U-shaped (Dillingham, 1981b) and inverted-U shaped (Root, 1981) relationships between disability resulting from accidental injury and age have also been reported. Fatalities caused by accidents also rise with increasing age (Root, 1981; Dillingham, 1981b). Kossoris (1940) showed that this relationship held for both males and females: the over-60 worker death-rate was three times, while the over-50 worker death-rate was twice, that of a 21–25 year-old worker.

Mitchell (1988) examined the effects of different occupations and different industries upon temporary and permanent disabilities and fatalities due to industrial accidents. She found that occupational differences within industries explained more of the variance in disability and fatality rates than did differences among industries. Further, a regression analysis suggested that risk of temporary injuries was greatest for employees under age 25 whereas, for permanent disabilities, the risk for older workers tended to be slightly higher than for the working population as a whole. Fatalities were also higher for workers aged 65 and older than for the sample average. The age–job risk profiles for all types of injury were virtually flat for employees between the ages of 25 and 64. Although they were small in magnitude, the age coefficients remained significant with the inclusion of industry, occupation and compensation variables in the regression analysis. Given the evidence, it is unclear whether older groups are more of an accident risk than are younger groups. While injuries occur less frequently in older workers, they tend to be more severe. But injury rates vary with occupational affiliation and other factors, such as job experience, the key factor being accident risk. Whether older workers tend to be randomly or systematically assigned to higher risk tasks is likely to depend upon the type of industry or occupation being studied.

AGE, JOB SATISFACTION, AND MOTIVATION

Age Differences in Job Satisfaction: Empirical Studies

An important area of occupational ageing research concerns the attitudes and emotional reactions associated with work. Traditionally, such research has tended to fall into two areas—job satisfaction and motivation or job involvement. Job satisfaction has normally been defined in terms of affective responses (cf. Locke, 1976), whereas job motivation concerns evaluations of the importance of work and of the expected outcomes of work behaviour (for example Vroom, 1964). More recent research has tended to emphasise the interrelatedness of satisfaction and motivation. At a theoretical level, both emotion and motivation may be explained by process of cognitive appraisal, of the personal significance of events (Lazarus, 1984) or of causal relationships (Weiner, 1985). In occupational contexts, contemporary theories of job satisfaction propose that satisfaction is causally determined by job perceptions and appraisals (James & Tetrick, 1986). Empirically, too, job satisfaction and motivation tend to be positively correlated (Hanlon, 1986). In this section we discuss empirical research on age differences in job satisfaction and in job involvement and motivation, before discussing theoretical accounts of such age differences. We also consider two more specialised aspects of age differences in job satisfaction and motivation: their nature in professional and managerial groups, and the role of sex differences.

Several recent reviews of the relationship between age and job satisfaction (Davies & Sparrow, 1985; Bourne, 1982; Rhodes, 1983) conclude that job satisfaction is higher in older workers. Rhodes (1983) reviews 28 bivariate analyses, of which 22 show a positive relationship between age and satisfaction. The positive relationship is found both within national surveys of representative households (Weaver, 1980), and within specific plants or organisations (Stagner, 1985). Age and satisfaction are positively correlated in manual, clerical, and managerial occupations. (Rhodes, 1983; Opinion Research Corporation, 1980). Some reviews suggest that the age–satisfaction correlation appears to be more reliably positive within men than within women (Rhodes, 1983), particularly in national survey data (Stagner, 1985) while other studies, which have analysed longitudinal data from either US national (Bokemeier & Lacy, 1986) or regional samples (Hodson, 1989), indicate minimal differences in job satisfaction between men and women. Although, on average, women hold jobs that are inferior in many respects to those held by men, job satisfaction levels appear to be broadly comparable in women and men. Hodson (1989) suggests that women may use different reference groups, for example, homemakers, when evaluating their jobs and, as a result of sex differences in socialization, women may also be less likely to verbalize dissatisfaction with their work than are men.

There are inconsistencies in the data, though, particularly regarding the likelihood of curvilinear relationships between age and job satisfaction. A widely cited review of relatively early research (Herzberg *et al.*, 1957) found that in 17 studies out of 23, a U-shaped relationship between age and satisfaction was obtained: job satisfaction was lowest in the middle years. However, as Rhodes (1983) points out, very few studies published after the Herzberg *et al.* (1957) review have found this kind of relationship. Recent studies of supervisors (Singh & Singh, 1980) and of nurses (Kacmar & Ferris, 1989) do report a U-shaped relationship, although, in the latter study, the curvilinear relationship only emerged when job tenure was controlled. Satisfaction was lowest between 30 and 40. Kacmar & Ferris (1989) also cite four studies which have failed to find any significant relationship between age and job satisfaction. Recent studies of white-collar water workers (Hollingworth, Matthews & Hartnett, 1988) and of managers in a food service organisation (Meyer *et al.*, 1989) report a similar absence of correlation between age and job satisfaction. It has also been suggested that the relationship between age and satisfaction is monotonic up to age 60, after which there is a sharp dip preceding retirement (Saleh & Otis, 1964). Testing this hypothesis is difficult because of a dearth of studies with adequate numbers of over-sixties, but the pre-retirement dip does not seem to be a reliable finding (Davies & Sparrow, 1985).

A further possibility is that the association between age and satisfaction is monotonic and positive, but non-linear. Kalleberg & Loscocco (1983), using data from the 1972–73 Quality of Employment Survey, assessed job satisfaction in 1390 subjects, analysed as 10 age bands, with adequate numbers in the extreme bands of 16–20 ($N = 82$) and 61+ ($N = 84$). They found a relatively strong third-order polynomial component in the regression of age on satisfaction. Job satisfaction increased until the late thirties, but was then fairly constant until the late fifties, after which there was a further increase with satisfaction with age: the 61+ group showed the highest satisfaction level of all.

Other research has tested age differences in different aspects or facets of job satisfaction. In reviewing this research, Rhodes (1983) claims that the most sensitive facet of job satisfaction in relation to age is satisfaction with work itself, which has been found to increase linearly with age in a variety of different samples. Relationships between age and other aspects of job satisfaction, those related to pay, promotion, supervision, and co-workers, are not very reliable. However, there is a tendency for pay satisfaction to increase with age. Combining bivariate and multivariate studies, Rhodes (1983) cites four studies showing a positive relationship between age and pay satisfaction, four studies showing no relationship, and one study showing a negative relationship. Spector (1985) and Kacmar & Ferris (1989) also report generally positive relationships. Job satisfaction and perceived work alternatives tend to be negatively related (Hulin, Roznowski, & Hachiya, 1978) though less strongly in older workers than in younger workers (Pond & Geyer, 1987). Rhodes (1983) suggests that types of satisfaction other than intrinsic work satisfaction are determined mainly by the organisation and type of work involved, and so are insensitive to age.

Two types of explanation have been proposed for age differences in job satisfaction. On the one hand, there may be genuine changes with age in job attitudes and expectations. Theories of this kind are discussed in a subsequent section. Alternatively, the observed age differences may be an artefact of cohort differences, or of the confounding of age with other variables such as job tenure. Glenn, Taylor, & Weaver (1977) suggest that, compared to younger people, older people may be higher in job satisfaction because older cohorts tend to have less formal education, and hence lower expectations of the satisfactions to be gained from work. Two cross-sectional studies (Glenn, Taylor & Weaver, 1977; O'Brien & Dowling, 1981) have attempted to test for cohort effects on job satisfaction by testing age effects in conjunction with education and other variables associated with cohort membership. Taken together, these studies suggest that age differences in job satisfaction result from both cohort and ageing effects. Quasi-longitudinal studies of United States national survey data on job satisfaction, discussed by Davies & Sparrow (1985) and Kalleberg & Loscocco (1983), confirm that cohort effects are at most a partial explanation for age differences in job satisfaction. Kalleberg & Loscocco (1983, p. 89) 'observed a direct impact of chronological age on job satisfaction, which . . . reflects processes of adaptation to the work role'.

The most serious confounding factor in studies of age and job satisfaction is job tenure. However, age appears to remain positively correlated with job satisfaction even when tenure is controlled (Gibson & Klein, 1970; O'Brien & Dowling, 1981, Siassi, Crocetti, & Spiro, 1975); at least in male rather than female samples (Hunt & Saul, 1975). Kacmar & Ferris (1989) point out that tenure in the job and tenure working for current supervisor should be controlled as well as length of service, the usual measure of tenure. When all three measures were controlled, they found a linear, positive relationship between age and intrinsic job satisfaction, and U-shaped relationships between age and extrinsic sources of job satisfaction such as promotion and quality of supervision. Kalleberg & Loscocco (1983) report no significant interaction between age and occupational variables in the determination of job satisfaction. Rhodes (1983) reviews other multivariate studies, which suggest that the age–job satisfaction relationship is not mediated by other possible confounding factors such as family income, marital status, and occupational prestige.

Age Differences in Commitment to Work and Motivation: Empirical Studies

Hanlon (1986) describes a number of different aspects of commitment to work and motivation, which can be distinguished by factor analysis. For example,

Lawler & Hall (1970) and Cummings & Bigelow (1976) identified three empirically distinct dimensions—job involvement, intrinsic motivation, and higher order need satisfaction. Job involvement refers to the extent to which the job situation is central to the person and his or her identity. Intrinsic motivation concerns the person's need to perform well in the job, and higher order need satisfaction is described as the degree to which needs are actually satisfied (Lawler & Hall, 1970). Kanungo (1982) and Mistra et al. (1985) state that job involvement, the importance of the person's present job, should be distinguished from work involvement, the importance of work in general. A further construct is organisational commitment, the importance of the organisation for which the person currently works. Hanlon (1986) describes various additional constructs for gauging commitment to work, such as attitudes towards specific aspects of work. There appears to be a general but modest tendency for different measures of commitment to work to intercorrelate positively (Hanlon, 1986).

The two major reviews of age and commitment to work have been published by Rhodes (1983) and Hanlon (1986). Rhodes (1983) reviews 21 studies of job involvement, using measures such as the Lodahl & Kejner (1965) Job Involvement Scale. Of these studies, 18 show a positive relationship between age and job involvement, although correlations tend to be small in magnitude, typically +0.2 to +0.3 (Hanlon, 1986). The effect appears to generalise across a variety of cultures (Reitz & Jewell, 1979). Cherrington, Condie & England (1979) found that age was positively related to measures of the moral importance of work, pride in craftsmanship, and the importance of work over friends, in a sample of 3053 workers in 53 companies. Studies of this kind suggest that older workers show greater adherence to 'traditional' work values than younger workers. Job involvement also appears to be more stable over time in older workers than in younger workers (Lorence & Mortimer, 1985). In contrast to studies of job performance and of job satisfaction, there are few indications of curvilinear relationships between age and job involvement.

Three out of four multivariate studies reviewed by Rhodes (1983) confirmed the validity of the age–job involvement relationship, although other factors such as the characteristics of the job or organisation appear to be stronger determinants of job involvement than age. Rabinowitz, Hall, & Goodale (1977) found that age and job involvement were unrelated when job tenure and four other variables were controlled. In contrast, Wagner et al. (1987) found that age was a stronger predictor of job involvement than organisational tenure. Wagner et al. (1987) point out that there is generally no linear relationship between job involvement and tenure, although there may be a curvilinear relationship. Hanlon (1986) found that age was positively related to job involvement, and negatively related to work role involvement, in bivariate analyses. The relationship with work effort was an inverted-U, with peak effort in the 35–44 age group. However, only the effect of age on work involvement remained significant when other variables were controlled. In particular, Hanlon's (1986) data suggest that effects of age on job involvement may be mediated by job satisfaction, which tends to be positively correlated with both age and job involvement. Other studies of work involvement (Warr, Cook & Wall, 1979) and of work role centrality (Mannheim, 1975) show no association with age.

Rhodes (1983) also found that 17 out of 21 studies showed that organisational commitment increased with age. A recent study of 535 salespeople (Ornstein, Cron, & Slocum, 1989) found no significant age differences in organisational commitment, although job involvement increased with age. In contrast, Stevens, Beyer & Trice (1978) found that age was positively related to organisational commitment even when job involvement and other variables such as tenure were controlled. In general, multivariate studies of organisational commitment provide mixed results: Rhodes (1983) suggests that the age dependence of organisational commitment may depend on occupation. Age also seems to be positively related to internal or intrinsic job motivation (Rhodes, 1983) and to pride in job accomplishment (Susman, 1973).

Theories of Age Differences in Job Satisfaction and Job Involvement

Thus far, we have seen that there is quite strong evidence for modest increases in job satisfaction and job involvement with age. If changes in job involvement are mediated by changes in job satisfaction, as Hanlon (1986) suggests, then the two kinds of age difference may share a common causal mechanism. Next, we discuss possible explanations for real changes with age in these constructs. First, age may affect expectancies and beliefs about work, which in turn affect emotion and motivation. Second, work attitudes may be subject to well-defined developmental or cyclical stages. Third, age differences in job satisfaction may result from changes in general life stress, rather than from changes in work-specific attitudes.

The dominant theory of work motivation has been expectancy theory (Vroom, 1964; Atkinson & Feather, 1986). Motivation is determined by the perceived value of extrinsic and intrinsic rewards of the job, and by beliefs about the efficacy of work effort in attaining those rewards. There has been rather little research on age differences in expectancy motivation, although two studies (Arvey & Neel, 1976: Heneman, 1973) have found that older workers are less likely to believe that increased effort will produce desired benefits. However, age differences in locus of control, reflecting the person's belief in their ability to control their environment, appear to be negligible (Kausler, 1982).

It has been suggested that job satisfaction increases with age because older workers actually do have jobs which are more rewarding or more congruent with their needs or values (Quinn, Staines, & McCullough, 1974; Wright & Hamilton, 1978). Not surprisingly, salaries and other extrinsic rewards do rise with age (Kalleberg & Loscocco, 1983), at least for white-collar workers (Wright & Hamilton, 1978). Byrne & Reinhart (1989) found a correlation of 0.33 between age and occupational level within a sample of 432 professional and managerial employees of the Australian Public Service. However, as described above, satisfaction with pay is relatively weakly related to age. People may well expect salaries to rise with age, so that pay satisfaction reflects pay relative to the salary deemed appropriate for the person's age and occupation. Intrinsic rewards, such as the degree of challenge of the job and the fulfilment obtained from work, also increase with age (Kalleberg & Loscocco, 1983), as would be expected from the increases with age in intrinsic motivation discussed previously. This effect may reflect the greater time available to older workers in which to find personally satisfying work (Wright & Hamilton, 1978).

Age may also affect the value put on job rewards. Campbell, Converse, & Rodgers (1976) suggest that job satisfaction rises with age because people's expectancies become 'ground down' by experience, so that older workers are more easily satisfied than younger ones. However, two studies of the 1972–73 Quality of Employment Survey (Wright & Hamilton, 1978; Kalleberg & Loscocco, 1983) fail to support this view. Kalleberg & Loscocco (1983) conclude that intrinsic and financial rewards are valued more strongly by younger workers, although Wright & Hamilton's (1978) analysis suggests that different aspects of intrinsic and financial reward may be differentially related to age. Older workers appear to value job security and some extrinsic rewards such as fringe benefits more strongly than do younger workers (Holley, Field, & Holley, 1978; Porter, 1963). Loscocco (1980) showed that the effects of intrinsic rewards on job satisfaction decreased with increasing age, but the relationship between financial rewards and job satisfaction were similar across age groups. Multivariate analyses presented by Kalleberg & Loscocco (1983) suggest that age differences in rewards and values account for only part of the association between age and job satisfaction. Rhodes (1983) reviews other research on age differences in needs, much of which is inconclusive. Thus, the expectancy theory of age changes in attitudes to work receives some support from studies of job rewards and their value to the person. Job satisfaction rises with age at least in part because the job is perceived as more intrinsically and extrinsically rewarding. Changes in reward value may also be implicated but their exact role is unclear.

This analysis leaves open the question of the relative importance of changes in the appraisal of the job situation, as opposed to changes in the objective nature of the job. One approach to developmental changes in attitudes to work is provided by the concepts of life stages and career stages. Levinson's (1986) life stage model proposes that adult life is characterised by a linear succession of stages, such as early, middle and late adulthood. Each stage is divided into substages associated with specific age ranges. Each substage is associated with specific tasks to be accomplished, many of which are concerned with career development. These tasks will influence the way in which work is perceived, and hence job satisfaction and involvement. For example the mid-life transition (40–45) is associated with a task of questioning the importance of work, so that job satisfaction and involvement are likely to decline. Thus, the life stage model aims simply to interpret differences in job attitudes associated with chronological age. The career stage model (Super, 1984) also proposes a sequence of stages, termed trial, establishment, maintenance and decline, but they are not rigidly linked to specific ages are as life stages. Moreover, people tend to recycle through the stages during major transitions, such as changing jobs. The model predicts that job attitudes should vary with career stage.

Ornstein, Cron, & Slocum (1989) point out that although the ideas of life and career stages have been influential, there have been few direct tests of the models. Their own study looked at the associations between various work-related attitudes and life and career stage. Life stage was operationalised as age bands and career stage was assessed by a questionnaire on career concerns. Although support for both models was mixed, Ornstein, Cron, & Slocum (1989) found that career stage was a stronger predictor of attitudes to the work itself, such as measures of job involvement, organisational commitment, and overall job satisfaction. Life stages were more successful as predictors of attitudes related to career decisions. Further evidence for a link between job satisfaction and career stages was obtained by Shirom & Mazeh (1988) who found a five-year periodicity in the relationship between job satisfaction and seniority in a sample of 900 Israeli teachers, which they attributed to major career transitions such as changing job. Career stage also seems to moderate the relationship between job complexity and job satisfaction (Gould, 1979).

In summary, stage models provide theoretical grounds for supposing that job attitudes and perceptions, and hence job satisfaction and involvement, may vary with the person's adaptation to the work role. Relevant empirical work on stage models is very limited, but these models may be useful in accounting for age differences in work expectancies. Furthermore, to the extent that age/life stage is confounded with career stage, it may be important to distinguish empirically between these two variables.

Another possibility is that age differences in job satisfaction are associated with age differences in life stress generally, rather than with age differences in attitudes to work. To date, there is no research which has tested this hypothesis directly, but some clues to the importance of life stress can be obtained. Stress and job satisfaction appear to be intimately related: low job satisfaction is associated with a variety of stress symptoms (Hollingworth, Matthews & Hartnett, 1988). A recent meta-analysis (Tait, Padgett & Baldwin, 1990) estimates the correlation between job satisfaction and life satisfaction to be 0.44, in a sample of almost 20000. Older people experience fewer major life events than younger people (Folkman *et al.* 1987), so it is possible that increases in job satisfaction with age reflect a general decrease in life stress. Folkman *et al.* (1987) found that older people also report a lower level of daily hassles than younger people, although the older sample in this study were retired. However, age also appears to be negatively related to job stress (Hendrix, Ovalle & Troxler, 1985). Older people also report lower levels of stress associated with specific activities such as driving (Dorn, Matthews, & Glendon, 1990). Levels of the neuroticism personality trait, which is associated with individual differences in sensitivity to stress, decline markedly during adulthood (Eysenck & Eysenck, 1976).

Minor psychiatric symptomatology, as measured by the Minnesota Multiphasic Personality Inventory (MMPI), shows little consistent change with age, though, although different subscales show different regressions with age (Gynther, 1979). The incidence of depressive symptoms actually seems to increase in the elderly, although this may be attributable to an increase in somatic problems (Zemore & Eames, 1979). One study of an occupational sample found that older workers were both higher in job satisfaction, and lower in psychiatric symptoms (Siassi, Crocetti, & Spiro, 1975), but Srole *et al.* (1962) obtained a positive association between age and psychiatric symptoms.

There may also be qualitative as well as quantitative differences in life stress with age. Although older people experience fewer total life events, they are subject to more events involving loss, such as bereavements. Folkman *et al.* (1987) found that older people tend to use more passive, intrapersonal, and emotion-focused coping than younger people. Age differences of this kind may reflect the changing nature of the type of stressor to which older people are subjected (McCrae, 1982). The impact of stressors may also vary with age. For example, being widowed is more strongly associated with mental hospital admission in younger people than in older people (Cochrane, 1988). Thus, future research could usefully investigate whether age differences in job satisfaction are associated with age differences in life stress, coping strategy, or the appraisal of job-related stressors.

AGE AND WITHDRAWAL BEHAVIOUR

Withdrawal behaviour encompasses both absenteeism and turnover (Muchinsky, 1977), but the extent to which these two forms of behaviour are related remains in some doubt (Lyons, 1972; Porter & Steers, 1973). Withdrawal behaviour can be costly both to organizations and to individuals (Mowday, Porter, & Steers, 1982; Steers & Rhodes, 1978; Taylor, 1979), and in consequence numerous empirical studies of withdrawal behaviour have been conducted and various models of the psychological processes and organizational factors held to be involved have been put forward (Brooke, 1986; Brooke &

Price, 1989; Muchinsky, 1977; Nicholson, Brown, & Chadwick-Jones, 1977; Price, 1977).

Indices of absenteeism have included frequency measures, i.e. number of times absent; severity measures, i.e. duration or days absent; attitudinal absences, i.e. frequency of one-day absences; and medical absences, i.e. frequency of absences of three days or longer (Huse & Taylor, 1962). Additional indices were analysed by Chadwick-Jones et al. (1971). These included reasons for absence other than holidays, rest days, or sickness, for example, lateness; worst day of the week ('Blue Monday' or Friday); and time lost for reasons other than leave. The frequency index has been reported to be the most reliable and consistent measure of absence across studies (see Muchinsky, 1977). Since absenteeism indices have varying psychometric properties, different, and sometimes conflicting, results have been obtained.

From the above indices, two absence types emerge: these are unavoidable (sickness, involuntary, sanctioned, or certificated) absence (Nicholson, Brown, & Chadwick-Jones, 1977) and avoidable (casual, voluntary, unsanctioned and uncertificated) absence, which probably accounts for about a third of the total time lost (Hedges, 1977). Blau (1984) points out that it is important that research takes into account the situation for a particular type of absence behaviour, whether it is excused or unexcused for reasons relating to job characteristics, sickness in the family, personal reasons, or general tardiness.

The main measures of absenteeism are absence frequency and the duration of each period of absence. In most studies of avoidable absence, absence frequency falls with increasing age (Garrison & Muchinsky, 1977; Nicholson, Brown, & Chadwick-Jones, 1977; Watson, 1981), though positive (Woska, 1972) and non-significant (Hammer & Landau, 1981) relationships have also been reported. The avoidable absence measure has been viewed as an indicator of work motivation by Nicholson (1977), who explained the lower rates of avoidable absenteeism in men as a reflection of an age-related need for regularity and stability. However, most studies have found that older men incur more unavoidable absence than do younger men, though negative, non-significant, and curvilinear relationships have also been reported (see Nicholson, Brown, & Chadwick-Jones, 1977).

An early study by Schenet (1945) found that, on average, women showed higher frequency of absence (both avoidable and unavoidable) than did men; this might be explained in terms of differences between men and women in the level of domestic responsibility and/or in the centrality of the work role (Isambert-Jamati, 1962). Patterns of unavoidable absence in women, relative to age, are predominantly twofold; either older women incur higher unavoidable absenteeism rates than do younger women (Baumgartel & Sobol, 1959) or age and absenteeism are unrelated (Nicholson & Goodge, 1976; Ilgen & Hollenback, 1977). But, as in the case of men, negative (Ilgen & Hollenback, 1977) and curvilinear (Hedges, 1977) relationships have also been reported. No clear-cut pattern of avoidable absence in women is apparent, and positive, negative, inverted-U, and null relationships between age and avoidable absence in women have been reported in various studies (see Nicholson, Brown, & Chadwick-Jones, 1977).

Attitudinal factors, for example, job satisfaction, job involvement (Nicholson, 1977) and organizational commitment (Mowday, Porter & Steers, 1982), and organizational variables, such as conditions of pay (Farrell & Stamm, 1988) and organizational permissiveness (Nicholson & Johns, 1985), may moderate the relationship between age and absenteeism (Brooke & Price, 1989). Early studies reported a negative relationship between job satisfaction and absenteeism (see Rhodes, 1983), a finding confirmed by later studies (Newman, 1974; Waters & Roach, 1971, 1973). However, no significant relationships were found between absenteeism and satisfaction with pay, promotion, supervision, and co-workers (Waters & Roach, 1973; Newman, 1974). Meta-analyses of studies examining the relation between absenteeism and job satisfaction also obtain weak negative relationships between composite measures of job satisfaction and total time lost, between satisfaction and absence frequency (Hackett & Guion, 1985; Scott & Taylor, 1985), and between satisfaction and other measures of absence (Hackett & Guion, 1985). Farrell & Stamm (1988), in the only meta-analysis of the job satisfaction–absenteeism relationship to include age, found that age, and also sex, were poorer predictors of absence than were attitudinal and organizational factors such as job involvement, task significance, task variety, and pay. Multi-factorial causal models of attendance behaviour have also been advanced (Steers & Rhodes, 1978), extended (Brooke, 1986), tested, and revised (Brooke & Price, 1989). It is argued that age itself is a weak predictor of attendance behaviour but that the effects of other age-related variables account for differences in attendance. However, neither for measures of absence nor for measures of attendance behaviour is there any clear evidence that any relationship with age is strongly influenced by attitudinal factors or organizational variables.

Apart from absenteeism, withdrawal behaviour also takes the form of turnover (Mobley, 1982). As with absenteeism, several measures of turnover have been employed. Again, a distinction is made between avoidable (Dalton, Krackhardt, & Porter, 1981) or voluntary turnover (Mowday & Spencer, 1981), unavoidable or involuntary turnover, and total turnover (Beehr & Gupta, 1978). Involuntary turnover comprises dismissal, mandatory retirement, and sickness (Stumpf & Dawley, 1981); and total turnover includes all forms of voluntary and involuntary turnover. Mobley et al. (1979) observed that what is included as voluntary turnover may differ from study to study, and cited pregnancy as an example. Abelson (1987) found no significant difference between unavoidable leavers and stayers, but job satisfaction, organizational commitment, job tension and withdrawal cognitions, such as those outlined by Mobley, Horner, & Hollingsworth (1978), discriminated unavoidable leavers from avoidable leavers.

Several investigators (e.g., Angle & Perry, 1981) have pointed to the importance of investigating the relationship between absenteeism and turnover. Some studies obtain a positive relationship (Newman, 1974); absenteeism has thus sometimes been seen as a precursor of turnover (Jackson, 1983). On the other hand, absenteeism can be regarded as an alternative to turnover, which explains negative relationships between the two kinds of behaviour (Fitzgibbons & Moch, 1980; Williams *et al.*, 1979). Other studies have reported no relationship between absenteeism and turnover (Mowday & Spencer, 1981; Angle & Perry, 1981; Nicholson, Wall & Lischeron, 1977). Muchinsky's (1977) review indicated that, in general, absenteeism is positively associated with turnover at an 'individual' or one-sample level, but, at a 'group level', for example, samples taken from a number of departments within one company, the relationship between absenteeism and turnover is more tenous. The different relationships between absenteeism and turnover may result from the different measures of absenteeism used in different studies, and/or the confounding of potential mediating variables, such as labour market conditions (Behrend, 1953), economic factors (Muchinsky & Morrow, 1980), unemployment levels (Shikiar & Freudenberg, 1982), job satisfaction (Locke, 1976) and organizational attitudes (Mowday, Porter & Steers, 1982). Several authors have proposed explanatory models of the relationship between absenteeism and turnover (Johns & Nicholson, 1982; Mobley, 1982; Thompson & Terpening, 1983; Wolpin & Burke, 1985), although the usefulness of such models appears to depend on the measures used (Wolpin & Burke, 1985).

There is strong support for an overall negative relationship between age and turnover (Werbel & Bedeian, 1989). This is in spite of the various measures used (Rhodes, 1983). However, it should be noted that age accounts for only 7% of the variance in turnover rates (Mobley *et al.*, 1979) and turnover is likely to be more strongly influenced by other factors, for example, job performance (McEvoy & Cascio, 1987), internal work motivation (Aldag & Brief, 1977), and organizational commitment (Angle & Perry, 1981; Arnold & Feldman, 1982; Bluedorn, 1982; Farrell & Peterson, 1984). Porter & Steers (1973) have used 'intentions to quit' as a predictor of withdrawal. Wolpin & Burke (1985) and Cotton & Tuttle (1986) found that the propensity to leave, or the intention to quit, was the best predictor of voluntary turnover. Social desirability is positively related to age and negatively associated with intentions to quit (Werbel & Bedeian, 1989). It has been consistently found that older workers show less turnover intention (Arnold & Feldman, 1982; Gupta & Beehr, 1979; Jamal, 1981; Martin & Hunt, 1980; Miller, Katerberg & Hulin, 1979). This is likely to be due to the greater commitment seen among older employees (Luthans, Baack, & Taylor, 1987), since commitment is negatively associated with turnover intention (MacFarlane Shore & Martin, 1989). But there may also be occupational variations in the relationship between age and commitment, which may explain differences between studies reporting a positive relationship between age and commitment (Bluedorn, 1982; Michaels & Spector, 1982) and those obtaining a non-significant relationship (Bluedorn, 1982; Steers, 1977; Stevens, Beyer, & Trice, 1978). In addition, the effects of job dissatisfaction are greater on the intention to quit rather than on turnover itself (Mobley, Horner, & Hollingsworth, 1978; Martin & Hunt, 1980) as are the effects of career mobility (Miller, Katerberg & Hulin, 1979) and the opportunity to find attractive career alternatives (Thompson & Terpening, 1983). These variables, and withdrawal cognitions such as 'thinking of quitting', 'intent to search' 'intent to leave' and the 'probability of finding an acceptable job with another employer' (Mobley, Horner, & Hollingworth, 1978) are likely to affect the relationship between age and turnover. Withdrawal behaviour as a whole should be viewed as a process involving psychological, sociological, and economic factors (Muchinsky & Morrow, 1980). Age differences in withdrawal behaviour may be more readily explained in terms of age differences in the predictors of withdrawal behaviour obtained from recent models (e.g. Brooke & Price, 1989).

RETIREMENT

The idea that people should relinquish paid employment in exchange for a pension at a fixed chronological age, regardless of their capacity to continue working effectively, or of their willingness to do so, is relatively recent. The first old-age insurance legislation, which provided for a standard retirement age of 70, was introduced in Germany in 1889. By 1914, Austria, the United Kingdom, France and Sweden had begun to develop national retirement systems, but the United States did not establish such a system until 1935 (for a history of retirement in the United States see Graebner, 1980, and for accounts of the development of retirement in different industrialised countries see Markides & Cooper, 1987). Atchley (1982, p. 263) defines retirement as a 'substantial reduction in employment accompanied by income from a retirement pension or personal savings'. Pampel & Park (1986) suggest that this definition applies well to men in advanced industrial societies, but less well to women in industrialised countries or to men and women in developing countries. They proposed a broader definition of retirement as 'withdrawal from the labour force during old age' Pampel & Park, 1986 (p. 934). Palmore et al., (1985) distinguished between 'subjective retirement', defined in terms of respondents' assessments of their employment status, and 'objective retirement' defined in terms of the number of hours worked and whether or not the respondent was in receipt of public and/or private pension income. Gibson (1987) observes that among Black Americans aged 55 and over a new type of retiree is emerging, 'the unretired-retired', who do not derive their income primarily from retirement sources, who do not regard themselves as retired and for whom there is no clear division between work and non-work. Parnes & Less (1983) point out that the use of different measures of retirement, for example, pension coverage, labour market withdrawal, or subjective report, will affect the number of people who are deemed to be retired and hence any conclusions that may be drawn. Research on retirement has focused both on factors affecting the retirement decision, in individuals who can retire voluntarily, and on those influencing the adjustment to retirement in voluntary and involuntary retirees. Most psychological research has investigated the adjustment to retirement in groups, usually of men, meeting normal retirement criteria, as implied by Atchley's (1982) definition.

The Retirement Decision

The choice of retirement age, where such a choice is available, is likely to be influenced by a variety of factors, including the kinds of retirement options available, the benefits associated with them, estimates of inflation trends, the individual's financial commitments, the level of job satisfaction, perceived health status, labour market conditions, and societal retirement norms. The retirement decision is thus affected not only by personal circumstances but by the wider economic and social context. For both men and women, the principal factors affecting the decision to retire appear to be health status and retirement income (Gratton & Haug, 1983; McGoldrick & Cooper, 1980), although, on the basis of longitudinal data, George, Fillenbaum, & Palmore (1984) reported that for women age was the only significant predictor of the retirement decision. In general, people who report their health to be relatively poor, and who perceive their retirement income to be adequate, are more likely to decide to retire, especially if they are also dissatisfied with their job, or feel that they are unable to cope with its demands (Schmitt & McCune, 1981; Walker & Price, 1976). Workers who retire early frequently hold relatively low-status jobs, requiring minimal levels of skill, offering few opportunities for the exercise of autonomy or responsibility, and often imposing considerable physical demands (Barfield & Morgan, 1972; Jacobson, 1972a,b; Sheppard, 1976). Early retirees tend to be semi-skilled or unskilled workers and to have been employed in industries where contractions in employment opportunities have been particularly severe (Mirkin, 1987). In a British study of early retirement, Laczko et al. (1988) reported that, compared to non-manual workers, manual workers were more likely to have taken early retirement because of redundancy, and to have significantly lower post-retirement incomes. Furthermore, Laczko et al. (1988) suggested that since the 1970s ill-health may have become a less significant determinant of early retirement, as also appears to have been the case in the United States (Sherman, 1985). For workers retiring early on health grounds, who may comprise over 40% of early retirees among white American workers and over 50% among black American workers (Parnes & Nestel, 1981), the loss of income can be quite considerable. In contrast, the self-employed, managers, and professional workers possessing high educational and occupational status, and people in primary sector employment are less likely to retire early and more likely to continue working beyond the normal retirement age (Fillenbaum, 1971; Hayward & Hardy, 1985; Mitchell, Levine, & Pozzebon, 1988; Sheppard, 1976). Perhaps as a consequence of their greater work satisfaction, older workers, particularly those who are near to the normal retirement age, may be more reluctant than younger workers to take early retirement, even when no loss of retirement income is involved. However, positive attitudes towards work do not generally appear to be associated with negative attitudes towards retirement (Atchley, 1971; Fillenbaum, 1971; Goudy, Powers, & Keith, 1975). Compared to single individuals, dual-earner couples tend to delay retirement (Anderson, Clark, & Johnson, 1980) with the decision to retire being collaboratively determined, taking into account not only the personal circumstances of one member of the couple, but also those of the spouse (Henretta & O'Rand, 1983). In general, however, the husband's earnings and pension entitlements exert a stronger effect on the wife's retirement decision than do the wife's on the husband's (Henretta & O'Rand, 1983).

Adjustment to Retirement

Many, if not most, men and women make the transition from work to retirement fairly easily. Only a small minority of retirees, fewer than 20%, report that they miss their former jobs (Atchley, 1976), and the loss of the work role does not appear to exert a significant negative effect on personal happiness (Beck, 1982). Survey data indicate that most retirees are reluctant to return to work, with estimates of those who would choose to do so varying from 2% to 33% (Stagner, 1979). But retirement does not preclude labour market activity. In the United States about one-sixth of retirees were in the labour force in 1980, with males compulsorily retired through mandatory retirement plans having the highest labour force participation rate (Parnes & Less, 1983). Male retirees were also more likely to work if their wives had a job. Palmore et al., (1985) analysed longitudinal data obtained in various American national surveys conducted during the 1970s and found that between 27 and 37% of men, and between 22 and 26% of women, worked after retirement, though these percentages fell with increasing age, and there was considerable variation in the number of hours worked per week. Not surprisingly, income and health, the factors which are most influential in determining the retirement decision, are also the most significant determinants of the adjustment to retirement (Beck, 1982; Chatfield, 1977; George &

Maddox, 1977; Prentis, 1980). The minority of individuals who adjust poorly to retirement, estimated in American studies to be about one-third of retirees, are more likely to experience either financial or health problems, or both (Atchley, 1976). The main reason given by retirees for working, or wishing to work, is to obtain additional income (Palmore *et al.*, 1985), although boredom or dissatisfaction with retirement, age, the type of job held prior to retirement, and health are also related to the likelihood of working (Parnes & Less, 1983; Stagner, 1979).

Retirement and old age are associated with reduced income, particularly among widows. Older women are more likely to be poor than are older men (Duncan & Smith, 1989; Gratton & Haug, 1983), and women constitute the great majority of the 'old elderly'), a group that is especially vulnerable to poverty; in the United States in 1980, for example, 1.5 million of the population aged 85 and over were women, while only 0.68 million were men (Longino, 1988). Nevertheless, in many industrialised countries the risk of poverty among the elderly now appears to be lower than that of the population on average (Holtzmann, 1989). Although there is considerable variation across industrialised countries in the degree of income inequality among the elderly (see, e.g. Hedstrom & Ringen, 1987), in general the economic position of the elderly has improved in industrialised countries in recent years, in some countries considerably (Duncan & Smith, 1989; Holtzmann, 1989; Walker, Hardman, & Hutton, 1989). Duncan & Smith (1989) observed that the average income of elderly family units in the United States increased by 55% (in constant 1982 dollars) between 1967 and 1984. While the proportion of total family income contributed by earnings fell by over a half during this period, the proportion coming from property income (interest, dividends, rent and income from estates and trusts) doubled, and the proportions contributed by Social Security benefits and by occupational and other pensions each increased by over a quarter. Walker, Hardman, & Hutton (1989) also observed an improvement in the relative economic position of pensioners in the United Kingdom between 1970 and 1985, due mainly to an increase in income from state benefits and, to a lesser extent, from occupational pensions. However, in their analysis of age and income in seven industrialised countries (Canada, Germany, Israel, Norway, Sweden, the United Kingdom, and the United States), Hedstrom & Ringen (1987) noted that the disposable income of 65–74 year-olds in the United Kingdom, adjusted for family size, was only 76% of the population average, while for those aged 75 and over it was 67%. The respective averages for the remaining six countries were 94% and 82%, illustrating 'how far behind their compatriots in the other countries are the elderly in Britain' (Hedstrom & Ringen, 1987, pp. 234–235).

Just as the relative economic position of the elderly has been improving over the past few decades, so has their relative health. For example, a comprehensive analysis of data from the US National Health Interview Survey, involving about 120000 people, indicated that substantial advances in relative health among the elderly occurred over the period 1961–81 (Palmore, 1986). However, the effects of retirement on health are often considered to be deleterious, a viewpoint encapsulated in what has been termed 'retirement impact theory' (see Rowland, 1977, for discussion). The theory sees retirement as a stressful life event resulting in physical disorders that may well prove fatal; it thus suggests that retirement is associated with a higher level of mortality than would be expected on the basis of age alone, although since poor health is a frequent determinant of the decision to retire early (Morrison, 1983; Parnes, 1983), health status may be confounded with employment status in studies of the impact of early retirement. Moreover, ideal comparison groups for normal retirees may be difficult to obtain (Haynes, McMichael, & Tyroler, 1979). The evidence relating to retirement impact theory is inconclusive (Minkler, 1981), although it does not appear that retirement *per se* is strongly associated with an increase in mortality rates. Haynes, McMichael, & Tyroler (1979), for example, examined mortality rates over a five-year post-retirement period in a large cohort of American rubber tyre workers who either retired at the normal age of 65, or took early retirement between the ages of 62 and 64. They found that for early retirees, who had experienced poorer health prior to retirement than had normal retirees, mortality rates were significantly higher than expected for the first, fourth, and fifth years following retirement. But for normal retirees mortality rates were lower than expected for the first two years, about equal to the expected rate for the third and fourth years, and again lower than expected in the fifth; the lower rate observed in the fifth year persisted for up to 10 years after retirement (Haynes, McMichael, & Tyroler, 1977). Interestingly, low socio-economic status predicted mortality only for normal retirees; among early retirees higher socio-economic status was associated with a higher mortality rate. Adams & Lefebvre (1981) examined mortality rates over a four-year period following normal retirement in a large cohort of Canadian men and women. Mortality rates were lower than expected among men for the first year following retirement, but were subsequently higher. For women, mortality rates were lower than expected throughout the four-year period. Changes in mortality rates following retirement may be related to the various stages of retirement that have been suggested by some researchers, notably Atchley (1976). Atchley proposed that there are seven such stages, two in the pre-retirement period, the remote stage and the near stage, and five during retirement itself, the honeymoon stage, the disenchantment stage, the reorientation stage, the stability stage and the termination stage. Evidence for the existence of all of these stages is somewhat equivocal (see Ekerdt, Bosse, & Levkoff, 1985), but the honeymoon stage of retirement, for which there is some support, does seem to be associated with lower than expected mortality rates, at least among normal retirees.

Most studies concerned with the effects of retirement on physical health have employed interviews or self-report measures of health status. Results from such studies suggest that around 40% of retirees claim that their health has improved following retirement, and the perception of improved health appears to be due in part to the reduction of occupational stress associated with the loss of the work role (see, e.g. Ekerdt, Bosse, & LoCastro, 1983). Self-report measures of health status are poorly correlated with physicians' evaluations, which tend to be less favourable. But longitudinal studies incorporating both self-report data and physicians' evaluations do not indicate that retirement exerts any substantial effect upon physical health (Streib & Schneider, 1971; Palmore et al., 1979). Similarly, retirement would seem to exert a minimal impact on mental health and well-being, although not surprisingly those in poor health, in adverse financial circumstances, or with few social contacts are likely to report lower levels of well-being (see Kasl, 1980). Involuntary early retirees have also been found to have lower levels of retirement satisfaction (Price, Walker & Kimmel, 1979).

Since the retirement period generally overlaps with the post-parenting period, retirement enables husbands and wives to spend more time with one another, and several cross-sectional studies of marital satisfaction suggest that marital adjustment improves in later life (e.g. Johnson et al., 1986; Rollins & Cannon, 1974). However, the 'upswing' in marital satisfaction during retirement, when it occurs, may have more to do with the termination of active parenting than with the cessation of paid employment. Lee & Shehan (1989) found no indication of any increase in marital satisfaction following retirement, and suggested that this might result from the unequal division of domestic labour, with wives continuing to perform the great majority of household tasks, even though the husband is no longer working. This view receives some support from the finding that wives who continued to work following their husband's retirement, while, presumably, still carrying a heavy domestic workload, had significantly lower levels of marital satisfaction than did wives in couples with any other employment status combination. Keith (1985) found that women who had never married reported greater happiness in retirement than did women who were widowed, separated, or divorced, partly, perhaps, because their economic circumstances were likely to be more favourable as a result of their relatively unbroken work records.

Retirement also increases the opportunity to participate in leisure activities. The amount of activity in general, and the number of leisure activities in particular, have been shown to be associated with the level of retirement satisfaction (Knapp, 1977; Markides & Martin, 1979; O'Brien, 1981). In a survey of five different investigations of leisure activity in retirement conducted by different researchers, with sample sizes ranging form 65 to 2797, Roadburg (1981) found that watching television, reading/writing, and visiting family and friends, were the leisure activities most frequently cited by retired people. As might be expected, from the forties onwards participation in active leisure pursuits, such as exercise and sport, tend to decline with age, while participation in 'core' types of leisure, such as family, social, and home-based activities, remain at a relatively high level (Kelly, Steinkamp & Kelly, 1986). Havighurst (1961, 1977) has argued that many of the 'meanings' of leisure are the same as those of work, for example, opportunities for experiencing variety, for exercising creativity, for utilising skills, for obtaining prestige and status, and for establishing and maintaining contact with friends. Hence, following retirement, leisure can be viewed as a replacement for work, and as serving the same functions as did work in the pre-retirement phase. But the attributes of activity which are associated with job satisfaction (e.g. skill utilization and variety) do not appear to be the attributes of leisure activity which predict life satisfaction in the retired (O'Brien, 1981); the attribute most often found to relate to life satisfaction in retirement is social interaction, (see, e.g. Lemon, Bengtson, & Peterson, 1972; Okun et al., 1984), and, in particular, the perceived quality of social interaction, rather than merely the amount (Gibson, 1986); other attributes of leisure activity seem to be only weakly related to well-being. Further, since studies of leisure and well-being are correlational, the direction of any causal relation between the two characteristics is unclear. Underlying differences in, for example, socio-economic status may be predictors of both. Life satisfaction in retirement appears to be a function of socio-economic status, health, and the quality and frequency of social interactions.

In many industrialised countries, then, there is a tendency for workers to embark on retirement earlier, and to enjoy retired status for longer. Successive cohorts of retirees are healthier and more prosperous, and most people appear to make a good adjustment to the experience of retirement. Since the world's elderly population, those aged 65 years and over, is currently growing at a much faster rate (about 2.8% per year) than is the population as a whole (about 1.7% per year), and since by age 65 the great majority of workers in industrialised countries will have retired, the number of retirees is also increasing rapidly. Elderly dependency ratios are projected to continue to increase both in industrialised and developing countries: in the United States, for example, the elderly dependency ratio is projected to more than double, from 19 to 39% between 1985 and 2060 (Chen, 1987). The public expenditure implications of the increase in the numbers of elderly people have thus become matters of some concern (Holtzmann, 1989). Although the developing countries contain about three-quarters of the world's population, their populations are predominantly youthful and only just over half (53%) of the global elderly population live in such countries. But by 2025 nearly 70% of the world's elderly will come from developing countries, in many of which the extent of public pension provision appears at present to be inadequate.

Rising elderly dependency ratios are not an inevitable consequence of population ageing, since non-demographic variables, such as the number of working women, the age at which young people typically enter the labour force, and the age at which workers typically retire, all affect labour force participation rates, and hence the number of workers available to support both elderly and child dependents (Clark, 1984; Falkingham, 1989). Various policy options have been advanced to alleviate the increasing tax burden on the working population resulting from population ageing, either by reducing the number of dependents, thereby reducing the size of the numerator in the elderly dependency ratio, or by increasing the number of potential 'supporters' (Chen, 1987) thereby increasing the size of the denominator. Raising the standard retirement age, equalizing retirement ages for men and women, and reversing the current trend towards earlier retirement, would achieve both objectives, and some countries are beginning to adopt such policies. The United States, for example, is to phase in an increase in the standard retirement age from 65 to 67 between 2000 and 2027, and in Japan the standard retirement age for women is being raised from 55 to 60 by the year 2000; other reforms of public pension provision are also being considered by many industrialised countries. (see Holtzmann, 1989). But as Falkingham (1989) points out, pensioners constitute a large and growing proportion of the electorate, and, at least in the United States, the elderly are increasingly more likely to use their votes than are younger people (Preston, 1984); middle-aged voters, with their own old age in prospect, may also be more likely to align themselves with the dependency concerns of the elderly population. The tendency for public expenditures to be especially amenable to the political influence of the elderly and their supporters is widespread. In a cross-national study of the determinants of public pension expenditure in 48 industrialised and developing countries at four time points, 1960, 1965, 1970, and 1975, Pampel & Williamson (1985) found that the percentage of people aged 65 and over and the extent of social insurance programme experience were significant predictors of the level of pension expenditures, with the percentage of elderly people having a particularly strong effect both in industrialising and in advanced industrial democracies. It may be difficult, therefore, especially in industrialised countries, for policies directed at reforming public pensions to be sustained, unless they are supported by older voters. The recent trend towards earlier retirement, favoured by many governments, employers, labour unions, and by a significant proportion of older workers, albeit for somewhat different reasons, may also be difficult to reverse. Employers will continue to recruit older workers, and may even attempt to entice the elderly out of retirement, when younger workers are scare; it is worth noting that some British companies, faced with a growing shortage of school-leavers, are now beginning to 'target' older workers and retirees (Metcalf & Thompson, 1990). Yet it seems virtually certain that unless their relative economic position deteriorates markedly, most retired individuals will need to be persuaded to return to the labour force, and that the incentives to do so will need to be extremely attractive. It is possible, as Chen (1987) has suggested, that elderly people could be encouraged to continue working, or to re-enter the labour force, through job redesign, job reassignment, and other improvements to the quality of the working environment. But the test of whether there has been any fundamental shift with respect to age discrimination in employment, and to attitudes to the older worker, will come when younger workers are no longer in short supply.

ACKNOWLEDGEMENTS

The preparation of this chapter was supported in part by a grant from the United Kingdom Economic and Social Research Council. We are grateful to Ian Glendon and Ann Taylor for their comments on earlier versions of the manuscript.

Correspondence address
Dr D. R. Davies, Human Factors Research Unit, Aston Business School, Aston University, Aston Triangle, Birmingham, B4 7ET, UK

REFERENCES

Abelson, M. A. (1987) Examination of avoidable and unavoidable turnover. *Journal of Applied Psychology*, **72**, 382–386.

Adams, O., & Lefebvre, J., (1981). Retirement and mortality. *Aging and Work*, **4**, 115–120.

Aldag R. J. & Brief, A. P. (1977) Age and reactions to task characteristics. *Industrial Gerontology*, **2**, 223–229.

Anderson, K. K., Clark, R. L., & Johnson, T. (1980) Retirement in dual career families. In Clark R. L. (ed.) *Retirement Policy in an Aging Society*. Durham, NC: Duke University Press.

Angle, H. L., & Perry, J. L. (1981) An empirical assessment of organizational effectiveness. *Administrative Science Quarterly*, **26**, 1–13.

Arnold, H. J., & Feldman, D. C. (1982) A multivariate analysis of the determinants of job turnover. *Journal of Applied Psychology*, **67**, 350–360.

Arvey, R. D. (1979) Unfair discrimination in the employment interview: legal and psychological aspects. *Psychological Bulletin*, **86**, 736–765.

Arvey, R. D., & Muscio, S. J. (1973) Test discrimination, job performance and age. *Industrial Gerontology*, **16**, 22–29.

Arvey, R. D., & Neel, C. W. (1976) Motivation and obsolescence in engineers. *Industrial Gerontology*, **3**, 113–120.

Atchley, R. C. (1971) Retirement and work orientation. *Gerontologist*, **11**, 29–32.

Atchley, R. C. (1976) *The Sociology of Retirement*. New York: Schenkman.

Atchley, R. C. (1982) Retirement as a social institution. *Annual Review of Sociology*, **8**, 263–287.

Atkinson, J. W., & Feather, N. T. (1986) *A Theory of Achievement Motivation*. New York: Wiley.

Avolio, B. J., & Barrett, G. V. (1987) Effects of age stereotyping in a simulated interview. *Psychology and Aging*, **2**, 56–63.

Avolio, B. J. & Waldman, D. J. (1987) Personnel aptitude test scores as a function of age, education and job type. *Experimental Aging Research*, **13**, 109–113.

Axelbank, R. G. (1972) The position of the older worker in the American labor force. In G. M. Chatto (ed.), *Employment of the Middle-aged.* Springfield, IL: C. C. Thomas.

Barfield, R. E., & Morgan, J. (1972) *Early Retirement: The Decision and the Experience.* Ann Arbor, Michigan: University of Michigan, Institute for Social Research.

Barrett, G. V., Mihal, W. L., Panek, P. E., Sterns, H. L., & Alexander, R. A. (1977) Information processing skills predictive of accident involvement for younger and older commercial drivers. *Industrial Gerontology,* 4, 173–182.

Baumgartel, H., & Sobol, R. (1959) Background and organizational factors in absenteeism. *Personnel Psychology,* 12, 431–443.

Beck, S. H. (1982) Adjustment to and satisfaction with retirement. *Journal of Gerontology,* 37, 616–624.

Becker, E. H. (1984) Self-employed workers: An update to 1983, *Monthly Labor Review,* July, 14–18.

Beehr, T. A., & Gupta, N. (1978) Note on the structure of employee withdrawal. *Organizational Behaviour and Human Performance,* 21, 23–79.

Behrend, H. (1953) Absence and labour turnover in a changing economic climate. *Occupational Psychology,* 27, 69–79.

Belbin, E. (1958) Methods of training older workers. *Ergonomics,* 1, 207–221.

Belbin, R. M. (1953) Difficulties of older people in industry. *Occupational Psychology,* 27, 177–190.

Belbin, R. M. (1955) Older people and heavy work. *British Journal of Industrial Medicine,* 12, 309–319.

Belbin, R. M., & Clarke, S. (1971) International trends in employment. *Industrial Gerontology,* 9, 18–23.

Bernstein, V., Hakel, M. D., & Harlan, A. (1975) The college-student as interviewer: A threat to generalizability? *Journal of Applied Psychology,* 60, 266–268.

Birren, J. E., Woods, A. M., & Williams, M. V. (1980) Behavioral slowing with age— causes, organization and consequences. In L. W. Poon (ed.), *Aging in the 1980s.* Washington DC: American Psychological Association.

Blau, G. J. (1984) Relationship of extrinsic, intrinsic and demographic predictors to various types of withdrawal behaviours. *Journal of Applied Psychology,* 70, 442–450.

Bluedorn, A. C. (1982) A unified model of turnover from organizations. *Human Relations,* 35, 135–153.

Blumberg, M. (1980) Job switching in autonomous work groups. An exploratory study in a Pennsylvania coal mine. *Academy of Management Journal,* 23, 287–306.

Bokemeier, J. L., & Lacy, W. B. (1986) Job values, rewards, and work conditions as factors in job satisfaction among men and women. *Sociological Quarterly,* 28, 189–204.

Bould, S. (1980) Unemployment as a factor in early retirement decisions. *American Journal of Economics and Sociology,* 11, 123–126.

Bourne, B. (1982) Effects of aging on work satisfaction, performance and motivation. *Aging and Work,* 5(1), 37–47.

Boyle, A. J. (1980) 'Found experiments' in accident research: Report of a study of accident rates and implications for future research. *Journal of Occupational Psychology,* 53, 53–56.

Britton, J. O. & Thomas, J. R. (1973) Age and sex as employment variables: Views of employment service interviewers. *Journal of Employment Counseling,* 10, 180–186.

Brooke, P. P. (1986) Beyond the Steers and Rhodes model of employee attendance. *Academy of Management Review,* 11, 345–361.

Brooke, P. P. & Price, J. L. (1989) The determinants of employee absenteeism: An empirical test of a causal model. *Journal of Occupational Psychology,* 62, 1–19.

Byrne, D. G. & Reinhart, M. I. (1989) Work characteristics, occupational achievement and the Type A behaviour pattern. *Journal of Occupational Psychology*, **62**, 123–134.

Campbell, A., Converse, P. E. & Rodgers, W. L. (1976) *The Quality of American Life: Perceptions, Evaluations and Satisfactions*. New York: Russell Sage Foundation.

Casey, B. (1984) Recent trends in retirement policy and practice in Europe and the USA: An overview of programmes directed to the exclusion of older workers and a suggestion for an alternative strategy. In P. K. Robinson, J. Livingston & J. E. Birren (eds), *Aging and Technological Advances*. New York: Plenum Press.

Cattell, R. B. & Kline, P. (1977) *The Scientific Analysis of Personality and Motivation*. New York: Academic Press.

Cerella, J. (1985) Information processing rates in the elderly. *Psychological Bulletin*, **98**, 67–83.

Chadwick-Jones, J. K., Brown, C. A., Nicholson, N., & Sheppard, C. (1971) Absence measures: Their reliability and stability in an industrial setting. *Personnel Psychology*, **24**, 463–470.

Charness, N. (1979) Components of skill in bridge. *Canadian Journal of Psychology*, **33**(1), 1–16.

Charness, N. (1981) Search in chess: Age and skill differences. *Journal of Experimental Psychology: Human Perception and Performance*, **7**, 467–476.

Charness, N. (1983) Age, skill and bridge bidding: A chronometric analysis. *Journal of Verbal Learning and Verbal behavior*, **22**, 406–416.

Charness N. (1985) Age and problem-solving performance. In N. Charness (ed.), *Aging and Human Performance*. Chichester: Wiley.

Chatfield, W. F. (1977) Economic and sociological factors influencing life satisfaction of the aged. *Journal of Gerontology*, **35**, 593–599.

Chelius, J. R. (1979) Economic and demographic aspects of the occupational injury problem. *Quarterly Review of Economics and Business*, **19**, 65–70.

Chen, Y-P. (1987) Making assets out of tomorrow's elderly. *Gerontologist*, **27**, 410–416.

Cherrington, D. K., Condie, S. K., & England, J. L., (1979) Age and work values. *Academy of Management Journal*, **22**, 617–623.

Chirikos, T. N., & Nestel, G. (1981) Impairment and labor market outcomes: A cross-sectional and longitudinal analysis. In H. S. Parnes (ed.), *Work and Retirement: A Longitudinal Study of Men*. Cambridge, Massachusetts: MIT Press.

Clark, R. L. (1984) Aging and labor force participation. In P. K. Robinson, J. Livingston & J. E. Birren (eds), *Aging and Technological Advances*, New York: Plenum Press.

Clay, H. M. (1956) A study of performance in relation to age at two printing works. *Journal of Gerontology*, **11**, 417–424.

Cleveland, J. N., & Landy, F. J. (1981) The influence of rater and ratee age on two performance judgements. *Personnel Psychology*, **34**, 19–29.

Cobb, B. B., Nelson, P. L., & Mathews, J. J. (1973) *The Relationships of Age and ATC Experience to Job Performance*. FAA Civil Aeromedical Institute.

Cochrane, R. (1988) Marriage, separation and divorce. In S. Fisher & J. Reason (eds), *Handbook of Life Stress, Cognition and Health*. Chichester: Wiley.

Cole, S. (1979) Age and scientific performance. *American Journal of Sociology*, **84**, 958–977.

Colledge, M., & Bartholemew, R. (1980) The long-term unemployed: some new evidence. *Department of Employment Gazette*, **88**, 9–12.

Connor, C. L., Walsh, P. R., Litzelman, D. K., & Alvarez, M. G. (1978) Evaluation of job applicants: The effects of age versus success. *Journal of Gerontology*, **33**, 246–252.

Cotton, J. L., & Tuttle, J. M. (1986) Employee turnover: A meta-analysis and review with implications for research and theory. *Academy of Management Review*, **11**, 55–70.

Craft, J. A., Doctors, S. I., Shkop, Y. M., & Benecki, T. J. (1979) Simulated management perceptions, hiring decisions and age. *Aging and Work*, **2**, 95–102.

Cronbach, L. J. (1984) *Essentials of Psychological Testing*, 4th edn. New York: Harper & Row.

Crook, G. H., & Heinstein, M. (1958) *The Older Worker in Industry*. Institute of Industrial Relations, University of California, Berkeley.

Cummings, T. G., & Bigelow, J. (1976) Satisfaction, job involvement, and intrinsic motivation: An extension of Lawler and Hall's factor analysis. *Journal of Applied Psychology*, **57**, 339–340.

Dalton, D. R., Krackhardt, D. M., & Porter, L. W. (1981) Functional turnover: An empirical assessment. *Journal of Applied Psychology*, **66**, 716–721.

Dalton, G. W. & Thompson, P. H. (1971) Accelerating obsolescence of older engineers. *Harvard Business Review*, **49**, 57–68.

Daniel, W. W. (1974) *National Survey of the Unemployed*. London: Political and Economic Planning.

Davies, D. R., & Parasuraman, R. (1982) *The Psychology of Vigilance*. London: Academic Press.

Davies, D. R. & Sparrow, P. R. (1985) Age and work behaviour. In N. Charness (ed.), *Aging and Human Performance*. Chichester: Wiley.

De Viney, S., & O'Rand, A. M. (1988) Gender–cohort succession and retirement among older men and women, 1951 to 1984. *Sociological Quarterly*, **29**, 525–540.

Dillingham, A. E. (1979) The injury risk structure of occupations and wages. PhD dissertation, Cornell University.

Dillingham, A. E. (1981a) Sex differences in labour market injury risk. *Industrial Relations*, **20**, 117–122.

Dillingham, A. E. (1981b) Age and workplace injuries. *Aging and Work*, **4**, 1–10.

Dorn, L., Matthews, G., & Glendon, A. I. (1990) Personality correlates of driver stress. Paper presented to the European Association of Personality Psychology. Fifth European Conference on Personality, Universita Degli Studi di Roma, Italy, 12/15 June, 1990.

Duncan, G. J., & Smith, K. R. (1989) The rising affluence of the elderly: How far, how fair, and how frail. *Annual Review of Sociology*, **15**, 261–289.

Easterlin, R. A., Crimmins, E. M., & Ohanian, L. (1984) Changes in labor force participation of persons 55 and over since World War II: Their nature and causes. In P. K. Robinson, J. Livingston, & J. E. Birren, (eds), *Aging and Technological Advances*. New York: Plenum Press.

Ekerdt, D. J., Bosse, R., & Levkoff, S. (1985) An empirical test for phases of retirement: findings from the normative aging study. *Journal of Gerontology*, **40**, 95–101.

Ekerdt, D. J., Bosse, R., & LoCastro, J. S. (1983) Claims that retirement improves health. *Journal of Gerontology*, **38**, 231–236.

Eisenberg J. (1980) Relationship between age and effects upon work: A study of older workers in the garment industry. Doctoral dissertation, City University of New York, 1980. Dissertation Abstracts International, 41(4A), 1682 (University Microfilms No. 8023–666).

Elias, P. K., Elias, M. F., Robbins, M. A. & Gage, P. (1987) Acquisition of word-processing skills by younger, middle aged, and older adults. *Psychology and Aging*, **2**, 340–348.

Eysenck, H. J., & Eysenck, S. B. G. (1976) *Manual of the Eysenck Personality Questionnaire (Junior and Adult)*. London: Hodder and Stoughton.

Faley, R. H., Kleiman, L. S., & Lengnick-Hall, M. L. (1984) Age discrimination and personnel psychology: A review and synthesis of the legal literature with implications for future research. *Personnel Psychology*, **37**, 327–350.

Falkingham, J. (1989) Dependency and aging in Britain: A re-examination of the evidence. *Journal of Social Policy*, **18**, 211–233.

Farrell, D., & Peterson, J. C. (1984) Commitment, absenteeism, and turnover of new employees: A longitudinal study. *Human Relations*, **37**, 681–692.

Farrell, D., & Stamm, C. L. (1988) Meta-analysis of correlates of employee absenteeism. *Human Relations*, **41**, 211–227.

Fillenbaum, G. G. (1971) The working retired. *Journal of Gerontology*, **26**, 82–89.

Fitzgibbons, D., & Moch, M. (1980) Employee absenteeism: A multiple analysis with replication. *Organizational Behaviour and Human Performance*, **26**, 349–372.

Folkman, B., Lazarus, R. S., Pimley, S. & Novacek, J. (1987) Age differences in stress and coping processes. *Psychology and Aging*, **2**, 171–184.

Garrison, K. R. & Muchinsky, P. M. (1977) Attitudinal and biographical predictors of incidental absenteeism. *Journal of Vocational Behaviour*, **10**, 221–230.

George, L. K., Fillenbaum, G. G., & Palmore, E. (1984) Sex differences in the antecedents and consequences of retirement. *Journal of Gerontology*, **34**, 86–93.

George, L. K. & Maddox, G. L. (1977) Subjective adaptation to loss of the work role: A longitudinal study. *Journal of Gerontology*, **32**, 456–462.

Giambra, L. M. & Quilter, R. E. (1988) Sustained attention in adulthood: A unique, large-sample, longitudinal and multicohort analysis using the Mackworth clock-test. *Psychology and Aging*, **3**, 75–83.

Gibson, D. M. (1986) Interaction and well-being in old age: Is it quantity or quality that counts? *International Journal of Aging and Human Development*, **24**, 29–40.

Gibson, J. J., & Klein, S. M. (1970) Employee attitudes as function of age and length of service reconceptualization. *Academy of Management Journal*, **13**, 411–425.

Gibson, R. C. (1987) Reconceptualizing retirement for black Americans. *Gerontologist*, **27**, 691–698.

Giniger, S., Dispenzieri, A., & Eisenberg, J. (1983) Age, experience and performance on speed and skill jobs in an applied setting. *Journal of Applied Psychology*, **68**, 469–475.

Gist, M., Rosen, B., & Schwoerer, C. (1988) The influence of training method and trainee age on the acquisition of computer skills. *Personnel Psychology*, **41**, 255–265.

Glenn, N. D., Taylor, P. A., & Weaver, C. N. (1977) Age and job satisfaction among males and females: a multivariate, multisurvey study. *Journal of Applied Psychology*, **62**, 189–193.

Gordon, M. E. & Fitzgibbon, W. J. (1982) Empirical test of the validity of seniority as a factor in staffing decions. *Journal of Applied Psychology*, **67**, 311–319.

Gordon, M. E., Cofer, J. L., & McCullough, P. M. (1986) Relationships among seniority, past performance, inter-job similarity and trainability. *Journal of Applied Psychology*, **71**, 518–521.

Goudy, W. J., Powers, E. A., & Keith, P. (1975) Work and retirement: A test of attitudinal relationships. *Journal of Gerontology*, **30**, 193–198.

Gould, S. (1979) Age, job complexity, satisfaction, and performance. *Journal of Vocational Behavior*, **14**, 209–223.

Graebner, W. (1980) *A History of Retirement: The Meaning and Function of an American Institution, 1885–1978*. New Haven, CT: Yale University Press.

Gratton, B., & Haug, M. R. (1983) Decision and adaptation: Research on female retirement. *Research on Aging*, **5**, 59–76.

Green, R. F. (1969) Age–intelligence relationship between ages sixteen and sixty-four: a rising trend. *Developmental Psychology*, **1**, 618–627.

Greenberg, L. (1960) Productivity of older workers, *Gerontologist*, **1**, 38–41.

Griew, S. (1958) A study of accidents in relation to occupation and age. *Ergonomics*, **2**, 17–23.

Griew, S. (1959) Methodological problems in industrial ageing research. *Occupational Psychology*, **33**, 36–45.

Griew, S., & Tucker, W. A. (1958) The identification of job activities associated with age differences in the engineering industry. *Journal of Applied Psychology*, **42**, 278–282.

Gupta, N. & Beehr, T. A. (1979) Job stress and employee behaviors. *Organizational Behaviour and Human Performance*, **23**, 373–387.

Gynther, M. D. (1979) Aging and personality. In Butcher J. N. (ed.), *New Developments in the Use of the MMPI*. Minneapolis: University of Minnesota Press.

Hackett, R. D. & Guion, R. M. (1985) A re-evaluation of the absenteeism-job satisfaction relationship. *Organizational Behaviour and Human Decision Processes*, **35**, 340–381.

Haefner, J. E. (1977a) Race, age, sex and competence as factors in employer selection of the disadvantaged. *Journal of Applied Psychology*, **62**, 199–202.

Haefner, J. E. (1977b) Sources of discrimination among employees: A survey investigation. *Journal of Applied Psychology*, **62**, 265–270.

Hale, A. R., & Hale, M. (1971) Accidents in perspective. *Occupational Psychology*, **44**, 115–121.

Hale, A. R., & Hale, M. (1972) *A Review of the Industrial Accident Literature*. London: Her Majesty's Stationery Office.

Hammer, T. H. & Landau, J. (1981) Methodological issues in the use of absence data. *Journal of Applied Psychology*, **66**, 574–581.

Hanlon, M. D. (1986) Age and commitment to work—A literature review and multivariate analysis. *Research on Aging*, **8**, 289–316.

Hansen, C. P. (1989) A causal model of the relationship among accidents, biodata, personality, and cognitive factors. *Journal of Applied Psychology*, **74**, 81–90.

Havighurst, R. J. (1961) The nature and values of meaningful free-time activity. In R. W. Kleemeier (ed.) *Aging and Leisure*. New York: Oxford University Press.

Havighurst, R. J. (1977) Life-style and leisure patterns in the later years. In R. A. Kalish (ed.), *The Later Years: Social Applications of Gerontology*. Monterey, California: Brooks Cole.

Haynes, S. G., McMichael, A. J., & Tyroler, H. A. (1977) The relationship of normal, involuntary retirement to early mortality among U.S. rubber workers. *Social Science and Medicine*, **11**, 105–114.

Haynes, S. G., McMichael, A. J., & Tyroler, H. A. (1979) Survival after early and normal retirement. *Journal of Gerontology*, **33**, 269–278.

Hayward, M. D. & Hardy, M. A. (1985) Early retirement processes among older men—Occupational differences. *Research on Aging*, **7**, 491–515.

Hedges, J. N. (1977) Absence from work measuring the hours lost. *Monthly Labor Review*, **100**, 16–23.

Hedstrom, P., & Ringen, S. (1987) Age and income in contemporary society: A research note. *Journal of Social Policy*, **16**, 227–239.

Heneman, H. G. III (1973) Relationship between age and motivation to perform on the job. *Industrial Gerontology*, **16**, 30–36.

Hendrix, W. H., Ovalle, N. K., & Troxler, R. G. (1985) Behavioral and physiological consequences of stress and its antecedent factors. *Journal of Applied Psychology*, **70**, 188–201.

Henretta, J. C., & O'Rand, A. (1983) Joint retirement in the dual worker family. *Social Forces*, **62**, 505–520.

Heron, A., & Chown, S. (1960) Semi-skilled and over forty. *Occupational Psychology*, **34**, 264–274.

Herzberg, F., Mausner, B., Peterson, R. P., & Capwell, D. F. (1957) *Job Attitudes: Review of Research and Opinion*. Pittsburgh: Psychological Service of Pittsburgh.

Hodson, R. (1989) Gender differences in job satisfaction: Why aren't women more dissatisfied? *Sociological Quarterly*, **30**, 385–399.

Holley, W. H., Jr, Field, H. S., & Holley, B. B. (1978) Age and reactions to jobs: An empirical study of paraprofessional workers. *Aging and Work*, **1**, 33–40.

Hollingworth, C., Matthews, G., & Hartnett, O. M. (1988) Job satisfaction and mood: An exploratory study. *Work and Stress*, **2**, 225–232.

Holtzmann, R. (1989) Pension policies in the OECD countries: Background and Trends. In J. Eekelaar & D. Pearl (eds) *An Aging World—Dilemmas and Challenges for Law and Social Policy*. Clarendon Press, Oxford (UK) and Nihon Kajo Publishing Co., Ltd (Japan).

Horner, K. L., Rushton, J. P., & Vernon, P. A. (1986) Relation between aging and research productivity. *Psychology and Aging*, **1**, 319–324.

Horner, P. (1980) Construction and implementation of an alternative performance rating scale and possible age group and managerial level effects on performance ratings. Unpublished MA thesis, Wayne State University.

Hulin, C. L., Roznowski, M., & Hachiya, D. (1985) Alternative opportunities and withdrawal decision. Empirical and theoretical discrepancies and an integration. *Psychological Bulletin*, **97**, 233–250.

Hunt, J. W., & Saul, P. M. (1975) The relationship of age, tenure, and job satisfaction in males and females. *Academy of Management Journal*, **18**, 690–702.

Huse, E. F., & Taylor, E. K. (1962) The reliability of absence measures. *Journal of Applied Psychology*, **46**, 159–160.

Ilgen, D. R., & Hollenback, J. H. (1977) The role of job satisfaction in absence behaviour. *Organizational Behaviour and Human Performance*, **19**, 148–161.

International Labour Office (1962) *Report to the Director General*. Geneva: ILO.

International Labour Office (1962) *Yearbook of Labour Statistics*. Geneva: ILO.

International Labour Office (1970) *Yearbook of Labour Statistics*. Geneva: ILO.

International Labour Office (1988) *Yearbook of Labour Statistics*. Geneva: ILO.

Isambert-Jamati, V. (1962) Absenteeism among women workers in industry. *International Labour Review*, **85**, 248–261.

Jackson, S. E. (1983) Participation in decision making as a strategy for reducing job-related strain. *Journal of Applied Psychology*, **68**, 3–20.

Jacobson, D. (1972a) Willingness to retire in relation to job strain and type of work. *Industrial Gerontology*, 1972, 65–68.

Jacobson, D. (1972b) Fatigue-producing factors in industrial work and preretirement attitudes. *Occupational Psychology*, **46**, 193–199.

Jamal, M. (1981) Shift work related to job attitudes, social participation and withdrawal behaviour: A study of nurses and industrial workers. *Personnel Psychology*, **34**, 552–563.

James, L. R., & Tetrick, L. E. (1986) Confirmatory analytic tests of three causal models relating job perceptions to job satisfaction. *Journal of Applied Psychology*, **71**, 77–82.

Johns, G. (1978) Attitudinal and nonattitudinal predictors of two forms of absence from work. *Organizational Behaviour and Human Performance*, **22**, 431–444.

Johns, G., & Nicholson, N. (1982) The measure of absence: New strategies for theory and research. *Research in Organizational Behaviour*, **4**, 127–172.

Johnson, D. R., White, L. K., Edwards, J. N., & Booth, A. (1986) Dimensions of marital quality: Toward methodological and conceptual refinement. *Journal of Family Issues*, **7**, 31–49.

Jolly, T., Creigh, S., & Mingay, A. (1980) Age as a factor in employment. Research Paper No. 11. London: Dept. of Employment.

Kacmar, K. M., & Ferris, G. R. (1989) Theoretical and methodological considerations in the age-job satisfaction relationship. *Journal of Applied Psychology*, **74**, 201–207.

Kalleberg, A. L., & Loscocco, K. A. (1983) Aging, values, and rewards: Explaining age differences in job satisfaction. *American Sociological Review*, **48**, 78–90.

Kanungo, R. N. (1982) Measurement of job and work involvement. *Journal of Applied Psychology*, **67**, 341–349.

Kasl, S. V. (1980) The impact of retirement. In C. L. Cooper and R. Payne (eds), *Current Concerns in Occupational Stress*. Chichester: Wiley.

Kasschau, P. L. (1976) Perceived age discrimination in a sample of aerospace employees. *The Gerontologist*, **16**, 166–173.

Kasschau, P. L. (1977) Age and race discrimination reported by middle-aged and older persons. *Social Forces*, **55**, 728–742.

Kausler, D. H. (1982) *Experimental Psychology and Human Aging*. New York: Wiley.

Keith, P. M. (1985) Work, retirement, and well-being among unmarried men and women. *Gerontologist*, **25**, 411–416.

Kelleher, C. H., & Quirk, D. A. (1973) Age, functional capacity and work: An annotated bibliography. *Industrial Gerontology*, **19**, 80–98.

Kelly, J. R., Steinkamp, M. W. & Kelly, K. R. (1986). Later life leisure: How they play in Peoria. *The Gerontologist*, **26**, 531–537.

King, H. F. (1956) An attempt to use production data in the study of age and performance. *Journal of Gerontology*, **11**, 410–416.

Kinsella, K. (1988) *Aging in the Third World*. Washington, DC: US Bureau of the Census.

Kingson, E. R. (1981a) The health of very early retirees. *Aging and Work*, **4**, 11–22.

Kingson, E. R. (1981b) Involuntary early retirement. *Journal of the Institute of Socioeconomic Studies*, **7**, 27–39.

Kleiman, L. S., & Durham, R. S. (1981) Performance appraisal, promotion, and the courts: A critical review. *Personnel Psychology*, **34**, 103–121.

Knapp, M. R. J. (1977) The activity theory of aging: An examination in the English context. *The Gerontologist*, **17**, 553–559.

Kossoris, M. D. (1940) Relation of age to industrial injuries. *Monthly Labor Review*, **51**, 789–804.

Kossoris, M. D. (1948) Absenteeism and injury experience of older workers. *Monthly Labor Review*, **67**, 10–19.

Kutscher, R. E., & Walker, J. F. (1960) Comparative job performance of office workers by age. *Monthly Labor Review*, **83**, 39–43.

Laczko, F., Dale, A., Arbers, S. & Gilbert, G. N. (1988) Early retirement in a period of high unemployment. *Journal of Social Policy*, **17**, 313–333.

Lawler, E. E. III, & Hall, D. T. (1970) Relationship of job characteristics to job involvement, satisfaction, and intrinsic motivation. *Journal of Applied Psychology*, **54**, 305–312.

Lazarus, R. S. (1984) On the primacy of cognition. *American Psychologist*, **39**, 124–129.

Lee, J. & Clemons, T. (1985) Factors affecting employment decisions about older workers. *Journal of Applied Psychology*, **70**, 785–788.

Lee, G. R., & Shehan, C. L. (1989) Retirement and marital satisfaction. *Journal of Gerontology*, **44**, 227–230.

Lemon, B. W., Bengtson, V. L., & Peterson, J. A. (1972) Activity types and life satisfaction in a retirement community. *Journal of Gerontology*, **27**, 511–523.

Levinson, D. J. (1986) A conception of adult development. *American Psychologist*, **41**, 3–13.

Lifson, K. A. (1953) Errors in time-study judgments of industrial work pace. *Psychological Monographs*, **67**, Whole No. 355.

Locke, E. A. (1976) The nature and causes of job satisfaction. In M. D. Dunnette (ed.), *Handbook of Industrial and Organisational Psychology*. Chicago: Rand McNally.

Locke-Connor, C., & Walsh, P. R. (1980) Attitudes toward the older job applicant: Just as competent but more likely to fail. *Journal of Gerontology*, **35**, 919–927.

Lodahl, T. M., & Kejner, M. (1965) The definition and measurement of job involvement. *Journal of Applied Psychology*, **49**, 24–33.

Longino, C. F. (1988) A population profile of very old men and women in the United States. *Sociological Quarterly*, **29**, 559–564.

Lorence, J., & Mortimer, J. T. (1985) Job involvement through the life course—A panel study of three age groups. *American Sociological Review*, **50**, 618–638.

Loscocco, K. A. (1980) Age differences in job satisfaction. Unpublished master's paper, Department of Sociology, Indiana University.

Love, D. O., & Torrence, W. D. (1989) The impact of worker age on unemployment and earnings after plant closings. *Journal of Gerontology*, **44**, 190–195.

Luthans, F., Baack, D., & Taylor, L. (1987) Organizational commitment: Analysis of antecedents. *Human Relations*, **40**, 219–236.

Lyons, T. F. (1972) Turnover and absenteeism: a review of the relationships and shared correlates. *Personnel Psychology*, **25**, 271–281.

McAuley, W. J. (1977) Perceived age discrimination in hiring: Demographic and economic correlates. *Industrial Gerontology*, **4**, 21–28.

McCrae, R. R. (1982) Age differences in the use of coping mechanisms. *Journal of Gerontology*, **37**, 454–460.

McDowd, J. M., & Craik, F. I. M. (1988) Effects of aging and task difficulty on divided attention performance. *Journal of Experimental Psychology: Human Perception and Performance*, **14**, 267–280.

McEvoy, G. M., & Cascio, W. F. (1987) 'Do good or poor performers leave?' A meta-analysis of the employee turnover process. *Academy of Management Journal*, **30**, 744–762.

McEvoy, G. M., & Cascio, W. F. (1989) Cumulative evidence of the relationship between employee age and job performance. *Journal of Applied Psychology*, **74**, 11–17.

McFarlane Shore, L., & Martin, H. J. (1989) Job satisfaction and organizational commitment in relation to work performance and turnover intentions. *Human Relations*, **42**, 625–638.

McGoldrick, A., & Cooper, C. L. (1980) Voluntary early retirement – taking the decision. *Employment Gazette*, August, 859–864.

Makeham, P. (1980) Economic aspects of the employment of older workers. Research Paper No. 14. London: Dept. of Employment.

Mannheim, B. (1975) A comparative study of work centrality, job rewards and satisfaction. *Sociology of Work and Occupations*, **2**, 79–102.

Markides, K. S., & Cooper, C. L. (eds) (1987) *Retirement in Industrialised Societies*. Chichester: Wiley.

Markides, K., & Martin, H. W. (1979) A causal method of predicting life satisfaction among the elderly. *Journal of Gerontology*, **34**, 86–93.

Martin, T. N., & Hunt, J. G., (1980) Social influence and intent to leave: A path-analytic process model, *Personnel Psychology*, **33**, 505–528.

Metcalf, H. & Thompson, M. (1990) *Older Workers: Employers' Attitudes and Practices*. Institute of Manpower Studies Report No. 194. University of Sussex.

Metzner, H. & Mann, F. C. (1953) Employee attitudes and absences. *Personnel Psychology*, **6**, 467–485.

Meyer, H. H. (1970) The validity of the in-basket test as a measure of managerial performance. *Personnel Psychology*, **23**, 297–307.

Meyer, J. P., Paunonen, S. V., Gellatly, I. R., Goffin, R. D., & Jackson, D. N. (1989) Organizational commitment and job performance: it's the nature of the commitment that counts. *Journal of Applied Psychology*, **74**, 152–156.

Michaels, C. E., & Spector, P. E. (1982) Causes of employee turnover: A test of the Mobley, Griffith, Hand & Meglino model. *Journal of Applied Psychology*, **67**, 53–59.

Miller, H. E., Katerberg, R. & Hulin, C. L. (1979) Evaluation of the Mobley, Horner and Hollingsworth model of employee turnover. *Journal of Applied Psychology*, **64**, 509–517.

Minkler, M. (1981) Research on the health effects of retirement: An uncertain legacy. *Journal of Health and Social Behavior*, **22**, 117–130.

Mirkin, B. A. (1987) Early retirement as a labor force policy: an international overview. *Monthly Labor Review*, March, 19–33.

Mistra, S., Kanungo, R. N., von Rosensteil, L., & Stuhler, E. A. (1985) The motivational formulation of job and work involvement: A cross-national study. *Human Relations*, **38**, 501–518.

Mitchell, O. S. (1988) The relation of age to workplace injuries. *Monthly Labor Review*, **111**, 8–13.

Mitchell, O. S., Levine, P. B., & Pozzebon, S. (1988) Retirement differences by industry and occupation. *The Gerontologist*, **28**, 545–551.

Mobley, W. H. (1982) Some unmeasured questions in turnover and withdrawal research. *Academy of Management Review*, **7**, 111–116.

Mobley, W. H., Griffith, R. W., Hand, H. H., & Meglino, B. M. (1979) Review and conceptual analysis of the employee turnover process. *Psychological Bulletin*, **86**, 493–522.

Mobley, W. H., Horner, S. O. & Hollingsworth, A. T. (1978) An evaluation of precursors of hospital employee turnover. *Journal of Applied Psychology*, **63**, 408–414.

Morrison, M. H. (1979) International developments in retirement flexibility. *Aging and Work*, **2**, 221–234.

Morrison, M. H. (1983) Health circumstances; a major factor in retirement decisions. *Aging and Work*, **6**, 89–92.

Motowidlo, S. J. (1982) Relationship between self-rated performance and pay satisfaction among sales representatives. *Journal of Applied Psychology*, **67**, 209–213.

Mowday, R. T., Porter, L. W., & Steers, R. M. (1982) *Employee–Organization Linkages: The Psychology of Commitment, Absenteeism and Turnover*. New York: Academic Press.

Mowday, R. T., & Spencer, D. G. (1981) The influence of task and personal characteristics on employee turnover and absenteeism incidents. *Academy of Management Journal*, **24**, 634–642.

Muchinsky, P. M. (1977) Employee absenteeism: A review of the literature. *Journal of Vocational Behaviour*, **10**, 316–340.

Muchinsky, P. M., & Morrow, P. C. (1980) A multidisciplinary model of voluntary employee turnover. *Journal of Vocational Behaviour*, **17**, 263–290.

Murrell, K. F. H. (1959) Major problems of industrial gerontology. *Journal of Gerontology*, **34**, 275–279.

Murrell, K. F. H., & Griew, S. (1958) Age structure in the engineering industry—a study of regional effects. *Occupational Psychology*, **32**, 1–13.

Murrell, K. F. H., & Griew, S. (1965) Age, experience and speed of response. In A. T. Welford & J. E. Birren (eds) *Behavior, Aging and the Nervous System*. Springfield, IL: Charles C. Thomas.

Murrell, K. F. H. & Tucker, W. A. (1960) A pilot job study of age-related causes of difficulty in light engineering. *Ergonomics*, **3**, 74–79.

Murrell, K. F. H., Griew, S., & Tucker, W. A. (1957) Age structure in the engineering industry: a preliminary study. *Occupational Psychology*, **31**, 1–19.

Nelson, T. C. (1980) The age structure of occupations. In P. K. Ragan (ed.), *Work and Retirement: Policy issues*. Los Angeles, University of California: Andrus Gerontology Center.

Newman, J. E. (1974) Predicting absenteeism and turnover: A field comparison of Fishbein's model and traditional job attitude measures. *Journal of Applied Psychology*, **59**, 610–615.

Nicholson, N. (1977) Absence behavior and attendance motivation: A conceptual synthesis. *Journal of Management Studies*, **14**, 231–252.

Nicholson, N., Brown, C. A., & Chadwick-Jones, J. K. (1977) Absence from work and personal characteristics. *Journal of Applies Psychology*, **62**, 319–327.

Nicholson, N., & Goodge, P. M. (1976) The influence of social, organizational and biographical factors on female absence. *Journal of Management Studies*, **13**, 234–254.

Nicholson, N., & Johns, G. (1985) The absence culture and the psychological contract—Who's in control of absenteeism? *Academy of Management Review*, **10**, 397–407.

Nicholson, N., Wall, T., & Lischeron, J. (1977) The predictability of absence and propensity to leave from employees' job satisfaction and attitudes toward influence in decision-making. *Human Relations*, **30**, 499–514.

O'Brien, G. E., & Dowling, P. (1981) Age and job-satisfaction. *Australian Psychologist*, **16**, 49–61.

O'Brien, G. E. (1981) Leisure attributes and retirement satisfaction. *Journal of Applied Psychology*, **66**, 371–384.

Okun, M. A., Stock, W. A., Haring, M. J. & Witter, R. A. (1984) The social activity, subjective well-being relation. *Research on Aging*, **6**, 45–65.

O'Rand, A. M. & Henretta, J. C. (1982) Delayed career entry, industrial pension structure and retirement in a cohort of unmarried women. *American Sociological Review*, **47**, 365–373.

O'Rand, A. M. & Maclean, V. M. (1986) Labour market, pensions rule structure and retirement benefit promise for long-term employees. *Social Forces*, **65**, 224–240.

Opinion Research Corporation (1980) *Strategic Planning for Human Resources: 1981 and Beyond*. Princeton, NJ: Opinion Research Corporation.

Ornstein, S., Cron, W. L., & Slocum, J. W. (1989) Life stage versus career stage—A comparative test of the theories of Levinson and Super. *Journal of Organizational Behavior*, **10**, 117–133.

Padley, R., (1947) Studies on age and wastage in industrial populations: I. Age and incidence. *British Journal of Occupational Medicine*, **1**, 213–237.

Palmore, E. (1986) Trends in the health of the elderly. *Gerontologist*, **26**, 298–302.

Palmore, E. B., Burchett, B. M., Fillenbaum, G. G., George, L. K., & Wallman, L. M. (1985) *Retirement: Causes and Consequences*. New York: Springer.

Palmore, E., Cleveland, W. P., Nowlin, J. B., Ramm, D., & Siegler, I. C. (1979)

Stress and adaptation in later life. *Journal of Gerontology*, **34**, 841–851.

Palmore, E. B., & Manton, K. (1973) Ageism compared to racism and sexism. *Journal of Gerontology*, **28**, 363–369.

Pampel, F. C., & Park, S., (1986) Cross-national patterns and determinants of female retirement. *American Journal of Sociology*, **91**, 932–955.

Pampel, F. C., & Tanaka, K., (1986) Economic development and female labor force participation: A reconsideration. *Social Forces*, **64**, 599–619.

Pampel, F. C., & Weiss, J. A. (1983) Economic development, pension policies, and the labor-force participation of aged males; A cross-national, longitudinal approach. *American Journal of Sociology*, **89**, 350–372.

Pampel, F. C., & Williamson, J. B. W. (1985) Age structure, politics, and cross-national patterns of public pension expenditure. *American Sociological Review*, **50**, 782–799.

Parnes, H. S. (1983) Health, pension policy and retirement. *Aging and Work*, **6**, 93–103.

Parnes, H. S., Gagen, M. G., & King, R. H. (1981) Job loss among long service workers. In H. S. Parnes (ed.), *Work and Retirement: A Longitudinal Study of Men*. Cambridge, MA: MIT Press.

Parnes, H. S., & King, R. (1977) Middle-aged job losers. *Industrial Gerontology*, **4**, 77–95.

Parnes, H. S., & Less, L. (1983) *From Work to Retirement: The Experience of a National Sample of Men*. Columbus, Ohio: Ohio State University Center for Human Resource Research.

Parnes, H. S., & Nestel, G. (1981) The retirement experience. In H. S. Parnes (ed.), *Work and Retirement*. Cambridge, MA: MIT Press.

Pond, S. B., & Geyer, P. D. (1987) Employee age as a moderator of the relation between perceived work alternatives and job satisfaction. *Journal of Applied Psychology*, **72**, 552–557.

Ponds, R. M., Brouwer, W. H., & Van Wolffelaar, P. C. (1988) Age differences in divided attention in a simulated driving task. *Journal of Gerontology*, **43**(6), 151–156.

Porter, L. W. (1963) Job attitudes in management: II. Perceived importance of needs as a function of job level. *Journal of Applied Psychology*, **47**, 141–148.

Porter, L. W., & Steers, R. M. (1973) Organization, work, and personal factors in employee turnover and absenteeism. *Psychological Bulletin*, **80**, 151–176.

Powell, M. (1973) Age and occupational change among coal miners. *Occupational Psychology*, **47**, 37–49.

Prentis, R. S. (1980) White-collar working women's perception of retirement. *Gerontologist*, **80**, 90–95.

Preston, S. H. (1984) Children and the elderly: Divergent patterns for America's dependents. *Demography*, **21**, 435–457.

Price, J. L. (1977) *The Study of Turnover*. Ames: Iowa State University Press.

Price, J. L., Thompson, P. H., & Dalton, G. W. (1975) A longitudinal study of technological obsolescence. *Research Management*, Nov. 1975, 22–28.

Price, K. F., Walker, J. W., & Kimmel, D. C. (1979) Retirement timing and retirement satisfaction. *Aging and Work*, **2**, 235–245.

Pursell, E. D., Dossett, D. L., & Latham, G. P. (1980) Obtaining valid predictors by minimizing rating errors in the criterion. *Personnel Psychology*, **33**, 91–96.

Quadagno, J. (1988) Women's access to pensions and the structure of eligibility rules: Systems of production and reproduction, *Sociological Quarterly*, **29**, 541–558.

Quinn, J. F. (1979) Wage determination and discrimination among older workers. *Journal of Gerontology*, **34**, 728–735.

Quinn, R. P., Staines, G. L., & McCullough, M. R. (1974) *Job Satisfaction: Is There a Trend?* Manpower Research Monograph No. 30, US Department of Labor. Washington DC: US Government Printing Office.

Rabinowitz, S., & Hall, D. T. (1977) Organizational research on job involvement. *Psychological Bulletin*, **84**, 265–288.

Rabinowitz, S., Hall, D. T., & Goodale, J. G. (1977) Job scope and individual differences as predictors of job involvement: Independent or interactive? *Academy of Management Journal*, **20**, 273–281.

Reitz, H. J. & Jewell, L. N. (1979) Sex, locus of control and job involvement – 6 – country investigation. *Academy of Management Journal*, **22**, 72–80.

Rhodes, S. R. (1983) Age-related differences in work attitudes and behavior: A review and conceptual analysis. *Psychological Bulletin*, **93**, 328–367.

Richardson, I. M. (1953) Age and work: a study of 489 men in heavy industry. *British Journal of Industrial Medicine*, **10**, 269–284.

Roadburg, A. (1981) Perceptions of work and leisure among the elderly. *The Gerontologist*, **21**, 142–145.

Rollins, B. C., & Cannon, K. L. (1974) Marital satisfaction over the life cycle: A re-evaluation. *Journal of Marriage and the Family*, **36**, 271–282.

Rones, P. L. (1983) The labor market problems of older workers. *Monthly Labor Review*, May, 3–19.

Root, N. (1981) Injuries at work are fewer among older employees. *Monthly Labor Review*, **104**, 30–34.

Rosen, B., & Jerdee, T. H. (1976a) The nature of job-related age stereotypes. *Journal of Applied Psychology*, **59**, 511–512.

Rosen, B., & Jerdee, T. H. (1976b) The influence of age stereotypes on managerial decisions, *Journal of Applied Psychology*, **61**, 428–432.

Rowland, K. F. (1977) Environmental events predicting death for the elderly. *Psychological Bulletin*, **84**, 349–372.

Saleh, S. D., & Otis, J. L. (1964) Age and level of job satisfaction. *Personnel Psychology*, **17**, 424–430.

Salthouse, T. (1984) Effects of age and skill in typing. *Journal of Experimental Psychology: General*, **113**, 345–371.

Salthouse, T. (1985) Speed of behavior and its implications for cognition. In J. E. Birren & K. W. Schaie (eds), *Handbook of the Psychology of Aging (2nd edn)*. New York: Van Nostrand Reinhold.

Salthouse, T. (1988) Aging and skilled performance. In A. Colley & J. Beech (eds), *The Acquisition and Performance of Cognitive Skills*. Chichester: Wiley.

Salthouse, T., Kausler, D. H., & Saults, J. S. (1988) Utilization of path-analytic procedures to investigate the role of processing resources in cognitive aging. *Psychology and Aging*, **3**, 158–166.

Salthouse, T., & Somberg, B. L. (1982) Skilled performance: Effects of adult age and experience. *Journal of Experimental Psychology: General*, **111**, 176–207.

Salvendy, G. (1972) Effects of age on some test scores of production criteria. *Studia Psychologica*, **14**, 186–189.

Schenet, N. (1945) An analysis of absenteeism in one war plant. *Journal of Applied Psychology*, **29**, 27–39.

Schmitt, N., & McCune, J. T. (1981) The relationship between job attitudes and the decision to retire. *Academy of Management Journal*, **24**, 795–802.

Schwab, D. P., & Heneman, H. G. III (1977) Effects of age and experience on productivity. *Industrial Gerontology*, **4**, 113–117.

Scott, K. D., & Taylor, G. S. (1985) An examination of conflicting findings on absenteeism — a meta-analysis. *Academy of Management Journal*, **28**, 599–612.

Semyonov, M. (1980) The social context of women's labor force participation: A comparative analysis. *American Journal of Sociology*, **86**, 534–550.

Sheppard, H. L. (1970) On age discrimination. In H. L. Sheppard (ed.), *Towards an Industrial Gerontology*. Cambridge, MA: Schenkman.

Sheppard, H. L. (1976) Work and retirement. In R. H. Binstock and E. Shanas (eds), *Handbook of Aging and the Social Sciences*. New York: Van Nostrand Reinhold.

Sheppard, H. L., & Rix, S. E. (1977) *The Graying of Working America: The Coming Crisis in Retirement Age Policy*. New York: Free Press.

Sherman, S. R. (1985) Reported reasons retired workers left their last job: Findings from the 1982 New Beneficiary Survey. *Social Security Bulletin*, **48** (March), 27.

Shikiar, R., & Freudenberg, R. (1982) Unemployment rates as a moderator of the job disatisfaction–turnover relation. *Human Relations*, **35**, 845–856.

Shirom, A., & Mazeh, T. C. (1988) Periodicity in seniority–job satisfaction relationship. *Journal of Vocational Behaviour*, **33**, 38–49.

Siassi, I., Crocetti, G., & Spiro, H. R. (1975) Emotional health, life and job satisfaction in aging workers. *Industrial Gerontology*, **2**, 289–296.

Simonton, D. K. (1988) Age and outstanding achievement—What do we know after a century of research? *Psychological Bulletin*, **104**, 251–267.

Singh, S. P., & Singh, A. P. (1980) The effect of certain social and personal factors on job satisfaction of supervisors. *Psychological Studies*, **25**, 129–132.

Slater, R. (1972) Age discrimination in Great Britain. *Industrial Gerontology*, **1**, 42–58.

Slater, R. (1973) The end of the road at forty? *Personnel Management*, **5**, 31–35.

Smith, J. M. (1969) Age and occupation: a classification of occupations by their age structure. *Journal of Gerontology*, **24**, 412–418.

Smith, J. M. (1973) Age and occupation: the determinants of male occupational age structures - Hypothesis H versus Hypothesis A, *Journal of Gerontology*, **28**, 484–490.

Smith, J. M. (1974) Age and occupation: a review of the use of occupational age structures in industrial gerontology. *Industrial Gerontology*, **1**, 42–58.

Smith, J. M. (1975) Occupations classified by their age structure. *Industrial Gerontology*, **2**, 209–215.

Smith, J. M. (1981) Over forties in manual and technical work. In C. L. Cooper & D. P. Torrington (eds), *After Forty*. Chichester: Wiley.

Smith, M. W. (1953) Older workers' efficiency in jobs of various types. *Personnel Journal*, **32**, 19–23.

Snyder, C. J., & Barrett, G. V. (1988) The Age Discrimination in Employment Act: A review of court decisions. *Experimental Aging Research*, **14**, 3–47.

Sobel, I. (1970) Economic changes and older worker utilization patterns. In P. M. Paillet & M. E. Bunch (eds) *Age, Work and Automation*. Basle: Karger.

Sorrentino, C. (1981) Unemployment in international perspective. In B. Showler & A. Sinfield (eds), *The Workless State*, Oxford: Martin Robertson.

Sparrow, P. R., & Davies, D. R., (1988) Effects of age, tenure, training and job complexity on technical performance. *Psychology and Aging*, **3**, 307–314.

Spector, P. E. (1985) Measurement of human service staff satisfaction: Development of the Job Satisfaction Survey. *American Journal of Community Psychology*, **13**, 693–713.

Spirduso, W. W. (1980) Physical fitness, aging, and psychomotor speed: A review. *Journal of Gerontology*, **35**, 850–865.

Sprague, N. (1970) Preface. In H. L.Sheppard (ed). *Towards an Industrial Gerontology*. Cambridge, MA: Schenkman.

Srole, L., Langner, T. S., Michael, S. T., Opler, M. K., & Rennie, T. A. C. (1962) *Mental Health in the Metropolis: The Midtown–Manhattan Study*, vol. 1. New York: Mc-Graw-Hill.

Stagner, R. (1971) An industrial psychologist looks at industrial gerontology. *Aging and Human Development*, 2, 29–37.

Stagner, R. (1979) Propensity to work: An important variable in retiree behavior. *Aging and Work*, 2, 161–171.

Stagner, R. (1985) Aging in industry. In J. E. Birren & K. W. Schaie (eds), *Handbook of the Psychology of Aging* (2nd edn). New York: Van Nostrand Reinhold.

Steers, R. M. (1977) Antecedents and outcomes of organizational commitment. *Administrative Science Quarterly*, 22, 46–56.

Steers, R. M., & Rhodes, S. R. (1978) Major influences on employee attendance: A process model. *Journal of Applied Psychology*, 63, 391–407.

Stevens, A. F. (1929) Accidents of older workers: Relation of age to extent of disability. *Personnel Journal*, 8, 138–145.

Stevens, J. M., Beyer, J. M., & Trice, H. M. (1978) Assessing personal, role, and organizational predictors of managerial commitment. *Academy of Management Journal*, 21, 380–396.

Stones, M. J. & Kozma, A., (1985) Physical performance. In N. Charness (ed.), *Aging and Human Performance*. Chichester: Wiley.

Streib, G. F., & Schneider, J. J. (1971). *Retirement in American Society*, Ithaca, New York: Cornell University Press.

Stumpf, S. A., & Dawley, P. K. (1981) Predicting voluntary and involuntary turnover using absenteeism and performance indices. *Academy of Management Journal*, 24, 148–163.

Super, D. E. (1984) Career and life development. In D. Brown & L. Brooks (eds), *Career Choice and Development*. San Francisco: Jossey-Bass.

Surry, J. (1977) *Industrial Accident Research*. Toronto: Labour Safety Council.

Susman, G. I. (1973) Job enlargement: Effects of culture on worker responses. *Industrial Relations*, 12, 1–15.

Tait, M., Padgett, M. Y., & Baldwin, T. T. (1990) Job and life satisfaction: A reevaluation of the strength of relationship and gender effects as a function of the date of study. *Journal of Applied Psychology*, 74, 502–507.

Taylor, D. E. (1979) Absent workers and lost work hours. *Monthly Labor Review*, 102, 51–53.

Taylor, R. N. (1975) Age and experience as determinants of managerial information processing and decision-making performance. *Academy of Management Journal*, 18, 74–81.

Teiger, C. (1989) Le vieillissement différentiel dans et par le travail: un vieux problème dans un contexte récent. *Travail Humain*, 52, 21–56.

Thackray, R. I. & Touchstone, R. M. (1981) *Age-related Differences in Complex Monitoring Performance*. (Tech. Rep. FAA-AM-81-12). Washington, DC: Federal Aviation Administration.

Thompson, K. R., & Terpening, W. D. (1983) Job-type variations and antecedents to intention to leave: a content approach to turnover. *Human Relations*, 36, 655–682.

Trites, D. K., & Cobb, B. B. (1962) *Problems in Air Traffic Management: III. Implications of Age for Training and Job Performance of Air Traffic Controllers*. FAA Civil Aeromedical Research Institute, Report No. 62-3.

Tuckman, J., & Lorge, I. (1952) Attitudes toward older workers. *Journal of Applied Psychology*, 36, 149–153.

US Department of Labor (1957) *Comparative Job Performance by Age: Large Plants in the Men's Footwear and Household Furniture Industries.* Bulletin No. 1223, Washington DC.

Van Zelst, R. H. (1954) The effect of age and experience upon accident rate. *Journal of Applied Psychology,* **38,** 313–317.

Vernon, H. M. (1945) Prevention of accidents. *British Journal of Industrial Medicine,* **2,** 1–9.

Verrillo, R. T. & Verrillo, V. (1985) Sensory and perceptual performance. In N.Charness (ed.), *Aging and Human Performance.* Chichester: Wiley.

Vroom, V. H., (1964) *Work and Motivation.* New York: Wiley.

Wagner, J. A., Ferris, G. R., Fandt, P. M., & Wayne, S. J. (1987) The organizational tenure-job involvement relationship—A job-career experience explanation. *Journal of Occupational Behaviour,* **8,** 63–70.

Waldman, D. A., & Avolio, B. J. (1986) A meta-analysis of age differences in job performance. *Journal of Applied Psychology,* **71,** 33–38.

Walker, A. (1985) Early retirement: release or refuge from the labour market? *Quarterly Journal of Social Affairs,* **1,** 211–229.

Walker, J. W., & Price, K. F. (1976) Retirement policy formulation: a systems perspective. *Personnel Review,* **5,** 39–43.

Walker, R., Hardman, G., & Hutton, S. (1987) The occupational pension trap: Towards a preliminary empirical specification. *Journal of Social Policy,* **18,** 578–593.

Walsh, R. P., & Connor, C. L. (1980) Old men and young women: How objectively are their skills assessed? *Journal of Gerontology,* **34,** 561–568.

Wanner, R. A., & McDonald, L. (1983) Ageism in the labor market: Estimating earnings discrimination against older workers. *Journal of Gerontology,* **38,** 738–744.

Waters, L. K., & Roach, D. (1971) Relationship between job attitudes and two forms of withdrawal from the work situation. *Journal of Applied Psychology,* **55,** 92–94.

Waters, L. K., & Roach, D. (1973) Job attitudes as predictors of termination and absenteeism: Consistency over time and across organizational units. *Journal of Applied Psychology,* **57,** 341–342.

Watson, C. J. (1981) An evaluation of some aspects of the Steers and Rhodes model of employee attendance. *Journal of Applied Psychology,* **66,** 385–389.

Warr, P., Cook, J. & Wall, T. (1979) Scales for the measurement of some work attitudes and aspects of psychological well-being. *Journal of Occupational Psychology,* **52,** 129–148.

Weaver, C. N. (1980) Job satisfaction in the United States in the 1970s. *Journal of Applied Psychology,* **65,** 364–367.

Weiner, B. (1985) An attributional theory of achievement motivation and emotion. *Psychological Review,* **92,** 548–573.

Welford, A. T. (1958) *Ageing and Human Skill.* London: Oxford University Press.

Welford, A. T. (1977) Motor performance. In J. E. Birren & K. W. Schaie (eds) *Handbook of the Psychology of Aging.* New York: Van Nostrand.

Welford, A. T. (1985) Changes of performance with age: An overview. In N. Charness (ed.), *Aging and Human Performance.* Chichester: Wiley.

Welford, A. T., & Speakman, D. (1950) The employability of older people. In *The Aged and Society.* London: Industrial Relations Research Association.

Werbel, J. D., & Bedeian, A. G. (1989) Intended turnover as a function of age and job performance. *Journal of Organizational Behaviour,* **10,** 275–281.

Williams, A., Livy, B., Silverstone, R., & Adams, P. (1979) Factors associated with labour turnover among ancilliary staff in two London hospitals. *Journal of Occupational Psychology,* **52,** 1–16.

Wolpin, J., & Burke, R. J. (1985) Relationships between absenteeism and turnover: A function of the measures? *Personnel Psychology*, **38**, 57–74.

Woska, E. (1972) Sick leave incentive plans: A benefit to consider. *Public Personnel Review*, **133**, 21–24.

Wright, J. D., & Hamilton, R. F. (1978) Work satisfaction and age: some evidence for the job change hypothesis. *Social Forces*, **56**, 1140–1158.

Zemore, R., & Eames, N. (1979) Psychic and somatic symptoms of depression among young adults, institutionalized aged and noninstitutionalized aged. *Journal of Gerontology*, **31**, 805–807.

Chapter 6

METHODOLOGICAL ISSUES IN PERSONNEL SELECTION RESEARCH

Heinz Schuler and Andreas Guldin

University of Hohenheim, Federal Republic of Germany

INTRODUCTION

The period under review, 1986–89, saw significant increase in the publication and discussion of methodological issues. Therefore, only a sample of works published in the main journals and a comparatively small number of books and articles could be included in this chapter. For a better understanding of methodological developments in some cases, we have referred to literature earlier than 1986.

The chapter begins with a review of validity concepts and validation research. Based on the changing conceptions of validity, interesting validation models were proposed including performance domains as well as predictor systems. In construct validation a tendency to multimodal approaches can be recognized, creatively making use of ideas and procedures that come partly from outside industrial and organizational psychology (I/O)—e.g., Brunswik's principles of symmetry and Sternberg's information processing work. Explanations for the underestimation of selection methods—e.g. the employment interview— appeared, and suggestions for more adequate statistical treatments in predictive validation were put forward. An attempt was made to make generalizability theory more attractive for applied research after 20 years of rather passive respect for this useful alternative to classical reliability theory. The importance or even sufficiency of general cognitive ability in employment has been discussed. The proponents of validity generalization, the most lively field of methodological innovation, do have a decisive answer to this question. But their methods, too, seem to be open to improvement.

The next section is devoted to utility analysis using language that seems to be closer to that of business than psychologists' concepts of validity. The 'Archilles heel of utility' is still seen in the estimation of performance variation

International Review of Industrial and Organizational Psychology 1991 Volume 6
Edited by C. L. Cooper and I. T. Robertson © 1991 John Wiley & Sons Ltd.

(SD_Y), so several attempts have been made to improve estimates of actual performance distributions, or even do without them, and use archival data. Now, SD_Y estimates from different approaches can be compared. Enrichment of utility estimations through capital-budgeting methodology can bring psychology even closer to business administration. Finally, a new general model has been suggested as an approach to utility.

Within the frame of decision models, interesting work has been carried out on strategies or 'policies' of (individual) decision makers. As a new method, HYPAG was suggested for configuration-based analysis of multivariate data. It compares decision-makers' individual hypotheses about their decision processes with objective observations of their behavior and tests the resulting models. Expert–novice comparisons resulted in several, but overall rather small, differences in decision-making strategies between these groups.

In the section 'psychometric considerations' we have to note that Item Response Theory (IRT) still does not receive much attention by applied psychologists, although work is reported that demonstrates its utility as an analytic tool for a number of problems. One of them is the question of test fairness. For investigating fairness we suggest a distinction between three levels of bias in relating predictor and criterion. Other topics in psychometric research have been temporal stability or the measurement of change, reliability, and the aggregation of raw scores. Finally, we would like to consider the '(non)equivalence of quality of measured behavior' as a probable influence on predictor–criterion linkages.

While many topics in this review deserve—and occasionally get—a comprehensive treatment of their own, this is especially true for developments in statistical techniques. The range and breadth of new research on statistical issues is large. A future volume of the *International Review of Industrial and Organizational Psychology* will contain a chapter devoted to statistical developments of relevance to personnel selection; accordingly this chapter does not include a section on statistical methods.

VALIDITY AND VALIDATION

As far as the semantics of validity and validation are concerned, fundamental conceptual issues seem to be settled. According to the American Psychological Association in coauthorship with two other associations (American Educational Research Association, American Psychological Association, & National Council of Measurement in Education, 1985, p. 9) validity 'refers to the appropriateness, meaningfulness, and usefulness of the specific inferences made from test scores'. Test validation is defined as 'the process of accumulating evidence to support such inferences'. Many ways of accumulating evidence may contribute to any particular inference, but validity as an epistemological category should be conceived as a unitary concept. The object of validation is, strictly speaking, not the test itself but 'specific uses of a test'.

The Society for Industrial and Organizational Psychology (1987) discusses *Principles for the Validation and Use of Personnel Selection Procedures*, stating that the kind of inference in personnel selection 'is ultimately an inference about probable job behavior' (p. 4) thereby referring to the importance of job analysis and of the definition and measurement of criteria. Within the idea of validity being a unitary concept, however, the traditional trinity—content, criterion, and construct—is maintained, albeit as validation strategies, discussed as interrelated approaches which deliver specific contributions to empirically based evidence.

The inappropriateness of logical separation of 'types of validity' has been trenchantly stressed by Landy (1986). He argued that American jurisdiction is partly responsible for the rigid perpetuation of the formerly useful but nowadays scientifically obsolete distinction among the three validation models. According to Landy (1986, p. 1188), 'validity studies are attempts to develop a theory of performance that explains how an individual can (or will) meet the demands of a particular job'. For the development and testing of such theories diverse information can be used as there are different kinds of inferences that can be made from a test score. In this sense, Landy suggests that validation should be considered as a process of hypothesis testing, intended to collect the best available evidence to rule out alternative explanations for the relationship between test performance and job performance. This position goes beyond Anastasi's frequently quoted notion (Anastasi, 1988) that in principle, all validity is construct validity. Landy's venture stimulated renewed interest in validity issues; for example, Hogan & Nicholson (1988) explicitly referred to his concept when they stated that measurement-based research is formally identical with any other type of scientific inquiry. Wainer & Brown (1988) edited a book on test validity including several articles concerned with conceptual issues; one general tenor is the dominant role that theory building and hypothesis testing ought to play in validation.

So we can say that validation can be understood as a set of principles to investigate the heuristic value of a diagnostic strategy—or, even more generally formulated, an epistemological tool restricted only by conventions rather than principle. This conception is as relevant to the theoretical problem of the relationship between theories and data as to the practical question of which ways validation models can be used to determine adequacy. As in other kinds of acquisitions of knowledge, single investigations are seldom decisive when a question of some importance and complexity is investigated. This means that no methodology requiring rigid action can be ideal. Opinions on the validity of certain strategies, tools, or decisions are built up from a variety of single items of information, which stem only in part from empirical validations and also include results from theoretically related investigations and even prescientific observations and convictions. In this sense, a methodology in need of relatively homogeneous material may not be ideal or ultimate. Meta-analysis, for example, may seem to be too restrictive in its present state to integrate this wide informational potential, and thus must not be mistaken for a meta-theory on validity. At the same time we should be cautious not to formulate (meta-)theoretical concepts that are too far from our goals in applied validation research.

Models of Validation

If the line of reasoning in the preceding paragraph is correct, validation is not restricted to a handful of methods usually subsumed under this label—in 9 out of 10 studies correlational techniques—, but can be extended to virtually all methods reported in this article or, even further, in textbooks on research design and evaluation. This may be a reasonable consequence; it is opposed, however, by increasing ambiguity concerning validity conclusions in science and users' decisions in practice. To ask for 'the validity of a certain test' would then be naive, and we would have to face an even longer road from research to practical use of selection instruments.

Reductions of this complexity are prompted by the argument that although the traditional 'trinitarian' concept of validity—the distinction of predictive, content-, and construct-related facets—may be an oversimplification, all strategies are not equally appropriate. This supports some kind of faceting at least for pragmatic reasons (Guion, 1987; Society for Industrial and Organizational Psychology, 1987; Moser & Schuler, 1989).

Sussmann & Robertson (1986) refer to Cook & Campbell (1976) to distinguish four 'kinds of validity': statistical conclusion, internal, construct, and external validity (generalization over a facet and from sample to universe). Explicitly separating validity (logic of inferences) from validation (the process of research using a specific design), Sussmann and Robertson compare 11 criterion-related validation designs according to their 'validity', i.e. 'the best approximation to the truth or falsity' (Cook & Campbell, 1976, p. 37). For each of the designs shown in Table 1, the authors discuss its suitability to test aspects of the four facets of validity. In Sussman and Robertson's evaluation, the selection procedure is the major design property that influences the validity of validation studies. No specific design, however, is considered appropriate for all purposes, so the authors suggest the use of validation research programs including different designs. A 'theory-driven approach to validity', also referring to Cook and Campbell's validity categories, is suggested by Chen & Rossi (1987) for research in program evaluation. Their central argument is that a model or theory—instead of only a research design—should be formulated in a program evaluation; the modeling process should include the identification and control of potential threats to validity. The suggested measures to control these threats

Table 1—Eleven Validation Study Designs with Timing of Test and Performance Measurement and with Selection Decision (from Sussmann & Robertson, 1986)

Design	Sequential stage				
	Before employment	*Selection decision*	*At entry*	*After short tenure*	*After extended tenure*
1	X	R	—	—	P
2	—	R	X	—	P
3	X	E	—	—	P
4	—	E	X	—	P
5	X	X	—	—	P
6	—	R	—	X, P	—
7	—	R	—	—	X, P
8	—	E	—	X, P	—
9	—	E	—	—	X, P
10	—	E	—	—	X, P (CS)
11	—	E	—	—	A, P

Note. E = existing test(s); P = job performance measure(s); R = random selection; X = experimental test(s); A = archival data; CS = cross-sectional, present employees.

are sufficiently general also to be of significance in personnel selection research.

A rather elaborate model for personnel decision research is suggested by Binning & Barrett (1989). Referring to Landy's formulation of validation as theory building and hypothesis testing, they identify validation as collecting evidence for inferential linkages between predictor and performance constructs and measures. Personnel selection is then conceived as 'the process of identifying and mapping predictor samples of behavior to effectively overlap with performance domains. Validity, therefore, can be viewed as the extent to which these two construct systems overlap' (p. 481).

Binning and Barrett come to the conclusion that construct-related and content-related approaches represent the two basic ways of relating predictor measures to the performance domain, while the criterion-related approach can be understood as a research strategy for empirically assessing the quality of these behavior sampling processes. These authors develop a model of validation as personnel decision research which should be a stimulating heuristic for researchers in this field. Especially remarkable in this thoughtful analysis is the fact that the criterion side in validation is not given less weight than the predictor side.

One of the ubiquitous burdens in selection research is that we deal with traits or trait-like entities of relatively high abstraction levels. In Fiske's view (Fiske, 1987a, 1987b) there is no definitive separation of traits and methods, and all research using the multitrait–multimethod matrix (MTMM) has shown method effects to be the main cause of the explained variance. In principle, Fiske's pessimistic view is that there is no real possibility of empirically validating a personality trait. Dealing with short behavioral entities and precisely defined behavior-method units—low-level constructs—seems to be an opportunity partly to avoid problems with more general constructs. Work samples may be a promising attempt in this regard; on the other hand, comparisons between measurements from different operations require theories not only on the constructs but also on the processes involved in each method and in the eventual aggregation of results (Fiske, 1987a, 1987b).

Multimodal assessment of predictors and criteria may be a pragmatic approach in personnel psychology to be recommended (Schuler & Schmitt, 1987). A more systematic treatment of the problem is suggested by Wittman (1987). He argues that questions of reliability and validity are confused in the typical MTMM interpretation. Building on Brunswik's principles of symmetry and on Cattell's basic data relations matrix (BDRM), Wittmann suggests a multivariate reliability and validity theory (Wittman, 1987; in press). Essentials of this theory are the assumption of polythetic constructs and precise separation of reliability and validity questions by application of the 'four data-box conception', i.e. a reduction of Cattell's BDRM taxonomy to four boxes—a predictor box, an experimental treatment box, a nonexperimental treatment box, and a criteria box. Comparisons within these boxes are questions of reliability, whereas only comparisons between boxes have to be treated as questions of validity.

Schmitt (1989a) summarized what he considers promising alternatives to the MTMM approach in construct validation:

— The Borman, Rosse and Abrahms (1980) construction and empirical test of equivalent constructs in personality research;
— Frederiksen's (1986) process validation;
— The cognitive correlates approach represented by the work of Carroll (1979);
— Information processing work represented by Sternberg;
— Comparisons of experts and novices;
— The structural modeling approach represented by the work of Turban *et al.* (1989).

Two of these approaches will shortly be described here. Frederiksen (1986) suggested a procedure for test development and construct validation based on a theory of criterion performance. According to assumptions of a doctor's ability to solve medical problems, he constructed a criterion test. In parallel with this test, a predictor test for admission of students to medical school was constructed, but not requiring medical knowledge. A third set of variables, so-called process variables, was designed and administered as tests to investigate the critical processes or constructs in the predictor and the criterion data and thus evaluate hypotheses about diagnostic problem solving.

Turban *et al*. (1989) presented another approach that might be helpful in assessing construct validity of new tests. This approach, labeled construct equivalence, allows for replacing or amending valid tests currently in use with new test items, for example when the security of test items had been compromised. By using correlational analysis, structural modeling, and operational effects analysis, Turban *et al*. (1989) evaluated the equivalence of the new items and the test in use. In the case of their investigation, all three types of analysis led to the same conclusion, but the congeneric test model fitted their data best. As Schmitt (1989a) remarks, an interesting extension of this approach would be to measure the equivalence of test and criterion constructs.

Further combinations of methodologies in the construct validation process have been especially fruitful. Hammond, Hamm, & Grassia (1986) combined MTMM and Brunswik's representative design of experiments for generalizing results over conditions. Cote, Buckley & Best (1987) developed a set of guidelines to recommend how three alternative construct validation methodologies—confirmatory factor analysis, MTMM, and analysis of variance—can be used in combination, dependent on the characteristics of the data set.

In general, structural equation models are increasingly used in validation research (James & James, 1989). One type of structural equation models, confirmatory factor analysis (CFA), is being frequently used for validation of criteria as well as of predictors. For example, Vance *et al*. (1988) used Widaman's approach to assessment of convergent and discriminant validity of multitrait–multimethod data for contrasting alternative performance models. The use of second-order confirmatory factor analysis was suggested by March & Hocever (1988) as a more powerful approach to multitrait–multimethod analyses. If mutliple indicators of each scale (i.e. items or subscales) are at hand, these items or subscales can define first-order factors, and trait or method factors can be posited as second-order factors. In this way, several weaknesses of the usual method of application of CFA can be avoided, for example the failures to correct appropriately for measurement error due to weak trait or method effects. An even more general solution was proposed by Rindskopf & Rose (1988) who place second-order models in a hierarchy of factor analysis models to show how the fit of various models can be compared.

To overcome the problem of criterion-related validation for small samples—as is usual in the context of most organizations—a synthetic validation strategy is sometimes used. The principles of synthetic validity is to decompose a task into its elements and infer the total validity of a selection tool from the validity of its elements. Hollenbeck & Whitener (1988) proposed a new approach to synthetic validity by integrating and extending three existing models. The main difference to former models of synthetic validity is that Hollenbeck and Whitener use sampling theory and matrix algebra to show that the order of validation and aggregation need not be fixed (although comparability requires the same procedure for each person within one investigation). Moser *et al.* (1989) discussed the applicability of validation strategies to job and task analysis instruments. They concluded that both reliability and validity concepts can be used in a manner comparable to convenient person-specific assessment devices, provided that an analogy between the concept of trans-situational consistency (consistency of a person across different situations) used in personality psychology and 'transpersonal consistency' (consistency of a job across different job holders) in the frame of job analysis can be drawn.

Validation Research

In the course of this chapter, methodological treatments of predictors and criteria are not separated. Traditionally, research on criterion validation has not been extensive, although demands for progress have been renewed in the period under review (cf. Cascio, 1987; Frederiksen, 1986; Guion, 1987). Impulses for increasing interest in recent years might have been given by results of meta-analyses showing different validities for all kinds of predictors when related to different criteria (Schmitt *et al.*, 1984). Direct comparisons of supervisory ratings and results-oriented performance data showed substantial differences (Heneman, 1986). The same was true in a study reported by Sackett, Zedeck & Fogli (1988) where, additionally, correlations between typical and maximum performance were low. Meyer (1987) found that cognitive ability tests were highly predictive of managerial promotional progress, but almost uncorrelated with supervisory ratings.

Among the more theoretical or methodological contributions in the period under review were suggestions by Dickinson (1987) for evaluating the validity and accuracy of performance ratings. Dickinson used a design combining the multitrait–multimethod and person perception designs to isolate the influence of rater, ratee, and context factors on the quality of performance ratings. Schmidt, Hunter, & Outerbridge (1986) demonstrated how validity generalization can be instrumental in construct analyses of supervisory ratings and other performance measures. Intended as 'the beginning of a generalizable task taxonomy' (p. 447), Vance *et al.* (1989) tested a covariance structure model that related several classes of predictors to five classes of criteria-rated performance by supervisor, peers, and self, a work sample test, and training success; the task performance model received support for each of three categories of tasks.

Methods for measuring rater agreement and making inferences about the accuracy of inter-observer agreement data were described by Uebersax (1988). Using a model related to signal detection theory and Item Response Theory, Uebersax demonstrated that considerable improvements in traditional reliability estimates are possible, for example by combining opinions of multiple raters by decision rules based on the accuracy of the ratings. Even under the relatively ideal circumstances of expert raters in sports, however, there are ceilings in the reliability and validity of performance ratings, as Weekley & Gier (1989) showed.

Suggestions for improving construct validity of assessment center ratings were made by Bycio, Alvares, & Hahn (1987) who recommended eliciting more ability-related behaviors within the exercises reducing cognitive demands placed on assessors.

Studies in the context of validity generalization had shown that estimates of personnel selection experts were superior to small-sample validity studies (Schmidt et al., 1983). Now Hirsh, Schmidt, & Hunter (1986) have shown that even the estimates of less experienced judges are as accurate as those obtained from small-sample empirical studies. Compared to experts' estimates, however, the less experienced judges' estimates contained less information and more random error as well as more systematic error. While experts underestimated validities on average, novices overestimated them.

One of the puzzles in validity research has been why research can come up with astoundingly low validities for methods that every user is convinced of—especially the traditional employment interview. This may be the reason for the relatively high number of interview studies among the altogether low number of validations in recent years, most of them showing high reliabilities and validities for structured and job-related interviews (Eder & Ferris, 1989). Hunter & Hirsch (1987) suggested that the unstructured, not explicitly job-related, interview measured primarily those nonperformance-related components that are also included in supervisory ratings (e.g. self-presentation); thus its validity can be interpreted as incremental validity.

Dreher, Ash, & Hancock (1988) argued that the common practice of collapsing data across several interviewers results in underestimates of validity coefficients, as individuals usually show constant rating effects or consistent differences in their use of a response scale. Individual mean differences—i.e. consistently more or less lenient ratings—are included as error variance and thus reduce the magnitude of the overall validity coefficient.

Martin (1989) extended this argument to a variety of criterion-related studies. Not only does generalization to every other predictor, where several raters give less than fully reliable responses, seem appropriate, but the same should be true for criterion data consisting of ratings from multiple sources. If either the predictor or the criterion is based on data collapsed across multiple sources, the calculated validity coefficients may be underestimated. However, in the case of a positive correlation between the subgroup means of the predictor and the criterion, coefficients may also be overestimated. This might be relevant in the context of fairness issues, where inflated aggregate correlation coefficients could result in the erronous impression of equal validity for different subgroups. If subgroup means are negatively correlated, on the other hand, an underestimate of validity can be expected.

Martin (1989) additionally pointed out that it is also necessary that all predictor variances have to be equal if an overall validity coefficient is to provide an estimate of the weighted average validity coefficients for all individuals. So adjustments for subgroup differences in the standard deviations may be necessary in order to interpret the overall coefficient as the weighted average of the subgroup validities.

A number of further problems in interview validation, especially in experimental studies—which could be partly generalized to other assessment tools—were discussed by Dreher & Maurer (1989) and by Kacmar, Ratcliff & Ferris (1989).

Evidence for construct validity of life history prediction systems (biographical inventories) was reviewed by Klimoski (1988). Robertson (1989) discussed the main approaches to exploring construct validity in managerial selection and assessment, introducing concepts of situational strength and construct stability. Robertson refered to a notion of Adler & Weiss (1988) that most research in I/O psychology involves situations that are 'strong', thus minimizing variance caused by person variables. Robertson argued that construct-related evidence should be used as a main basis of selection only in the case of stable constructs and weak but stable situations.

To test the hypothesis that abstract constructs are more difficult to measure than concrete constructs, Cote & Buckley (1987) categorized 70 studies according to the type of constructs measured. Attitude measures had the least trait variance (29·8%) and the highest method/error-variance, personality and aptitude measures accounted for 39·1 and 39·5% respectively, and for job performance (assumed to be represented by the most concrete constructs), the trait variance was 46·5%.

The 'classical' function of construct validation—i.e. to enhance scientific understanding of traits and measures—was demonstrated by two studies carried out by Pulakos, Borman, & Hough (1988). Cognitive ability and personality construct measures showed predictable patterns of correlations with rating criteria measuring different performance areas. In a study reported by Schuler (1989), a structured interview intended to measure service orientation showed the same correlation pattern with relevant dimensions of personality tests as a paper-and-pencil test which was developed to measure the same construct.

For all empirical validation research, it should be kept in mind that competitive tests of theories by comparing the predictive or relational strength of factors or variables have to be fair in the sense that comparisons require equivalent operations. Cooper & Richardson (1986) demonstrated that different kinds of operations, manipulations, or measurements can lead to erroneous conclusions about different qualities of the theories or variables on test.

Maier (1988) reminded us that reasons for inaccurate validity coefficients may lie in the conditions of data collection, including incompetencies of test administrators, and suggested the exercising of quality control during the statistical analysis. Smith *et al.* (1986) presented 'guidelines for clean data' and suggested rules for avoiding and detecting errors while collecting, analyzing, and storing data, and for correcting data sets.

Generalizability Theory

A notable basis for validity theory and validation research can be generalizability theory (GT). This concept, proposed by Cronbach *et al.* (1972), has been widely recognized but scarcely used in applied fields. Recently, an attempt was made by Shavelson, Webb, & Rowley (1989) to familiarize psychological researchers with this concept.

The basic idea of GT is the reinterpretation of reliability. In classical test theory reliability is defined as the ratio of true- to observed-score variance, each observed score being a sum of true score and error. In GT, error is understood not as a homogeneous term, but error variance is composed from a variety of sources. Thus the characteristic score of a person is a generalization over all intended observations including all relevant error components. This typical value is called the person's 'universe score' (Cronbach *et al.*, 1972). The question posed by GT, then, is how accurately a person's observed score in a given situation allows generalization over a defined range of situations.

Shavelson, Webb, & Rowley (1989) compare the logic of identifying error components to that of a factorial analysis of variance. Each of the multiple error components can be estimated separately, and measurements can be designed to minimize specific errors for a particular purpose.

In principle, calculation of a generalizability coefficient is carried out dividing the estimated person variance component by the estimated observed score variance, in analogy to the reliability coefficient in classical test theory. But GT distinguishes between relative decisions and absolute decisions. Relative decisions result from ranking of persons (e. g. for a certain job) and thus concern the dependability of differences between persons. Absolute decisions refer only to the individual scores without relating them to scores of other persons (e.g. in criterion-referenced tests). So, the GT generalizability coefficient—the ratio of the universe-score variance to the expected observed score variance, an intraclass correlation—includes only error components associated with ranking of individuals for the relative case and, additionally, error terms associated with facets (e.g. occasions, raters, and items) for absolute decisions (Shavelson, Webb, & Rowley, 1989, p. 925).

In GT, two types of designs are distinguished—generalizability (G) studies and decision (D) studies. Roughly speaking, G studies define the universe and the measurement parameters, while D studies are the applied form, specifying the interpretation in a given context. For both types of designs, Shavelson, Webb, & Rowley (1989; referring to several studies in press) report new developments in GT. One line of development concerns the treatment of fixed facets in D-study designs by averaging over measures from different situations or conducting separate G-studies for each fixed facet. Another relates to the objects of measurement, taking the perspective that not only persons but any facet in research design may be regarded as the object of measurement (e.g. item parameters as indicators of successful change).

Additionally, a Bayesian approach and a restricted maximum likelihood estimation are reported as new procedures for estimating variance components to avoid the problem of unstable and negative estimates common in ANOVA. Finally, for multiple scores—as is common in personnel psychology—the problem of forming a composite arises. Shavelson and his coworkers compared four weighting schemes and ended up with high G coefficients for multivariate composites based on the variance of dimension scores and for weights derived from confirmatory factor analysis (as opposed to unit weights and expert judgements).

The *G*-factor in Employment

A different kind of g is meant by the g-factor in employment (testing). The highest common factor for a set of mental tests is usually labelled 'general ability' or 'g'. A complete issue of the *Journal of Vocational Behavior* addressed the relevance of general ability or general intelligence for personnel selection.

Jensen (1986) discussed the question of whether g should be understood as an artefact of the method of constructing psychometric tests (including the operations of factor analysis) or whether g represents some natural phenomenon that exists independently of statistical procedures. In support of the view that g is a natural phenomenon in its own right, Jensen refers to biological correlates of g that are independent of psychometrics and factor analysis, including heritability of test scores, familial correlations, inbreeding depression, evoked potentials, and choice reaction time.

In a comparison of different sample sizes, Thorndike (1986) demonstrated that in double cross-validation designs with small sample sizes, the uniform general factor score was clearly superior to specific weights. But when separately tailored sets of regression weights were derived from large samples, they provided an increase of 10–15% in the prediction compared to a general factor measure. Hunter (1986) reviewed data from military studies and from the US Employment Service (mostly performance ratings as criteria) clearly showing that general cognitive ability predicts success better than do tailored aptitude composites. Hunter interprets these data to be 'consistent with the data on job knowledge which shows that the main reason for the validity of general cognitive ability is that it predicts learning' and that it measures 'the ability to innovate and prioritize in dealing with situations that deviate from those encountered in prior training' (p. 358). This may mean that general ability exerts its influence by 'managing' the other abilities, skills, and knowledges possessed by the individual (Arvey, 1986). Consistent with prior publications, Hunter's review of meta-analyses of hundreds of studies shows that general cognitive ability predicts performance in all jobs, whether performance is measured as performance ratings, training success, or work samples. Linn's review of partly the same data, however, results in multiple correlations that are 'well below Hunter's adjusted summary validity coefficients' (Linn, 1986, p. 440). Also, Prediger (1989) found in reviewing 34 studies that g was insufficient as a descriptor of work-relevant abilities.

Gottfredson & Crouse (1986) conclude by reviewing earlier work by Crouse that academic ability is largely one-dimensional and that 'non-academic tests' seem to predict career success only insofar as they correlate with academic tests. The most highly g-loaded tests were the best predictors of later success. (In spite of this, Crouse concludes from his data that using the Scholastic Aptitude Test (SAT) only marginally improves the prediction of college success possible from high school record). In Gottfredson's theory of occupational inequalities (Gottfredson, 1986), validity of occupational selection by (general) intelligence plays a crucial role in status differentiation among occupations; improved efficiency of g-selection should lead to more social and especially racial inequality. Contradictory arguments were forwarded by Humphreys (1986b).

Validity Generalization

If the number of publications, symposia, and discussions is an indicator of scientific importance, then meta-analysis can probably be regarded as the most important methodological innovation in psychology within recent decades.

The argument is convincing: if it is true that statistical treatment of data is superior to intuitive treatment within single studies, the same should be true for the combination of results from several studies. Problems of data selection and weighting may be solved both in the clinical and in the statistical type of conclusion, but the solutions for the latter are more clearly set out and open to discussion and improvement.

The most important insight for personnel selection research was made possible by the type of meta-analysis Schmidt & Hunter (1977) proposed under the title of validity generalization (VG)—namely, that variations of validity coefficients between single studies using the same selection methods are mostly determined by sampling errors and other artefacts. Thereby, psychologists' beliefs in differential validity or moderating effects were radically challenged. By then, psychological researchers were very eager to avoid type I errors, but have largely neglected type II errors, this prevented them from concluding that their selection instruments had general ('generalizable') validity.

The artefacts that can be reduced by combining single study results via VG can be summarized as follows (Hunter & Schmidt, 1989):

— Sampling errors resulting from small sample sizes;
— Attenuation of study results produced by error of measurement in the dependent and in the independent variable;
— Attenuation of study results produced by dichotomization of the dependent and of the independent variable;
— Variation in results produced by range variation on the independent variable;
— Attrition artefacts on the dependent variable (selective loss of subjects).

Several slightly different VG procedures seem to get this done equally well and lead to the same general conclusions regarding the effectiveness of a predictor measure (Burke, Raju, & Pearlman, 1986). Not only quantitative knowledge can result from VG but also qualitative, theoretical advancement. If validation is theory building or hypothesis testing (Landy, 1986) then many tests of theories were and still are insufficient, being based on weak data.

In this chapter the many studies applying VG cannot even be mentioned. Several meta-analyses had been carried out concerning the validity of specific cognitive aptitudes predicting performance in specific jobs (Hunter & Hirsh, 1987). Cognitive ability has been the primary domain in VG research (Hunter & Schmidt, 1989), but also studies related to other predictors or criteria in personnel psychology have been conducted. In the period under review, several reviews on meta-analysis have been published, for example, Bangert-Drowns (1986), Hunter & Hirsh (1987), Hunter & Schmidt (1989), Jansen et al., (1986), Schmidt (1988) and Wolf (1986). For readers not well acquainted with the manifold criticism of VG up to 1985, the extensive discussion led by Schmidt et al. (1985) and Sackett et al. (1985) is recommended. Many arguments currently exchanged can be found in these sources.

We restrict further citations to selected publications representing some relevant lines of development or discussion. Among the many aspects James, Demaree, & Mulaik (1986) and James et al. (1988) criticized and Schmidt, Hunter, & Raju (1988) rejected, one consideration has been widely neglected in VG work: interpretation of meta-analytic results require judgement calls by the researcher (Wanous, Sullivan, & Malinak, 1989; Guzzo, Jackson & Katzell, 1987). To reduce subjectivity, VG procedures can be regarded as based on structural equations for observed validities in order to identify causes for variation in validity distributions and formulate explanatory models (James, Demaree, & Mulaik, 1986). Alexander & Borodkin (1989) derived an idex of fit for results in VG from the Schmidt & Hunter (1977) ratio of explained to observed variances and showed that it possessed a number of desired criteria.

Understanding VG as an explanatory approach will give way to uses of this method as a powerful tool for theory building and hypothesis testing. Hunter (1986) and Schmidt, Hunter, & Outerbridge (1986) give an example of this kind of work by formulating a path analytical model for the relationship of ability, job knowledge, work sample performance, and supervisor ratings. The results were interpreted in the way that cognitive ability predicts job performance, in large part because it predicts learning and job mastery (Hunter & Schmidt, 1989). Contributions to performance theories can also be made by comparisons of different criteria for test validation (e.g. Nathan & Alexander, 1988). Applications of VG to job classification often leads to less differentiation and thus gives impulses to theoretical reorientation; for example, a recently conducted review of General Aptitude Test Battery (GATB) data using VG resulted in the conclusion that the present classification of jobs into five job families is of little value as performance is predicted by essentially the same formula for all jobs (Hartigan & Wigdor, 1989).

An ongoing problem is the question of how to detect true situational specificity. Second-order sampling error is high as long as study samples are not homogeneous and not sufficiently numerous to allow separate evaluations of moderators. Monte Carlo simulations testing the Schmidt–Hunter 75% ratio, the Callender–Osburn procedure, and a chi-square test resulted in nondetection of small true differences regardless of sample sizes and numbers of studies; moderate true differences were not detected in small numbers of studies or small sample sizes (Sackett, Harris, & Orr, 1986). A study by Spector & Levine (1987) which concluded that the usual estimates of sampling error variance is biased was rejected by Callender & Osburn (1988). Contrary to Spector & Levine (1987), Rasmussen & Loher (1988) found equal power and type I error rates for the Schmidt and Hunter ratio and the U-statistic. Effects of true reliability distributions on VG estimates were investigated by Paese & Switzer (1988). Size of errors increased proportionally as sample sizes increased, leading to overestimates of artefactual variance. Alexander *et al.* (1989) suggested four empirically based distributions as adjuncts to the Schmidt–Hunter distribution of range restriction, dependent on the nature of the predictor and the type of setting.

The 90% credibility value as a basis of 'transportability' of test validities was questioned by Kemery, Mossholder, & Dunlap (1989). Millsap (1988) recommended two new approaches to determine credibility intervals around true validity values, especially in the case of small or moderate numbers of studies integrated into VG. Providing an alternative unbiased correction for sampling error, Hedges (1989) could demonstrate that the usual correction is not seriously biased as was claimed by James, Demaree, & Mulaik (1986).

Conceptual problems in VG methodology lead Jansen *et al.* (1986) to a Bayesian remodeling of the procedure. Among other criticisms they point to the absence of a deductive phase of deriving the validity value to be expected in a future study. According to these authors, VG is not proof against violations of the model assumptions underlying the method. Another attempt to develop a Bayesian model of VG was made by Hedges (1988).

Rosenthal & Rubin (1986) and Raudenbush, Becker, & Kalaian (1988) proposed solutions for the multivariate case. Rosenthal and Rubin presented a method for obtaining a single summary effect size estimate from multiple effect sizes. Raudenbush, Becker, and Kalaian, building on this work, propose the use of a generalized least-squares regression approach for analyzing multiple effects.

Concluding Remarks

The comprehension of validity as a unitary concept seems to be stabilizing, and parts of the entire controversy may turn out as issues of semantics. Validation, then, can be understood as a set of principles to investigate the heuristic value of a diagnostic strategy. As a type of measurement-based research, validation is formally identical with other types of scientific inquiry. Therefore, open-mindedness toward concepts developed outside our narrow field of personnel selection should be obligatory to improve our strategies.

What should not be a consequence of a more theory-oriented concept of validity is to depreciate 'simple' predictive validation studies. Meta-analysis has enabled us to base our knowledge on a more solid level and promises to contribute even to aptitude theory; but further insights, for example in respect of moderators, will depend on further empirical data. If these are not of flawless quality, meta-analytic conclusions cannot be better but instead may even lead to a false estimation of all methods of selection. So, within a validation research program, studies of criteria should always have a prominent place.

It should be kept in mind that most of the methodological issues reviewed in this chapter are in some sense measures to control threats to validity. For a comprehensive validation strategy, it would be worthwhile thinking of systematic ways of tracking errors in prediction—this seems not to have been done up to now. Even what we must regard as a very satisfying validity coefficient is characterized by more unexplained than explained variance. Pursuing the cases in which our predictions fail may lead to insights not included in our meta-analytic type of epistemology and thus improve later models and predictions.

UTILITY ANALYSIS

The usefulness of utility concepts within the frame of personnel psychology may be seen in the unique opportunity of bridging over the communicative gap between psychologists and managers in the case of impending decisions on future personnel practices such as recruitement, selection, training, turnover, etc.

Managers are used to evaluating companies' actions in terms of money, psychologists tend to illustrate the effectiveness of psychological instruments/actions in terms of validity. Thus if the two groups want or need to exchange information for the purpose of decision making, a 'common language' will be required. Utility concepts may be considered as such a language because they contain both unitless psychological quantities like validity coefficients or mean standardized test scores and economic factors such as SD_Y (standard deviation of job performance in dollars) converting psychological quantities in the 'metric of money'. However, it is still a fact that psychologists have been quite adamant on their genuine classical terms of evaluation such as validity.

Determining utility of selection methods and other personnel practices through the use of decision theoretic equations was derived more than 30 years ago by both Brogden (1949) and Cronbach & Gleser (1965). Although these devices of utility have existed for a long time, their broad application in personnel psychology has not happened due to the 'Archilles heel of utility' (Cronbach & Gleser, 1965, p. 121)—the SD_Y and the previous belief that this crucial parameter could only be estimated by complex and expert cost-accounting procedures (e.g. Roche, 1965). Nevertheless, interest in utility calculations of personnel practices has recently been renewed, mainly caused by new procedures of estimating the SD_Y parameter, shifting from cost-accounting to behaviorally based rating data. Schmidt et al. (1979) proposed a Global Estimation Model (GEM) using supervisory estimations of 'the value of the products and services produced' (p. 621). In addition, based on empirical findings (Hunter & Schmidt, 1982) that labor costs represent roughly half the cost of output and that the true value of SD_Y of work output falls somewhere in the range 40–70% of average annual salary, the 40% of mean salary was suggested as a conservative and suitable alternative for a SD_Y estimation. Finally, Cascio (1982) and Cascio & Ramos (1986) presented their CREPID Cascio–Ramos estimate of performance in dollars method combining a preceding job analysis with individual performance ratings of workers as two major steps for determining utility. Referring to these SD_Y estimation procedures several methodological aspects are in question, such as the convergence of the estimates or the interrater agreement. In addition, a better understanding of the estimation process itself conducted by the supervisors seems to be essential; furthermore, it is still a matter of discussion whether these utility concepts fulfil the task of being a 'common language' because Boudreau (1983a, b) and his associates (Boudreau & Berger, 1985) advocated an enrichment of the common concepts through capital-budgeting methods.

In the following section we will concentrate on the above-mentioned methodological issues and ignore specific applications of utility equations, although their use was recently extended from the original domain selection (cf. Barthel & Schuler, 1989; Cascio & Ramos, 1986; Schmidt et al., 1988) to other types of human resources management decisions such as turnover/layoff management (Boudreau, 1983b; Boudreau & Berger, 1985) training (Mathieu & Leonard, 1987), and performance feedback (Florin-Thuma & Boudreau, 1987).

SD_Y Estimation Procedures

The behaviorally based approaches of estimating SD_Y are real benchmarks in the history of utility analysis. However, some crucial points are still included, thus determining the needs of further research which should clarify the suitability of assumptions and provide constructive suggestions to decrease the procedural deficiencies of the SD_Y estimation processes. First, we will review recently discussed aspects of each of the two major behaviorally based SD_Y estimations, and secondly examine their convergence in general and with the 40–70% rule in particular. Due to the fact that the Schmidt et al. (1979) Global Estimation Method (GEM) was the first proposal, the bulk of research has focused on this.

Global estimation method (GEM) (Schmidt et al., 1979)

Besides the lack of any theoretical justification for the suggested estimation procedure of the financial value of performance (Raju, Burke, & Normand, 1990) it seems to be the distribution underlying the raters' estimates and the interrater variability which are the major problems of the GEM.

Concerning the distribution problem, Bobko, Karren, & Parkington (1983) found that the supervisor's estimates of SD_Y adequately reflected actual SD_Y of normally distributed sales revenue for sales counsellors, although the percentile estimates were quite different (e.g. rating more extreme percentiles), raters compressed the range between the 85th and 97th percentiles, resulting in an underestimation of SD_Y. Thus, these ratings threw at least some doubt upon the presumption that raters used a normally distributed variable as a cognitive basis for their rating process, even though the objective indicator of job performance, as in the Bobko, Karren, and Parkington study, was normally distributed.

The empirical results demonstrated no significant differences between the upper and lower SD_Y (Bobko, Karren, & Parkington, 1983; Burke & Frederick, 1984; Edwards, Frederick, & Burke, 1988; Greer & Cascio, 1987; Reilly & Smither, 1985). From a logical point of view, it should be noted that equivalence of the dollar value difference between the 85th and 50th percentiles and between the 50th and 15th percentiles is generally not an unequivocal indicator of a normal distribution as the raters' cognitive basis of the rating process because any symmetric distribution (e.g. rectangular) might also provide this equivalence.

Moreover, subjects often found the global estimation task difficult, refused to do it, or produced high interrater variability (e.g. Bobko, Karren, & Parkington, 1983, Mathieu & Leonard, 1987; Reilly & Smither, 1985; Rich & Boudreau, 1987). The severe weakness of interrater variability might be due to the fact that raters used different scales in making estimates. Herefore, Bobko, Karren, & Parkington (1983) found a significant correlation ($r = 0.70$) between the value of the 50th percentile (= raters' individual anchor) and the estimates of SD_Y; Wroten (1984) reported similar findings with a mean correlation of $r = 0.46$. These results made obvious the contradiction with the theoretical normality assumption of no covariance between estimates of mean score and standard deviation (Bobko, Karren, & Parkington, 1983).

Reilly & Smither (1985) stated that the interrater variability increased with an increase of informative cues relevant for the convertion of job performance to dollar value. In addition, they attributed interrater variance partly to at least two different interpretations of overall worth, because GEM requires raters to estimate the value of overall products and services, and in order to facilitate this estimation of dollar value raters should consider the cost of hiring an outside firm to provide these services. Boudreau (1983a), however, has pointed out correctly that the value of products and services need not be equal to the cost of obtaining them from an outside firm.

A substantial reduction of interrater variability was achieved by Burke & Frederick (1984, 1986) and Edwards, Frederick, & Burke (1988), modifying the original procedure in the following way to establish an equivalent anchor for all raters on the dollar value performance scale: First, the supervisors estimated the 50th percentile, the average 50th percentile estimate of all raters was then fed back to each rater individually. Second, the estimation of remaining percentiles was conducted by every rater. Furthermore, besides varying feedback modes Burke & Frederick (1984, 1986) used an additional percentile (97th) for the SD_Y estimation.

As a conclusion to the reviewed studies the following is advisable for GEM applications:

— To train raters on the assumptions, computations, and interpretations of percentiles to eliminate possible unwanted interrater variability;
— To provide an anchor for the scale by an individual feedback procedure of the average 50th percentile to reduce interrater variability;
— To eliminate any ambiguity in interpretations of the questionnaire;
— To take more than the usual three percentiles into account in order to check whether the essential assumption of a normal distribution of job performance being really in the mind of any rater is not violated.

The 40–70% rule (Hunter & Schmidt, 1982)

Due to the summarized difficulties in applying the GEM, an easily applicable SD_Y estimation has been proposed. As mentioned above, the 40–70% rule is only a rule of thumb based on the empirically found relation between mean salary and mean work output, and the fact that the SD_Y of dollar-criterion performance can be estimated as being between 40 and 70% of annual salary (Hunter & Schmidt, 1982; Schmidt & Hunter, 1983). Being cautious, with the lowest possible value being inserted in the utility calculations, 40% of the mean salary provides a likely estimate of SD_Y.

Cascio–Ramos estimate of performance in dollars (CREPID)
(Cascio, 1982; Cascio & Ramos, 1986)

Compared with the Schmidt *et al.* proposals of global SD_Y estimation, the CREPID estimates SD_Y from a detailed analytical procedure. This includes a job analysis, a separate rating and weighting of the identified major job activities, and finally the measurement of the job holders' performance which provides the distribution of overall job performance from which SD_Y can be deduced.

Edwards, Frederick, & Burke (1988) pointed out that CREPID is a rather time-consuming costly procedure. Thus, the 'utility of CREPID' could be increased substantially by using archival job performance data of employees. Edwards, Frederick, & Burke. (1988) demonstrated empirically the adequacy of this kind of data for CREPID procedures. Concerning the accuracy of CREPID ratings, Reilly & Smither (1985) reported an interrater reliability of $r = 0.87$, and Greer & Cascio (1987) one of $r = 0.70$. In addition to this objective measurement of accuracy, the subjectively perceived accuracy of CREPID is also high, because managers evaluated their own ratings in the CREPID procedure as more accurate compared with their estimations using the GEM (Edwards, Frederick, & Burke, 1988).

From direct comparison of the two procedures the following results were reported:

1. The CREPID procedure produced smaller estimations compared with the GEM (Edwards, Frederick, & Burke, 1988; Greer & Cascio, 1987; Reilly & Smither, 1985; Weekley *et al.*, 1985). Moreover, Greer & Cascio (1987) investigated the GEM and CREPID estimation of SD_Y using an estimation based on a cost-accounting approach as a standard for comparing the behaviourally based methods. Because of substantial differences only between the CREPID estimation and the cost-accounting-based SD_Y, they concluded 'the results provide strong support for the accuracy of the Global Estimation Model, whereas the CREPID approach appears to underestimate SD_Y' (p. 592). Note that in this comparative

study the cost-accounting-based procedure was regarded as a measure of 'truth'—this need not be the case, hence, the previous interpretation should be looked at cautiously. Finally, Greer and Cascio (1987) demonstrated that the CREPID method produced a much tighter range of values compared with the GEM, had the highest degree of face validity, and that the CREPID model produced a mean value of worth that was 98% (only 56% by the GEM) of that produced by the cost-accounting-based approach.

2. A conclusive assessment of a possible convergence of CREPID and/or GEM SD_Y estimates with the 40–70% rule is impossible—some studies have demonstrated convergence, others have not (see Table 2).

3. From a theoretical point of view, the three considered methods differ in their valuation context (Edwards, Frederick, & Burke, 1988; Raju, Burke, & Normand, 1990; Steffy & Maurer, 1988). CREPID and the 40–70% rule have the same valuation base—salary. Salary, a service cost, is what economists and accountants refer to as an *ex post* valuation (i.e. an asset or entity's current value to the organization or the owner), whereas the GEM is based on an *ex ante* valuation (i.e. an asset of an investment's contribution to the expected gross proceeds or the net present value resulting from its use by the organization). As Steffy and Maurer pointed out, we should not necessarily expect convergent results from procedures based on different valuation contexts.

Raters' Processes Implied in the Estimation of SD_Y

The reviewed facets of SD_Y estimation make it obvious that the applied procedures like GEM and CREPID are based on judgements of supervisors.

Table 2—Overview of Studies Investigating the Convergence of SD_Y Estimates from CREPID and/or GEM with the 40–70% Rule

Studies/Method	CREPID	GEM
Bobko (1983)	+	n.u.
Burke & Frederick (1984)	−	n.u.
Burke & Frederick (1984)	−	n.u.
Cascio & Ramos (1986)	n.u.	+
Edwards, Frederick, & Burke (1988)	−	−
Greer & Cascio (1987)	+	+
Hunter & Schmidt (1982)	+	n.u.
Reilly & Smither (1985)	−	−
Rich & Boudreau (1987)	+	n.u.
Weekley *et al.* (1985)	+	+

Note: + = values did not differ significantly from values of the 40–70% rule; − = values did differ significantly from values of the 40–70% rule; n.u. = method not used in the study.

As such, even the most sophisticated models for overcoming likely economic limitations (see following subsection) need scrutiny at their source. Thus, as Bobko, Karren, & Kerkhar (1987) demanded, 'a better understanding of the processes underlying human judgements of overall worth' (p. 91) must be approached. Bobko, Karren, and Kerkhar proposed two complementary devices to unravel the dimensions from which SD_Y might be derived: process tracing (asking raters to report the factors considered) considered to be a more descriptive method and policy capturing being the quantitative complement which involves estimating the degree of determination of policies by relevant informative cues.

As previously discussed, the interpretation of instructions, the meaning of percentiles, and the shape of the distribution of the relevant variables are of great importance for the rating process. Moreover, both GEM and CREPID— whether intentionally or not—exclude SD_Y estimations which a rater may have in mind: negative values, especially at low performance percentiles. Burke & Federick (1984) and Weekley et al. (1985) have reported negative estimations of worth at the 15th percentile performance level. A revision of overall estimation procedures allowing negative estimates may reflect the internal scale of raters in a better way, furthermore, some 'true' zero point could be identified. In principle, employees below such a point cost an organization more than they are worth (Bobko, Karren, & Kerkhar, 1987).

Whether normative utility models reflect managerial decision processes adequately was recently investigated by Florin-Thuma & Boudreau (1987) and Orr, Sackett, & Mercer (1989). The latter used a policy-capturing approach to see whether supervisors considered both prescribed behaviors, such as 'create and run test' or 'use utilities' and so-called nonprescribed behaviors, e.g. 'team cooperation', 'company orientation', and 'contribution to morale', when making judgements about work performance of computer programmers. The supervisors attached dollar values to 50 profiles of hypothetical workers which consisted of 10 prescribed and the three mentioned nonprescribed behavioral dimensions. The results indicated the use of nonprescribed behavior for dollar judgements of work performance, these behaviors accounted for an additional 13% of variance. Applying utility analysis to a performance feedback intervention in a small retail organization Florin-Thuma & Boudreau (1987) provided 'the first empirical examination of the relationship between the normative prescriptions of the utility model and actual managerial decisions' (p. 695). Their results revealed differences in these two decision models. On the one hand, the managers estimated utility parameters such as cost of offered products or cost of the intervention inaccurately, and underestimated the dimension of the problem itself and the potential effectiveness of performance feedback. On the other hand, they considered several negative factors not present in the normative utility model such as customer dissatisfaction, employee dislike, or slower service. However, taking these supplementary negative factors into account, the utility model's basic finding of sufficient performance feedback payoffs was not altered.

Besides investigations of correspondence between managerial decision processes and normative utility models, Murphy (1986) emphasized the influence of applicants' decision processes like the acceptance or rejection of a job offered on the utility estimation. Usually the proportion of initial offers accepted is less than 100%. Under realistic circumstances (with the regression coefficient of $b_{yx} = -0.20$ for predicting ability (y) from probability of accepting a job offer (x)) currently used utility formulas could overestimate utility gains by 30–80%.

Improvements of Utility Estimations Through Capital-budgeting Methodology

Capital-budgeting techniques have been influencing utility models of human resource (HR) programs in two directions. First, in order to reflect the economic realities of organizations more adequately, complementing financial parameters were included in utility equations. Second, based on the argument that personnel programs should be regarded as investment options competing with other investments, the decisive power of utility equations was enhanced through methods evaluating risk and uncertainty of estimated utilities.

Boudreau (1983a, b), Boudreau & Berger (1985), and Cronshaw & Alexander (1985) demonstrated how currently applied utility formulas could easily be altered to account for three basic financial/economic concepts: variable costs, taxes and discounting.

1. Variable costs: sales or service values differ from service costs which differ from net benefits (service value minus service costs) produced by an HR intervention. Improving sales values might require additional support costs, these variable costs are also relevant for utility estimates.
2. Tax: most organizations pay taxes, thus net benefits and implementation costs of a HR program are influenced by tax rates.
3. Discounting: returns can often be invested to earn interest; thus the interest rate earned on program returns over several time periods should be incorporated into selection utility.

Noncapital-budgeting methods with payoff functions considering only the value of output as sold will probably overestimate the utility of HR programs.

Furthermore, the proposers of investment models acknowledged that organizations seldom invest in a selection program to use it once only. Therefore an 'employee flow' model (Boudreau, 1983b) was suggested to account for temporal changes of utility variables due to the fact that consecutively better-selected cohorts of employees determine net benefit differently compared with the product 'single cohort effect $\times$ number of applications of the program'.

Uncertainty and risk are the two most relevant parameters when managers have to decide. Consequently, if utility estimations were planned as a decision aid, it would be necessary to illustrate whether or not the implementation of an HR program might be a risky decision due to the (un-)certainty of predicted payoffs. Concerning the variability in utility estimations, the work of Alexander & Barrick (1986) is orientated toward the parameter with the likely largest measurement error, SD_Y, providing an estimation formula for standard error of projected dollar gains in utility analysis.

In addition, several utility applications have addressed possible variability in utility through sensitivity analysis (e.g. Barthel & Schuler, 1989; Boudreau, 1983a, Boudreau & Berger, 1985; Cronshaw et al., 1987; Florin-Thuma & Boudreau, 1987; Rich & Boudreau, 1987; Schmidt, Mack, & Hunter, 1984). In sensitivity analysis each of the utility parameters is varied from its lowest to its highest value, holding other values constant. The utility estimates resulting from each combination of parameter values are examined to determine the relative influence of parameters by deciding which parameters' variability has the greatest effect on utility estimates. Even more connected with the studies of the advocates of capital-budgeting approach, two further methods for estimating uncertainty were conducted, given under the headings below:

(1) Break-even analysis

Such an analysis is carried out by calculating the lowest value of any individual utility parameter (or parameter combination) that would still yield a positive total utility value. These parameters were labelled 'break-even' values due to the fact that they equal the HR program's benefits with costs. For the most frequently investigated utility parameter SD_Y, Boudreau (1989) summarized empirical findings applying break-even analysis: 'Without exception, the break-even SD_Y values fell below 60% of the estimated SD_Y values' (p. 249). (See also: Cascio & Ramos, 1986; Cronshaw et al., 1987; Florin-Thuma & Boudreau, 1987; Rich & Boudreau, 1987).

(2) Monte Carlo analysis of utility value variability

Monte Carlo analysis requires empirically based or at least assumed distributions for any utility parameter; in each trial, a value for each utility parameter is 'chosen' randomly from the distributions. Unlike the three other methods mentioned, a Monte Carlo simulation can vary many parameters at once, and thus, can reflect interdependencies. Rich & Boudreau (1987), by using this approach, discovered that SD_Y heavily influenced the utility value distribution. Consistent with other studies (Bobko, Karren, & Parkington, 1983; Burke &

Frederick, 1984; Schmidt, Mack, & Hunter, 1984), the SD_Y values were positively skewed. Moreover, their analysis supported the need of further research into the estimation process itself: First, they calculated SD_Y variability of the raters' estimates under the assumption of pure measurement error; second, they assumed that SD_Y variability might reflect not only measurement error but also true situational differences observed by different estimators. Their results clearly indicated the dependence of utility value distribution on the different theoretical assumptions concerning SD_Y estimates.

Although recent criticism (Hunter, Schmidt, & Coggin, 1988) reminded us of specific circumstances (e.g. absence of investment) limiting the possible application of capital-budgeting techniques, this approach undoubtedly enriched and improved further approaches to the utility of HR programs. As such, due to the increasing complexity of these estimation models, it remains questionable whether this approach will be successful in creating a 'common language' for psychologists and managers.

A New Approach to Utility

Based on a clarifying presentation of implicit assumptions of current models, a new utility analysis approach was presented by Raju, Burke, & Normand (1990). Current utility analysis equations make the following two major assumptions:

1. The relationship between the dollar value of an employee's performance (Y) and the predictor score (X) is linear.
2. The correlation between an employee's observed job performance R (usually a supervisory rating) and X is equal to the correlation between X and Y (i.e. $\rho_{XR} = \rho_{XY}$).

The tenability of the second assumption in particular is questionable. In practice, due to measurement error, the sufficient condition of $\rho_{RY} = 1$ for that assumption is extremely unlikely.

Thus Raju, Burke, & Normand (1990) differentiated between the levels of observed and latent variables and proposed a linear relationship between *true* job performance R_t and *true* dollar value of an employee's job performance (Y_t) and equality of $\rho_{XR_t} = \rho_{XY_t}$ with the index t indicating true score. The following regression equation illustrates the new utility approach:

$$Y_t = AR_t + B \tag{1}$$

where

Y_t = true score of dollar value of employee's job performance,

R_t = true score of job performance rating,
A = slope of the function,
B = scaling constant.

Conceptually, an employee's true worth to an organization is the same whether it is measured in financial terms or with a rating scale. In addition, R_t can easily be estimated from the test score X and its reliability.

What is new about this approach?

The parameter A and the normally used SD_Y have the same function in utility equations, namely to translate the product of the validity coefficient and mean standard predictor score into the appropriate dollar value—thus, this seems to be no innovation at all.

More innovative are the following aspects:

1. The proposed model links performance ratings and dollar value of job performance explicitly and directly. By doing this the 'conjoint measurement' of dollar value of job performance including (a) the dimensions of job performance, (b) the different values of job (components) to an organization, and (c) their interdependencies was broken up into its component parts and a plausible regression model combining these components is offered.
2. By showing that CREPID and 40–70% are just special cases obtaining $A \times SD_R$, the new utility approach can be regarded as the more general model.
3. The parameter A is unitless, hence the unit can easily be changed depending on the type of organization, type of job performance rating, etc.
4. A theoretically valuable distinction between observed and latent variables was made.

Concluding Remarks

As concluding remarks, two principal points may be stated. First, although the behaviorally based estimation procedures of SD_Y certainly facilitate the application of utility analysis, and capital-budgeting methodology enriched it substantially, the calculation of the utility of actions within HR management is far from being a routinely applied procedure. Consequently the strengths and advantages of utility analysis should be made evident to responsible people in HR management. To make it even worse, the increasing sophistication of utility analysis and the intermethod variance of SD_Y estimates may counteract the goal of bridging over the communicative gap between psychologists and managers in the area of business administration. Therefore, more investigations of the (lack of) convergence of SD_Y estimates from different methods is essential to determine the validity of SD_Y estimates.

Second, the weak point of all suggested SD_Y estimation procedures is still the completely unknown cognitive process of the raters when estimating SD_Y. Thus, further research should be strongly based upon results and methodology from research areas like information-integration and prediction under uncertainty.

DECISION MODELS

Besides the prerequisite of a preceding job or task analysis, any personnel selection procedure roughly consists of three sequential steps: first, based on the job analysis, applicants' psychological features are described; second, these features are evaluated, weighted, and integrated, frequently with strong reference to the prediction of chosen job criteria; and finally a classification/placement or selection decision for each applicant is made. Whereas the measurement and description of psychological features might be regarded as a genuine task of psychodiagnostics, the second and third steps are constituents of decision models.

Within the frame of 'decision models' mainly two types of models are usually differentiated:

1. *Individual heuristic model of the decision maker.* This model of individual heuristics used by decision makers contains individual implicit rules of information integration, evaluation, weighting, and, finally, decision making. Usually these processes are labelled 'clinical judgement'.
2. *Statistical decision model.* This kind of model consists of normative, explicit rules of assignment of an applicant to a job (or task, training, etc.). Based on previous applicant data these rules are empirically evaluated by maximizing true assignments and minimizing false assignments. A supplement to this optimizing might be utility models considering utility gains due to different decisions (see previous section).

The focus of recent publications is unequivocally on the individual model. Concerning statistical models a real innovation can be seen in score band procedures for selection (Cascio, Alexander, & Barrett, 1988), which lay down passing grades with score bands of a predictor (usually defined by the standard error of measurement) and selecting individuals in the highest scoring band at random. In the case of more openings than the number of candidates in the highest band, all candidates in the highest score band are accepted and for the still available openings all candidates in the second band are considered and randomly selected.

In addition, as statistical decision models, elaborated concepts for uni- and multivariate data using cut-off models, linear and nonlinear regressions, profile analysis, classification methods like discriminant analysis or nonparametric configural methods have existed for quite a long time (for comprehensive overviews see Cascio, 1987; Dunnette & Borman, 1979). However, probably due to the requirements of the application of these methods—large data sets, computer programs, and at least the users' sufficient understanding of the sophisticated mathematical/statistical background—these methods are seldom used (cf. Zedeck & Cascio, 1984).

In our overview we will concentrate on attempts elaborating on the individual model of decision makers such as policy-capturing methods, comparisons of decisions from experts and novices, approaches making individual implicit heuristics explicit by transforming rules of decision makers into computer programs, and erroneous heuristics in decision tasks.

Policy Capturing Approaches

Since 1971, the year of the fundamental publication of Slovic and Lichtenstein, policy capturing is a common method for investigating the integration and relative weighting of single items of information into a judgment or a decision.

The commonly applied basic model to estimate the amount of variance in decisions 'captured' by decision makers' 'individual policy' of using informational cues is linear regression. The crucial theoretical point is the assumed linear regression model itself, which may—but certainly need not—reflect the true cognitive individual model of decision makers. With policy capturing both inter-individual differences in the degree of prediction of decisions and intra-individual consistency concerning the relative weight of the information used for a decision can be estimated.

Recently published work applying policy-capturing methodology in personnel selection decisions:

1. Confirmed again the superiority of statistical models in predicting job performance (Dougherty, Ebert, & Callender, 1986);
2. Showed again that, although relevant job information about applicants still had the largest direct influence on personnel decisions, irrelevant job information such as sex, race, etc. also influenced managerial decisions (Barr & Hitt, 1986; Huber, Neale, & Northcraft, 1987a). This was even the case where managers were directed towards specific relevant job information with job descriptions (Hitt & Barr, 1989). In contrast to this, Tosi & Einbender (1985) concluded from their results that providing decision makers with more data of the job itself and relevant job characteristics of an applicant would reduce the exhibited bias;
3. Demonstrated an increase in consistency of informational cues used by decision makers when they were provided with estimates based on mechanical/statistical models of their own prior decisions (Peterson & Pitz, 1986).

Hypotheses agglutination (HYPAG): A Method for Configuration-based Analysis of Multivariate data

In heuristics the common statistical procedures, for example regression or variance analyses, often seem to be unsatisfactory because the formal structure of these model does not fit typical descriptions of dependencies among facts in human language such as 'if A . . . , then B . . . ' . In addition, models based on configurations, i.e. combinations of specific values in the concerning variables, match the logical structure of hypotheses in human language substantially better. Wottawa (1987) specified 'the stating of a configuration is formally equivalent to the combination of the values in the applied variables by "and", the agglutination of various configurations corresponds to the use of "or"' (p. 69).

Wottawa (1987) developed a new configuration-based method called 'hypotheses agglutination' (HYPAG), which he applied to personnel selection and classification, marketing research, and an analysis of well-being of shift-workers. Within HYPAG the individual process model of a decision maker is (re-)constructed, therefore individual, implicit hypotheses are transformed into explicit ones by using decision-makers' individual explanations and objective observations of their decision behavior. These explicit models are testable by parameter estimations like the hit rate of the formulated configural decision model of past/actual decisions. From a methodological point of view, HYPAG has two considerable advantages:

1. In contrast to policy-capturing approaches no a priori assumption of an underlying information-integration model is made. Whereas in policy-capturing linear regression functions as an implicit information-integration model, HYPAG reconstructs and tests the individual model of a decision maker.
2. Compared with other configurational techniques, HYPAG neither requires an underlying latent model as in latent class analyses nor are all considered variables used in order to define a configurational type as in configuration frequency analysis (e.g. Goodman, 1978; Krauth & Lienert, 1973).

A major deficiency of HYPAG can be seen in the lack of an adequate error model, making it difficult to identify the one 'best' model because usually several models have acceptable hit rates of 90–95% and the intermodel differences are often minimal (Wottawa, 1987).

Expert–Novice Comparison

A third approach to uncover decision makers' models is the comparison of strategies used by experienced (e.g. personnel managers), and inexperienced persons (e.g. students), making decisions in the same decision task (for an overview see Chi, Glaser, & Rees, 1982).

The major results of recent studies (Barr & Hitt, 1986; Hitt & Barr, 1989) are summarized as follows:

1. The effect size of the factor 'managers vs students' was rather small (10% of explained variance) in selection decision tasks.
2. Both groups used irrelevant job informational cues for their decisions. Additionally, no substantial difference in the degree of using these irrelevant cues was found between the groups.
3. Both groups used a complex information-integration model demonstrated by significant higher-order interactions of informative cues in both groups.
4. Students had the tendency to use more variables than managers for their decisions.
5. Students rated applicants higher than did experienced managers.

Heuristics in Biased Decisions

Huber, Neale, & Northcraft (1987b) demonstrated the influence of both framing and the salience of selection-related costs on decisions. Framing was manipulated by inducing a 'rejecting' (identifying those applicants who should not be invited to an interview) or an 'accepting' (identifying those applicants who should be invited to an interview) selection strategy, cost salience was manipulated by making selection-related costs either implicit or explicit. The results showed that the mean acceptance threshold for applicant selection—operationalized as the lowest 'probability of success'—was higher for decision makers under the condition of the 'accepting' strategy. Furthermore, decision makers with a rejection strategy accepted more candidates for an interview than decision makers with the acceptance strategy. Invitation rates differed only, however, when selection-related costs were salient. Finally, salient selection-related costs raised the acceptance of the threshold of success probability, increased decision-processing time, and reduced the invitation rate of candidates for an interview.

In contradiction to Binning et al. (1988), Peek Phillips & Dipboye (1989) demonstrated an erroneous influence of pre-interview impressions on heuristics in selection interviews, causing an evaluation of applicants' interview performance which maintained initial impressions through a kind of self-fulfilling consistency heuristic.

Using an interactive computer paradigm Keinan (1987) investigated effects of raters' stress on heuristics. She demonstrated that stressed raters showed a significantly stronger tendency to offer solutions before all available alternatives had been considered (premature closure) and to scan information within the decision process nonsystematically. Furthermore, Srinivas & Motowidlo (1987) showed that raters' stress caused more inaccurate ratings.

Finally, as a prerequisite for any heuristic of selection choices, the decision makers' ability to differentiate personality types associated with occupational groups was investigated. The findings were inconclusive: Paunonen, Jackson, & Oberman (1987) and Paunonen & Jackson (1987) presented results showing that decision makers had reliable, accurate, and different conceptions about personality characteristics of different jobs and prototypical job incumbents. In case of multifaceted job activities, more salient job components were overweighted at the expense of others. Contradictory to these results, Anderson & Shackleton (1990) found no significant differences in their field study comparing personality profiles of accepted candidates across 14 job functions.

Concluding Remarks

With regard to work recently published, it is unquestionable that the focus was on individual and not on statistical decision models. According to individual models, traditional methodology such as policy-capturing and expert–novice comparison are predominantly used. However, the usually assumed a priori models of information-integration (e.g. linear regression) limit the results of these normative investigations to a description of empirical data under an assumed a priori model; moreover, it is impossible to investigate *individual cognitive processes* in decision making using an *a priori model* of information integration *normatively*. Thus, nonnormative models (like HYPAG) reflecting intra- and interindividual different decision models seem to be methodologically more progressive. Work on heuristics could have supported these progressive approaches, but the lack of a theoretical framework led to the problem of heuristics being likely to be valid only for the very often artificial situations in which they occurred.

PSYCHOMETRIC CONSIDERATIONS

Out of the manifold interactions of psychometrics and personnel selection, we would like to exemplify two directions of mutual influence.

First, new psychometric theories like Item Response Theories (IRT) which may change test applications in personnel selection, and second, new psychometric considerations concerning current problems resulting from applying instruments of psychological measurement, for example the fairness of tests.

Concerning test fairness, we would like to focus on a more psychometric perspective, therefore, a very brief preceding introduction into IRT is essential.

Besides being a prerequisite of our approach to fairness, IRT contains further noteworthy methodological improvements for test application.

Finally, besides 'the thrill of the latest methodological issues' there is still some routine work to be done, and accordingly we refer to recently published papers giving useful advice and results. Furthermore, as a kind of psychometric outlook, we would like to discuss the nonequivalence of qualities of measured behavior such as typical and maximum influencing the predictor–criterion relationship.

Item Response Theory (IRT)

The relevance of IRT for personnel selection is obvious although applications of this theory in day-to-day activities of an I/O psychologist are exceptions. A prerequisite for any selection decision is the diagnosis of applicants. Diagnosis is based on data concerning psychological constructs. For measuring psychological constructs a measurement model is inevitably required—IRT provides measurement models on psychological processes underlying a person's response to a question (an item).

Basic implications of IRT measurement models are summarized below, for detailed introductions to the mathematically quite sophisticated IRT we recommend both classical texts such as Rasch (1960), Birnbaum (1968), and Fischer (1974) or new introductory presentations (Hulin, Drasgow, & Parsons, 1983; Hambleton and Swaminathan, 1985):

1. An observed behavior (=response) in a test is an indicator of a latent trait. The relationship between the unidimensional latent trait and the observable response is a probabilistic one. In other words, IRT models the relation between an individual's standing on a latent characteristic and the item responses.

2. The probability of a response is determined only by person and item parameters. This is formally illustrated in equation (2):

$$P(A_i) = f_i(pe_v, it_i) \tag{2}$$

where

$$P(A_i) = \text{probability of response } A \text{ to item } i,$$
$$f_i = \text{function of } pe_v \text{ and } it_i \text{ to calculate } P(A_i),$$
$$pe_v = \text{standing on the latent psychological characteristic}$$
$$\text{of the individual } v,$$
$$it_i = \text{item characteristic(s) of item } i.$$

Dependent on the model, there is more than one item characteristic proposed, for example, in the Rasch model only the item difficulty is a constituent, whereas Birnbaum (1968) added another item parameter to his model—the discrimination power of an item.

The function f_i, called the item-characteristic curve (ICC), is monotonic, but not necessarily linear. Frequently an S-shaped curve such as the cumulative ogive describes the probabilities of an item response and the score on the latent trait. Thus, regarding a single item response, differences in the probability of a response to the item depend only on different standings on the dimension of the latent trait.

3. 'Item and person parameter estimates are invariant in the sense that neither the choice of examinee samples from the examinee population of interest nor the choice of test items from the item population will affect the item and ability parameter' (Hambleton, 1986, p. 416).

Whether measurement models derived from IRT are superior to models based on classical test theory (CTT) depends on the measurement purpose, therefore a final answer is neither possible nor desirable (van der Linden, 1986). However, for actual practice in personnel psychology, IRT applications offer a respectable amount of potential improvement (Thissen & Steinberg, 1988). As discussed later in detail, IRT models provide analytic tools for questions of fairness (see page 247), they also facilitate substantially procedures of test construction or testing such as adaptive testing, rule-based item construction, and item banking.

Moreover, they would help to overcome typical obstacles of CTT-based tests such as

— The dependence of examinees' scores on the sample of administered items and on the sample of tested examinees, which makes different item analyses and (re-)normations of raw scores necessary;
— Interpretive deficiencies when the conditions of standardization (e.g. application of the same test several times to the same testees) are violated;
— The diagnostic insufficiency of test scores not being an exhaustive statistic;
— The fact that reliability of CTT tests might decrease for extreme (low/high) score levels, whereas IRT models may provide exactly the same reliability for any level of the latent trait.

In practice, the application of IRT is limited to ability or aptitude tests, and, besides the above-mentioned favorable opportunities, requires several essential features such as sophisticated computer programs, unidimensional constructs, and unequivocal indicators of an item response model fit to data which seriously restrict its broad application. However, for practical diagnostic problems in personnel selection, IRT may function as a powerful analytical tool. For example, concerning the practical problem of detecting inappropriateness of examinees' scores, Drasgow, Levine, & McLaughlin (1987) suggested several IRT-based indices even when the test has satisfactory measurement properties. For example, faking good, lucky guessing, or copying answers from a more talented neighbour may result in spuriously high scores because although easy items were not answered, more difficult items were answered in the indicative direction. Response sets, language difficulties, or registration errors on the answer sheet may result in spuriously low scores. The most important finding of this study was that some indices provide nearly optimal detection rates for inappropriate scores when spuriously high scores were connected with low latent trait scores and vice versa, whereas identifying inappropriate scores from examinees where abilities were near average was insufficient.

The detection of inappropriate scores is a matter of substantial interest for personnel selection because employing false high scorers may considerably reduce the utility of tests, therefore Drasgow & Guertler (1987) suggested a decision-theoretic utility model.

Test Fairness—the Problem of True or False Subgroup Differences

In personnel selection, test fairness is still an important topic. Because of restricted space we can only recommend the works of Gottfredson (1988), Schmidt (1988), Schmitt (1989b), Schmitt & Noe, 1986), and Seymour (1988) as comprehensive overviews.

In addition, the problem of fairness is multifarious. Societal, social, ethical, and legal aspects as well as policies (Allen, 1988; Bolick, 1988; Delahunty, 1988; Goldstein & Patterson, 1988; Gottfredson, 1988; Seymour, 1988; Sharf, 1988) and, finally, the subjective facet of fairness, say applicants' perception of fairness (Bies, 1987; Bies & Moag, 1986; Cropanzano & Folger, 1989; Folger & Konovsky, 1989; Greenberg, 1986) were also discussed intensively. However, we would like to concentrate on fairness from a psychometric viewpoint.

Recent empirical studies concentrated on the following aspects:

1. Race effects on performance measures (Ford, Kraiger, & Schechtman, 1986; Kraiger & Ford, 1985; Pulakos *et al.*, 1989);
2. Age effects on performance measures (Cleveland, Festa, & Montgomery, 1988; Waldman & Avolio, 1986);
3. Sex effects on selection decisions (Biggs & Beutell, 1986; Gilmore, Beehr, & Love, 1986; Graves & Powell, 1988; Olian, Schwab, & Haberfeld, 1988; for an overview see Powell, 1987);
4. Effects of sex-typed stereotypes for applicants and jobs on employment decisions (Glick, Zion, & Nelson, 1988; Heilman, Martell, & Simon, 1988).

A more psychometric approach to fairness

Results of fairness research indicate that sizable differences in mean performance on selection instruments and smaller differences on mean job performance measures exist between majority and minority groups. Regarding fairness as a genuine psychometric quality of psychological measurement and prediction, the cardinal question seems to be: *'Do true scores of individuals from different subgroups predict true scores of the same individuals from these different subgroups on a job performance measure for every subgroup equally exactly?'*

A thorough analysis of this cardinal question reveals several implications which are illustrated in Table 3. For investigating fairness of psychological instruments we suggest a distinction between three levels of bias relevant to fairness:

Level 1 is regarded as measurement bias for both predictor and criterion. A measurement instrument should be regarded as fair if and only if no interaction of the variable 'subgroup' and the measurement instrument (=item) within the process of measurement occurs. A rather inappropriate indicator of such an interaction is the proportion of correct answers between subgroups 'because the proportion-correct statistic confounds measurement bias with between-group differences in the attribute measured by the test' (Drasgow, 1987, p. 20; same: Humphreys, 1986a; Linn & Drasgow, 1987). Better evidence is provided by using concepts of item response theory.

In terms of this theory, measurement equivalence (= no bias) 'holds when individuals with equal standing on the trait measured by the test but sampled from different subpopulations have equal expected observed test scores' (Drasgow, 1987, p. 19).

Therefore, when item-characteristic curves, determined by slope and difficulty parameters, are not the same for a majority and a minority group an item is said to be biased (Drasgow, 1987; Humphreys, 1986a; Thissen & Steinberg, 1988; Thissen, Steinberg, & Gerrard, 1986). In the case of the same item-characteristic curves for both groups, differences in observed scores can be interpreted as true because of measurement equivalent differences. However, note finally that all items could be biased equally, such bias remains undetectable.

Table 3—Levels of Bias Relevant for the Evaluation of Fairness of Psychological Measures

	Predictor	*Criterion*
Level 1	Item	Item
Level 2	Test	Scale
Level 3	←————————————→	

Level 2 is considered as a cumulative measurement bias. Ordinarily, responses to several items are integrated as generally test scores—not item scores—are the basis of predictions. Because measurement bias on level 1 is a necessary but not a sufficient condition for a biased total score, the cumulative measurement bias should be analyzed in any case of measurement bias on level 1. Therefore, test-characteristic curve (TCC) values, which represent the expected overall score as a function of the latent trait, can be calculated and cumulative measurement bias can be identified by comparing the TCC of a set of unbiased items with the TCC of the complete item set. Only substantial differences support the hypothesis of a cumulative measurement bias, which is for practical reasons more relevant than the measurement bias. Due to the biased items in different directions, it might occur that the cumulative measurement bias is marginal because the divergent effects of biased items cancel each other out when summed up to a total score (Drasgow, 1987; Thissen, Steinberg, & Gerrard, 1986).

Level 3 is proposed to represent a relational bias because the relation between predictor and criterion, not necessarily the two variables themselves, is biased. A relational bias occurs when a bivariate measure of the association of a predictor and criterion is not identical across relevant subpopulations. The general approach to relational bias is called differential prediction.

A pure relational bias can only be detected if no evidence for bias on levels 1 and 2 was found; on the other hand, no relational bias may occur when criterion and predictor are massively but equally biased on levels 1 and/or 2.

As discussed above, it is obvious that levels of bias are not independent, thus we suggest, for more psychometrically orientated fairness research, a top-down strategy, starting on level 1 and finishing on level 3. Curiously enough, the history of fairness research reveals a down-top approach. In principle, the strategy should always be applied for predictor as well as for criterion, though prior research—especially on levels 1 and 2—on criteria is rather sparse.

Remarks Concerning Psychometric Day-to-day Problems: Temporal Stability, Reliability, Aggregation of Raw Scores

In addition to the broader topics 'fairness' and 'IRT', some recently published papers are quite noteworthy because they deal with aspects more relevant to the day-to-day work of I/O psychologists, for example the measurement of change which is closely related to the question of temporal stability of test scores, considerations of reliability and aggregation of raw or previously standardized scores to total scores.

Measurement of change

Gardner & Neufeld (1987) examined the simple difference score ($D = Y - X$) in three different correlational analyses. Again, they impressively confirmed the equivocal nature of the complex difference score D by showing that the calculated correlations are influenced by interdependent and compensating factors like the ratio of variance of Y and X, the correlations r_{DY} and r_{DX}, etc. Hence, when using D, the calculation of further statistics like the variance ratio of Y and X is essential if ambiguity of interpretation is to be reduced.

A methodologically innovative approach towards assessment of change was presented by Bryk & Raudenbush (1987) proposing a two-stage hierarchical linear model. At the first stage, a within-subject model expresses the status on a given trait as a function of individual growth curves. The second stage consists of a between-subject analysis, whereby varying individual growth parameters are investigated with respect to differences in background and experience of the testees. In addition, Yarnold (1988) derived methods based on classical test theory for evaluating change for $N = 1$.

Reliability

For the purpose of test construction and evaluation the work of Fleishman & Benson (1987) is to be recommended. They presented successively built-up linear structural relationship (LISREL) models as a complete research programme for measurement models (parallel method, tau-equivalent, congeneric with and without correlated error) and reliability, except internal consistency.

Cronbach (1988) compared new and old methods estimating internal consistency, Huynh (1986) derived a formula for the reliability of the maximum score when several test scores are obtained for a given examinee and the highest score is to be assigned as the only test score for that examinee. Huynh showed that the maximum score is more reliable than each of the single other scores, but less reliable than their composite score.

Concerning forced-choice scales, Tenopyr (1988) demonstrated that some artifactually high internal consistency reliability could be generated as a result of scale interdependence, thus encouraging false confidence of users in the psychometric properties of a scale/test. In addition, Johnson, Wood & Blinkhorn (1988) pointed out psychometric restrictions of ipsative personality tests in general. In particular they stated: 'reliabilities of ipsative tests overestimate, sometimes severely, the actual reliability of the scales: in fact, the whole idea of error is problematical' (p. 154).

Finally, for personnel selection purposes, the exploration of temporal stability of self-report personality inventories from Schuerger, Zarrella, & Hotz (1989) is certainly a matter of interest. Their major results based on 89 separate studies were as follows:

—Consistent with prior findings, the prime determinant of test–retest reliability is the length of the time interval between the two measurements: the longer the interval the smaller the reliability coefficient.

—Factors with only marginal effects on the reliability were the age of testees and the average number of items per scale. Subjects' gender and sample size were unrelated to reliability.

Aggregation of raw scores

In their discussion of the problem of aggregating raw scores Gardner & Erdle (1984, 1986) and Stevens & Aleamoni (1986) emphasized that an aggregate of raw scores implies differential weighting of the aggregated components, whereas an aggregation of prior standardized scores has equal weights for the components. Due to the fact that the implicit different weighting might be unintentional and perhaps inappropriate, aggregation of previously standardized raw scores is more recommendable, all the more so because differential weights of components, when appropriate, can easily be used when aggregating standardized scores.

A Psychometric Outlook: (Non)equivalence of Qualities of Measured Behaviour

Recently published works in the area of trainability and skill acquisition dealt indirectly with a further psychometric aspect influencing the predictor–criterion relation: the (non)equivalence of qualities of measured behavior/behavioral dispositions.

Apart from its psychodiagnostic label, such as extraversion or intelligence, any behavior can be classified as rare, most likely, individuals' upper/lower limit, automatic or consciously controlled, etc. These aspects represent qualities of measured behaviour such as frequency, extremity, and ability to control, far more qualities are certainly relevant. From a psychodiagnostic angle the qualities of measured behavior determine the kind of sensibly psychodiagnostic statements. Moreover, these qualities are not interchangeable (although they are probably correlated) when psychodiagnostic conclusions are drawn, for example a person acting very often (=typical) in a neurotic way does not necessarily show extreme (=maximum) neurotic behavior and vice versa. Note that the qualities of behavior are not limited to predictors but are also of relevance for criteria.

Although a refined and overall taxonomy does not exist, we would like to illustrate the influence of (non)equivalence of qualities of measured behavior on the predictor–criterion relation reviewing recent research on the qualities 'typical vs maximum' behaviour in the area of trainability and 'automatic versus consciously controlled' behavior in the area of skill acquisition.

For the measurement of trainability several suggestions have been made (Guthke, 1988, 1982; Robertson & Downs, 1989 Siegal, 1983):

1. Score of the posttest;
2. Difference between the scores of the post-and the pretest, considered as a measurement of the gain through learning;
3. Error score related to the number of errors made by the testee while learning to fulfill the task;
4. Rating by an expert observer (usually a trainer) for predicting the applicant's likely performance in training or target task.

Whether or not these measures are equal, is still inconclusive—reported correlations between (1) and (2) or (3) and (4) are always positive but show a great variation. From a theoretical point of view (1) and (2) measure the effect of learning, whereas (3) and (4) are an evaluation of the learning process itself.

In the field of organizational psychology, Robertson & Downs (1989) combined the concepts of work samples and trainability resulting in work-sample tests of trainability. Their recent meta-analysis revealed the following results: Trainability test scores (3) and (4) had been correlated with training success and job performance. While the mean validity coefficient for error scores ($\bar{r}$ = .48) and ratings ($\bar{r}$ = .41) as predictors for training performance are quite sufficient, though the variability was rather high, the predictive mean validity for error scores ($\bar{r}$ = .20) and rating ($\bar{r}$ = .24) for job performance was noticeably lower.

Reilly & Israelski (1988) found the same relation of validity coefficients for different criteria ($\bar{r}$ = .39 for job and $\bar{r}$ = .49 for training performance) when evaluating the criterion validity of the trainability test 'minicourse' (i.e. standardized training material representative of the content of a full-scale training/job presented in the learning period; predictor: combination of time-to-complete a training module and test performance).

The theoretically interesting explanation of the difference of mean validity coefficients due to kind of criterion (training or job performance) was offered by Robertson & Downs (1989): ' . . . trainability tests and training criteria may be more indicative of maximum performance, and job criteria more indicative of typical performance' (p. 406). Considering the aspect of typical vs maximum behavior, four combinations of predictor–criterion pairs can be derived (Table 4).

Especially with reference to Sackett, Zedeck, & Fogli's (1988) findings that measurements of typical and maximum job performance of newly employed and current supermarket cashiers correlated very low (range: $\bar{r}$ = .08 – $\bar{r}$ = 0.32), it seems rather likely that in case of the predictor–criterion combinations (2) and (3): validity coefficients are attenuated because of the qualitative noncorrespondence of measured performance.

The psychometric implication of these findings are quite obvious: if we presume that individuals' typical and maximum behaviors concerning a trait are different, validity research has to take the configuration of predictor scores

Table 4—Combinations of predictor–criterion with typical/maximum performance

		Criterion	
		Typical	*Maximum*
Predictor	*Typical*	1	2
	Maximum	3	4

of typical or maximum behavior into account in order to predict job performance, which consists of typical or maximum behavior too.

Concerning the quality 'ability to control', recent investigations (Ackerman, 1987, 1989; Henry & Hulin, 1987, 1989;. Schneider, Dumais, & Shiffrin, 1984) of skill acquisition demonstrated the influence of (non)equivalence of predictor and criterion on predictive validity.

Empirically, when longitudinal data of the ability–performance relations were collected, a frequent finding was the following pattern of correlations (called 'simplex structure'): the correlation coefficients between ability measures, assessed at time i, and performance, assessed successively at times $i + 1, \ldots, i + k$, decrease as a function of the number of intervening trials and the highest correlations occur between adjacent trials independent from the position towards i.

Though Hulin and Henry claimed the simplex structure as ubiquitous, Ackerman (1989) stated with reference to several studies that this is not the case. Moreover, he presented a new information-processing perspective on patterns of validity coefficients from longitudinal data. According to this view, two different information processes might be required for performance on a task:

Automatic processes

Their attributes are fast, effortless, not easily altered by a subject's conscious control and they allow operations with other information components within or between tasks. Typical skilled behaviors which imply automatic processes are driving a car, playing a piano etc. These processes may be developed only through extensive practice under consistent conditions. Consistency refers to the invariance of

— Rules of information processing;
— Components of processing;
— Sequencies of information-processing components used by a subject to master a task.

Controlled processes

Their attributes are slow, effortful, and amenable to quick alterations under a subject's conscious control. Controlled processes are developed when task requirements are novel or the task does not fit to the mentioned aspects of consistency.

Regarding ability tests as tasks requiring controlled processes and taking the aspect of (non)equivalence of measured behaviour into account, Ackerman's (1987) proposals of two different trends for the ability–performance relation over time can easily be assigned to the cases of predictor–criterion equivalence and nonequivalence respectively:

1. Nonequivalence: for tasks that allow for development of automatic processing over time, validity coefficients will decline when ability factors of general intelligence (= controlled processes) are included as predictors.
2. Equivalence: For tasks that require controlled processing, the validity coefficients of broad intellectual abilities remain stable or even increase over time.

Reanalysing several older studies with different sets of data—measurements of changes in variability with practice, within-task performance intercorrelations, and task performance over time intercorrelated with reference tests—Ackerman confirmed his predictions.

Concluding Remarks

Our aim in this section was to demonstrate the usefulness of psychometric theories for considerations of typical problems of applications of psychological instruments. Discussing test fairness, we exemplified this by demonstrating the utility of IRT as an analytic tool. We hope that our proposal of three different interdependent levels of test fairness can contribute to a clarification of the discussion of test fairness; moreover, if research proceeded from level 1 to level 3, true differences of subgroups in predictors and criteria will be identified and can be labelled as such. Apart from the problem of test fairness, the favorable opportunities of IRT are not sufficiently taken into consideration: IRT may serve as a basis for new testing concepts such as adaptive testing, for new considerations of traditional research concepts like content validity or as a general measurement model of behaviour for the rating of job performance.

Finally, we suggested the (non)equivalence of qualities of measured behavior as a factor influencing predictor–criterion validity. Mentioning our rough ideas, we hope to start the ball rolling forward a thoroughly constructed taxonomy of qualities of measured behavior, which could be a further tool to clarify predictor–criterion relationships in advance.

ACKNOWLEDGEMENTS

For their thoughtful comments and advice on earlier versions of this chapter we would like to thank the editors, Cary Cooper and Ivan Robertson, and Uwe Funke, Klaus Moser, Neal Schmitt, and Heinrich Wottawa.

Correspondence address
Universität Hohenheim, Lehrstuhl für Psychologie, Postfach 70 05 62, D-7000 Stuttgart 70, Federal Republic of Germany.

REFERENCES

Ackerman, P. L. (1987) Individual differences in skill learning: An integration of psychometric and information processing perspectives. *Psychological Bulletin*, **102**, 3–27.

Ackerman, P. L. (1989) Within-task intercorrelations of skilled performance: Implications for predicting individual differences? (A comment on Henry and Hulin, 1987). *Journal of Applied Psychology*, **74**, 360–364.

Adler, S., & Weiss, H. M. (1988) Recent developments in the study of personality and organizational behavior. In C. L. Cooper & I. T. Robertson (eds), *International Review of Industrial and Organizational Psychology 1988*. Chichester: Wiley.

Alexander, R. A., & Barrick, M. R. (1987) Estimating the standard error of projected dollar gains in utility analysis. *Journal of Applied Psychology*, **72**, 475–479.

Alexander, R. A., & Borodkin, L. J. (1989) A goodness-of-fit index for validity generalization. Paper presented at the 5th Annual Conference of the Society for Industrial and Organizational Psychology, Atlanta.

Allen, W. B. (1988) Rhodes handicapping, or slowing the pace of integration. *Journal of Vocational Behavior*, **33**, 365–378.

American Educational Research Association, American Psychological Association, and National Council of Measurement in Education (1985) *Standards for Educational and Psychological Testing*. Washington DC: American Psychological Association.

Anastasi, A. (1988) *Psychological Testing*, 6th edn. New York: Macmillan.

Anderson, N., & Shackleton, V. (1990) Decision making in the graduate selection interview: A field study. *Journal of Occupational Psychology*, **63**, 63–76.

Arvey, R. D. (1986) General ability in employment: a discussion. *Journal of Vocational Behavior*, **29** (special issue), 415–420.

Arvey, R. D., Miller, H. E., Gould, R., & Burch, P. (1987) Interview validity for selecting sales clerks. *Personnel Psychology*, **40**, 1–12.

Bangert-Drowns, R. L. (1986) Review of developments in meta-analytic method. *Psychological Bulletin*, **99**, 388–399.

Barthel, E. & Schuler, H. (1989) Nutzenkalkulation eignungsdiagnostischer Verfahren am Beispiel des biographischen Fragebogens. [Utility calculation in the case of a biographical questionnaire.] *Zeitschrift für Arbeits- und Organisationspsychologie*, **33**, 73–83.

Barr, S. H., & Hitt, M. A. (1986) A comparison of selection decision models in manager versus student samples. *Personnel Psychology*, **39**, 599–617.

Bies, R. J. (1987) The predictment of injustice: The management of moral outrage. In L. L. Cummings and B. M. Staw (eds), *Research in Organizational Behavior*. Greenwich, CT: JAI Press.

Bies, R. J., & Moag, S. J. (1986) Interactional justice: Communication criteria of fairness. In R. J. Lewicki, B. H. Sheppard & M. Z. Bazerman (eds), *Research on Negotiation in Organizations*. Greenwich, CT: JAI Press.

Biggs, D. L., & Beutell, N. J. (1986) Job applicants' sex and marital status as determinants of evaluations of resumes. *Psychological Reports*, **58**, 767–773.

Binning, J. F., & Barrett, G. V. (1989) Validity of personnel decisions: A conceptual analysis of the inferential and evidential bases. *Journal of Applied Psychology*, **74**, 478–494.

Binning, J. F., Goldstein, M. A., Carcia, M. F., & Scattaregia, J. H. (1988) Effects of preinterview impressions on questioning strategies in same-and opposite-sex employment interviews. *Journal of Applied Psychology*, **73**, 30–37.

Birnbaum, A. (1968) Some latent trait models and their use in inferring an examinee's ability. In F. M. Lord and M. R. Novick (eds), *Statistical Theories of Mental Test Scores*. Reading MA: Addison-Wesley.

Bobko, P., Karren, R., and Kerkar, S. P. (1987) Systematic research needs for understanding supervisory-based estimates of SD_y in utility analysis. *Organizational Behavior and Human Decision Processes*, **40**, 69–95.

Bobko, P., Karren, R., & Parkington, J. J. (1983) Estimation of standard deviations in utility analyses: An empirical test. *Journal of Applied Psychology*, **68**, 170–176.

Bolick, C. (1988) Legal and policy aspects of testing. *Journal of Vocational Behavior*, **33**, 320–330.

Borman, W. C., Rosse, R. L. & Abrahams, N. M. (1980) An empirical construct validity approach to studying predictor–job performance links. *Journal of Applied Psychology*, **65**, 662–671.

Boudreau, J. W. (1983a) Economic considerations in estimating the utility of human resource productivity improvement programs. *Personnel Psychology*, **36**, 551–557.

Boudreau, J. W. (1983b) Effects of employee flows on utility analysis of human resource productivity improvement programs. *Journal of Applied Psychology*, **68**, 170–176.

Boudreau, J. W. (1989) Selection utility analysis: A review and agenda for future research. In M. Smith and I. T. Robertson (eds), *Advances in Selection and Assessment*. Chichester: Wiley & Sons.

Boudreau, J. W. & Berger, C. J. (1985) Decision-theoretic utility analysis applied to employee separations and acquisitions. *Journal of Applied Psychology*, **70**, 581–612.

Brogden, H. E. (1949). When testing pays off. *Personnel Psychology*, **2**, 133–154.

Bryk, A. S., & Raudenbush, S. W. (1987) Application of hierarchical linear models to assessing change. *Psychological Bulletin*, **101**, 147–158.

Burke, M. J., and Frederick, J. T. (1984) Two modified procedures for estimating standard deviations in utility analyses. *Journal of Applied Psychology*, **69**, 482–489.

Burke, M. J., & Frederick, J. T. (1986) A comparison of economic utility estimates for alternative SD_y estimation procedures. *Journal of Applied Psychology*, **71**, 334–339.

Burke, M. J., Raju, N. S., & Pearlman, K. (1986) An empirical comparison of the results of five validity generalization procedures. *Journal of Applied Psychology*, **71**, 349–353.

Bycio, P., Alvares, K. M., & Hahn, J. (1987) Situational specifity in assessment center ratings: A confirmatory factor analysis. *Journal of Applied Psychology*, **72**, 463–474.

Callender, J. C., & Osburn, H. G. (1988) Unbiased estimation of sampling variance of correlations. *Journal of Applied Psychology*, **73**, 312–315.

Carroll, J. B. (1979) Measurement of ability constructs. In *Construct Validity in Psychological Measurements*. Proceedings of a collaquium on theory and application in education and employment. Princeton, NJ: Educational Testing Service.

Cascio, W. F. (1982) *Costing Human Resources: The Financial Impact of Behavior in Organizations*. Boston, MA: Kent.

Cascio, W. F. (1987) *Applied Psychology in Personnel Management*, 3rd edn. Englewood Cliffs, NJ: Prentice-Hall.

Cascio, W. F., Alexander, R. A., & Barrett, G. V. (1988) Setting cutoff scores: Legal, psychometric, and professional issues and guidelines. *Personnel Psychology*, **41**, 1–24.

Cascio, W. F., & Ramos, R. A. (1986) Development and application of a new method for assessing job performance in behavioral/economic terms. *Journal of Applied Psychology*, **71**, 20–28.

Chen, Huey-Tsyh, & Rossi, P. H. (1987) The theory-driven approach to validity. *Evaluation and Program Planning*, **10**, 95–103.

Chi, M. T. H., Glaser, R., & Rees, E. (1982). Expertise in problem solving. In R. Sternberg (ed.) *Advances in the Psychology of Human Intelligence*. Hillsdale, NJ: Erlbaum.

Cleveland, J. N., Festa, R. M., & Montgomery, L. (1988) Applicant pool composition and job perceptions: Impact on decisions regarding an older applicant. *Journal of Vocational Behavior*, **32**, 112–125.

Cook, T. D., & Campbell, D. T. (1976) The design and conduct of quasi-experiments and true experiments in field settings. In M. D. Dunnette (ed.), *Handbook of Industrial and Organizational Psychology*. Chicago: Rand McNally.

Cooper, W. H., & Richardson, A. J. (1986) Unfair comparisons. *Journal of Applied Psychology*, **71**, 179–184.

Cote, J. A., & Buckley, M. R. (1987) Estimating trait, method, and error variance: Generalizing across 70 construct validation studies. *Journal of Marketing Research*, **24**, 315–318.

Cote, J. A., Buckley, M. R., & Best, R. J. (1987). Combining methodologies in the construct validation process: An empirical illustration. *The Journal of Psychology*, **121**, 301–309.

Cronbach, L. J. (1988) Internal consistency of tests: Analyses old and new. *Psychometrika*, **53**, 63–70.

Cronbach, L. J. & Gleser, G. C. (eds) (1965) *Psychological Tests and Personnel Decisions*, 2nd edn. Urbana: University of Illinois Press.

Cronbach, L. J., Gleser, G. C., Nanda, H., & Rajaratnam, N. (1972) *The Dependability of Behavioral Measurements: Theory of Generalizability of Scores and Profiles*. New York: Wiley.

Cronshaw, S. F., Alexander, R. A. (1985) One answer to the demand for accountability-selection utility as an investment decision. *Organizational Behavior and Human Performance*, **35**, 102–118.

Cronshaw, S. F., Alexander, R. A., Wiesner, W. H., & Barrick, M. R. (1987) Incorporating risk into selection utility: Two models for sensitivity analysis and risk simulation. *Organizational Behavior and Human Decision Processes*, **40**, 270–286.

Cropanzano, R., & Folger, R. (1989) Referent cognitions and task decision autonomy: Beyond equity theory. *Journal of Applied Psychology*, **74**, 293–299.

Delahunty, R. J. (1988) Perspectives on within-group scoring. *Journal of Vocational Behavior*, **33**, 463–477.

Dickinson, T. L. (1987) Designs for evaluating the validity and accuracy of performance ratings. *Organizational Behavior and Human performance*, **40**, 1–21.

Dougherty, T. W., Ebert, R. J., & Callender, J. C. (1986) Policy capturing in the employment interview. *Journal of Applied Psychology*, **71**, 9–15.

Drasgow, F. (1987) Study of the measurement bias of two standardized psychological tests. *Journal of Applied Psychology*, **72**, 19–29.

Drasgow, F., & Guertler, E. (1987) A decision-theoretic approach to the use of appropriateness measurement for detecting invalid test and scale scores. *Journal of Applied Psychology*, **72**, 10–18.

Drasgow, F., Levine, M., & McLaughlin, M. (1987) Detecting inappropriate test scores with optimal and practical appropriateness indices. *Applied Psychological Measurement*, **11**, 59–79.

Dreher, G. F., Ash, R. A., & Hancock, P. (1988) The role of the traditional research design in underestimating the validity of the employment interview. *Personnel Psychology*, **41**, 315–327.

Dreher, G. F., & Maurer, S. D. (1989) Assessing the employment interview: Deficiencies associated with the existing domain of validity coefficients. In R. W. Eder & G. F. Ferris (eds), *The Employment Interview: Theory Research, and Practice*. Newbury Park: Sage.

Dunnette, M. A., & Borman, W. C. (1979) Personnel selection and classification systems. *Annual Review of Psychology*, **30**, 477–525.

Eder, R. W., & Ferris, G. F. (1989) *The Employment Interview. Theory, Research and Practice*. Newbury Park: Sage.

Edwards, J. E., Frederick, J. T., & Burke, M. J. (1988) Efficacy of modified CREPID SD_ys on the basis of archival organizational data. *Journal of Applied Psychology*, **73**, 529–535.

Fischer, G. H. (1974) *Einführung in die Theorie psychologischer Tests*. [Introduction to the theory of psychological tests.] Bern: Huber.

Fiske, D. W. (1987a) On understanding our methods and their effects. *Diagnostica*, **33**, 188–194.

Fiske, D. W. (1987b) Construct invalidity comes from method effects. *Educational and Psychological Measurement*, **47**, 285–307.

Fleishman, J., & Benson, J. (1987) Using LISREL to evaluate measurement models and scale reliability. *Educational and Psychological Measurement*, **47**, 925–939.

Florin-Thuma, B. C., & Boudreau, J. W. (1987) Performance feedback utility in a small organization: Effects on organizational outcomes and managerial decision processes. *Personnel Psychology*, **40**, 693–713.

Folger, R., & Konovsky, M. A. (1989) Effects of procedural and distributive justice on reactions to pay raise decisions. *Academy of Management Journal*, **32**, 115–130.

Ford, J. K., Kraiger, K., & Schechtman, S. L. (1986) Study of race effects in objective indices and subjective evaluations of performance: A meta-analysis of performance criteria. *Psychological Bulletin*, **99**, 330–337.

Frederiksen, N. (1986) Construct validity and construct similarity: methods for use in test development and test validation. *Multivariate Behavioral Research*, **21**, 3–28.

Gardner, R. C., & Erdle, S. (1984) Aggregating scores: To standardize or not to standardize. *Educational and Psychological Measurement*, **44**, 813–821.

Gardner, R. C., & Erdle, S. (1986) Aggregating standard scores or raw scores: Whither the controversy? *Educational and Psychological Measurement*, **46**, 533–536.

Gardner, R. C., & Neufeld, R. W. J. (1987) Use of the simple change score in correlational analyses. *Educational and Psychological Measurement*, **47**, 849–864.

Gilmore, D. C., Beehr, T. A., & Love, K. G. (1986) Effects of applicant sex, applicant physical attractiveness, type of rater and type of job on interview decisions. *Journal of Occupational Psychology*, **59**, 103–109.

Glick, P., Zion, C., & Nelson, C. (1988) What mediates sex discrimination in hiring decisions? *Journal of Personality and Social Psychology*, **55**, 178–186.

Goldstein, B. L., & Patterson, P. O. (1988) Turning back the Title VII Clock: The resegregation of the American work force through validity generalization. *Journal of Vocational Behavior*, **33**, 452–462.

Goodman, L. A. (1978) *Analyzing Qualitative/Categorical Data*. London: Addison-Wesley.

Gottfredson, L. S. (1986) Societal consequences of the g factor in employment. *Journal of Vocational Behavior*, **29** (special issue), 379–410.

Gottfredson, L. S. (1988) Reconsidering fairness: A matter of social and ethical priorities. Journal of Vocational Behavior, **33**, 293–319.

Gottfredson, L. S., & Crouse, J. (1986) Validity versus utility of mental tests: example of the SAT. *Journal of Vocational Behavior*, **29** (special issue), 363–378.

Graves, L. M., & Powell, G. N. (1988) An investigation of sex discrimination in recruiters' evaluations of actual applicants. *Journal of Applied Psychology*, **73**, 20–29.

Greenberg, J. (1986) Determinants of perceived fairness of performance evaluations. *Journal of Applied Psychology*, **71**, 340–342.

Greer, O. L., & Cascio, W. F. (1987) Is cost accounting the answer? Comparison of two behaviorally based methods for estimating the standard deviation of job performance in dollars with a cost-accounting-based approach. *Journal of Applied Psychology*, **72**, 588–595.

Guion, R. M. (1987) Changing views for personnel selection research. *Personnel Psychology*, **40**, 199–213.

Guthke, J. (1982) The learning test concept—an alternative to the traditional static intelligence test. *The German Journal of Psychology*, **6**, 306–324.

Guthke, J. (1988) Das Lerntestkonzept als Alternative bzw. Ergänzung zum Intelligenzstatustest—was hat es uns gebracht und wie geht es weiter?—Versuch einer Bilanzierung und Trendanalyse. [The learning test concept as an alternative and supplement, respectively, to status–diagnostic intelligence tests—An evaluative summary and trend analysis.] *Bericht über den 36. Kongreß der Deutschen Gesellschaft für Psychologie in Berlin 1988*, vol. 2, 213–228.

Guzzo, R. A., Jackson, S. E., & Katzell, R. A. (1987) Meta-analysis analysis. *Research in Organizational Behavior*, **9**, 407–442.

Hambleton, R. (1986) The changing conception of measurement: A commentary. *Applied Psychological Measurement*, **10**, 415–421.

Hambleton, R., & Swaminathan, H. (1985) *Item Response Theory: Principles and Applications*. Boston: Kluwer-Nijhoff.

Hammond, K. R., Hamm, R. M., & Grassia, J. (1986) Generalizing over conditions by combining the multitrait–multimethod matrix and the representative design of experiments. *Psychological Bulletin*, **100**, 257–269.

Hartigan, J. A., & Wigdor, A. K. (eds) (1989) *Fairness in Employment Testing*. Washington, DC: National Academy Press.

Hedges, L. V. (1988) The meta-analysis of test validity studies: Some new approaches. In H. Wainer & H. I. Braun (eds), *Test Validity*. Hillsdale, NJ: Erlbaum.

Hedges, L. V. (1989) An unbiased correction for sampling error in validity generalization studies. *Journal of Applied Psychology*, **74**, 469–477.

Heilmann, M. E., Martell, R. F., & Simon, M. C. (1988) The vagaries of sex bias: Conditions regulating the undervaluation, equivaluation, and overvaluation of female job applicants. *Organizational Behavior and Human Decision Processes*, **41**, 98–110.

Heneman, R. L. (1986) The relationship between supervisory ratings and results-oriented measures of performance: A meta-analysis. *Personnel Psychology*, **39**, 811–826.

Henry, R. A., & Hulin C. L. (1987) Stability of skilled performance across time: Some generalizations and limitations on utilities. *Journal of Applied Psychology*, **72**, 457–462.

Henry, R. A., & Hulin C. L. (1989) Changing validities: Ability–performance relations and utilities. *Journal of Applied Psychology*, **74**, 365–367.

Hirsh, H. R., Schmidt, F. L., & Hunter, J. E. (1986) Estimation of employment validities by less experienced judges. *Personnel Psychology*, **39**, 337–344.

Hitt, M. A., & Barr, S. H. (1989) Managerial selection decision models: Examination of configural cue processing. *Journal of Applied Psychology*, **74**, 53–61.

Hogan, R., & Nicholson, R. A. (1988) The meaning of personality test scores. *American Psychologist*, **43**, 621–626.

Hollenbeck, J. R., & Whitener, E. M. (1988) Criterion-related validation for small sample contexts: An integrated approach to synthetic validity. *Journal of Applied Psychology*, **73**, 536–544.

Huber, V. L., Neale, M. A., & Northcraft, G. B. (1987a) Judgment by heuristics: Effects of ratee and rater characteristics and performance standards on performance-related judgments. *Organizational Behavior and Human Decision Processes*, **40**, 149–169.

Huber, V. L., Neale, M. A., & Northcraft, G. B. (1987b) Decision bias and personnel selection strategies. *Organizational Behavior and Human Decision Processes*, **40**, 136–147.

Hulin, C. L., Drasgow, F., & Parsons, C. K. (1983) *Item Response Theory: Application to Psychological Measurement*. Homewood IL: Dow-Jones Irwin.

Humphreys, L. G. (1986a) An analysis and evaluation of test and item bias in the prediction context. *Journal of Applied Psychology*, **71**, 327–333.

Humphreys, L. G. (1986b) Commentary. *Journal of Vocational Behavior*, **29** (special issue), 421–437.

Hunter, J. E. (1986) Cognitive ability, cognitive aptitudes, job knowledge, and job performance. *Journal of Vocational Behavior*, **29** (special issue), 340–362.

Hunter, J. E., & Hirsh, H. (1987) Applications of meta-analysis. In C. L. Cooper & I. T. Robertson (eds), *International Review of Industrial and Organizational Psychology 1987* Chichester: Wiley.

Hunter, J. E., & Schmidt, F. L. (1982) Fitting people to jobs: The impact of personnel selection on national productivity. In M. E. Dunnette & E. A. Fleishman (eds), *Human Performance and Productivity: Human Capability Assessment*. Hillsdale, NJ: Erlbaum.

Hunter, H. E., & Schmidt, F. L. (1989) Meta-analysis: facts and theories. In M. Smith & I. Robertson (eds), *Advances in Selection and Assessment*. Chichester: Wiley.

Hunter, J. E., Schmidt, F. L., & Coggin, T. D. (1988) Problems and pitfalls in using capital budgeting and financial accounting techniques in assessing the utility of personnel programs. *Journal of Applied Psychology*, **73**, 522–528.

Huynh, H. (1986) On the reliability of the extreme score. *Psychometrika*, **51**, 475–478.

James, L. R., Demaree, R. G., and Mulaik, S. A. (1986) A note on validity generalization procedures. *Journal of Applied Psychology*, **71**, 440–450.

James, L. R., Demaree, R. G., Mulaik, S. A., & Mumford, M. D. (1988) Validity generalization: rejoinder to Schmidt, Hunter, and Raju 1988. *Journal of Applied Psychology*, **73**, 673–678.

James, L. R., and James, L. A. (1989) Causal modelling in organizational research. In C. L. Cooper & I. T. Robertson (eds), *International Review of Industrial and Organizational Psychology*. Chichester: Wiley & Sons.

Jansen, P. G. W., Roe, R. A., Vijn, P., and Algera, J. A. (1986) *Validity Generalization Revisited*. Delft: University Press.

Jensen, A. R. (1986) G: artifact or reality? *Journal of Vocational Behavior*, **29** (special issue), 301–331.

Johnson, C. E., Wood, R., & Blinkhorn, S. F. (1988) Spuriouser and spuriouser: The use of ipsative personality tests. *Journal of Occupational Psychology*, **61**, 153–162.

Kacmar, K. M., Ratcliff, S. L., & Ferris, G. R. (1989) Employment interview research:

Internal and external validity. In R. W. Eder & G. F. Ferris (eds), *The Employment Interview: Theory, Research, and Practice* Newbury Park: Sage, pp. 32–41.

Keinan, G. (1987) Decision making under stress: Scanning of alternatives under controllable and uncontrollable threats. *Journal of Personality and Social Psychology*, **52**, 639–644.

Kemery, E. R., Mossholder, K. W., & Dunlap, W. P. (1989) Meta-analysis and moderator variables: a cautionary note on transportability. *Journal of Applied Psychology*, **74**, 168–170.

Kemery, E. R., Mossholder, K. W., and Roth, L. (1987) The power of the Schmidt and Hunter additive model of validity generalization. *Journal of Applied Psychology*, **72**, 30–37.

Klimoski, R. (1988) Construct validity in life history prediction systems. Paper presented at 24th International Congress of Psychology, Sydney.

Kraiger, K., & Ford, J. K. (1985) A meta-analysis of ratee race effects in performance ratings. *Journal of Applied Psychology*, **70**, 56–65.

Krauth, J., & Lienert, G. A. (1973) *KFA—Die Konfigurations-Frequenzanalyse und ihre Anwendung in Psychologie und Medizin.* [Configuration frequency analysis and its application in psychology and medicine.] Freiburg: Adler.

Landy, F. L. (1986) Stamp collecting versus science. Validation as hypothesis testing. *American Psychologist*, **41**, 1183–1192.

Linn, R. B. (1986) Comments on the g factor in employment testing. *Journal of Vocational Behavior*, **29** (special issue), 438–444.

Linn, R. L., & Drasgow, F. (1987) Implications of the Golden Rule settlement for test construction. *Educational Measurement Issues and Practice*, **6**, 13–17.

Maier, M. H. (1988) On the need of quality control in validation research. *Personnel Psychology*, **41**, 497–502.

Marsh, H. W., & Hocevar, D. (1988) A new, more powerful approach to multitrait–multimethod analyses: Application of second-order confirmatory factor analysis. *Journal of Applied Psychology*, **73**, 107–117.

Martin, S. L. (1989) How traditional research designs can over- and underestimate criterion-related validity coefficients. Paper presented at the annual meeting of the American Psychological Association, New Orleans.

Mathieu, J. E., & Leonard, R. L., Jr (1987) An application of utility concepts to a supervisor skills training program: A time-based approach. *Academy of Management Journal*, **30**, 316–335.

Meyer, H. H. (1987) Predicting supervisory ratings versus promotional progress in test validation studies. *Journal of Applied Psychology*, **72**, 696–697.

Millsap, R. E. (1988) Tolerance intervals: alternatives to credibility intervals in validity generalization research. *Applied Psychological Measurement*, **12**, 27–32.

Moser, K., & Schuler, H. (1989) The nature of psychological measurement. In P. Herriot (ed.) *Handbook of Assessment in Organizations*. Chichester: Wiley.

Moser, K., Donat, M., Schuler, H., & Funke, U. (1989) Güte Kriterien von Arbeitsanalyseverfahren. [Criteria for job analysis methods.] *Zeitschrift für Arbeitswissenschaft*, **43**, 65–72.

Murphy, K. R. (1986) When your top choice turns you down: Effect of rejected offers on the utility of selection tests. *Psychological Bulletin*, **99**, 133–138.

Nathan, B. R., & Alexander, R. A. (1988) A comparison of criteria for test validation: A meta-analytic investigation. *Personnel Psychology*, **41**, 517–535.

Olian, J. D., Schwab, D. P., & Haberfeld, Y. (1988) The impact of applicant gender compared to qualifications on hiring recommendations. *Organizational Behavior and Human Decision Processes*, **41**, 180–195.

Orr, J. M., Sackett, P. R., & Mercer, M. (1989) The role of prescribed and nonprescribed behaviors in estimating the dollar value of performance. *Journal of Applied Psychology*, **74**, 34–40.

Paese, P. W., & Switzer III, F. S. (1988) Validity generalization and hypothetical reliability distributions: A test of the Schmidt–Hunter procedure. *Journal of Applied Psychology*, **73**, 267–274.

Paunonen, S. V., & Jackson, D. N. (1987) Accuracy of interviewers and students in identifying the personality characteristics of personnel managers and computer programs. *Journal of Vocational Behavior*, **31**, 26–36.

Paunonen, S. V., Jackson, D. N., & Oberman, S. M. (1987). Personnel selection decisions: Effects of applicant personality and the letter of reference. *Organizational Behavior and Human Decision Processes*, **40**, 96–114.

Peek Philips, A., & Dipboye, R. L. (1989) Correlational tests of predictions from a process model of the interview. *Journal of Applied Psychology*, **74**, 41–52.

Peterson, D. K., & Pitz, G. F. (1986) Effect of input from a mechanical model on clinical judgment. *Journal of Applied Psychology*, **71**, 163–167.

Powell, G. N. (1987) The effects of sex and gender on recruitment. *Academy of Management Review*, **12**, 731–743.

Prediger, D. J. (1989) Ability differences across occupations: More than g. *Journal of Vocational Behavior*, **34**, 1–27.

Pulakos, E. D., Bosman, W. C., & Hough, L. M. (1988) Test validation for scientific understanding: Two demonstrations of an approach to studying predictor–criterion linkages. *Personnel Psychology*, **41**, 703–716.

Pulakos, E. D., Schmitt, N., & Ostroff, C. (1986) A warning about the use of a standard deviation across dimensions within ratees to measure halo. *Journal of Applied Psychology*, **71**, 29–32.

Pulakos, E. D., White, L. A., Oppler, S. H., & Borman, W. C. (1989) Examination of race and sex effects on performance ratings. *Journal of Applied Psychology*, **74**, 770–780.

Raju, N. S., Burke, M. J., & Normand, J. (1990). A new approach to utility analysis. *Journal of Applied Psychology*, **75**, 3–12.

Rasch, G. (1960) *Probabilistic Models for Some Intelligence and Attainment Tests.* Copenhagen: Danmarks Paedogogiske Institut.

Rasmussen, J. L., & Loher, B. T. (1988) Appropriate critical percentages for the Schmidt and Hunter meta-analysis procedure: Comparative evaluation of type I error rate and power. *Journal of Applied Psychology*, **73**, 683–687.

Raudenbush, S. W., Becker, B. J., & Kalaian, H. (1988) Modelling multivariate effect sizes. *Psychological Bulletin*, **103**, 111–120.

Reilly, R. R., & Israelski, E. W. (1988) Development and validation of minicourses in the telecommunication industry. *Journal of Applied Psychology*, **73**, 721–726.

Reilly, R. R., & Smither, J. W. (1985) An examination of two alternative techniques to estimate the standard deviation of job performance in dollars. *Journal of Applied Psychology*, **70**, 651–661.

Rich, J. R., & Boudreau, J. W. (1987) The effecrs of variability and risk in selection utility analysis: An empirical comparison. *Personnel Psychology*, **40**, 55–84.

Rindskopf, D., & Rose, T. (1988) Some theory and applications of confirmatory second-order factor analysis. *Multivariate Behavioral Research*, **23**, 51–67.

Robertson, I. T. (1989) Construct validity in managerial selection and assessment. In B. J. Fallon, H. P. Pfister, & J. Brebner (eds), *Advances in Industrial Organizational Psychology*. Amsterdam: Elsevier.

Roche, W. J., Jr (1965) A dollar in fixed-treatment employee selection. In L. J.

Cronbach & G. C. Gleser (eds), *Psychological Testing and Personnel Decisions*. Urbana: University of Illinois Press.

Rosenthal, R., & Rubin, D. B. (1986) Meta-analytic procedures for combining studies with multiple effect sizes. *Psychological Bulletin*, **99**, 400–406.

Sackett, P. R., Harris, M. M. & Orr, J. M. (1986) On seeking moderator variables in the meta-analysis of correlational data: a Monte Carlo investigation of statistical power and resistance to type I error. *Journal of Applied Psychology*, **71**, 302–310.

Sackett, P. R., Schmitt, N., Tenopyr, M. L., Kehoe, J., & Zedeck, S. (1985) Commentary on forty questions about validity generalization and meta-analysis. *Personnel Psychology*, **38**, 697–798.

Sackett, P. R., Zedeck, S. & Fogli, L. (1988) Relation between mesures of typical and maximum job performance. *Journal of Applied Psychology*, **73**, 482–486.

Schmidt, F. L. (1988). The problem of group differences in ability test scores in employment selection. *Journal of Vocational Behavior*, **33**, 272–292.

Schmidt, F. L., & Hunter, J. E. (1977) Development of a general solution to the problem of validity generalization. *Journal of Applied Psychology*, **62**, 529–540.

Schmidt, F. L., & Hunter, J. E. (1983) Individual differences in productivity: An empirical test of estimates derived from studies of selection procedure utility. *Journal of Applied Psychology*, **68**, 407–414.

Schmidt, F. L., Hunter, J. E., Croll, P. R., & McKenzie, R. C. (1983) Estimation of employment test validities by expert judgement. *Journal of Applied Psychology*, **68**, 590–601.

Schmidt, F. L., Hunter, J. E., McKenzie, R. C., & Muldrow, T. (1979) The impact of valid selection procedures on work force productivity. *Journal of Applied Psychology*, **64**, 609–624.

Schmidt, F. L., Hunter, J. E., & Outerbridge, A. N. (1986) Impact of job experience and ability on job knowledge, work sample performance, and supervisory ratings of job performance. *Journal of Applied Psychology*, **71**, 432–439.

Schmidt, F. L., Hunter, J. E., Outerbridge, A. N., & Trattner, M. H. (1988) The economic impact of job selection methods on size, productivity, and payroll costs of the federal work force: An empirically based demonstration. *Personnel Psychology*, **39**, 1–29.

Schmidt, F. L., Hunter, J. E., Pearlman, K., & Hirsh, H. R. (1985) Forty questions about validity generalization and meta-analysis. *Personnel Psychology*, **38**, 697–798.

Schmidt, F. L., Hunter, J. E., & Raju, N. S. (1988) Validity generalization and situational specificity: A second look at the 75% rule and Fisher's z transformation. *Journal of Applied Psychology*, **73**, 665–672.

Schmidt, F. L., Mack, M. J., & Hunter, J. E. (1984) Selection utility in the occupation of U.S. park ranger for three modes of test use. *Journal of Applied Psychology*, **69**, 490–497.

Schmitt, N. (1989a) Construct validity in personnel selection. In B. J. Fallon, H. P. Pfister & J. Brebner (eds), *Advances in Industrial Organizational Psychology*. Amsterdam: Elsevier.

Schmitt, N. (1989b). Fairness in employment selection. In M. Smith & I. T. Robertson (eds), *Advances in Selection and Assessment*. Chichester: Wiley.

Schmitt, N., Gooding, R. Z., Noe, R. A., & Kirsch, M. (1984) Meta-analysis of validity studies published between 1964 and 1982 and the investigation of study characteristics. *Personnel Psychology*, **37**, 407–422.

Schmitt, N., & Noe, R. A. (1986) Personnel selection and equal employment opportunity. In C. L. Cooper & I. T. Robertson (eds), *International Review of Industrial and Organizational Psychology*. Chichester: Wiley.

Schneider, W., Dumais, S. T., & Shiffrin, R. M. (1984) Automatic and control processing and attention. In R. Parasuaraman & D. R. Davies (eds), *Varieties of Attention*. New York: Academic Press.

Schuerger, J. M., Zarrella, K. L., & Hotz, A. S. (1989) Factors that influence the temporal stability of personality by questionnaire. *Journal of Personality and Social Psychology*, **56**, 777–783.

Schuler, H. (1989) Construct validity of a multimodal employment interview. In B. J. Fallon, H. P. Pfister & J. Brebner (eds), *Advances in Industrial Organizational Psychology*. Amsterdam: Elsevier.

Schuler, H., & Schmitt, N. (1987) Multimodale Messung in der Personalpsychologie. [Multimodal measurement in personnel psychology.] *Diagnostica*, **33**, 259–271.

Seymour, R. T. (1988) Why plaintiffs' counsel challenge tests, and how they can successfully challenge the theory of 'validity generalization'. *Journal of Vocational Behavior*, **33**, 331–363.

Sharf, J. C., (1988) Litigating personnel measurement policy. *Journal of vocational Behavior*, **33**, 235–271.

Shavelson, R. J., Webb, N. M., & Rowley, G. L. (1989) Generalizability theory. *American Psychologist*, **44**, 922–932.

Siegal, A. I. (1983) The miniature job training and evaluation approach: Additional findings. *Personnel Psychology*, **36**, 41–56.

Slovic, P., & Lichtenstein, S. (1971) Comparison of Bayesian and regression approaches to the study of information processing in judgement. *Organizational Behavior and Human Performance*, **6**, 649–744.

Smith, P. C., Budzeika, K. A., Edwards, N. A., Johnson, S. M., & Bearse, L. N. (1986) Guidelines for clean data: Detection of common mistakes. *Journal of Applied Psychology*, **71**, 457–460.

Society for Industrial and Organizational Psychology (1987) *Principles for the Validation and Use of Personnel Selection Procedures*, 3rd end. College Park, MD: Author.

Spector, P. E., & Levine, E. L. (1987) Meta-analysis for integrating study outcomes: A Monte Carlo study of its susceptibility to type I and type II errors. *Journal of Applied Psychology*, **72**, 3–9.

Srinivas, S., & Motowidlo, S. J. (1987) Effects of raters' stress on the dispersion and favorability of performance ratings. *Journal of Applied Psychology*, **72**, 247–251.

Sussmann, M., & Robertson, D. V. (1986) The validity of validity: An analysis of validation study designs. *Journal of Applied Psychology*, **71**, 461–468.

Steffy, B. D., & Maurer, S. D. (1988) The dollar-productivity impact on the human resource function: Conceptualization and measurement. *Academy of Management Review*, **13**, 271–286.

Stevens, J. J., & Aleamoni, L. M. (1986) The role of weighting in the use of aggregate scores. *Educational and Psychological Measurement*, **46**, 523–531.

Tenopyr, M. L. (1988) Artifactual reliability of forced-choice scales. *Journal of Applied Psychology*, **73**, 749–751.

Thissen, D., & Steinberg, L. (1988) Data analysis using item response theory. *Psychological Bulletin*, **104**, 385–395.

Thissen, D., Steinberg, L., & Gerrard, M. (1986) Beyond group-mean differences: The concept of item bias. *Psychological Bulletin*, **99**, 118–128.

Thorndike, R. L. (1986) The role of general ability in prediction. *Journal of Vocational Behavior*, **29** (special issue), 332–339.

Tosi, H. L., & Einbender, S. W. (1985) The effects of the type and amount of information in sex discrimination research: A meta-analysis. *Academy of Management Journal*, **28**, 712–723.

Turban, D. B., Sanders, P. A., Francis, D. J., & Osburn, H. G. (1989) Construct equivalence as an approach to replacing validated cognitive ability selection tests. *Journal of Applied Psychology*, **74**, 62–71.

Uebersax, J. S. (1988). Validity inferences from interobserver agreement. *Psychological Bulletin*, **104**, 405–416.

Vance, R. J., Coovert, M. D., MacCallum, R. C., & Hedge, J. W. (1989) Construct models of task performance. *Journal of Applied Psychology*, **74**, 447–455.

Vance, R. J., MacCallum, R. C., Coovert, M. D., & Hedge, J. W. (1988) Construct validity of multiple job performance measures using confirmatory factor analysis. *Journal of Applied Psychology*, **73**, 74–80.

van der Linden, W. (1986) The changing conception of measurement in education and psychology. *Applied Psychological Measurement*, **4**, 325–332.

Wainer, H., and Brown, H. I. (eds) (1988) *Test Validity*. Hillsdale, NJ: Erlbaum.

Waldman, D. A., & Avolio, B. J. (1986). A meta-analysis of age differences in job performance. *Journal of Applied Psychology*, **71**, 33–38.

Wanous, J. P., Sullivan, S. E., & Malinak, J. (1989) The role of judgment calls in meta-analysis. *Journal of Applied Psychology*, **74**, 259–264.

Weekley, J. A., Frank, B., O'Connor, E. J., & Peters, L. H. (1985) A comparison of the three methods of estimating the standard deviation of performance in dollars. *Journal of Applied Psychology*, **70**, 122–126.

Weekley, J. A., & Gier, J. A. (1987) Reliability and validity of the situational interview for a sales position. *Journal of Applied Psychology*, **72**, 484–487.

Weekley, J. A., & Gier, J. A. (1989) Ceilings in the reliability and validity of performance ratings: The case of expert raters. *Academy of Management Journal*, **32**, 213–222.

Wittmann, W. W. (1987). Grundlagen erfolgreicher Forschung in der Psychologie: Multimodale Diagnostik, Multiplismus, multivariate Reliabilitäts- und Validitätstheorie [Multimodal diagnostics, multiplism, multivariate reliability and validity theory]. *Diagnostica*, **33**, 209–226.

Wittmann, W. W. (in press). Multivariate reliability theory: Principles of symmetry and successful validation strategies. In J. R. Nesselroade & R. B. Cattell (eds), *Handbook of Multivariate Experimental Psychology*, 2nd edn. New York: Plenum Press.

Wolf, F. M. (1986) *Meta-analysis: Quantitative Methods for Research Synthesis*. Beverly Hills: Sage.

Wottawa, H. (1987) Hypotheses Agglutination (HYPAG): A method for configuration-based analysis of multivariate data. *Methodika*, **1**, 68–92.

Wroten, S. P. (1984) Can supervisors really estimate SD_y? In S. P. Wroten (Chair), *Overcoming the Futilities of Utility Applications: Measures, Model, and Management*. Panel discussion conducted at the meeting of the APA, Toronto.

Yarnold, P. R. (1988) Classical test theory methods for repeated-measures $N = 1$ research designs. *Educational and Psychological Measurement*, **48**, 913–919.

Zedeck, S., & Cascio, W. F. (1984) Psychological issues in personnel decisions. *Annual Review of Psychology*, **35**, 461–518.

Chapter 7

MENTAL HEALTH COUNSELING IN INDUSTRY

Naomi G. Swanson and Lawrence R. Murphy
Motivation and Stress Research Section
National Institute for Occupational Safety and Health
USA[1]

PURPOSE AND INTRODUCTION

Industrial mental health counseling programs have existed in the workplace since 1915 (Burlingame, 1947). These programs were motivated by a suspected link between the emotional problems of workers and various organizational behaviours; e.g. accidents (Greenwood, 1918), dismissals (Jarrett, 1920), and morale and turnover (Mayo, 1934). This chapter critically reviews the literature on mental health counseling in industry, and suggests ways to strengthen these programs.

Mental health counseling, as defined here, encompasses a range of counseling techniques. These techniques include the interview approach of the Human Relations School (e.g. Dickson, 1945), as well as more conventional psychotherapeutic approaches, offered both on-site and by external providers, such as community mental health centers. Counselors (always nonmanagerial) have ranged from nonprofessionals, trained in nondirective listening techniques (e.g. Rogerian approach), to professionals such as social workers, clinical psychologists, and psychiatrists. The counseling programs have involved one or more therapeutic sessions with an employee who is seeking assistance for personal or job-related emotional distress. The primary objective of the majority of these programs has been the improvement of worker productivity; that is, to detect emotional problems impairing work performance and to restore troubled workers to full productivity.

The scope of this article is restricted to industrial mental health counseling as defined above. Other types of industrial counseling services (i.e. testing of

[1] The opinions, recommendations and conclusions expressed in this chapter are not necessarily those of the National Institute for Occupational Safety and Health.

job applicants, orienting new employees, stress management training, and career, financial, and substance abuse counseling) were not included, although it is recognized that some of these services do have mental health counseling components. Also excluded from this review are primary prevention programs such as health promotion programs. While such programs may have considerable potential for improving mental health in the workplace, health promotion was rarely included in the industrial mental health counseling literature. (See Roman & Blum, 1988, for a discussion of the structure and goals of health promotion programs.)

Sources for this review included journals and books in the areas of psychology, sociology, social work, business, and medicine, with a focus on literature from the United States. Articles were also drawn from trade publications. A shortcoming of many of these reports is that they are primarily descriptive and/or anecdotal in nature; few industrial mental health programs have been rigorously investigated for their efficacy.

The present chapter reviews the history of industrial mental health programs, describes their current status, and delineates their shortcomings. Finally, desirable components of a comprehensive mental health program, which overcome many of these shortcomings, are identified.

HISTORY

The first industrial psychiatric service in the United States was established at the Cheney Silk Company in 1915, after management discovered that emotional problems among workers '. . .cost the company more in production than accidents and disease' (Burlingame, 1947, p. 549). Unfortunately, this program has not been described in further detail in the literature.

Two other early programs of note were those of Metropolitan Life, which employed a full-time psychiatrist in 1922 (Giberson, 1937), and the R. H. Macy Company, which began a psychiatric mental health service in 1924 (Anderson, 1929). Both programs were implemented to rehabilitate 'maladjusted' or 'problem' employees in order to reduce health, absenteeism, productivity, and disciplinary problems, and were reportedly highly successful in their efforts.

Interest in counseling programs was very limited during the Depression years of the 1930s. An exception was the work of Elton Mayo at the Hawthorne, Illinois plant of the General Electric Company. Studies conducted by Mayo demonstrated the importance of human interaction in worker adjustment, reaction to change, and productivity (Mayo, 1945). In Mayo's view, industry had not paid as much attention to the psychological welfare of workers as to technological progress. Mayo felt that counseling enabled employees to better relate to, and cooperate with, coworkers and supervisors (Smith, 1962).

In 1936, Mayo established a counseling program which was staffed by nonprofessionals trained in the interview method of counseling (i.e. nondirective counseling), and which was available to all workers on the plant floor (Wilensky & Wilensky, 1951). The counselors circulated through work areas 'interviewing' workers about personal and work-related problems. The purpose of interviewing was to provide workers with an emotional outlet, not to resolve the problem itself. The counselors were not qualified to provide therapy for psychological disturbances.

According to Wilensky & Wilensky (1951), the program was implemented as a means for management to control and direct worker attitudes and motivation. Counselors' reports to management emphasized worker adjustments to employer demands, and counselors were at times asked to provide information about employee attitudes toward employer actions such as layoffs and downgrading of work. The effectiveness of the program was never accurately measured, and proponents argued that its good effects '. . .have to be accepted at least partially on faith' (Wilensky & Wilensky, 1951, p. 280).

Historically, there has been a greater interest by industry in mental health counseling services as a means of promoting worker efficiency and productivity during times of extraordinary pressure on productivity. Such pressures were evident during both world wars. The depleted workforce during the Second World War required the recruitment into the workforce of women, older workers, and the handicapped, individuals typically not a part of the labour force. The heightened production demands during this period, coupled with the inexperience of these workers, increased management concerns regarding absenteeism, accidents, and illness (Rosenbaum & Romano, 1943). During the immediate post-war years, the reintegration into the workforce of veterans carrying emotional burdens of battlefield experiences created additional concerns. McLean (1973) describes several post-war programs established for war veterans in the United States, Britain, and the Soviet Union.

During the 1940s and 1950s, counseling programs were established in a number of companies such as Caterpiller Tractor Company (Weider, 1947), DuPont (Gordon, 1953), Prudential Insurance Company (Levinson, 1956), Tennessee Valley Authority (McAtee, 1951), International Business Machines Corporation, and American Fore Insurance Group (Levinson, 1983). In general, these programs offered brief psychotherapy and concentrated on treating emotionally distressed workers and improving relations between supervisors and workers for purposes of reducing turnover, absenteeism, illness, and accidents. The programs were reportedly quite successful in this regard. McAtee (1951), for example, reports improvements in attendance, attitude, and productivity among those receiving psychotherapy for anxiety neuroses at the Tennessee Valley Authority.

Complementing the growth of counseling programs in industry, Harry Levinson established a Division of Industrial Mental Health at the Menninger Foundation in 1956, which he then directed for 14 years. Levinson and Menninger urged the establishment of in-house mental health centers in industry, providing data to establish the role of stress in absenteeism, alcoholism, and accidents. In addition, Levinson conducted week-long seminars for executives and occupational physicians directed towards identifying and managing stresses in organizations. These efforts added impetus to the establishment of industrial counseling programs (Levinson, 1983).

According to Smith (1962) and Wilensky & Wilensky (1951), the industrial counseling programs of the 1940s and 1950s were often based on the view that an emotionally disturbed ('irrational') worker was one who was uncooperative with management, and that this uncooperativeness could be overcome by allowing the worker to express feelings and personal concerns. These programs were perceived by labor as manipulative and as a means to 'keep labor happy' while increasing productivity and discouraging labor union activity (Smith, 1962, section 8, p. 34). For this reason, labor was suspicious of many of these programs, and their participation in industrial mental health programs was quite limited until the 1950s, when several unions implemented their own programs for members. These programs were often similar in content to those provided by industry (i.e. brief psychotherapy), but differed in that they were funded and accessed through a union. Some representative union-sponsored mental health programs included psychiatric services established for the Teamster's Local 688 in St Louis in 1946, and for the Retail Clerks Local 770 in Los Angeles in 1959. In Virginia, the United Mine Workers of America established mental health clinics in several communities in the 1950s. More recently, the Amalgamated Clothing Workers of America established a program in which mental health personnel were made available to members in both the factories and the union halls (McLean, 1973, Austin & Jackson, 1977).

Few new industrial mental health programs were implemented during the 1960s and early 1970s. However, since the late 1970s US industry has shown a much greater interest in establishing mental health programs than at any other time in the past. This burgeoning interest apparently has resulted from changes brought about by a number of converging economic and social factors. First, dramatic changes have occurred in the demographics of the workforce and the service sector of the economy has greatly expanded in the last 20 years. Of the 23.3 million new jobs created between 1970 and 1984, 22 million were in service industries (Stern, 1988). These newer white-collar and service industry jobs are more likely to produce mental stress and mental stress claims than blue-collar and manufacturing jobs (DeCarlo, 1987), perhaps, in part, because many of these jobs involve rapidly changing technologies, or are unskilled, low-paying jobs (Stern, 1988). Second, society has revised its attitude toward mental health, and no longer regards severe maladjustment as the sole determinant of the need for psychological assistance (Leonards, 1981). Accordingly, there is less social stigma attached to seeking and receiving help for emotional problems. Third, the productivity of the US workforce became a prime concern of management in the 1970s. Consequently, attention was focused on various human resource management techniques in an effort to increase productivity (Roman & Blum, 1988), and industry became increasingly willing to provide treatment for workers' emotional problems, regardless of etiology. Finally, there was a greater awareness of the risks to an employee's health, and the costs to the organization, of occupational stress. For example, the costs of worker's compensation claims for stress-related disorders nearly tripled between 1979 and 1983, and accounted for about 12% of all claims in 1985 (DeCarlo, 1987). Industry is attempting to reduce these costs with health promotion campaigns, stress management programs, and employee assistance programs (EAPs) offering mental health counseling services. The results of these efforts appear promising. A number of studies have shown dramatic reductions in health care costs (medical insurance claims, or medical facility usage) for individuals suffering from emotional distress who received brief psychotherapy (Cummings & Vanden Bos, 1981; Jameson, Shuman & Young, 1978; Jones and Vischi, 1979; Schlesinger et al., 1983).

CURRENT STATUS

Employee Assistance Programs (EAPs)

Currently, the most popular vehicle for employee mental health services in the United States appears to be the EAP. Estimates place the current number of EAPs in the United States at over 10 000 (BNA Special Report, 1987), with over 60% of the Fortune 500 companies having an EAP of some sort (Dixon, 1988). The situation appears to be similar in Canada; Santa-Barbara (1984) estimates that 10% of the Canadian workforce has access to an EAP.

Examples of EAPs abound in the literature of the last few years. These include EAPs at Detroit Edison (Nadolski & Sandonato, 1987), Presbyterian Hospital (Lesser & Cavaseno, 1986), US Department of Health and Human Services (Maiden, 1988), Russell Corporation (Gam et al., 1983), New York City (Rostain, Allan, & Rosenberg, 1980), CIGNA Corporation (Hook, 1988), Control Data (Bergmark, 1986), Gates Rubber Company (Busche, 1981), Seagrams of Canada (Chandler et al., 1988), Association of Flight Attendants (Feuer, 1987), in the newspaper industry (Rich, 1987) and in the hospital industry (Howard & Szczerbacki, 1988).

Origins of EAPs

EAPs are job-based programs which assist employees with personal or job-related problems which directly or indirectly affect their job performance. They have their roots in the occupational alcohol programs (OAPs) begun in the 1940s by Alcoholics Anonymous (Trice & Schonbrunn, 1981). Such programs offered an alternative to dismissing employees whose job performance had severely deteriorated due to alcohol abuse. OAPs increased in frequency from approximately 50 in the early 1950s to 500 by 1970 (Stern, 1988). A boost for these programs occurred in 1970 when Congress passed the Comprehensive Alcohol Abuse and Alcoholism Prevention Bill which mandated alcoholism programs for federal employees (Askt, 1976). In 1971, the newly established National Institute on Alcohol Abuse and Alcoholism (NIAAA) began funding research and development of alcohol-related assistance programs, and began actively promoting the establishment of such programs (Dubreuil & Krause, 1983). In 1978, a NIAAA survey of 300 companies with assistance programs found that the most successful programs provided assistance for a wide range of personal problems, rather than for substance abuse alone. From these findings came a NIAAA position paper endorsing broad-based EAPs (Roman, 1981). Since this time, EAPs have been characterized by a wide range of services. The guiding principle of EAPs is that it is more cost effective to rehabilitate a formerly competent employee than to hire and train a replacement. Indeed, Rotham (1986) estimates that it costs 60% more for the latter than the former approach.

Organizational structure of EAPs

EAPs can be either internal to the organization (typically part of the personnel, human resources or medical departments), or external, free-standing organizations which provide services to industry. Such external agencies include consulting firms, hospitals, and community mental health centers (Brill, Herzberg, & Speller, 1985). Very large firms (over 10 000 employees) are more likely, for economic reasons, to sponsor in-house programs (Madonia, 1985), while smaller firms, singly or in consortia, often contract with external agencies (Brill, Herzberg, & Speller, 1985; Dixon, 1988).

There are a variety of forms of EAPs, ranging from simple referral services (i.e. troubled employees are referred to appropriate community resources) to direct treatment (i.e. trained mental health professionals provide counseling). A few EAPs have an organizational development component, which focuses on revision of company policies in an effort to influence employee health (Klarreich, Francek, & Moore, 1985). A handful of other EAPs offer health promotion services, such as stress management, time management, and interpersonal skills training (Parcell, 1985).

Treatment through an EAP is typically initiated via one of two referral methods. The first method is supervisory referral, which occurs in response to declining job performance. Supervisory referral is generally an outcome of a 'constructive confrontation' strategy (Trice and Roman, 1972). The confrontation takes place between the supervisor and the employee, and the focus is on poor work performance, not personal problems. The constructive element of the strategy is the provision of EAP services to the worker while still employed. Repeated confrontations become necessary if work performance does not improve and, ultimately, the supervisor may need to precipitate a crisis and specify progressively more serious consequences (i.e. enter a treatment program or face job layoffs, reductions in pay, or job termination).

Constructive confrontation has been successful in work settings for a number of reasons. First, the focus is on work performance, not the employees' personal (nonoccupational) behaviour, as the former is a legitimate concern for employers. Second, the workplace has significant preventive potential since impaired job performance can be an early indicator of emotional distress. Third, it is more difficult for the troubled employee to use denial mechanisms when confronted with documented evidence of impaired work performance. Finally, the threat of disciplinary actions, even job loss, is a powerful motivating factor for most workers (Beyer & Trice, 1982).

Self-referral is the second referral method. Here, the employee initiates contact with the EAP and obtains counseling independent of supervisory awareness. No information is provided to the employer about the content of the contact, or the identity of the employee. Self-referral is the preferred referral method, under the assumption that employee problems will be addressed before job performance is affected (Santa-Barbara, 1984).

Despite concern over the focus of EAPs on the individual worker, rather than organizational interventions, unions are typically supportive of EAPs and their activities (particularly with respect to substance abuse counseling). Joint labor–management administration of EAPs, or the establishment of union programs, is not uncommon (Blum & Roman, 1988).

EAP Components

The structure of EAPs vary widely among specific programs, but most include a set of company policies and procedures for identifying and responding to employee personal or emotional problems that interfere with work performance (Walsh, 1982). Most programs have a written company policy, formalized procedures for identification and referral, assurance of confidentiality, and health insurance coverage for outpatient treatment. Less uniformity among programs has been found for employee education, supervisory orientation and training, and provision of services for employee dependents.

Walsh & Hingson (1985) reviewed the EAP literature and identified six (6) areas of program variability:

1. Content and formality of company policies and procedures;
2. Mechanisms for problem identification and referral;
3. Involvement of company functional units such as medical, personnel, and industrial relations, as well as union activity;
4. In-house vs external resources;
5. Distribution of problems (diagnoses) treated;

6. Staffing (psychologists, social workers, recovered alcoholics, nurses, physicians, psychiatrists, etc.).

Despite variations in program components, the following are believed to be essential ingredients of an effective EAP (MacLeod, 1985; Walsh, 1982; Wrich, 1984):

1. Commitment and support from top management;
2. A clear, written set of policies and procedures that outlines the purpose of the EAP and how it functions in the organization;
3. Close cooperation with local union(s);
4. Training of supervisors on their role in problem identification;
5. Education of employees and promotion of EAP services to foster widespread utilization throughout the company;
6. A continuum of care, including referral to community agencies and follow-up of each case;
7. An explicit policy on confidentiality of employee information;
8. Maintenance of records for program evaluation purposes;
9. Coverage of EAP services by company health insurance benefits.

Effectiveness of EAPs

Proponents of EAPs point to the cost effectiveness of these programs. A widely cited study of the Kennecott Copper Corporation EAP found a 52% reduction in absenteeism among the utilizers, and an overall reduction in worker's compensation costs of 74.6% and in health care costs of 55.4% (Skidmore, Balsam, & Jones, 1974). Busche (1981) reported a 43% reduction in medical visits to the company clinic at the Gates Rubber Company the first year following implementation of an EAP. Based on figures obtained six months after implementation of EAPs in 16 units operated by the US Department of Health and Human Services, Maiden (1988) estimated a cost–benefit ratio of 1 : 7 after five years. Use of sick leave dropped by 74–80% among users of EAP services at United Air Lines, and the program director reported a 1 : 16.35 dollar return in reduced absenteeism alone (Wrich, 1984).

Although EAPs are routinely promoted as successful, they are rarely evaluated using well-controlled, scientific methodologies. To understand this apparent disparity, it is necessary to appreciate various levels of program evaluation and the wide range of outcome measures used to evaluate program 'success'. Indicators of EAP program success have included:

1. The percentage of employees who enter treatment;
2. The percentage that return to work after treatment;

3. Changes in the status of the personal problem after treatment;
4. Improved work performance;
5. Cost-savings to the company.

Using these types of measures, EAPs achieve uniformly positive results. For example, in a recent national interview survey of 480 private sector companies with EAPs, Blum & Roman (1986) found EAP success rates of 60–68%.

In their review of EAP evaluation research, Kurtz, Googins, & Howard (1984) found relatively few studies that employed any type of comparison group and no studies that randomly assigned employees to study groups. The concern here is that without valid comparison groups or random assignment of employee to groups, there is no good reason to suspect that the treatments under study, as opposed to a host of other factors, produced the observed results. Indeed, nonspecific effects are common in the clinical literature (Kazdin & Wilcoxin, 1976) and in worksite stress management studies (Murphy, 1984).

One confounding variable in EAP evaluation research is selection bias; employees most likely to succeed are screened into the EAP, while the more incorrigible or less likely to succeed are screened out. Trice & Beyer (1984) elaborated other possible selection biases and designed a study to estimate such bias. Two types of selection bias were discussed:

1. Employees identified by managers as having a personal problem but who were discharged, laid off, retired, voluntarily quit, died, or were otherwise separated from the company instead of being referred to the EAP.
2. Employees who were referred to the EAP but did not complete the treatment program, or were 'lost to follow-up', for reasons including those listed in (1) above.

The authors concluded that selection biases in EAPs account for a relatively small percentage (8%) of the high success rates commonly reported for EAPs (Trice & Beyer, 1984).

Beyond the methodological criticisms, little research has addressed other key topics, such as the comparative effectiveness of alternative treatment strategies (e.g. Alcoholics Anonymous, psychotherapy, relaxation training, etc.), inpatient vs outpatient treatment plans, company in-house vs external EAPs, constructive confrontation of employees vs formal discipline, and identification and assessment of EAP selection biases (Walsh & Hingson, 1985). Notable exceptions are studies by Trice & Beyer (1984), which addressed the relative significance of components of EAPs (i.e. constructive confrontation vs formal discipline).

Finally, barriers to EAP evaluation are noteworthy. Foremost among these barriers are limited access by evaluation researchers and issues of employee confidentiality. Walsh & Hingson (1985) supplied convincing evidence of the former. In their study, all but one of 68 companies declined an offer to participate in an evaluation study, most on the basis of logistical and ethical concerns inherent in randomized experiments. Violations of employee confidentiality, or even the impression of violation, is another significant barrier to evaluation research, especially in external EAPs. Since the assurance of confidentiality is crucial to the success of the EAP, many EAP providers are reluctant to provide sensitive employee data to researchers.

Future directions

EAPs are evolving into fully integrated mental health care delivery systems tied closely to health benefit plans. Large companies typically have three separate mechanisms by which mental health services can be offered: worker's compensation, EAPs, and group health insurance plans. Trends indicate that by the year 2000 all these programs will be combined into one package (George-Perry, 1988). Additionally, in some companies, EAPs are now providing advice and direction regarding the selection of health care benefit plans and/or the development of mental health preferred provider organizations (PPOs) (Dixon, 1988; George-Perry, 1988).

NonEAP Programs

Although EAPs are currently the dominant purveyors of industrial mental health counseling programs, less comprehensive programs are also found in the workplace. For example, formal and informal employee support groups have been formed for employees working in highly stressful work environments (e.g. intensive care units or oncology clinics). As reviewed by Weiner & Caldwell (1981), these groups typically consist of 6–12 workers who meet at scheduled intervals and are led by a mental health professional. The purpose is to help the workers deal with work-related stress and conflicts, and the expression and release of emotions is encouraged. Weiner & Caldwell (1981) claim that these groups are successful, pointing to data showing better morale, reduced turnover/absenteeism, and reductions in reported stress levels.

ISSUES FOR THE FUTURE

Weaknesses of Current Industrial Mental Health Counseling Programs

It is clear that the emotional health of workers is becoming an increasing concern of industry due to both health cost and productivity considerations. While industrial mental health counseling programs fill a need in their current form, they do suffer from a number of weaknesses. Criticisms of current programs focus on the points given under the headings below.

Reactive treatment approach

According to Balgopal (1989) and Forrest (1983), mental health counseling programs in industry are reactive rather than proactive. The emphasis is on treating problems after they arise, rather than preventing their occurrence, although the costs of preventing mental illnesses may ultimately be far less than the costs of a strict treatment approach (Orlans, 1986). Additionally, worker-focused counseling does not contribute to the resolution of problems of workplace origin. A better approach, according to Balgopal (1989), is to examine the organization for intrinsic stressors, such as work pacing, or excessive productivity demands, which may negatively impact worker mental health.

The concept of the troubled employee

According to Lee and Rosen (1984) the primary focus of many mental health counseling programs has been on the 'problem' or 'troubled' employee, commonly defined as an employee who displays impaired work performance due to personal problems. This approach, including the supervisory referral procedure, has several drawbacks. Supervisory referral may be resisted by supervisors who are concerned about repercussions affecting the 'labeled' employee (Rostain, Allen, & Rosenberg, 1980). This approach also implies that employees who cannot adjust to the work environment have emotional problems (Lee & Rosen, 1984), and may foster disregard of unhealthy or stressful working conditions (Balgopal, 1989).

Ambiguity regarding the client

A third criticism concerns the client of the mental health program: is the company the client or the individual worker? Orlans (1986) noted that some of the goals and objectives of counseling (e.g. accurate problem identification, problem-focused coping, employee self-actualization) may be in conflict with those of the organization (i.e. increased productivity, reduced health care costs, reduced worker compensation claims, etc.). Furthermore, according to McLean (1983, p. 60), occupational mental health counselors must acknowledge that their allegiance is to the overall mission, or well-being, of the organization. Unless care is taken to place the emphasis on the emotional well-being of the worker, a mental health program may be perceived as a means of social control and enforcement of company policy (Rhodes, 1978). At least one report describes 'subtle coercion' from supervisors and coworkers on employees voluntarily entering treatment (Lee & Rosen, 1984). This perception is reinforced by the fact that occupational mental health programs have typically been aimed at the worker, rather than at management.

The contribution of working conditions to emotional strain

Both Balgopal (1989) and Brody (1988) point out that providers of remedial services may have little appreciation of working conditions and organizational practices or policies which give rise to emotional strain. Knowledge of working conditions, work roles, and company practices can facilitate the treatment process, particularly if the emotional problem has its roots at the workplace. Dubreuil & Krause (1983) argue that therapists must be sensitive to the ways in which clinical problems can interact with work factors. Similarly, McLean (1983) suggests that counselors examine the fit between workers and their job demands to determine if these demands are contributing to disability.

Involvement in organizational change

Technological change places stress on organizations, particularly changes which involve downsizing organizations or workgroups, job redesign, retraining efforts, etc. For example, a survey of large United Kingdom organizations, found that 'change' was cited as the most important current stressor affecting employees (Orlans, 1986). According to McLean (1983), mental health specialists need to become actively involved in organizational change processes to ease the impact of these changes on the psychological health of the workers.

Aspects of Comprehensive Industrial Mental Health Programs

As noted earlier, few of the industrial mental health programs reviewed in this article offered preventive, as well as treatment, components. Most programs utilized educational efforts as a means of promoting the counseling services, and a few have additionally offered health promotion services. However, none combined mental health counseling and health promotion services with education/training directed at the recognition of psychological disorders and underlying risk factors, or with job/organizational design efforts.

In 1988, the US National Institute for Occupational Safety and Health (NIOSH) published a National Strategy for the Prevention of Work-related Psychological Disorders. The document was compiled by a panel of experts (internal and external to NIOSH) in the area of occupational stress, as well as by representatives from labor and management. One of the components of the national strategy centered on comprehensive industrial mental health programs composed of counseling, education/training, and job design interventions. It was recognized that the exact structure of comprehensive mental health programs may vary from industry to industry, and company to company, as each has its own unique blend of risk factors and types of mental health services needed. However, the strategy suggests that an industrial mental health program contain elements from the components given under the headings below (NIOSH, 1988).

Mental health services

The scope and content of mental health programs need to be adjusted according to local factors, such as the nature of the work performed and the special needs of the workforce. All programs should offer, at a minimum, basic psychological support in areas common to any workforce, such as, personal crisis management, alcohol/chemical dependency, marital/family counseling, and stress management. These services need to have both treatment and primary prevention components. More specialized concerns, notably impending retirement, layoff, and relocation or other job-specific problems, may require additional effort and expertise. Mechanisms can be established for input from consultants in occupational mental health. Counseling services should be integrated into the overall occupational health care program, and need to be developed with input from all relevant departments, as well as from workers, and management (Lee & Rosen, 1984).

Mental health programs need to be constructed so that there is an opportunity for collective, as well as individual, interventions; that is, interventions which seek to change aspects of the organization or work environment, as well as those which seek to change the individual worker. In addition, feedback from mental health counseling programs, in aggregate form to protect confidentiality, is a good source of information to help identify and remedy organizational problems.

Within small firms where the establishment of on-site programs for psychological health services may not be feasible, a liaison or network can be established with local mental health or social service agencies to provide a bridge between troubled workers and treatment facilities. Formalized relationships could be developed so that routine referral is possible, and mental health personnel from the agencies can be enlisted readily for specialized programs. State or local mechanisms could be developed to assist small firms in seeking appropriate mental health services.

Educational training services

There is a need to educate workers, management, labor, and health and safety personnel in how to recognize psychological disorders and the underlying risk factors. Such training may include: awareness and appreciation of emotional disorders as occupational health problems; understanding of both work and non-work risk factors; recognition of individual and organizational manifestations of emotional disorders; means of reducing stressful working conditions and personal risks; and the scope of treatment.

There is also a need for educating managers in both the mental health consequences of poor job design, and in work-related causes of psychological disorders and necessary control measures. Such training should reach all levels of management. In addition, Rostain, Allen & Rosenberg (1980) recommend that managers be trained in how to approach the issue of employee counseling.

Information about occupational factors influencing mental health can be placed in corporate news letters. This is especially pertinent because of the job-specific nature of many risk factors. Mental health issues, additionally, can be incorporated into regular health and safety meetings and into meeting notes and labor newsletters. Finally, telenetworks which provide public access to prerecorded health information can be offered to provide individual workers with mental health information and counseling sources.

Job and organizational design feedback

As much research attests, the design of jobs has important influences on employee mental health (e.g. Caplan, *et al.*, 1975; Cooper & Marshall, 1976). Because of their access to organizations and employee populations, industrial mental health counseling programs have great potential for improving employee mental health. For this potential to be realized, however, industrial mental health programs will need to evolve to a more comprehensive level than is currently the case. Developments in this evolution should include the addition of primary prevention components and provisions of feedback to organizations with respect to work environment stressors. In light of the sensitivity of worker confidentiality, such feedback needs to be provided in a manner that prevents individual worker identification. Provision of summary statistics, for example, would protect the confidentiality of workers yet permit organizations to pinpoint stress problems that can serve as a starting point for more in-depth stress assessment studies.

Other types of feedback from an industrial mental health program could take the form of organizational characteristics that generate worker distress and identification of high stress departments or work areas. Provision of this type of feedback requires that mental health counselors become familiar with principles of organizational behavior and the dynamics of work environment/health relationships. This approach may require adding occupational mental health specialists to the counseling program staff and/or providing occupational mental health training to existing staff.

SUMMARY

The high costs to organizations of health care, rising worker's compensation for stress-related disorders, competitive pressures facing US businesses, and technological changes occurring in the workplace suggest that interest in industrial mental health programs will continue into the next decade. For these programs to be successful, they will need to evolve towards more comprehensive programs in which primary, preventive interventions are coupled with more traditional treatment strategies. This evolution will also require that mental health counseling program providers develop competencies in the areas of organizational behaviour and industrial/organizational psychology. Finally, there is a concomitant need for evaluation of these comprehensive programs, using scientifically rigorous designs, to establish their cost effectiveness and their ultimate effects on employee mental health.

Correspondence address
Motivation and Stress Research Section, National Institute for Occupational Safety and Health, Robert A. Taft Laboratories, 4676 Columbia Parkway, Cincinnati, Ohio 45226, USA.

REFERENCES

Anderson, V. V. (1929) *Psychiatry in Industry*, New York: Harper.

Askt, E. L. (1976) *Federal Legislation Relating to Alcohol Abuse and Alcoholism.* Rockville, MD: NIAAA.

Austin, M. J., & Jackson, E. (1977) Occupational mental health and the human services: A review. *Health and Social Work*, 2, 93–118.

Balgopal, P. R. (1989) Occupational social work: An expanded clinical perspective. *Social Work*, 34, 437–442.

Bergmark, R. E. (1986) Employee assistance programs: Trends and principles, *Journal of Business and Psychology*, 1, 59–68.

Beyer, J. M., & Trice, H. M. (1982) Design and implementation of job based alcoholism programs: Constructive confrontation strategies and how they work. In *Occupational Alcoholism: A Review of Research Issues.* DHHS (ADM) Publication No. 82-1184, Washington, DC: US Government Printing Office.

Blum, T. C., & Roman, P. M. (1986) Alcohol, drugs, and EAPs: New data from a national study. *The Almacan*, May, 20–23.

Blum, T. C., & Roman, P. M. (1988) Purveyor organizations and the implementation of employee assistance programs. *The Journal of Applied Behavioral Science*, 24, 397–411.

BNA Special Report (1987) *Employee Assistance Programs: Benefits, Problems and Perspectives*, Washington, DC: Bureau of National Affairs.

Brill, P., Herzberg, J., & Speller, J. L. (1985) Employee assistance programs: An overview and suggested roles for psychiatrists. *Hospital and Community Psychiatry*, 36, 727–732.

Brody, B. E. (1988) Employee assistance programs: An historical and literature review. *American Journal of Health Promotion*, 2, 13–19.

Burlingame, C. C. (1947) Psychiatry in industry. *American Journal of Psychiatry*, 103, 549–553.

Busche, E. J. Jr. (1981) Developing an employee assistance program. *Personnel Journal*, 60, 708–711.

Caplan, R. D., Cobb, S., French, J. R. Jr, Harrison, R. V., & Pinneau, S. R. Jr

(1975) *Job Demands and Worker Health: Main Effects and Occupational Differences*, DHEW (NIOSH) Publication No. 75-160. Washington, DC: US Government Printing Office.

Chandler, R. G., Kroeker, B. J., Fynn, M., & MacDonald, D. A. (1988) Establishing and evaluating an industrial social work programme: The Seagram, Amherstburg experience. *Employee Assistance Quarterly*, 3, 243–253.

Cooper, C. L., & Marshall, J. (1976) Occupational sources of stress: a review of the literature relating to coronary heart disease and mental ill health. *Journal of Occupational Psychology*, 49, 11–28.

Cummings, N., & VandenBos, G. (1981) The twenty year Kaiser-Permanente experience with psychotherapy and medical utilization. *Health Policy Quarterly*, 1, 159–175.

DeCarlo, D. T. (1987) New legal rights related to emotional stress in the workplace. *Journal of Business and Psychology*, 1, 313–325.

Dickson, W. J. (1945) The Hawthorne plan of personnel counseling. *American Journal of Orthopsychiatry*, 15, 343–347.

Dixon, K. (1988) Employee assistance programs: A primer for buyer and seller. *Hospital and Community Psychiatry*, 39, 623–627.

Dubreuil, E., & Krause, N. (1983) Employee assistance programs: Industrial and clinical perspectives, *New Directions for Mental Health Services*, 20, 85–94.

Feuer, B. (1987) Innovations in employee assistance programs: A case study at the Association of Flight Attendants. In A. W. Riley & S. J. Zaccaro (eds), *Occupational Stress and Organizational Effectiveness*. New York: Praeger.

Forrest, D. V. (1983) Employee assistance programs in the 1980's: Expanding career options for counselors. *The Personnel and Guidance Journal*, 62, 105–107.

Gam, J., Sauser, W. I. Jr, Evans, K. L., & Lair, C. V. (1983) Implementing an employee assistance program. *Journal of Employment Counseling*, 20, 61–69.

George-Perry, S. (1988) Easing the costs of mental health benefits. *Personnel Administrator*, 33, 62–67.

Giberson, L. G. (1937) Nervous health in industry. *Personnel Journal*, 15, 255–259.

Gordon, G. (1953) Industry's problem children. *National Safety News*, February, 32–33, 81–84.

Greenwood, M. A. (1918) A report on the cause of wastage of labour in munition factories. *Medical Research Council*. London: HMSO.

Hook, E. (1988) Successful approaches to helping troubled employees. *Risk Management*, June, 70–71.

Howard, J. C., & Szczerbacki, D. (1988) Employee assistance programs in the hospital industry. *Health Care Management Review*, 13, 73–79.

Jameson, J., Shuman, L., & Young, W. (1978) The effects of outpatient psychiatric utilization on recovery from surgery and heart attacks: An analysis of the literature. *American Journal of Public Health*, 72, 141–151.

Jarrett, M. C. (1920) The mental hygiene of industry: Report of progress on work undertaken under the Engineering Foundation of New York City. *Mental Hygiene*, 4, 867–884.

Jones, K., & Vischi, T. (1979) Impact of alcohol, drug abuse and mental health treatment on medical care utilization: A review of the research literature. *Medical Care*, 17, (suppl), 1–82.

Kazdin, A. S., & Wilcoxin, L. A. (1976) Systematic desensitization and non-specific treatment effects: A methodological evaluation. *Psychological Bulletin*, 83, 729–756.

Klarreich, S., Francek, J., & Moore, C. (eds), (1985) *The Human Resources Management Handbook*, New York: Praeger.

Kurtz, N. R., Googins, B., & Howard, W. C. (1984) Measuring the success of occupational alcoholism programs, *Journal of Studies on Alcohol*, **45**, 33–45.

Lee, S. S., & Rosen, E. A. (1984) Employee counseling services: Ethical dilemmas. *The Personnel and Guidance Journal*, **62**, 276–280.

Leonards, J. T. (1981) Corporate psychology: An answer to occupational mental health. *The Personnel and Guidance Journal*, **60**, 47–51.

Lesser, J. G., & Cavaseno, V. H. (1986) Establishing a hospital's employee assistance program. *Health and Social Work*, **11**, 126–132.

Levinson, H. (1956) Employee counseling in industry. *Bulletin of the Menninger Clinic*, **20**, 76–84.

Levinson, H. (1983) Clinical psychology in organizational practice, In J. S. J. Manuso (ed.), *Occupational Clinical Psychology*. New York: Praeger.

McAtee, O. A. (1951) The establishment and function of an industrial mental hygiene service. *American Journal of Psychiatry*, **107**, 623–627.

McLean, A. A. (1973) Occupational mental health: Review of an emerging art. In R. L. Noland (ed.), *Industrial Mental Health and Employee Counseling*. New York: Behavioral Publications.

McLean, A. A. (1983) The psychiatrist's role in occupational mental health. *Advances in Occupational Mental Health*, **20**, 57–63.

MacLeod, A. G. S. (1985) EAPs and blue collar stress. In C. L. Cooper & M. J. Smith (eds), *Job Stress and Blue Collar Work*. London: John Wiley.

Madonia, J. F. (1985) Handling emotional problems in business and industry. *Social Casework*, **66**, 587–593.

Maiden, R. P. (1988) Employee assistance program evaluation in a federal government agency. *Employee Assistance Quarterly*, **3**, 191–203.

Margolis, B. L., Kroes, W. H., & Quinn, R. A. (1974) Job Stress: An unlisted occupational hazard. *Journal of Occupational Medicine*, **16**, 654–661.

Mayo, E. (1934) *The Human Problems of an Industrial Civilization*. New York: Macmillan.

Mayo, E. (1945) *The Social Problems of Industrial Civilization*. Cambridge, MA: Harvard University Graduate School of Business Administration.

Murphy, L. R. (1984) Occupational stress management: A review and appraisal. *Journal of Occupational Psychology*, **57**, 1–15.

Murphy, L. R. (1988) Workplace interventions for stress reduction and prevention. In C. L. Cooper and R. Payne (eds), *Causes, Coping and Consequences of Stress at Work*. New York: John Wiley.

Nadolski, J. N., & Sandonato, C. E. (1987) Evaluation of an employee assistance program. *Journal of Occupational Medicine*, **29**, 32–37.

National Institute for Occupational Safety and Health (NIOSH) (1988) *Proposed National Strategies for the Prevention of Leading Work-related Diseases and Injuries, Part 2*. Association of Schools of Public Health.

Orlans, V. (1986) Counselling services in organisations. *Personnel Review*, **15**, 19–23.

Parcell, C. (1985) Wellness vs illness: Which road are we taking? *EAP Digest*, **5**, 18–27.

Pelletier, K. R., & Lutz, R. (1988) Healthy people—healthy business: A critical review of stress management programs in the workplace. *American Journal of Health Promotion*, **2**, 5–12, 19.

Rhodes, W. C. (1978) Normality and abnormality in perspective. In J. Mearig (ed.), *Working for Children: Ethical Issues Beyond Professional Guidance*. San Francisco: Jossey-Bass.

Rich, C. (1987) Employee assistance programs: Prescription for stress in the press. *Employee Assistance Quarterly*, **3**, 25–34.

Roman, P. (1981) From employee alcoholism to employee assistance: An analysis of the de-emphasis on prevention and on alcoholism problems in work-based programs, *Journal of Studies on Alcoholism*, **42**, 244–272.

Roman, P. M., & Blum, T. C. (1988) Formal intervention in employee health: Comparisons of the nature and structure of employee assistance programs and health promotion programs. *Social Science and Medicine*, **26**, 503–514.

Rosenbaum, M., & Romano, J. (1943) Psychiatric casualties among defense workers. *American Journal of Psychiatry*, **100**, 314–319.

Rostain, H., Allan, P., & Rosenberg, S. (1980) New York City's approach to problem–employee counseling. *Personnel Journal*, **59**, 305–321.

Rothman, M. (1986) Mental health and the workplace: A case for employee assistance programs. *Compensation and Benefits Review*, **18**, 33–43.

Santa-Barbara, J. (1984) Employee assistance programs: An alternative resource for mental health service delivery. *Canada's Mental Health*, **32**, 35–38.

Schlesinger, H., Mumford, E., Glass, G., Patrick, C., & Sharfstein, S. (1983) Mental health treatment and medical care utilization in a fee-for-service system. *American Journal of Public Health*, **73**, 422–429.

Skidmore, R. A., Balsam, D. D., & Jones, O. (1974) Social work practice in industry. *Social Work*, **19**, 280–286.

Smith, K. U. (1962) *Behavior Organization and Work: A New Approach to Industrial Behavioral Science*. Madison, WI: College Printing and Typing Co.

Stenr, M. J. (1988) Economic change and social welfare: Implications for employees' assistance. *Employee Assistance Quarterly*, **3**, 7–23.

Trice, H. M., & Beyer, J. M. (1984) Work related outcomes of the constructive--confrontation strategy in a job based alcoholism program. *Journal of Studies on Alcoholism*, **45**, 393–404.

Trice, H. M., & Roman, P. (1972) *Spirits and Demons at Work: Alcohol and Other Drugs on the Job*. Ithaca, New York: Cornell University.

Trice, H., & Schonbrun, M. (1981) A history of job-based alcoholism programs—1900–1955. *Journal of Drug Issues*, **11**, 171–198.

Walsh, D. C. (1982) Employee assistance programs. *Millbank Memorial Quarterly*, **60**, 492–517.

Walsh, D. C., & Hingson, R. W. (1985) Where to refer employees for treatment of drinking problems. *Journal of Occupational Medicine*, **27**, 745–752.

Weider, A. (1947) A mental hygiene program in industry—a clinical psychological contribution. *Journal of Clinical Psychology*, **3**, 309–320.

Weiner, M. F., & Caldwell, T. (1981) Stresses and coping in ICU nursing II. Nurse support groups on intensive care units. *General Hospital Psychiatry*, **3**, 129–134.

Wilensky, J. L., & Wilensky, H. L. (1951) Personnel counseling: The Hawthorne case. *American Journal of Sociology*, **57**, 265–280.

Wrich, J. T. (1984) *The Employee Assistance Program*, Center City, Minnesota: Hazelden Educational Foundation.

Chapter 8

PERSON–JOB FIT: A CONCEPTUAL INTEGRATION, LITERATURE REVIEW, AND METHODOLOGICAL CRITIQUE

Jeffrey R. Edwards
Darden Graduate School of Business Administration
University of Virginia
USA

The concept of person–job (P–J) fit is ubiquitous in organizational behaviour (OB) and industrial/organizational (I/O) psychology. In essence, P–J fit implies that the person and job operate as joint determinants of individual and organizational outcomes (cf. Lewin, 1951; Murray, 1938). This basic notion underlies theoretical and empirical research in many areas of OB and I/O psychology, including motivation (Hackman & Oldham, 1980), job satisfaction (Locke, 1976), job stress (French, Caplan, & Harrison, 1982), and vocational choice (Holland, 1985).

An overview of the P–J fit literature reveals three basic deficiencies. First, despite the common emphasis on P–J fit across many areas of OB and I/O psychology, developments in these areas have largely occurred independently. This has produced streams of P–J fit research that are typically considered distinct, but actually share more similarities than differences. For example, P–J fit approaches to job satisfaction and job stress share many of the same constructs and operationalize these constructs in basically the same manner (cf. Dawis & Lofquist, 1984; French, Caplan, & Harrison, 1982). Nonetheless, most investigators have overlooked the fundamental similarities of these approaches or, in some cases, emphasized relatively minor differences (e.g. Shirom, 1982). Second, few attempts have been made to comprehensively review and critically evaluate empirical P–J fit research. As a result, there is no unified body of knowledge to justify the current widespread acceptance of P–J fit or to guide new developments in P–J fit research. Third, empirical

International Review of Industrial and Organizational Psychology 1991 Volume 6
Edited by C. L. Cooper and I. T. Robertson © 1991 John Wiley & Sons Ltd.

P–J fit research is repeatedly plagued with serious methodological problems. Though some investigators have acknowledged these problems, many have not, and viable solutions have not been implemented.

The purpose of this chapter is to address the deficiencies in the P–J fit literature summarized above. Specifically, this chapter will provide an integrative framework for P–J fit research, critically review and evaluate available empirical evidence, identify recurring methodological problems, and propose solutions to these problems. The chapter will conclude with recommendations for future research in this important area of investigation.

THE DOMAIN OF PERSON-JOB FIT RESEARCH

Though the boundaries defining a given domain of research are occasionally stated a priori, they often must be inferred from common themes embodied in accumulated research. This is particularly true when new boundaries are drawn across traditionally separate domains, as in the present discussion. A clear statement of a research domain is critical, in that it allows us to distinguish research that falls within this domain from research that is related but conceptually distinct. These distinctions are particularly important in the following review, where they provide criteria for the inclusion of relevant studies and guide the subsequent interpretation of these studies.

The domain of P–J fit research put forth here (see Figure 1) was derived from common themes in areas of I/O psychology and OB research that emphasize the fit, congruence, matching, contingency, or joint influence of the person and job in the prediction of individual and organizational outcomes. Though many areas were considered, the primary sources were job satisfaction (Dawis & Lofquist, 1984; Katzell, 1964; Lawler, 1981; Locke, 1969, 1976; Porter, 1964), motivation (Hackman & Oldham, 1980; Kulik, Oldham, & Hackman, 1987; Lee, Locke, & Latham, 1989; Locke et al., 1981), job stress (French, Caplan, & Harrison, 1982; McGrath, 1976), and vocational choice (Holland, 1985). Though these areas differ in specific terminology and emphasis, several common themes are clearly evident.

One theme is the emphasis on two broad classes of corresponding person and job constructs. The first class concerns employee desires and job supplies available to meet those desires. These constructs are central to P–J fit theories of job satisfaction (Dawis & Lofquist, 1984; Locke, 1969, 1976), job stress (French, Caplan, & Harrison, 1982; Schuler, 1980), vocational choice (Holland, 1985), and motivation, particularly goal-setting theory (Lee, Locke, & Latham, 1989; Locke et al., 1981). Desires have been described in various terms, such as psychological needs (Dawis & Lofquist, 1984; French, Caplan, & Harrison, 1982; Porter, 1964), goals (Lee, Locke, & Latham, 1989; Locke et al., 1981), values (Chatman, 1989; Locke, 1969, 1976), interests (Campbell & Hansen, 1981), and preferences (Pryor, 1987). Though theoretical distinctions among

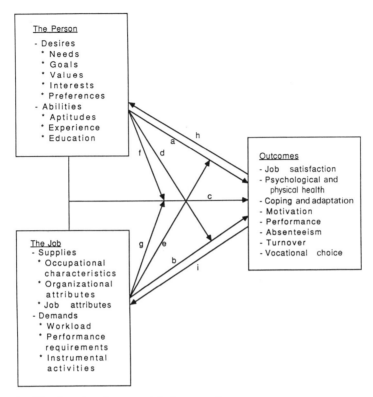

Figure 1 The domain of person–job fit research

these variations are worth noting (for discussions, Locke, 1969; Rokeach, 1973; Super, 1973), each refers to the attractiveness of various job attributes to the employee and, therefore, may be considered under the general rubric of desires. Job supplies range from general occupational characteristics (Holland, 1985) to specific organizational and job attributes, such as pay (Lawler, 1981), participation in decision-making (Alutto & Belasco, 1972), role clarity (Lyons, 1971), and characteristics comprising enriched jobs (Cherrington & England, 1980).

The second class of corresponding person and job constructs concerns job demands and employee abilities available to meet those demands. These constructs are most evident in P–J fit theories of job stress (Beehr & Bhagat, 1985; French, Caplan, & Harrison, 1982; McGrath, 1976), though they have also been posited as predictors of performance (Dunnette, 1976; Waldman & Spangler, 1989) and retention and promotion (Dawis & Lofquist, 1984). Abilities have typically been desribed in terms of employee aptitudes (Dawis & Lofquist, 1984; Desmond & Weiss, 1973) or proxies for aptitudes, such as experience (French, Caplan, & Harrison, 1982), and education (Drexler & Lindell, 1981; French, Caplan, & Harrison, 1982), though they are occasionally inferred from structural job attributes, most notably job decision latitude (Karasek, 1979). Job demands have included quantitative and qualitative work load (French & Caplan, 1972), requirements for adequate job performance (Rosman & Burke, 1980), and activities instrumental to the receipt of valued outcomes (Harrison, 1985; McGrath, 1976).

A second theme is the importance of commensurate measurement of person and job constructs. Commensurate measures express the person and job in terms of the same content dimensions (Caplan, 1987; French, Caplan, & Harrison, 1982; Graham, 1976, Lewin, 1951; Rounds, Dawis, & Lofquist, 1987). For example, commensurate measures of fit between employee desires and job supplies regarding pay would assess the amount of pay desired by the employee and, in a parallel fashion, the amount of pay received by the employee. Commensurate measurement is evident in the instrumentation of P–J fit theories of job satisfaction (Porter, 1962; Weiss et al., 1966), job stress (Caplan et al., 1980), and vocational choice (Holland, 1979). Several investigators have argued that such measures are essential because they provide a logical basis for calculating fit indices, particularly difference scores (e.g. French, Rogers, & Cobb, 1974; Kahn, 1970). However, methodological problems regarding the use of difference scores are widely known (Cronbach & Furby, 1970; Johns, 1981; Wall & Payne, 1973) and, as argued later, the reduction of person and job measures to a single index of any form severely hampers the interpretation of results. Nevertheless, commensurate measures are essential for theoretical reasons, in that they ensure the conceptual relevance of person and job measures to one another (Caplan, 1987). Returning to the previous example, combining a measure of actual pay with desires regarding any job attribute other than pay would render subsequent comparisons meaningless in terms of P–J fit (Kahn, 1970). Furthermore, the combined effects of noncommensurate person and job measures (e.g. worker background and job enlargement) are often interpreted in terms of P–J fit (Kulka, 1979). Such interpretations are readily justified only when commensurate person and job measures are actually used.

A third theme is the emphasis on the combined effects of the person and job rather than either in isolation. In its simplest form, the represents the direct effects of both the person and the job on outcomes. (Figure 1, arrows a and b). A far more common alternative is the reduction of person and job measures to a single index, typically a difference score or some transformation thereof (Figure 1, arrow c). This alternative is particularly common in P–J fit theories of job satisfaction (Dawis & Lofquist, 1984; Katzell, 1964; Locke, 1969, 1976; Porter, 1964) and job stress (French, Caplan, & Harrison, 1982; McGrath, 1976). Another common method of combining person and job measures is the calculation of a product term, reflecting the moderating effects of the person (e.g. value importance) on the relationship between the job and outcomes (Figure 1, arrow d), or the moderating effects of the job (e.g. opportunity for growth) on the relationship between the person and outcomes (Figure, 1 arrow e).[1] This method is evident in models of job satisfaction and stress that posit the strength or importance of a desire as a moderator of the relationship between job characteristics and outcomes (e.g. Evans, 1969; Lyons, 1971; Wanous & Lawler, 1972). Another set of moderating effects involves the impacts of the person (Figure 1, arrow f) or the job (Figure 1, arrow g) on the relationship between a combined index of the person and job (e.g. a difference score) and outcomes. This is most often represented by the use of importance to weight the difference between perceived and desired job attributes (Mobley & Locke, 1970; Rice et al., 1985; Wanous & Lawler, 1972). A final set of relationships is based on transactional (e.g. Schneider, 1983, 1987; Terborg, 1981) and cybernetic (Cummings & Cooper, 1979; Edwards, 1989) approaches to P–J fit, where the effects of individual and organizational outcomes on the person and job are also considered (Figure 1, arrows h and i).

A fourth theme involves the outcomes considered in P–J fit research (see Figure 1). These outcomes essentially represent the dependent variables emphasized in the various areas of I/O psychology and OB research upon which the present framework is based. By far, the outcome that has received the most attention is job satisfaction. However, studies have also examined outcomes primarily relevant to the employee, such as coping, adaptation, and psychological and physical health, as well as outcomes concerning the employee's role in the organization, such as motivation, performance, commitment, absenteeism, turnover, and vocational choice.

As presented here, the domain of P–J fit research excludes several related but distinct areas of investigation that, in some instances, have been viewed in terms of P–J fit. For example, studies of the moderating effects of general individual differences, such as Protestant work ethic and alienation from middle-class norms (Hulin & Blood, 1968; Turner & Lawrence, 1965), on the relationship between job characteristics and outcomes are often interpreted in terms of P–J fit. The most explicit example of this is provided by Kulik, Oldham, & Hackman (1987), who describe job characteristics theory (Hackman & Oldham, 1980) in terms of P–J fit, based on the premise that enriched jobs increase motivation and job satisfaction only for employees with high growth needs strength (GNS). However, close inspection reveals that the GNS measure contains few items that specifically address the desire for an enriched job (cf. Aldag & Brief, 1979; Cherrington & England, 1980). Therefore, the GNS

---

[1] Though these effects are represented by separate arrows to reflect their different theoretical origins, it should be emphasized that they both represent the interaction of the person and job and, hence, are statistically equivalent.

measure is not commensurate with measures of job enrichment, such as the Job Diagnostic Survey (Hackman & Oldham, 1975), and results from job characteristics research should not be considered direct tests of P–J fit. A similar lack of commensurate measurement is evident in studies of general individual differences (e.g. Hulin & Blood, 1968; Turner & Lawrence, 1965), in which the job is rarely characterized in the same terms as the individual.

Research into role stress (Jackson & Schuler, 1985; Kahn et al., 1964) has also been conceptualized in terms of P–J fit. For example, person–role conflict has been defined in terms of misfit between personal values and role requirements (Kahn et al., 1964; Rizzo, House, & Lirtzman, 1970). Likewise, quantitative and qualitative role overload are typically defined in terms of demands that exceed employee skills and abilities (French & Caplan, 1972). However, measures of role conflict and role overload rarely contain commensurate person and job indices, and single items that explicitly tap commensurate person and job constructs (e.g. performing work that suits one's values) are often confounded with items that do not (e.g. MacKinnon, 1978; Newton & Keenan, 1987; Rizzo, House, & Lirtzman, 1970). Hence, though conceptual definitions of role stress emphasize P–J misfit, most studies of role stress do not use measures that adequately represent commensurate person and job constructs.

Several areas of research employ commensurate measures but do not focus on both the person and job. For example, value congruence research (Kemelgor, 1982; Meglino, Ravlin, & Adkins, 1989; Posner, Kouzes, & Schmidt, 1985) focuses on the correspondence between the values of organizational members (e.g. supervisor and subordinate). As such, this research involves the fit between two or more persons rather than the person and job. Nonetheless the effects of value congruence are often interpreted in terms of P–J fit, based on the assumption that value congruence facilitates the attainment of desired job attributes (Kemelgor, 1982) or is inherently desirable and, therefore, yields satisfaction (Posner, Kouzes, & Schmidt, 1985). However, value congruence studies typically do not measure the desire for value congruence, nor do they measure desired and actual job attributes that are presumably contingent on value congruence. Hence, it is inappropriate to interpret the results of these studies in terms of P–J fit.

An analogous example is provided by studies of interpersonal agreement (Berger-Gross, 1982; Graen & Schiemann, 1978), which examine the similarity between employee perceptions of various job and organizational attributes. Because these studies typically contain no direct measure of the desires or abilities of the employee, their results should not be interpreted in terms of P–J fit. Similarly, research into social comparison processes (Goodman, 1977; Oldham et al., 1986) emphasizes the congruence between job attributes across employees (e.g. pay received by self and other). Though the job attributes obtained by other employees may partly influence employee preferences (Lawler, 1981; Locke, 1969; Michalos, 1985), these two constructs are conceptually distinct, and most studies provide no direct measure of employee preferences to verify this relationship (Huseman, Hatfield, & Miles, 1987).

Studies of the congruence between job attributes and employee expectations are also excluded from the P–J fit domain, in that expectations and desires, though often considered interchangeable are conceptually distinct (Locke, 1969). Expectations refer to beliefs regarding job conditions as they are anticipated to exist in the future. These beliefs do not necessarily involve conditions that are desirable, as when a layoff or plant closing is expected. Furthermore, empirical evidence indicates that, when desires are controlled, the relationship between expectations and job outcomes, such as job satisfaction, disappears (Greenhaus, Seidel, & Marinis, 1983; Locke, 1967). This does not exclude the possibility that expectations and desires are causally related. For example, expectations regarding future job conditions may shape employee preferences (Michalos, 1985), and preferences for certain job attributes may prompt the employee to take action to ensure their eventual attainment, thereby influencing expectations. Nonetheless, expectations and desires are distinct constructs, and research into the fit between job attributes and expectations should be considered related to, but distinct from, P–J fit research.

In summary, the domain of P–J fit research is characterized by commensurate person and job constructs hypothesized to jointly influence various individual and organizational outcomes. Two basic forms of fit are included, one involving the correspondence between employee desires and job supplies, and another involving the correspondence between employee abilities and job demands. P–J fit research may be considered a specific form of congruence research that focuses explicitly on commensurate person and job constructs. The broader domain of congruence research also includes research into individual differences (Hackman & Oldham, 1980; Hulin & Blood, 1968; Turner & Lawrence, 1965), value congruence (Kemelgor, 1982; Meglino, Rawlin, & Adkins, 1989; Posner, Kouzes, & Schmidt, 1985), interpersonal agreement (Berger-Gross, 1982; Graen & Schiemann, 1978), and social comparison processes (Goodman, 1977; Oldham et al., 1986). Several investigators have derived plausible hypotheses relating constructs within these areas and those contained within the domain of P–J fit (e.g. Lawler, 1981; Michalos, 1985). However, the constructs and processes represented within these areas are theoretically distinct, and research in one area should not be used to draw conclusions regarding another. Other areas of research are conceptually consistent with P–J fit (e.g. Kahn et al., 1964), but associated empirical research has generally not employed measures that allow valid inferences regarding P–J fit. Hence, P–J fit research focuses explicitly on commensurate person and job constructs as predictors of individual and organizational outcomes and, as such, falls within the broader context of congruence research. The following review will focus specifically on studies within the domain of P–J fit research as described above.

LITERATURE REVIEW

In selecting studies for the following review, three criteria were used. First, only studies within the domain of P–J fit research were reviewed. This included all studies using commensurate measures of the desires or abilities of the person and the supplies or demands of the job as predictors of individual and/or organizational outcomes. Studies using 'direct' measures of fit (i.e. those comparing the person and job within a single item) were included, provided these measures contained explicit and separate references to the person and job. Second, to ensure that some minimum criterion of scientific rigor had been met, only published studies were considered. Third, to focus explicitly on fit regarding the job, only field studies with samples from working populations were included. A handful of studies that met these criteria were nonetheless excluded because they did not adequately describe the operationalization of fit (e.g. Elizur & Tziner, 1977; Hughes, 1979; Salomone & Sheehan, 1985), the direction of the obtained effect (e.g. Abdel-Halim, 1979; Humphrys, 1981; West & Rushton, 1989), or whether the effect was significant (e.g. Coburn, 1975; Hackman & Lawler, 1971; Hulin & Smith, 1965; Locke, 1969; Sadler, 1970; Tannenbaum & Kuleck, 1978; Vroom & Deci, 1971). Computerized (ABI/Inform, PsychINFO) and ancestral (Cooper, 1982) searches of literature published from 1960 through 1989 yielded 92 studies that were included in the review. These studies are summarized in Table 1.

Given the substantial number of studies located, it seemed potentially useful to supplement the following narrative review with a meta-analysis (Hunter, Schmidt, & Jackson, 1982; Wolf, 1986). However, a meta-analysis was not conducted, for two reasons. First, despite differences in samples, measures, and operationalizations of fit, nearly every study reviewed found relationships that were significant and in the expected direction. Therefore, it is highly unlikely that the results of a meta-analysis would have substantively altered the conclusions of the narrative review (cf. Guzzo, Jackson, & Katzell, 1987). More importantly, nearly every study reviewed contained methodological flaws that seriously threaten the interpretability of the results obtained. Cumulating these results through a meta-analysis was not deemed a worthwhile pursuit.

The following review is organized in two sections corresponding to the two primary classes of P–J fit described earlier, i.e. the fit between employee desires and job supplies, and the fit between employee abilities and job demands. Within each class, studies are grouped according to the fit index used (algebraic difference, absolute difference, etc.) and, for each index, the

Table 1—Summary of Person–Job Fit Studies

Investigators	Sample	Content area(s)	Person measure	Job measure	Fit index	Findings
Alutto & Acito (1974)	75 industrial workers	Participation in decision-making	Preferred	Actual	$J–P$	Positive relationships with job satisfaction, job and organizational commitment, trust, and favorable attitudes toward company; negative relationship with tension
Alutto & Belasco (1972)	454 school teachers	Participation in decision-making	Preferred	Actual	$P–J$	U-shaped relationships with militant attitudes; no relationship with organizational commitment or trust
Alutto & Vredenburgh (1977)	197 nurses	Participation in decision-making	Preferred	Actual	$J–P$	Negative relationship with tension; no relationship with trust
Amerikaner, Elliot, & Swank (1988)	80 employee adults	Occupation	Preferred	Actual	$r_{P,J}$	No relationship with job satisfaction
Andrews & Farris (1972)	100 scientists	Time pressure	Optimal	Typical	$P–J$	No relationship with performance
Aranya, Barak, & Amernic (1981)	2148 American and Canadian accountants	Conventional occupation	Preferences, competencies, interests	Actual job	$P=J$ $P|J$	P=J positively related to satisfaction and commitment for Americans; conventional scores positively related to satisfaction for Americans and commitment for both samples

Continued

Table 1—Continued

Investigators	Sample	Content area(s)	Person measure	Job measure	Fit index	Findings
Barak & Meir (1974)	368 employed adults	Occupation	Attractiveness	Actual occupation	$P=J$ $P|J$	Positive relationship with satisfaction
Brandt & Hood (1968)	126 employed adults	Occupation	Liking	Actual occupation	$P=J$	Positive relationship with occupational satisfaction
Barrett (1978)	45 naval personnel	Variety, independence	Preferred	Actual	$|P-J|$	Negative relationship with job satisfaction
Beer (1966)	129 insurance company	Leader behavior (initiating structure, production emphasis, consideration, freedom of action); needs (security, social, esteem, autonomy, self-actualization)	Appropriate; importance	Actual	$J-P_{A,I}$ $J \times P_A$	No relationships with initiative or self-assurance
Betz (1984)	330 employed women	Security/safety, social, autonomy, esteem self-actualization	Should be	Actual	$J-P$	Positive relationship with job satisfaction for self-actualization fit
Betz (1969)	105 department store employees	Job attributes	Importance	Actual	$-|P-J|$	Positive relationship with job satisfaction

Study	Sample	Attribute	Needed	Actual	Discrepancy	Findings
Blau (1981)	123 bus drivers	Company policies, scheduling, personal danger	Needed	Actual	$P-J$ $P+J$	For company policies and scheduling, job satisfaction negatively related to $P-J$ for personal danger, job performance positively related to $P-J$; no significant relationships to $P+J$
Butler (1983)	104 DOT administrators, 98 bank employees	Intrinsic and extrinsic job attributes	Importance	Actual	P, J $P \times J$	Job satisfaction positively related to P and J; $P \times J$ interaction not significant
Cairo (1982)	83 employed adults	Occupation type	Liking	Actual occupation	$P = J$	No relationship with job or career satisfaction
Cherrington & England (1980)	3053 manufacturing workers	Job enrichment	Would like	Actual	P, J $P \times J$ $J\|P$	Job satisfaction positively related to actual job enrichment and negatively related to desired job enrichment; job performance positively related to actual job enrichment but unrelated to desired job enrichment; stronger relationship between job satisfaction and job enrichment for respondents who desired an enriched job
Cook & Wall (1980)	260 blue-collar workers	Social, self-esteem, autonomy, self-actualization	Would like	Actual	$P-J^\star$	Negative relationships with interpersonal trust, organizational commitment, and job satisfaction

Continued

Table 1—Continued

Investigators	Sample	Content area(s)	Person measure	Job measure	Fit index	Findings
Crosby (1982)	345 employed adults	Job attributes	Wanted	Actual	$J-P^\star$	Negative relationships with resentment
Dolliver, Irvin & Bigley (1972)	220 employed	Occupation type	Liking	Actual occupation	P/J	No relationship with job satisfaction
Dorr, Honea, & Posner (1980)	66 nurses, attendants, and ward clerks	Involvement, support, spontaneity, autonomy, practical orientation, anger/aggression, order/organization, program clarity, staff control	Ideal	Actual	$P-J$	Job satisfaction positively related to actual involvement, support, practical orientation, order/organization, and program clarity and negatively related to fit for involvement, support, autonomy, practical orientation, order/organization, and program clarity
Doty & Betz (1979)	88 sales managers	Realistic, investigative, artistic, social, enterprising, conventional	Preferences, competences, interests	Actual	P/J	Satisfaction positively related to social and enterprising scales
Drexler & Lindell (1981)	2286 US Army personnel	Training	Type of training	Job type	$P=J$	Positive relationship with job satisfaction
Dyer & Theriault (1976)	392 employed adults	Importance of determinants of pay increases	Should be	Actual	$P-J$	Negative relationship with pay satisfaction

Study	Sample	Content	Measure	Comparison	Index	Results
Feldman & Meir (1976)	167 employed women	Realistic, investigate, artistic, social, enterprising & conventional occupations	Preferences, competencies, interests	Actual	$P\|J$	Satisfaction positively related to interest in relevant occupation
French, Caplan, & Harrison (1982)	318 male blue- and white-collar workers	Job complexity role ambiguity, responsibility for persons, workload, overtime, income; length of service, education	Wanted; own level	Actual; required	$J-P$ $\|J-P\|$ $(J-P)>0$ $(J-P)<0$ $(J-P)/P$ $\|(J-P)/P\|$ $(J-P)/P<0$ $(J-P)/P<0$ $(J-P)^2$	Asymmetric V-shaped relationships between psychological strains and job complexity, role ambiguity, responsibility for persons, workload, education, and length of service; psychological strains negatively related to income $((J-P)/P)$ and positively related to overtime fit $(J-P)$; few relationships with physiological symptoms or health behaviors
Furnham & Shaeffer (1984)	82 employed adults	Occupation type	Preferences, competencies, interests	Actual	$P\|J$	Positive relationship with job satisfaction; negative relationship with mental strain
Gilbride (1973)	100 priests	Occupation type	Preference	Actual	$P\|J$	No relationship with resignation
Giles (1977)	260 nonsupervisory employees	Higher-order needs	Would like	Actual	$J-P$	Negative relationship with volunteering for a job enrichment program

Continued

Table 1—Continued

Investigators	Sample	Content area(s)	Person measure	Job measure	Fit index	Findings
Giles & Barrett (1971)	64 engineers and managers	Merit increases	Equitable	Hypothetical	J/P	For $J<P$, weak positive relationship; for $J>P$, strong positive relationship with pay satisfaction
Greenhaus, Seidel, & Marinus (1983)	125 employed adults	Task characteristics, interpersonal relationships, company practices	Preferred	Actual	$1-|P-J|^\star$	Positive relationship with job satisfaction
Hall, Schneider, & Nygren (1970)	141 professional foresters	Security, social, esteem, autonomy, self-actualization	Should be	Actual	$J-P$	Positive relationships with job challenge, job involvement, and professional identification, particularly for autonomy and self-actualization
Hener & Meir (1981)	126 registered nurses	Clinical area	Attractiveness	Actual area	$P=J$	Positive relationship with job satisfaction
Herman & Hulin (1973)	105 supervisory personnel	Security, social, esteem, autonomy self-actualization	Should be	Actual	$P-J$	Negative relationships with work pay, and promotion satisfaction

Study	Sample	Variables			$P-J$*	Findings
Hollenbeck (1989)	140 salespeople	Pay, work itself, supervision, coworkers	Should	Actual	$P-J$*	Negative relationship with job satisfaction and organizational commitment; positive relationship with job turnover; no relationship with organizational turnover
Hrebiniak (1974)	46 hospital employees	Participation in decision-making	Desired	Actual	$P-J$ $(P-J)/J$	$P-J$ negatively related to trust but unrelated to role tension or organizational commitment; $(P-J)/J$ unrelated to outcomes
Hrebiniak & Alutto (1972)	318 teachers, 395 nurses	Time spend on job activities; importance of advancement criteria	Ideal; should	Actual	$|P-J|$	Factors for advancement fit negatively related to commitment
Hrebiniak & Roteman (1973)	40 managers	Security, social, esteem, autonomy, self-actualization	Should be	Actual	$P-J$	Positive relationship with absenteeism for security, esteem, autonomy, and self-actualization fit
Imparato (1972)	349 hospital employees	Job attributes	Should be	Actual	$P-J$	Negative relationship with job satisfaction; higher satisfaction for respondents high on both P and J than those low on both P and J

Continued

Table 1—Continued

Investigators	Sample	Content area(s)	Person measure	Job measure	Fit index	Findings
Ivancevich (1979)	154 project engineers	Participation in decision-making	Desired	Actual	$P-\mathcal{J}$	Inverted U-shaped relationship with organizational commitment, work satisfaction, supervisor satisfaction, and performance; U-shaped relationship with role conflict, physical symptoms, and job tension; no relationship with self-esteem, attitudes toward company, motivation, role ambiguity, or fatigue
Ivancevich & Donnelly (1974)	261 salesmen, supervisors, and operating employees	Role clarity	Importance	Actual	$\mathcal{J}\|P$	Stronger positive relationships with job interest and job satisfaction and stronger negative relationships with tension, physical symptoms, and propensity to leave for respondents with high need for clarity
Klein & Wiener (1977)	54 managers	Occupation	Liking	Actual	$P\|\mathcal{J}$	No relationship with job satisfaction or mental health

Study	Sample	Attribute	Ideal	Comparison	Type	Findings
Korman (1967)	52 employed adults	Job attributes	Desired	Actual	P–J	Negative relationship with job satisfaction
Lachman & Aranya (1986)	1206 CPAs	Job attributes	Should be	Actual	P–J	Positive relationship with turnover intentions; negative relationships with job satisfaction and organizational and professional commitment
Laing, Swaney & Prediger (1984)	1372 employed adults	Occupation	Preferred	Actual	P–J	Positive relationship with staying in the same type of occupation
Lawler & Hall (1970)	291 scientists	Self-actualization, autonomy	Should be	Actual	P–J	No relationship with self-rated effort or performance
Lawler & Porter (1967)	148 managers	Security, social, esteem, autonomy, self-actualization	Should be	Actual	J–P	Positive relationship with effort and performance
Lefkowitz, Somers, & Weinberg (1984)	632 employed adults	Job attributes	Importance	Actual	P×J	Stronger relationship with job involvement for more important job attributes
London & Klimoski (1975)	153 registered nurses	Job complexity	Should	Actual	P–J	Performance lower for excess complexity than for optional or inadequate complexity; job satisfaction lower for inadequate complexity than for optional or excess complexity; satisfaction with peers higher for optional complexity than for excess or inadequate complexity

Continued

Table 1—Continued

Investigators	Sample	Content area(s)	Person measure	Job measure	Fit index	Findings
Lopez & Greenhaus (1978)	523 school employees	Job attributes	Would like	Actual	$\|P-J\|$	Negative relationship with job satisfaction
Lyons (1971)	156 nurses	Role clarity	Importance	Actual	J/P	Stronger positive relationship with job satisfaction and stronger negative relationships with intended and actual turnover for respondents with high need for clarity; negative relationship between role clarity and tension regardless of need for clarity
Meir & Engel (1986)	81 physicians	Social contact, mechanical, and sensation-seeking activities	Liking	Actual	$1-\|P-J\|$	Positive relationships with job satisfaction
Meir & Erez (1981)	109 engineers	Six job activities	Liking	Dominant activity	P/J	Positive relationship between liking of dominant activity and satisfaction
Meir & Melamed (1986)	74 female primary school teachers	Occupation	Preferences, competencies, interests	Actual	$P=J$	Positive relationship with occupational satisfaction; negative relationship with somatic symptoms; no relationship with work satisfaction or anxiety

		Occupation type	Preference; attractiveness	Actual occupation	$P=J$	
Melamed & Meir (1981)	227 employed men; 66 employed adults				$P=J$	Positive relationship with job satisfaction and engaging in leisure activities similar to one's job; negative relationship with seeking satisfaction through leisure activities
Michalos (1980)	357 clerical workers	Overall job	Goal	Actual	$J/P\star$	Positive relationships with job satisfaction
Michalos (1983)	291 employed adults	Overall job	Goal	Actual	J/P	Positive relationships with job satisfaction
Miles & Petty (1975)	152 government R&D employees	Role clarity	Importance	Actual	J/P	Stronger negative relationship with tension for respondents with high need for clarity
Mount & Muchinsky (1978)	362 employed adults	Realistic, investigative, social, enterprising, conventional	Preferences, competencies, interests	Actual job	$P=J$	Satisfaction higher for respondents in congruent jobs

Continued

Table 1—Continued

Investigators	Sample	Content area(s)	Person measure	Job measure	Fit index	Findings
O'Brien & Dowling (1980)	1383 employed adults	Skill utilization, influence, variety, pressure, interaction	Desired	Actual	$P, \mathcal{J}$ $P \times \mathcal{J}$ $\lvert P - \mathcal{J} \rvert$	Job satisfaction positively related to perceived influence, interaction, skill utilization and variety and desired interaction and pressure and negatively related to desired influence, skill utilization, and variety; relationship between job satisfaction and perceived skill utilization and variety stronger for those with high desires; relationship between job satisfaction and interaction and pressure positive only for those with low desires; relationship between job satisfaction and absolute difference fit negative for skill utilization, influence, and variety and positive for interaction
O'Brien & Humphrys (1982)	281 pharmacists	Skill utilization, influence, variety	Would like	Actual	$P \times \mathcal{J}$ $(P \times \mathcal{J})^2$ $(P \times \mathcal{J})^3$	Few significant effects for $P \times \mathcal{J}$ in predicting job satisfaction; no significant effects for $(P \times J)^2$ or $(P \times J)^3$

			Would like	Actual		
O'Brien & Stevens (1981)	192 factory workers	Influence	Would like	Actual	$P \times J$	Positive relationship between influence and satisfaction with coworkers only for those with high desires
Orpen (1974)	120 factory workers	Job attributes	Should	Actual	$J-P$	Positive relationship with job satisfaction
Payne (1970)	81 unskilled workers; 106 managers	Security, social, esteem, autonomy, self-actualization	Ought, Importance	Actual	$J-P_o$ $(J-P_o)/P_I$	For unskilled workers, neuroticism negatively related to $J-P_o$ and job adjustment positively related to $(J-P_o)/P_I$; for managers, job satisfaction positively related to $J-P_o$ and $(J-P_o)/P_I$
Pazy & Zin (1987)	175 employed adults	Occupation type; job attributes	Preferences, competencies, interests; desires	Actual	$P=J$ $|P-J|$	Occupational fit ($P=J$) positively related to organizational commitment but unrelated to professional commitment, job satisfaction or job involvement; job attributes fit ($|P-J|$) positively related to occupational commitment, professional commitment, and job satisfaction but unrelated to job involvement
Peiser & Meir (1978)	360 employed adults	Occupation	Attractiveness	Actual job	$P=J$	Positive relationship with satisfaction and seven-year stability of attractiveness ratings

Continued

Table 1—Continued

Investigators	Sample	Content area(s)	Person measure	Job measure	Fit index	Findings
Pelz & Andrews (1976)	534 scientists	Job attributes; influence	Importance; preferred	Actual	$J\text{–}P$	Performance quality positively related to J and $J\text{–}P$ for job attributes; no relationship with performance quantity
Phillips, Barrett, & Rush (1978)	60 blue-collar workers	Job attributes	Preferred	Actual	$|P\text{–}J|$	Negative relationship with job satisfaction
Porter & Lawler (1968)	563 managers	Security, social, esteem, autonomy, self-actualization	Should	Actual	$P\text{–}J$	Negative relationship with supervisor performance ratings for social, esteem, autonomy, and self-actualization; positive relationship with self-performance ratings for social
Rice, McFarlin, & Bennett (1989)	78 part-time workers	13 job facets	Wanted	Actual	$|P\text{–}J|$ $P \times J$	For most facets, satisfaction positively related to $|P\text{–}J|$ stronger relationship between satisfaction and perceived amount for those with high wanted amount
Rosman & Burke (1980)	130 sales personnel	12 job aptitudes	Competencies	Requirements	$|P\text{–}J|$	Negative relationship with job satisfaction; no relationship with self-esteem

Study	Sample	Content dimension			Indices	Results
Rounds, Davis & Lofquist (1987)	635 employed adults; 405 employed adults	Job attributes	Importance	Actual	$P=\mathcal{J}$ $P\times\mathcal{J}$ $r_{P,J}$ D^2 D'^2 D''^2 $P\times D^2$	Job satisfaction unrelated to $P=\mathcal{J}$ or $P\times\mathcal{J}$, positively related to $r_{P,J}$, and negatively related to D^2 indices
Scarpello & Campbell (1983)	185 R&D employees	18 job facets	Importance	Actual	D^2	Negative relationship with facet satisfaction
Schletzer (1966)	185 employed adults	Occupation type	Liking	Actual occupation	$P\|\mathcal{J}$	No relationship with job satisfaction
Sexton (1967)	83 manufacturing	Need for achievement, affiliation, autonomy, recognition, self-actualization	Importance	Actual	$P-\mathcal{J}$	No relationship with performance effectiveness
Sheridan & Slocum (1975)	35 managers; 59 machine operators	Job attributes	Should be; importance	Actual	$P_{SB}-\mathcal{J}$ $P_{I}\times\mathcal{J}$ $P_{I}\times(P_{SB}-\mathcal{J})$	For managers, $P_{I}\times\mathcal{J}$ positively related to performance 12 months earlier; for machine operators, $P_{SB}-\mathcal{J}$ negatively related to performance after controlling for $\mathcal{J}$
Slocum (1971)	87 supervisors; 132 managers	Security, social, esteem, autonomy, self-actualization	Should be	Actual	$\mathcal{J}-P$	Positive relationship with performance for social, esteem, autonomy, and self-actualization fit

Continued

Table 1—Continued

Investigators	Sample	Content area(s)	Person measure	Job measure	Fit index	Findings
Sorensen & Sorensen (1974)	264 CPAs	Professional and bureaucratic work experiences	Ideal	Actual	$J-P$	Positive relationships with job satisfaction; negative relationship with turnover intentions for professional experiences; positive relationship with turnover intentions for bureaucratic experiences
Swaney & Prediger (1985)	1688 employed	Occupation	Preferred	Actual	$|P-J|$	Negative relationship with interest in work
Tziner (1987)	400 industrial employees	Achievement climate	Preferred	Actual	P, J $P-J^\star$	J positively related to job satisfaction and commitment; P positively related to performance and commitment; $P-J^\star$ positively related to job satisfaction, performance, and commitment
Vaitenas & Wiener (1977)	150 employed adults	Occupation type	Liking	Actual occupation	$P|J$	Negative relationship with career change
Wanous (1974)	80 female operators	Variety, autonomy, task identity, task feedback	Would like	Actual	$J|P$	Stronger relationships with job satisfaction but not absenteeism or performance for respondents who desired variety, autonomy, task identity, task feedback, and other job characteristics

Wanous & Lawler (1972)	208 telephone company employees	23 job attributes	Should be, would like, importance	Actual	$J \times P$ $P_{SB}-J$ $P_{WL}-J$ $P_I \times (P_{SB}-J)$ $P_I \times (P_{WL}-J)$	Job satisfaction negatively related to all discrepancy indices; importance weighting did not increase the obtained relationships
Wanous & Zwany (1977)	208 telephone company employees	Existence, relatedness, growth	Importance	Actual	$P|J$	Relationship between importance and satisfaction negative for respondents with low supplies and positive for respondents with high supplies
White & Ruh (1973)	2755 manufacturing employees	Participation decision-making	Importance	Perceived amount	$P \times J$	No relationship with job involvement, motivation, or identification with company
White & Spector (1987)	496 city and county managers	Job attributes	Preferred	Actual	$J-P$	Positive relationship with job satisfaction
Wiener & Klein (1978)	101 managers	Occupation type	Liking	Actual occupation	$P|J$	Positive relationship with job satisfaction
Wiggins (1984)	123 school counselors	Occupation; realistic, investigative, artistic, social, enterprising, conventional	Liking	Actual occupation	$P=J$ $P|J$	Both fit indices positively related to job satisfaction
Wiggins (1976)	110 teachers	Realistic, investigative, artistic, social, enterprising, & conventional occupations	Appeal	Actual job	$P|J$	Satisfaction positively related to social and artistic interests and negatively related to realistic and conventional interests

Continued

Table 1—Continued

Investigators	Sample	Content area(s)	Person measure	Job measure	Fit index	Findings
Wiggins *et al.* (1983)	247 teachers	Realistic, investigative, artistic, social, conventional	Preferences	Actual type of teaching	$P=\mathcal{J}$	Positive relationship with satisfaction
Wright & Gutkin (1981)	60 teachers	Assessment, direct services, consultation, administration, and information activities	Desired	Actual	$P \cdot \mathcal{J}$	Satisfaction negatively related to actual assessment activities and positively related to actual service, actual consultation, and desired administration activities
Zytowski (1974)	75 employed adults	Occupation	Preference	Actual occupation	$P=\mathcal{J}$	Positive relationship with occupational satisfaction but not performance
Zytowski (1976)	882 employed adults	Occupation	Preference	Actual occupation	$P|\mathcal{J}$	No relationship with job satisfaction or job success; positive relationship with continuation in occupation

Note: When distinct content areas were collapsed into a single measure, a summary label (e.g. 'job attributes') is used rather than the original content areas. For fit indices, '$P|\mathcal{J}$' (read 'P, given '$\mathcal{J}$') refers to studies examining the relationship between the person and outcomes for different jobs. Similarly, '$\mathcal{J}|P$' (read '$\mathcal{J}$, given P') refers to studies examining the relationship between job attributes and outcomes for different persons. Subscripts were added to distinguish between multiple person measures when they were used differently in operationalizations of fit. '$P \cdot \mathcal{J}$' indicates that person and job measures were entered as simultaneous predictors of outcomes in a regression analysis. A superscript star ($\star$) indicates a 'direct assessment' of fit (see text).

specific type of person measure used. Studies that explicitly compared multiple fit indices are reviewed separately at the end of each section. Methodological problems specific to a given study are discussed with that study; problems common to multiple studies are discussed separately at the end of the chapter.

Fit Between Employee Desires and Job Supplies

Algebraic difference

By far, most empirical P–J fit research has focused on the fit between employee desires and job supplies, and the bulk of these studies have operationalized fit as an algebraic difference. Though a handful of these studies were conducted prior to 1960 (for a review, see Katzell, 1964), most followed the development of Porter's need satisfaction questionnaire (PNSQ; Porter, 1962). The PNSQ contains 13 items describing job attributes intended to reflect Maslow's need hierarchy, with two additional items reflecting pay and knowledge. For each item, respondents rate the current level ('is now'), desired (i.e. appropriate) level ('should be'), and importance of the indicated job attribute. The difference between current and appropriate responses ('should be' minus 'is now') is considered an index of need deficiency, whereas the negative of this difference ('is now' minus 'should be') is considered an index of need satisfaction (Porter, 1962).[2]

Most early studies using the PNSQ documented differences in need deficiency with respect to job level, job type, and other contextual variables (Cummings & ElSalmi, 1968; Haire, Ghiselli, & Porter, 1966; Porter, 1964; Porter & Lawler, 1964). Because these variables are considered determinants rather than consequences of need deficiency (Porter, 1964), they provide little information regarding the outcomes of P–J fit. Other early studies of the PNSQ focused primarily on its psychometric properties, particularly its correspondence with Maslow's theory (Wahba & Bidwell, 1976), rather than its relationship with individual and organizational outcomes.

Studies following the initial investigations of the PNSQ began to focus on its relationship with job satisfaction, performance, and other outcomes. For example, Orpen (1974) found a positive relationship between the total PNSQ need satisfaction score and job satisfaction. Similarly, Imparato (1972) found negative correlations between the total PNSQ need deficiency score and the five scales of the Job Descriptive Index (JDI; Smith, Kendall, & Hulin, 1969). Furthermore, JDI scores were significantly higher for respondents who scored above the midpoint on both components of the deficiency index ('is now' and

---

[2] Despite usage of the term 'satisfaction', it should be emphasized that the response format of the PNSQ does not elicit the employee's affective orientation toward work (i.e. satisfaction or dissatisfaction).

'should be') than those who scored below the midpoint on both components, indicating that satisfaction was contingent not only on the fit between desires and supplies, but also the absolute level of both components. Herman & Hulin (1973) found negative correlations between individual PNSQ need deficiency items and the JDI work, pay, and promotion satisfaction scales. However, PNSQ items presumably reflecting the same need dimension were not consistently related to satisfaction, offering no clear interpretation of these results.

Studies examining the relationship between the PNSQ and outcomes other than job satisfaction have also been reported. For example, Hrebiniak and Roteman (1973) scored the PNSQ for deficiencies in security, social, esteem, autonomy, and self-actualization needs and found positive relationships between absenteeism and all deficiencies except social. Slocum (1971) found that performance was positively related to the satisfaction of social, esteem, autonomy, and self-actualization needs, but not security needs. Lawler & Porter (1967) found that performance and effort were positively related to the satisfaction of security, social, esteem, autonomy, and self-actualization needs, with little difference in the strength of these relationships for different needs. Unfortunately, both of these studies purported to measure need deficiency, but subsequently interpreted their results in terms of need satisfaction, which somewhat obscures the exact nature of their results. Porter & Lawler (1968) found that deficiencies for social, esteem, autonomy, and self-actualization needs were negatively related to supervisor ratings of performance, whereas deficiencies for security needs were positively related to self-ratings of performance. Hall, Schneider, & Nygren (1970) found that the satisfaction of autonomy and self-actualization needs was positively related to job challenge, job involvement, and professional identification. Finally, Sheridan & Slocum (1975) conducted a 12-month panel study of managers and machine operators, examining the relationship between performance and total need deficiency. None of the concurrent, lead, or lagged correlations between performance and total need deficiency were significant. However, both samples contained fewer than 60 respondents, suggesting that these null results may have been partly attributable to low statistical power. Nonetheless, subsequent analyses revealed that, for the machine operator sample, the time 2 concurrent correlation between performance and need deficiency was negative after controlling for 'is now' scores. However, Sheridan & Slocum (1975) fail to note that these results simply reflect the relationship between performance and the 'should be' measure, holding 'is now' constant (cf. Wall & Payne, 1973) and, therefore, should not be interpreted in terms of need deficiency.

Studies using fit indices analogous to the PNSQ (i.e. the difference between 'should be' and 'is now') have typically found results consistent with those reviewed above. For example, in a sample of unskilled workers, Payne (1970) found that neuroticism was negatively related to social need satisfaction, and job adjustment was positively related to total need satisfaction. However, in a managerial sample, Payne (1970) found that job satisfaction was positively related to total need satisfaction and esteem, autonomy, and self-actualization need satisfaction, but not security and social need satisfaction. Wanous & Lawler (1972) found that job satisfaction was negatively related to need deficiencies regarding 23 job attributes. However, job satisfaction was more strongly related to the simple 'is now' measures than the need deficiency measures. Post-hoc analyses by Wall & Payne (1973) indicated that, after controlling for 'is now', relationships between job satisfaction and most deficiency measures were no longer significant. As noted by Wall & Payne (1973), these results should not be interpreted in terms of deficiency, but rather as the relationship between 'should be', holding 'is now' constant. Taken together, these results indicate that the need deficiency relationships found by Wanous & Lawler (1972) merely reflected the 'is now' component of the deficiency indices and, hence, were spurious.

More recent studies using analogous fit indices have found similar results. For example, Dyer & Theriault (1976) found that pay satisfaction was negatively related to need deficiency regarding the importance of various determinants of salary increases. Betz (1984) regressed a measure of life satisfaction on need deficiency indices regarding security/safety, social, autonomy, esteem, and self-actualization, but found a negative relationship only for the self-actualization index. Lachman & Aranya (1986) found that total need deficiency was positively related to turnover intentions and negatively related to job satisfaction and organizational and professional commitment.

Only two studies using measures analogous to the PNSQ did not find the anticipated results. Lawler & Hall (1970) found that self-rated effort and performance were unrelated to autonomy and self-actualization need deficiencies. Similarly, Beer (1966) failed to find a relationship between motivation (i.e. initiative, self-assurance) and need deficiencies regarding leader behavior. The null results found by Beer (1966) are at least partly attributable to low reliabilities for the motivation indices, none of which exceeded 0.43.

Three studies measured desires in terms of optimal ('ideal') rather than appropriate ('should') job attributes. Andrews & Farris (1972) found that the difference between typical and optimal time pressure displayed an inverted-U relationship with performance (i.e. usefulness, innovation, productivity) five years later, though these relationships did not reach significance. Sorensen & Sorensen (1974) operationalized fit by subtracting optimal from actual ratings of professional and bureaucratic work experiences. For professional experiences, this index was positively related to job satisfaction and negatively related to turnover intentions, but for bureaucratic experiences, this index was positively related to both job satisfaction and turnover intentions. The positive relationship between bureaucratic fit and turnover intentions was attributed to the presence of positive scores for this index, indicating that some respondents reported excess bureaucratic experiences. However, this explanation also implies that the relationship between bureaucratic fit and satisfaction should have been negative, but this was not the case. Finally, Dorr, Honea, & Posner (1980) found that job satisfaction was negatively related to optimal minus actual involvement, support, autonomy, practical orientation, order/organization, and program clarity. However, job satisfaction was also positively related to actual involvement, support, practical orientation, order/organization, and program clarity, suggesting that relationships between job satisfaction and fit may have been spurious.

Other studies have measured desires explicitly in terms of preferences (e.g. 'would like'). For example, White & Spector (1987) found that an index reflecting perceived minus preferred job attributes was positively related to job satisfaction. Similarly, Korman (1967) found that an index representing desired minus perceived job attributes was negatively related to job satisfaction, but only for employees with high self-esteem. Giles (1977) found that nonsupervisory employees with fulfilled higher-order preferences were less likely to volunteer for a job enrichment program, and Hrebiniak (1974) found that desired minus actual participation in decision-making was negatively related to interpersonal trust, but unrelated to role tension or organizational commitment. Wanous & Lawler (1972) found that job satisfaction was negatively related to scores representing 'would like' minus 'is now' for 23 job attributes. However, as with indices using 'should be', these relationships were smaller in absolute magnitude than those between job satisfaction and 'is now' measures. Furthermore, these relationships were no longer significant after controlling for 'is now' (Wall & Payne, 1973), suggesting that the results for fit were spurious. In a sample of bus drivers, Blau (1981) found that job satisfaction was negatively related to desired minus actual company policies and scheduling, whereas job performance was positively related to desired minus actual personal danger. However, for company policies and scheduling, job satisfaction was also positively related to actual amount and negatively related to desired amount, suggesting that its relationship with fit was spurious. Finally, Pelz & Andrews (1976) found that perceived minus desired influence over setting goals and objectives was unrelated to performance.

In perhaps the most comprehensive P–J fit study to date, French, Caplan, & Harrison, (1982; see also Caplan *et al.*, 1980) constructed three fit indices based on actual minus preferred job attributes, one consisting of the simple algebraic difference ('fit'), another setting all positive scores to zero ('deficiency'),[3] and another setting all negative scores to zero ('excess'). Results indicated that job complexity fit was negatively related to workload satisfaction

---

[3] Despite its name, it should be emphasized that greater scores on this index do not imply greater deficiency. Rather, lower scores indicate greater deficiency, and all positive scores were set to zero and, hence, considered equivalent.

and boredom, and responsibility for persons fit was positively related to job satisfaction and negatively related to boredom. Workload fit was negatively related to job and workload satisfaction and positively related to depression, anxiety, and irritation, and overtime fit was negatively related to job and workload satisfaction and positively related to anxiety and somatic complaints. Results for workload deficiency and excess were fairly consistent with those for workload fit, suggesting monotonic relationships with outcomes. However, for job complexity, deficiency and excess often exhibited opposite relationships with outcomes. For example, job satisfaction was unrelated to job complexity fit, but was positively related to deficiency and negatively related to excess. Furthermore, depression, anxiety, and irritation were positively related to job complexity excess but unrelated to job complexity deficiency. Though too numerous to summarize here, other results suggested similar asymmetries in relationships between fit and outcomes, indicating that the simple algebraic difference may have concealed curvilinear trends. However, Caplan et al., (1980) also reported numerous significant relationships for separate desires and supplies measures, suggesting that the relationships found for these fit indices simply reflected the effects of their components and, hence, were spurious.[4]

Several studies used direct measures of the discrepancy between perceived and preferred job attributes. Cook & Wall (1980) reported that a direct measure of wanting more than the current amount of 16 job attributes was negatively related to interpersonal trust, organizational commitment, and job satisfaction. Analogously, Crosby (1982) found that a direct measure of having more than wanted amount of various job attributes was negatively related to resentment. Hollenbeck (1989) found that direct measures of wanting more than current amount for pay, nature of work, supervision, and coworkers were negatively related to satisfaction and organizational commitment, positively related to job turnover, but unrelated to organizational turnover. Finally, Tziner (1987) found that a direct measure of wanting more than the current amount of achievement climate was positively related to job satisfaction, performance, and organizational commitment. In addition, after controlling for actual and preferred achievement climate, the relationship between fit and all outcomes remained significant. However, the reported relationships between fit and outcomes were *identical* before and after controlling for actual and preferred climate, implying that these measure were uncorrelated with fit. This is highly unlikely, since the fit measure conceptually represented a linear composite of the actual and preferred measures. Furthermore, since higher scores on the direct fit measure reflected inadequate achievement climate, a

---

[4]French, Caplan, & Harrison (1982) also report relationships between various fit indices and physiological outcomes. However, most of these relationships were 'low and uninformative' (Caplan et al., 1980, p. 227) and, therefore, are not reviewed here. For details, see Caplan et al., (1980) and French, Caplan, & Harrison (1982).

negative relationship with job satisfaction would be expected, though this contention could not be verified (A. Tziner, personal communication). For these reasons, these results should be considered with caution.

A number of studies using the algebraic difference between preferences and job supplies divided the sample into groups having too little, the preferred amount, and too much, thereby allowing the detection of curvilinear relationships with outcomes. Most of these studies focused on participation in decision-making. For example, Alutto & Belasco (1972) found that militant attitudes (i.e. support of union activities) demonstrated an asymmetric U-shaped relationships with desired minus actual participation, with highest scores for those who participated in fewer decisions than desired. Alutto & Acito (1974) found that, compared to those participating in the desired number of decisions, industrial workers who participated in fewer decisions than desired displayed more tension, less favorable attitudes toward the company, less job and organizational commitment, less trust, and less satisfaction with work, supervision, and promotion (no respondents reported participating in more decisions than desired). Similarly, Alutto & Vredenburgh (1977) found greater tension among nurses who participated in fewer decisions than desired than among those participating in the desired number of decisions (though several respondents reported participating in more decisions than desired, they were excluded from analyses). Ivancevich (1979) found that too much or too little participation was associated with higher tension and physical symptoms and lower organizational commitment, work satisfaction, supervisor satisfaction, and performance, but was unrelated to self-esteem, motivation, role ambiguity, fatigue, or attitudes toward the company. Finally, in a study focusing on job complexity fit, London and Klimoski (1975) found that, for self and supervisor performance ratings, performance was lower for excess complexity than for preferred or inadequate complexity. In contrast, satisfaction with work was lower for inadequate complexity than for preferred or excess complexity, whereas satisfaction with peers was higher for preferred complexity than for excess or inadequate complexity.

Finally, a handful of algebraic difference studies measured the person in terms of importance. Pelz & Andrews (1976) found that performance quality (but not quantity) was positively related to an index representing perceived amount minus importance regarding 13 job attributes. However, performance quality was also positively related to perceived amount, suggesting that its relationship with fit may have been spurious. Similarly, Wanous & Lawler (1972) found that job satisfaction was negatively related to importance minus 'is now' for 23 job attributes, but the presence of stronger positive relationships between job satisfaction and 'is now' measures suggests that these results may have been spurious. In contrast, Sexton (1967) found no relationship between importance minus availability of job attributes and performance effectiveness, and Beer (1966) found no relationship between a similar index and motivation (i.e. initiative, self-assurance). These inconsistent results are not surprising, given that importance is more appropriately conceived as a moderator of the relationship between job attributes and outcomes rather than the standard by which job attributes are compared (e.g. Mobley & Locke, 1970). Furthermore, using this index conveys the dubious assumption that an employee facing large amounts of important job attributes will react the same as an employee facing a small amount of unimportant job attributes (Evans, 1969; Wanous & Lawler, 1972).

Absolute difference

Several studies have operationalized fit as the absolute difference between employee desires and job supplies. Phillips, Barrett, & Rush (1978) found that job satisfaction was negatively related to the absolute difference between perceived and preferred job attributes. Similarly, Lopez & Greenhaus (1978) found that job satisfaction was negatively related to a summary index representing the absolute difference between the preferred and perceived amounts of 23 jobs attributes. Barrett (1978) also reported a negative relationship between job satisfaction and the absolute difference between preferred and actual variety and independence. Likewise, O'Brien & Dowling (1980) found that job satisfaction was negatively related to the absolute difference between desires and supplies for skill utilization, influence, variety, and social interaction. Hrebiniak & Alutto (1972; see also Alutto, Hrebiniak, & Alonso, 1971) found that organizational commitment was negatively related to the absolute difference between desired and supplies for advancement criteria, but not for time spent on various job activities. Swaney & Prediger (1985) found that expressed interest in work was negatively related to the absolute difference between actual and preferred occupational characteristics. Analogously, Meir & Engel (1986) found positive relationships between job satisfaction and one minus the absolute difference between the actual and preferred amounts of social contact, mechanical, and sensation-seeking activities. Finally, French, Caplan, & Harrison (1982) found that the absolute difference between preferred and actual job complexity was negatively related to job and workload satisfaction and positively related to boredom, depression, anxiety, irritation, and somatic complaints. An analogous index for workload was negatively related to job and workload satisfaction and positively related to boredom, depression, and irritation. For role ambiguity, this index was negatively related to job and workload satisfaction and positively related to boredom and depression, whereas for responsibility for persons, it was negatively related to job satisfaction and positively related to boredom. Though these results imply symmetric V-shaped relationships between fit and outcomes, it should be recalled that results for the deficiency and excess indices employed by French, Caplan, & Harrison (1982) indicate that many of these relationships were, in fact, asymmetrical.

Two studies employed the absolute value of direct measures of fit, in which zero represented the point where job supplies met desires. Rice, McFarlin, & Bennett (1989) found that, for 11 of 13 job facets, this index was negatively related to facet satisfaction. Analogously, Greenhaus, Seidel, & Marinus (1983) found that, for task characteristics, interpersonal relations, and company practices, the negative of this index was positively related to facet satisfaction.

Squared difference

Caplan *et al.* (1980) constructed indices representing the squared difference between actual and preferred workload, responsibility for persons, job complexity, and role ambiguity. Hierarchical regression was then used to examine the incremental variance explained by these indices over the corresponding simple algebraic difference indices. Results indicated significant incremental effects for role ambiguity in predicting boredom and job satisfaction, for responsibility for persons in predicting boredom, job satisfaction, and workload satisfaction, and for job complexity in predicting boredom, job satisfaction, workload satisfaction, anxiety, depression, and somatic complaints. For each job attribute, these results indicated that, when preceptions met preferences, job satisfaction reached its maximum, whereas the remaining outcomes reached their minima. However, it should again be noted that the symmetric U-shaped relationships implied by the squared difference are inconsistent with results for deficiency and excess indices, which suggested numerous asymmetrical relationships.

Three studies based on the Theory of Work Adjustment (Dawis & Lofquist, 1984) operationalized fit using D^2, representing the sum of squared differences between desires and supplies across multiple dimensions (Cronbach & Gleser, 1953). Each study measured desires using the Minnesota Importance Questionnaire (MIQ; Gay *et al.*, 1971) and supplies using ratings derived from the Minnesota Job Description Questionnaire (MJDQ; Borgen *et al.*, 1968). Scarpello & Campbell (1983) found that D^2 was negatively related to job satisfaction. In a more elaborate study, Rounds, Dawis, & Lofquist (1987) examined D^2, D'^2 (D^2 for normalized profiles; see Cronbach & Gleser, 1953), D^2 for elevation (i.e. the squared difference between profile means), and D^2 weighted by importance (MIQ scores). Relationships for weighted and unweighted D^2 were also examined for various subgroups, based on whether MIQ scores were greater or less than zero and/or each other. Results for six occupational samples indicated that, in general, satisfaction was negatively related to D^2 and D'^2 indices, though results for D^2 were more consistent for subgroups in which MJDQ scores were greater than MIQ scores. Unfortunately, Rounds, Dawis, & Lofquist (1987) do not mention that the subgrouping procedure simply sampled different portions of the surface representing the relationship between D^2 and satisfaction, nor do they test the differences between correlations obtained for different subgroups. For these reasons, it is difficult to draw firm conclusions from these results. In a second study, Rounds, Dawis, & Lofquist (1987) found negative relationships between job satisfaction and D^2, D'^2, D''^2 (D^2 for standardized profiles; see Cronbach & Gleser, 1953), and D'^2 weighted by importance. The strength of these relationships increased progressively from D^2, D'^2, D''^2 (weighting D'^2 by importance had little effect), but statistical tests regarding the differences between these correlations were not reported.

Ratio

A number of studies operationalized fit by dividing job supplies by employee desires. For example, Payne (1970) found that, in a sample of unskilled workers, total need satisfaction divided by need importance was unrelated to neuroticism or job adjustment, whereas in a managerial sample, this index was positively related to job satisfaction. Giles & Barrett (1971) found that the relationship between pay satisfaction and the ratio of actual to equitable merit increases represented a power function, with satisfaction increasing gradually as the actual merit increase approached the equitable merit increase, but rising rapidly as the actual merit increase exceeded the equitable merit increase. Finally, Michalos (1980, 1983) reported two studies using a direct assessment of the proportion of goals attained for various life areas, including work. In both studies this index was positively related to satisfaction with work.

Two studies used ratio indices constructed by dividing algebraic difference indices by the person or job measure included in the difference. Hrebiniak (1974) found that desired minus actual participation in decision-making divided by actual participation was unrelated to interpersonal trust, role tension, or organizational commitment. However, as indicated earlier, the algebraic difference index alone was negatively related to trust, suggesting that dividing by actual participation obscured this relationship. In contrast, French, Caplan, & Harrison (1980) found that actual minus preferred income divided by preferred income was positively related to workload satisfaction and negatively related to depression and somatic complaints.

Product

Three studies operationalized fit as the simple product of employee desires and job supplies. Beer (1966) found no relationship between motivation (i.e. initiative, self-assurance) and the product of actual and appropriate leader behavior. However, as indicated earlier, these relationships may have been attenuated by the low reliability of the motivation measures. Wanous & Lawler (1972) found that the product of importance and 'is now' for 23 job attributes was positively related to job satisfaction, though these relationships were slightly smaller than those for the simple 'is now' measures. Finally, Rounds, Dawis, & Lofquist (1987) constructed a dichotomous index representing high scores on both the MIQ and the MJDQ (i.e. the product of dummy coded MIQ and MJDQ measures) and found no relationship between this index and job satisfaction. Unfortunately, none of these studies used hierarchical analyses, after controlling for job supplies and importance, making it impossible to determine whether these indices explained additional variance beyond that associated with their components (Cohen, 1978).

Two studies constructed fit indices by multiplying need deficiency scores by importance. Wanous & Lawler (1972) used this technique for two sets of need deficiency measures, one measuring desires in terms of 'should be' and another in terms of 'would like'. Multiplying by importance did not increase the relationship between job satisfaction and either deficiency measure. Similarly, Sheridan & Slocum (1975) found that weighting total need deficiency by importance did not significantly increase its correlation with performance. However, as before, neither study appropriately controlled for need deficiency or importance before examining relationships for their product (Cohen, 1978).

Fortunately, more recent investigations have analyzed product indices using hierarchical regression or analysis of variance, which control for the components of the product and, hence, provide valid tests of the interaction between the person and job. White & Ruh (1973) found that participation in decision-making was positively related to job involvement, motivation, and identification with company, and that importance of participation did not moderate these relationships. Similarly, Butler (1983) found no significant interactions between perceived amount and importance of intrinsic and extrinsic job attributes in the prediction of job satisfaction. In contrast, Cherrington & England (1980) found a significant interaction between perceived and desired job enrichment, representing a stronger positive relationship between job satisfaction and job enrichment for those who desired job enrichment. O'Brien & Dowling (1980) found significant interactions between desires and supplies for social interaction, skill utilization, variety, and pressure in the prediction of job satisfaction. For skill utilization and variety, these interactions represented stronger positive relationships between job satisfaction and supplies for those with high desires, but for pressure and social interaction they represented positive relationships between job satisfaction and supplies only for those with low desires. Though the latter results are not easily explained, O'Brien & Dowling (1980) contend that they may have been partly caused by low reliabilities for the pressure and social interaction measures. O'Brien & Stevens (1981) found that the interaction between perceived and desired influence was significant in predicting satisfaction with coworkers, indicating a positive relationship only for those with high desires. In a more detailed study, O'Brien & Humphrys (1982) examined the interaction between desires and supplies for skill utilization, influence, and variety using the product, the product squared, and the product cubed. For the total sample, no significant interactions were found, though selected subsamples displayed significant interactions for the simple product index. Finally, Rice, McFarlin, & Bennett (1989) found significant interactions between perceived and wanted amounts of seven job facets in the prediction of facet satisfaction. For required effort, contact with clients/customers, and hours worked, these interactions represented positive relationships for employees with high wants and negative relationships for employees with low wants. For decision-making, autonomy, opportunity for promotion, health insurance coverage, and opportunity to learn new things, the relationship between supplies and satisfaction was stronger for employees with high wants, whereas for pay rate,. the relationship between supplies and satisfaction was stronger for employees with low wants.

Correlation

Two studies operationalized fit as the correlation between sets of commensurate person and job measures. In addition to the D^2 indices described above, Rounds, Dawis, & Lofquist (1987) created fit indices using the product–moment correlation, Spearman's rho, and Kendall's tau. Overall, results indicated positive relationships between these indices and satisfaction, though the relationships for the product–moment correlation were somewhat more consistent than those for rho or tau. More recently, Amerikaner, Elliot, & Swank (1988) operationalized fit as the rank-order correlation (i.e. Spearman's rho) between interest and occupation profiles containing six scores each, but found no relationship between this index and job satisfaction. It should be noted that a rank-order correlation is simply one minus the sum of squared differences between the ranked scores, rescaled for the number of scores ranked (Cohen & Cohen, 1983). Therefore, findings for this index may also be interpreted in terms of the negative of D^2. This is evidenced in Rounds, Dawis, & Lofquist (1987), where results for rho were essentially opposite of those for D^2.

Categorical agreement

A substantial number of studies have operationalized fit in terms of the categorical agreement between employee desires and job supplies. Most of these studies are based on Holland's theory of vocational choice (Holland, 1985; for earlier reviews, see Assouline & Meir, 1987, and Spokane, 1985). Holland (1985) postulates that employees attempt to choose occupations that are congruent with their preferences and abilities, and that this congruence will result in satisfaction, stability (i.e. low turnover), and achievement. Most studies of Holland's theory have measured the person using the Vocational Preference Inventory (VPI; Holland, 1977) or the Self-Directed Search (SDS; Holland, 1979). The VPI yields preference ratings regarding 84 occupations, whereas the SDS elicits preference, interest, and competency scores across a variety of activities and occupations. A third measure often used in the context of Holland's theory is the Strong Vocational Interest Blank (SVIB; Campbell, 1971) or its revision, the Strong–Campbell Interest Inventory (SCII; Campbell & Hansen, 1981). Typical scoring procedures for each measure yield six scores, reflecting realistic, investigative, artistic, social, enterprising, and conventional orientations (for a complete discussion of these orientations, see Holland, 1985). Occupations are then scored according to the same typology, typically based on the Occupations Finder (Holland, 1978), and an index reflecting the fit between the person and occupation is constructed.

The simplest fit index used in studies of Holland's theory is a dichotomy indicating whether the occupation ranked highest by the employee corresponds to their actual occupation (Holland, 1979). More complex indices have been derived that take into account scores on one or more of the remaining five dimensions (e.g. Iachan, 1984; Wiggins & Moody, 1981; Zener & Schnuelle, 1976). For all of these indices, studies using the SDS, VPI, SVIB, or SCII have generally found positive relationships between fit and satisfaction (Aranya, Barak, & Amernic, 1981; Brandt & Hood, 1968; Furnham & Schaeffer, 1984; Meir & Melamed, 1986; Melamed & Meir, 1981; Mount & Muchinsky, 1978; Wiggins, 1984; Wiggins et al., 1983), commitment (Aranya, Barak, & Amernic, 1981; Pazy & Zin, 1987), and seeking leisure activities similar to one's job (Melamed & Meir, 1981) and negative relationships with mental distress (Furnham & Schaeffer, 1984), somatic symptoms (Meir & Melamed, 1986), changing occupations (Laing, Swaney, & Prediger, 1984), and seeking satisfaction through leisure activities (Melamed & Meir, 1981). However, it should be noted that studies which used the SDS (i.e. Aranya, Barak, & Amernic, 1981; Furnham & Schaeffer, 1984; Meir & Melamed, 1986; Mount & Muchinsky, 1978; Pazy & Zin, 1987) implicitly confounded desires (i.e. preferences and interests) with abilities (i.e. competencies), thereby preventing an unambiguous interpretation of their results.

Categorical agreement studies using other measures have generally replicated the results reviewed above. Zytowski (1974) measured desires using the Kuder Preference Record (KRP; Kuder, 1946) and found that fit between actual and most preferred occupation was positively related to occupational satisfaction but unrelated to performance. Barak & Meir (1974) used Ramak, a measure of the attractiveness of eight occupational types, and found that fit between actual and most preferred occupation was positively related to occupational choice satisfaction. Later analyses using a five-point fit index (Peiser & Meir,

1978) again found that fit was positively related to occupational choice satisfaction, as well as stability of occupational attractiveness ratings across seven years. Hener & Meir (1981) used a measure of interest in nine clinical nursing areas and found that fit between actual clinical area and area of greatest interest was positively related to job satisfaction.

Two studies using the MIQ and the MJDQ operationalized fit using 'confidence band' indices, indicating the number of MIQ scores falling within a given distance (e.g. one standard deviation) from the relevant MJDQ score. These indices represent categorical agreement, in that each item is assigned a score of one if the MIQ score falls within the confidence band and a score of zero if it falls outside the band. Betz (1969) constructed confidence band indices using one standard deviation and one quartile as cutoffs and found positive relationships between both indices and job satisfaction. Rounds, Dawis, & Lofquist (1987) constructed indices using one and two standard deviations as cutoffs, but found no relationship between either index and job satisfaction. However, Betz (1969) collected MJDQ data directly from respondents, whereas Rounds, Dawis, & Lofquist (1987) relied on standardized occupational MJDQ ratings, which may partially explain these differing results.

Conditional desires

Several studies have operationalized fit by dividing a sample into subgroups based on a measure of job supplies and examining the relationship between employee desires and various outcomes within each group. This procedure is termed 'conditional desires', in that it reflects the relationship between desires and outcomes conditioned on the job.[5] Using this procedure, Feldman & Meir (1976) found that, across Holland's six occupational types, occupational satisfaction was positively related to the interest score for that occupation. However, like the SDS, their interest measure confounded preferences and competencies, making their results difficult to interpret. Barak & Meir (1974) used Ramak (a purer measure of preferences) and found that, across eight occupational types, occupational choice satisfaction was positively related to interest in that occupation. Using the SCII, Wiener & Klein (1978) found positive relationships between interest in one's occupation and satisfaction with work and supervision, but only for employees with long tenure. Similarly, Vaitenas & Wiener (1977) measured desires using the SVIB and found a negative relationship between career change and interest in one's occupation. Finally, Meir & Erez (1981) collected measures of the attractiveness of six types of activities in a sample of engineers and found a positive relationship between job satisfaction and strength of interest in one's

---

[5]This procedure may also be considered a method for detecting moderating effects of job supplies on the relationship between desires and outcomes (Arnold, 1982), though hierarchical regression is typically considered a superior method (Stone, 1988; Stone & Hollenbeck, 1984).

dominant activity. Unfortunately, none of these studies indicated whether correlations between satisfaction and the relevant occupation or activity scales were significantly higher than correlations for irrelevant scales, rendering their results somewhat inconclusive.

Several studies of conditional desires failed to find the expected results. For example, Schletzer (1966), Cairo (1982), and Dolliver, Irwin, & Bigley (1972) found no relationship between occupationally relevant SVIB scores and job satisfaction. Similarly, Klein & Weiner (1977) found no relationship between occupationally relevant SVIB scores and job satisfaction or mental health. Zytowski (1976) used the Kuder Occupational Interest Survey (KOIS; Kuder, 1966) and found that scores on occupationally relevant interest scales were unrelated to job satisfaction or self-rated job success, but were related to continuation in the relevant occupation across 12–19 years. However, each of these studies converted their respective interest measures into dichotomous or trichotomous indices, resulting in a loss of information and, hence, increasing the likelihood of a null result.

Several studies examined the relationship between desires and outcomes within a single occupation or associated with a single type of job attribute. For example, Aranya, Barak, & Amernik (1981) found that, in a sample of accountants, the SDS conventional scale was positively related to vocational satisfaction and professional commitment. Similarly, Doty & Betz (1979) found that, in a sample of sales managers, job satisfaction was positively related to the SDS and SCII social and enterprising scales but unrelated to the realistic, investigative, artistic, or conventional scales. Wiggins (1976) found that job satisfaction was greater for special educators who scored higher on the VPI social and artistic scales and lower on the VPI realistic and conventional scales. In a later study, Wiggins (1984) found that job satisfaction among school counselors was positively related only to their scores on the VPI social scale. An exception was reported by Gilbride (1973), who found that active and resigned priests did not differ in reported vocational preferences, including those presumably characteristic of the priesthood (i.e. social and artistic). Unfortunately, none of these studies tested whether correlations for the scale relevant to the particular occupation were stronger than correlations for other scales. Furthermore, because each study included a single occupational group, it is impossible to determine whether the relationships found would differ across occupations, which is necessary to demonstrate a congruence effect.

Finally, Wanous & Zwany (1977) reanalyzed data from Wanous & Lawler (1972), in which desires were measured in terms of the importance of job attributes rather than occupational interests. For the 'is now', importance, and satisfaction responses, scales were formed corresponding to existence, relatedness, and growth needs (Alderfer, 1972), and respondents were divided into three groups based on 'is now' score. For growth, the relationship between importance and satisfaction was negative for the low 'is now' group and positive for the high 'is now' group, and the difference between these correlations was significant. Results for existence and related were similar but less pronounced.

Conditional supplies

Several studies operationalized fit by dividing the sample into a subgroups sample based on a measure of desires and examining the relationship between job supplies and outcomes for each group. For example, three studies created subgroups based on the reported importance of role clarity (Ivancevich & Donnelly, 1974; Lyons, 1971; Miles & Petty, 1975). Taken together, these studies indicate that respondents who considered role clarity more important demonstrated stronger positive relationships between actual role clarity and job interest and job satisfaction, and stronger negative relationships between actual role clarity and tension, physical symptoms, and intended and actual turnover. In an analogous study, Lefkowitz, Somers, & Weinberg (1984) compared correlations between job satisfaction and the amount of various job attributes rated low and high in importance and found stronger relationships for attributes considered more important.

Two studies operationalizing fit in terms of conditional supplies measured desires in terms of preferences. Wanous (1974) found stronger positive relationships between job satisfaction and variety, autonomy, and, to a lesser extent, task identity and task feedback for respondents who desired these job characteristics. Similarly, Cherrington & England (1980) found stronger positive relationships between job enrichment and job satisfaction and performance for employees who desired an enriched job.

Sum

In an attempt to establish the validity of an algebraic difference index of fit, Blau (1981) compared it to an index representing the sum of preferred and actual job attributes. This index was unrelated to either job satisfaction or performance. As Blau (1981) notes, these null results are not surprising, given the atheoretical nature of this index.

Desires and supplies as simultaneous predictors

Three studies examined desires and supplies as simultaneous predictors of outcomes, using multiple regression analysis.[6] Cherrington & England

[6]Studies reporting bivariate correlations between desires, supplies, and outcomes (e.g. French, Caplan, & Harrison, 1982; O'Brien & Dowling, 1980) are not reviewed here, because interpreting these correlations in terms of the implied causal model (i.e. the effects of desires and supplies on outcomes) introduces the omitted variables problem (James, 1980). Studies reporting regression analyses including desires, supplies, and their product as simultaneous predictors (e.g. O'Brien & Dowling, 1980; O'Brien & Humphrys, 1982; O'Brien & Stevens, 1981) are also excluded, because the coefficients on desires and supplies are scale dependent in such analyses (Cohen, 1978).

(1980) found that job satisfaction was positively related to actual job enrichment and negatively related to desired job enrichment, whereas performance was positively related to actual job enrichment but unrelated to desired job enrichment. Wright & Gutkin (1981) used forward stepwise regression to analyze supplies and desires regarding five sets of job activities as predictors of job satisfaction. However, none of the resulting regressions happened to select commensurate person and job measures, rendering their results uninterpretable in terms of P–J fit. Finally, Tziner (1987) found that job satisfaction was positively related to actual achievement climate, performance was positively related to preferred achievement climate, and commitment was positively related to both actual and preferred achievement climate.

Comparisons of multiple indices

As indicated by the preceding review, several studies have employed multiple fit indices (e.g. Beer, 1966; Blau, 1981; Cherrington & England, 1980; French, Caplan, & Harrison, 1982; Hrebiniak, 1974; O'Brien & Dowling, 1980; Payne, 1970; Rice, McFarlin, & Bennett, 1989; Sheridan & Slocum, 1975; Wanous & Lawler, 1972). However, few studies statistically compared these indices as competing predictors of outcomes. An exception is Wanous & Lawler (1972), who conducted sign tests comparing relationships between job satisfaction and various need deficiency measures, both weighted and unweighted by importance, and found that relationships for simple 'is now' measures were significantly higher than those for 'is now' weighted by importance, which in turn were higher than weighted and unweighted 'would like' minus 'is now' and importance minus 'is now', which in turn were higher than weighted and unweighted 'should be' minus 'is now'.

Some studies conducted hierarchical tests of fit indices representing various nonlinear effects. For example, Caplan et al. (1980) and French, Caplan, & Harrison (1980) used hierarchical regression to determine whether indices representing curvilinear relationships (e.g. absolute difference, squared difference, deficiency, excess) explained additional variance in outcomes after controlling for their components (i.e. preferences and perceptions). However, they did not test which of these curvilinear indices displayed the strongest relationships with outcomes. Hence, it seems that relationships between fit and most outcomes was, for the most part, V-shaped and asymmetric, though it is impossible to determine whether certain representations of these relationships are more valid than others.

Other studies examining multiple indices have simply reported whether each index was significant. O'Brien & Dowling (1980) reported that the interaction and absolute difference between desires and supplies were both significantly related to job satisfaction. The present author conducted post-hoc analyses based on reported correlation matrices and found that, when entered as simultaneous predictors of job satisfaction, desires and supplies exhibited significant but opposite relationships. Taken together, the significant independent relationships for desires and supplies indicate that the surface relating desires and supplies to job satisfaction is sloped in both directions, whereas the interactions suggest that this surface has tilt, and relationships involving absolute differences suggest that it has curvature. Unfortunately, because no analyses simultaneously considered the slope, tilt, and curvature of this surface, it is difficult to draw firm conclusions from these results. Similarly, Rice, McFarlin, & Bennett (1989) reported that, for most of the 13 job facets examined, the relationship between facet satisfaction and the absolute value of a direct measure of fit remained significant after controlling for perceived amount, wanted amount, and the interaction between perceived and wanted amount. However, they did not test whether the absolute value or interactive forms of fit was more strongly related to job satisfaction. Furthermore, for many facets, perceived and wanted facet amounts were also significantly related to facet satisfaction. Hence, we can only conclude that the surface relating perceived and wanted facet amount to facet satisfaction has slope, tilt, and curvature, but the exact nature of this surface remains unclear.

Fit Between Employee Abilities and Job Demands

Compared to the substantial volume of research examining the fit between desires and job supplies, very few studies have examined the fit between abilities and job demands.[7] This is particularly surprising, in the light of the centrality of abilities–demands fit to several major theories of job stress (e.g. French, Caplan, & Harrison, 1982; McGrath, 1976). Given the small number of studies, they will be reviewed within a single section rather than separated by the fit index used. Rosman & Burke (1980) found that the absolute difference between competencies and requirements was negatively related to job satisfaction but unrelated to self-esteem. Using a categorical agreement index, Drexler & Lindell (1981) found that satisfaction was higher for army personnel whose training matched their current work assignment, though less than 1% of the variance in satisfaction was explained. French, Caplan, & Harrison (1980) measured employee abilities in terms of employee education

---

[7]It should again be noted that, in addition to preferences and interests, the SDS measures self-rated competencies (Holland, 1979). Therefore, relationships based on the SDS partly reflect abilities–demands fit. However, because the SDS is dominated by preference and interest items, studies using it were reviewed in the previous section. In the following section, problems created by confounding preferences, interests, and competencies within the SDS are discussed.

level and length of service and job demands in terms of required education level and length of service. Fit indices for length of service and education were created by subtracting abilities from demands and dividing the resulting index by abilities. This index was used in its raw form ('fit') and after setting all positive scores to zero ('deficiency'), setting all negative scores to zero ('excess'), and after taking the absolute value. Taken together, results for these indices indicate that deficiency for length of service was positively related to job satisfaction and negatively related to boredom, whereas deficiency for education was positively related to job and workload satisfaction and negatively related to boredom, depression, and somatic complaints. Though significant relationships for absolute value indices were also found, no relationships involving excess were significant, suggesting that these results were driven primarily by the region where demands fell short of abilities. Furthermore, because many relationships involving the separate demands and abilities measures were significant, results for the corresponding fit indices may have been spurious.

Summary

As indicated by the preceding review, the vast majority of empirical P–J fit research to date has focused on the fit between employee desires and job supplies. With few exceptions, these studies indicate that fit indices representing job supplies minus employee desires are positively related to job satisfaction. Relationships with job performance have been less consistent, including a mixture of positive (Ivancevich, 1979; Lawler & Porter, 1967; Porter & Lawler, 1968; Slocum, 1971; Tziner, 1987), negative (London & Klimoski, 1975; Porter & Lawler, 1968), and null results (Beer, 1966; Lawler & Hall, 1970; Pelz & Andrews, 1976; Sheridan & Slocum, 1975). These inconsistencies are partly attributable to different samples and job content dimensions, though they also probably reflect the omission of important variables, such as motivation, instrumentality, expectancy, intentions, and ability. Studies of other outcomes have demonstrated negative relationships with absenteeism (Hrebiniak & Roteman, 1973), turnover (Hollenbeck, 1989), and resentment (Crosby, 1982), and positive relationships with job involvement (Hall, Schneider, & Nygren, 1970), commitment (Alutto & Acito, 1974; Cook & Wall, 1980; Ivancevich, 1979; Hollenbeck, 1989; Tziner, 1987), trust (Alutto & Acito, 1974; Cook & Wall, 1980), and various indices of employee well-being (Alutto & Acito, 1974; Alutto & Vredenburgh, 1977; French, Caplan, & Harrison, 1980; Ivancevich, 1979). Algebraic difference studies measuring desires in terms of importance have found mixed results (Beer, 1966; Pelz & Andrews, 1976; Sexton, 1967; Wanous & Lawler, 1972). However, as stated earlier, these results are probably attributable to the dubious theoretical assumptions underlying this index.

Studies operationalizing fit as the absolute difference between desires and supplies have generally found negative relationships with job satisfaction (Barrett, 1978; French, Caplan, & Harrison, 1982; Greenhaus, Seidel, & Marinus, 1983; Lopez & Greenhaus, 1978; Meir & Engel, 1986; O'Brien & Dowling, 1980; Phillips, Barrett, & Rush, 1978; Rice, McFarlin, & Bennett, 1989), organizational commitment (Hrebiniak & Alutto, 1972), interest in work (Swaney & Prediger, 1985), and employee well-being (French, Caplan, & Harrison, 1981). Studies using the squared difference (or some variation thereof) have typically found similar results (Caplan et al., 1980; Rounds, Dawis, & Lofquist, 1987; Scarpello & Campbell, 1983). Taken together, these results suggest that some 'optimal' level may exist for many job supplies. However, some studies suggest that the relationships implied by absolute and squared difference indices may be asymmetric (e.g. Alutto & Belasco, 1972; French, Caplan, & Harrison, 1982; Giles & Barrett, 1971; London & Klimoski, 1975). Unfortunately, no studies explicitly tested whether the differences in slope implied by these asymmetries were significant.

Studies using ratio indices of fit have generally found positive relationships with job satisfaction (Giles & Barrett, 1971; French, Caplan, & Harrison, 1982; Michalos, 1980, 1983; Payne, 1970). However, none of these studies controlled for the components of the ratio, making it impossible to determine whether the ratio explained variance in outcomes beyond that accounted for by its components. A similar situation is evident in a number of studies using product indices of fit, which demonstrated positive relationships with job satisfaction but did not control for the components of the product (Sheridan & Slocum, 1975; Wanous & Lawler, 1972). Studies using hierarchical analyses have typically found significant moderating effects when the person is measured in terms of desires (Cherrington & England, 1980; O'Brien & Dowling, 1980; Rice, McFarlin, & Bennett, 1989), but not when the person is measured in terms of importance (Butler, 1983; White & Ruh, 1973).

Studies of categorical agreement have demonstrated consistent relationships with a variety of outcomes, most notably job and occupational satisfaction (Aranya, Barak, & Amernik, 1981; Barak & Meir, 1974; Betz, 1969; Brandt & Hood, 1968; Furnham & Schaeffer, 1984; Hener & Meir, 1981; Meir & Melamed, 1986; Melamed & Meir, 1981; Mount & Muchinsky, 1978; Peiser & Meir, 1978; Wiggins, 1984; Wiggins et al., 1983; Zytowski, 1974). Studies of conditional desires have also demonstrated consistent relationships with satisfaction (Aranya, Barak, & Amernik, 1981; Barak & Meir, 1974; Doty & Betz, 1979; Feldman & Meir, 1976; Meir & Erez, 1981; Vaitenas & Wiener, 1977; Wiener & Klein, 1978; Wiggins, 1976, 1984), though only Wanous and Zwany (1977) demonstrated that the relationship between satisfaction and desires differed significantly across groups. Studies of conditional supplies have found stronger relationships between supplies and outcomes for employees with higher desires (Cherrington & England, 1980; Ivancevich & Donnelly, 1974; Lefkowitz, Somers, & Weinberg, 1984; Lyons, 1971; Miles & Petty, 1975; Wanous, 1974), and each study adequately demonstrated the significance of this effect. However, all studies of conditional desires and supplies compared correlations across groups, whereas comparisons of regression slopes are required to appropriately evaluate the effect of interest (Stone & Hollenbeck, 1984).

Studies examining desires and supplies as simultaneous predictors have generally found differential relationships with outcomes (Cherrington & England, 1980; Tziner, 1987). In most cases, these relationships deviate from the form implied by commonly used fit indices. For example, operationalizing fit as an algebraic difference implies that relationships for the person and job are equal in magnitude but opposite in sign (Edwards & Cooper, 1990). In general, this pattern did not emerge in the studies reviewed, indicating that the constraint implied by the algebraic difference index may be inappropriate.

In sum, the studies reviewed here indicate that, across a variety of measures, samples, job content areas, and operationalizations, P–J fit has demonstrated the expected relationship with outcomes. Despite this seemingly overwhelming consensus, the results of these studies must be considered tentative, because serious methodological problems discussed in the following section are evident in nearly every study reviewed and, in many cases, render their results ambiguous and inconclusive. Fortunately, solutions to these problems are available which, if adopted, will enhance the conclusiveness of future P–J fit research.

METHODOLOGICAL ISSUES IN PERSON–JOB FIT RESEARCH

The preceding review noted methodological problems specific to individual P–J fit studies. In this section, problems characteristic of P–J fit research as a whole are discussed, and solutions to these problems are offered. These problems fall into four general categories, including sampling, design, measurement, and analysis. It should be emphasized that this discussion focuses specifically on problems that are particularly pressing in P–J fit research. Of course, this is not intended to imply that P–J fit research is not susceptible to problems that characterize OB and I/O psychology research in general (for discussions, see Bateman & Ferris, 1984; Bryman, 1988; Locke, 1986; McGrath, Martin, & Kulka, 1982; Mowday & Steers, 1979; Stone, 1978, 1986).

Sampling

Two major sampling problems are evident in empirical P–J fit research. First, most studies have relied on samples drawn from within a single job, company, or industry. As a result, the range of person measures is restricted, in that people with similar desires and abilities tend to select similar jobs (Holland, 1985). Similarly, the range of job measures is restricted, due to the limited variation in supplies and demands within a given job, company, or industry. Second, most studies have relied on rather small samples (i.e. less than 200). This also restricts the range of person and job measures and, furthermore, decreases the likelihood of including respondents whose person and job measures deviate substantially from one another. Taken together, these factors attenuate the estimated relationship between fit and outcomes. However, given the rather small number of studies reporting null results, it appears that the relationship between fit and outcomes is sufficiently robust to overcome this attenuation, at least in terms of reaching standard significance levels. Nonetheless, more accurate estimates will be obtained by employing large samples drawn from a variety of jobs, occupations, and industries. Existing studies that exemplify these features include French, Caplan, & Harrison (1982), Lefkowitz, Somers, & Weinberg (1984), O'Brien and Dowling (1980), Rounds, Dawis, & Lofquist (1987), Swaney & Prediger (1985), and Zytowski (1976).

Design

The primary problem regarding design in P–J fit research is the almost exclusive reliance on cross-sectional data. Consequently, the labeling of correlates of P–J fit as outcomes is necessarily ambiguous, and it is not difficult to construct plausible hypotheses involving reverse causality. For example, employees who are satisfied may display a sense of efficacy and enthusiasm, thereby garnering desirable job supplies. However, it is more likely that the relationship between fit and outcomes is bidirectional or, more precisely, cyclically recursive (Billings & Wroten, 1978), were misfit leads to negative outcomes, which in turn stimulate attempts to change job supplies and/or employee desires, thereby resolving misfit (cf. Chatman, 1989; Cummings & Cooper, 1979; Edwards, 1989; Schneider, 1983, 1987; Terborg, 1981). Unfortunately, current data are inadequate to detect these effects. To resolve this problem, future studies should employ repeated measures designs, thereby providing firmer ground for establishing causality and allowing the estimation of cyclically recursive relationships between fit and outcomes.

Measurement

Several major problems regarding measurement are evident in P–J fit research. Some of these problems concern commensurate measurement, which is required for adequate tests of P–J fit. Though the studies reviewed here were explicitly selected on the basis of commensurate measurement, many implemented procedures that risk diluting or eliminating the commensurate features of their measures. For example, several studies employed measures that were commensurate at the item level, but then summed these items to form overall person and job indices (e.g. Betz, 1969; Imparato, 1972; Lopez & Greenhaus, 1978; Orpen, 1974; Rounds, Dawis, & Lofquist, 1987; Sheridan & Slocum, 1975; Wanous, 1974). Without examining individual item variances and covariances, it is impossible to determine the relative contribution of items regarding specific job content dimensions to variation in the summary indices. Unless the contribution of these items happens to be the same for the person and job measures, the resulting summary indices will not be completely commensurate. Furthermore, because summary indices collapse conceptually distinct job content dimensions, their interpretation is confounded (Burt, 1976; Hattie, 1985; Hunter & Gerbing, 1982), and relationships involving specific job content dimensions are concealed. This is particularly problematic in P–J fit research, where the relationship between fit and outcomes often differs across job content dimensions (e.g. French, Caplan, & Harrison, 1982; Hall, Schneider, & Nygren, 1970; Mount & Muchinsky, 1978; Payne, 1970; Slocum, 1971).

Another problem involves the commensurate measurement of outcomes in P–J fit research. Though the importance of commensurate measurement of the person and job is widely discussed (e.g. Caplan *et al.*, 1980; Cherrington & England, 1980; French, Caplan, & Harrison, 1982; Kahn, 1970; Rounds, Dawis, & Lofquist, 1987), the commensurate measurement of outcomes has not been emphasized. Strictly speaking, fit regarding specific job content dimensions should only influence outcomes commensurate with that dimension. For example, the fit between actual and desired pay should influence pay satisfaction, but not satisfaction regarding other job facets. This principle is illustrated by Caplan *et al.* (1980), who found that workload fit demonstrated a stronger relationship with workload dissatisfaction than with any other outcome measure. Though several studies have employed commensurate person, job, and outcome measures (e.g. Betz, 1969; Dyer & Theriault, 1976; Giles & Barrett, 1971; Greenhaus, Seidel, & Marinus, 1983; Rice, McFarlin, & Bennett, 1989; Rounds, Dawis, & Lofquist, 1987), a number have measured fit and outcomes associated with different job facets (e.g. Alutto & Acito, 1974; Butler, 1983; Dorr, Honea, & Posner, 1980; Herman & Hulin, 1973; Imparato, 1972; Wright & Gutkin, 1981). Alternately, several studies have used global outcome measures, such as global job satisfaction (e.g. Cherrington

& England, 1980; Lopez & Greenhaus, 1978; Lyons, 1971; Meir & Engel, 1986; Orpen, 1974; Payne, 1970). Unfortunately, these measures conceal the relative contribution of satisfaction regarding specific job facets, making it impossible to determine whether commensurate outcome measurement exists. Furthermore, the use of global satisfaction measures confounds the relationship between fit and satisfaction with the relationship between facet and global satisfaction. Unless the latter relationship is perfect, tests of fit will be attenuated.

A third measurement problem involves inadequate distinction between desires–supplies fit and abilities–demands fit. For example, Blau (1981) initially defined misfit in terms of abilities and demands, but later measured the person and job in terms of desires and supplies. A more extreme example is provided by the SDS (Holland, 1979). As indicated earlier, the SDS contains measures of preferences, competencies, and interests. However, summary scores derived from the SDS confound these dimensions, making it impossible to determine whether associations between these scores and outcomes reflect desires–supplies fit, abilities–demands fit, or both. This problem is exacerbated by measures of the job typically used in conjunction with the SDS, which focus on occupation or job title and, hence, fail to distinguish between supplies and demands. By confounding desires–supplies and abilities–demands fit, important conceptual distinctions between these forms of fit are muddled, and differential relationships with outcomes are concealed (cf. Edwards & Cooper, 1990).

A fourth problem is the widespread focus on normatively desirable job attributes (e.g. pay, variety, challenge, participation in decision-making, role clarity) in studies of desires–supplies fit. For these attributes, responses to desires measures are often positively skewed and restricted in range, thereby hindering adequate tests of fit. Furthermore, these measures typically yield few observations where supplies exceed desires (e.g. Alutto & Acito, 1974; Alutto & Vredenburgh, 1977; French, Caplan, & Harrison, 1982; Porter, 1962). As a result, relationships between fit and outcomes primarily reflect deficiencies (i.e. the region in which supplies fall short of desires), and extrapolations to situations where supplies exceed desires are inappropriate.

A fifth problem is presented by the recent emergence of direct measures of fit, in which the person and job are compared within a single item (e.g. Cook & Wall, 1980; Crosby, 1982; Greenhaus, Seidel, & Marinus, 1983; Hollenbeck, 1989; Michalos, 1980, 1983; Rice, McFarlin, & Bennett, 1989; Tziner, 1987). In most cases, these measures represent attempts to avoid problems with the use of difference scores (e.g. Cronbach & Furby, 1970; Johns, 1981; Wall & Payne, 1973). However, these measures provide no guarantee that the *respondent* does not implicitly or explicitly calculate the difference between the relevant person and job dimensions in the process of providing a response. In fact, the construction of many direct measures of fit inherently primes the respondent to calculate a difference. For example, Rice, McFarlin, & Bennett, (1989) asked respondents to indicate whether they wanted more or less various job attributes, using a 5-point ranging from -2 to $+2$. Similarly, Cook & Wall (1980) used a 5-point verbally anchored response format ranging from 'I have more now than I really want' to 'I would like very much more'. It is not difficult to imagine that, in the process of providing a response, the respondent considers actual and desired amounts of the job attributes in question and subtracts one from the other, even if this calculation is intuitive and almost automatic. In any case, proponents of direct measures of fit provide no evidence that this process does not occur. If it does, then direct measures of fit are prone to the same problems as difference scores, because these problems are unaffected by whether the researcher or the respondent calculates the difference.

Direct measures of fit not only fail convincingly to avoid the problems with difference scores, they also introduce several additional problems that are not encountered when separate person and job measures are used. First, they presuppose the form of the relationship between fit and outcomes. For example, measures used by Cook and Wall (1980), Crosby (1982), Greenhaus, Seidel, & Marinus, (1983), Rice, McFarlin, & Bennett (1989), and Tziner (1987) presume a difference model (or some transformation thereof), whereas the measure used by Michalos (1980, 1983) presumes a ratio model. These representations may be inadequate, since the surface relating the person and job to outcomes may have slope, tilt, and curvature (e.g. O'Brien & Dowling, 1980; Rice, McFarlin, & Bennett, (1989). Second, they prevent the separate estimation of relationships involving the person and job, which may differ in magnitude and direction (e.g. Blau, 1981; Cherrington & England, 1980; French, Caplan, & Harris, 1982; Tziner, 1987; Wright & Gutkin, 1981). Third, they provide no mechanism for identifying situations where either the person or job is individually responsible for the relationships between fit and outcomes, as several studies have suggested (e.g. Dorr, Honea, & Posner, 1980; French, Caplan & Harrison, 1982; Pelz & Andrews, 1976; Wanous & Lawler, 1972). Finally, they necessarily confound person and job constructs, rendering their interpretation ambiguous (Burt, 1976; Hattie, 1985; Hunter & Gerbing, 1982).

Taken together, the measurement problems discussed above suggest the following recommendations. First, investigations of P–J fit should employ measures that reflect unidimensional and conceptually distinct job content dimensions, and should analyse these measures intact rather than collapsing them into summary indices. Second, fully commensurate sets of measures should be used, in which the person, the job, and outcomes each refer to the same job content dimension. Of course, general outcomes, such as absenteeism, turnover, and somatic complaints, are not readily expressed in terms of specific job content dimensions. However, it is likely that the relationship between fit and general outcomes is mediated by commensurate outcomes (e.g. facet satisfaction). If this is true, then measures of *both* sets of outcomes are required to appropriately represent the underlying process. Third, measures of desires and supplies should be clearly distinguished from measures of abilities and demands, in that these person and job factors are conceptually distinct and are likely to predict different outcomes. Fourth, studies should focus on a broad range of job attributes, particularly those that are likely to elicit wide variation in desirability responses (e.g. contact with coworkers, responsibility for persons, job complexity). Finally, direct measures of fit should be avoided in favor of separate measures of the person and job.

Analysis

Perhaps the most pressing problems associated with empirical P–J fit research involve methods of data analysis. Many of these problems result from the persistent tendency to reduce person and job measures into a single index, most often a difference score or some transformation thereof (e.g. absolute difference, squared difference). This tendency is apparently based on the belief that fit indices provide some advantage over separate person and job measures, either by representing some conceptually distinct construct or by contributing additional explanatory power. However, as argued below, fit indices provide neither of these advantages and, in most cases, yield ambiguous and potentially misleading results.

There are several reasons why fit indices provide no conceptual advantage over separate person and job measures. First, they contain no information beyond that provided by their components. For example, indices representing an algebraic difference are often considered distinct from their components because they provide 'relative' information, i.e. the degree to which the person and job deviate from one another. Though this information is not provided by either component *individually*, it is provided by both components considered *jointly*. Furthermore, most fit indices actually provide less information than that provided jointly by their constituent components. For example, algebraic difference indices discard information regarding the absolute level of person and job measures, which may be important in understanding the effects of fit. This was demonstrated by Imparato (1972), who found that respondents who desired and received larger amounts were more satisfied than those who desired and received smaller amounts. Indices representing absolute and squared differences fare worse, because they also discard directional information and, hence, eliminate the possibility of detecting asymmetries, such as those found by Alutto & Belasco (1972), French, Caplan, & Harrison (1982), and others.

Second, fit indices are necessarily multidimensional, because they collapse conceptually distinct constructs into a single measure (Hattie, 1985; Hunter & Gerbing, 1982). In most instances, the relative degree to which these indices reflect the person and job cannot be readily inferred, rendering their interpretation ambiguous. This is true even when the procedure used to construct the fit index is taken into account. For example, it is tempting to conclude that the correlations between an algebraic difference index and its components are approximately equal in magnitude but opposite in sign. However, these correlations are influenced heavily by the variances and covariances of the components (Cohen & Cohen, 1983). It can be easily demonstrated that changes in the variance of either component can cause the correlations between an algebraic difference index and its components to vary widely and even change in sign. The utility of indices whose interpretation is influenced by sample–specific factors, such as the variances obtained on the measures used, is obviously limited.

Third, fit indices generally do not meet criteria commonly used to establish construct validity (Cronbach & Meehl, 1955; Schwab, 1980). For example, Johns (1981) notes that the convergent validity of difference scores has not been demonstrated, because few studies report their relationship with independent attempts to measure the same underlying construct. The preceding review indicates that most other fit indices are subject to the same criticism. Johns (1981) also argues that difference scores fail to demonstrate discriminant validity, particularly when compared to their components. This was apparent in the preceding review, where correlations between algebraic difference indices and their components were large in magnitude (e.g. Caplan et al., 1980). This should not be surprising, since many fit indices are highly correlated with their components by construction and, therefore, cannot demonstrate discriminant validity.

Fit indices not only offer no apparent conceptual advantage over their constituent components, they also provide no explanatory power beyond that provided by their components and, in most cases, provide less. This results primarily from the fact that most fit indices simply represent a set of constraints on the parameters relating the person and job to outcomes. For example, algebraic difference indices implicitly constrain the coefficients on the person and job to be equal in magnitude but opposite in sign. Similarly, squared difference indices effectively introduce the person squared, the job squared, and the product of the person and job as predictors, with the constraint that the coefficients on the person squared and job squared are equal, and the coefficient on the product of the person and job is twice as large as these coefficients and opposite in sign. Absolute difference indices are substantively similar to squared difference indices, but statistically represent a piecewise linear model in which the coefficients on the person and job are equal in magnitude but opposite in sign, and the sign of both coefficients is reversed along the line where the person and job measures are equal. Most other indices can be similarly expressed as a set of constraints on models involving separate person and job variables, either in their original form or combined with higher-order transformations. Imposing these constraints cannot increase the amount of variance explained in outcomes and, in most cases, will decrease it. Moreover, the reliability of fit indices will usually be lower than the reliability of one or both component variables (Busemeyer & Jones, 1983; Dunlap & Kemery, 1988; Johns, 1981), which will further reduce the amount of variance explained.

In addition to reducing the amount of variance explained, fit indices often yield ambiguous and potentially misleading results. This is illustrated in the following example, using data from 177 entering Master of Business Administration (MBA) students and 165 participants in an executive education program. All respondents completed fully commensurate measures of supplies, desires, and satisfaction, with multiple items for each job content dimension. For illustration, two dimensions were selected, representing motivating and rewarding other for the MBA sample and the receipt of rewards and recognition for the executive sample. Because the MBA students were full-time and, hence, unemployed, they were asked to provide responses in reference to their most recent job. Four fit indices were constructed, including algebraic difference, absolute difference, squared difference, and product. Taken together, these indices represent the vast majority of those used in empirical P–J fit research to date (see Table 1).

Table 2 presents analyses of the relationships between these fit indices and satisfaction. Results for the algebraic difference index were significant, suggesting that satisfaction increases as supplies exceed desires and decreases as supplies fall short of desires. However, results for the absolute difference and squared difference indices were also significant, indicating that satisfaction decreased as supplies deviated from desires in either direction. The product index was positively correlated with satisfaction, but regression results indicated that, when desires and supplies were appropriately controlled, this relationship was no longer significant. Taken together, these results suggest that the relationship between fit and satisfaction is essentially the same for both samples, but the exact nature of this relationship remains unclear, given the significant results for all three difference indices.

Direct inspection of the data reveals that the preceding analyses are highly misleading. Figures 2 and 3 present three-dimensional graphs of the actual and predicted surfaces relating desires, supplies, and satisfaction. Within each figure, the first graph depicts the raw data, and the following four graphs represent estimate surfaces corresponding to the four fit indices analysed above.[8] For the MBA sample, the actual surface relating the person, the job, and satisfaction resembles a rounded hillside, with its primary slope along the line where the person and job are approximately equal. For the executive

---

[8] To facilitate inspection, surfaces corresponding to the raw data has been plotted using a distance-weighted least squares approximation, which allows the surface to flex locally to fit the data (McLain, 1974).

Table 2—The Relationship Between Satisfaction and Various Fit Indices

Index	MBA sample (n=177)				Executive sample (n=165)			
	r	b	ΔR^2	F	r	b	ΔR^2	F
J–P	0.334**	0.353	0.112	22.00**	0.331**	0.207	0.104	18.82**
|J–P|	−0.353**	−0.439	0.125	24.89**	−0.292**	−0.270	0.083	14.67**
$(J–P)^2$	−0.375**	−0.018	0.140	28.56**	−0.245**	−0.019	0.060	10.26**
J×P	0.521**	−0.001	0.000	0.04	0.522**	0.003	0.001	0.04

*p < 0.05; **p < 0.01.
Note: Regression results for the product index (J×P) correspond to a hierarchical model in which the person and job were controlled.

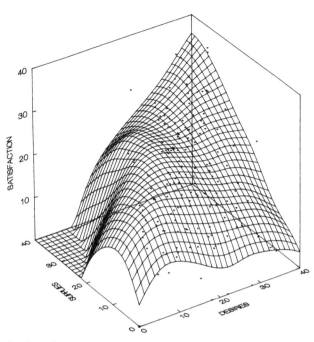

(a) Raw data

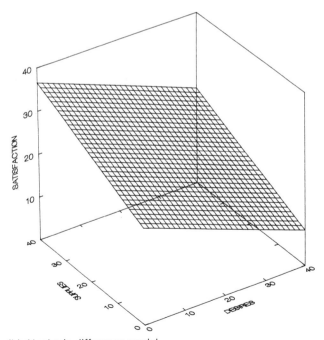

(b) Algebraic difference model

Figure 2 MBA sample

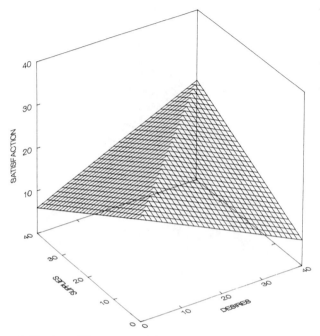

(c) Absolute difference model

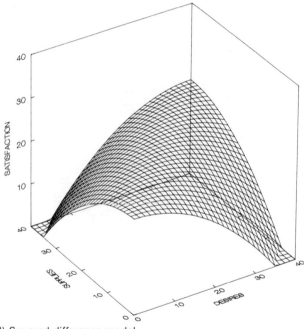

(d) Squared difference model

Figure 2 *cont.*

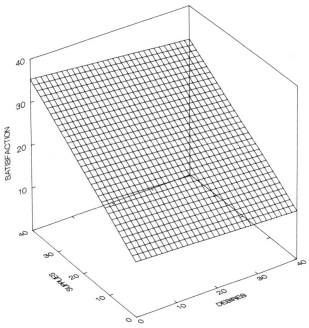

(e) Interactive model

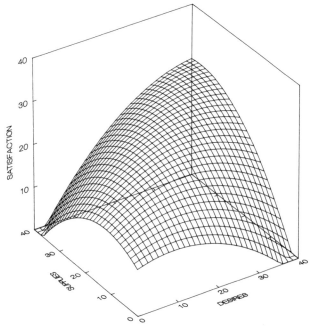

(f) Quadratic model

Figure 2 *cont.*

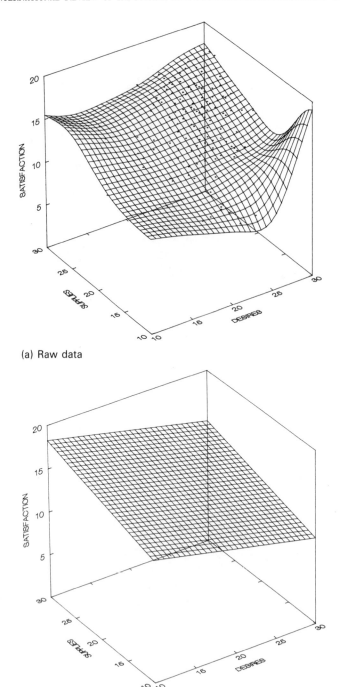

(a) Raw data

(b) Algebraic difference model

Figure 3   Executive sample

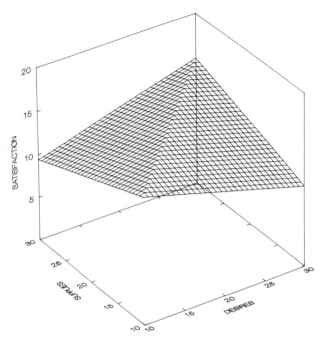

(c) Absolute difference model

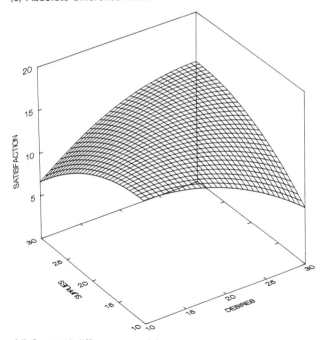

(d) Squared difference model

Figure 3 *cont.*

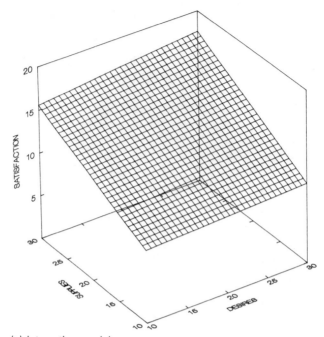

(e) Interactive model

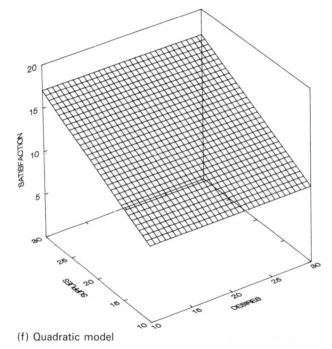

(f) Quadratic model

Figure 3 *cont.*

sample, the surface is simpler, resembling a plane with a positive slope along the supplies axis. Though there is curvilinearity in this surface at the low end of the supplies scale, this was caused by two outliers and, hence, should not be given undue consideration in the overall interpretation of the surface.

Surfaces estimated using the four fit indices analysed earlier provide rather poor representations of the actual data and, furthermore, fail to reflect the obvious differences between the two samples. For both samples, the algebraic difference index yielded a plane with a positive slope along the supplies axis and an equal but negative slope along the desires axis. Visual inspection reveals that these surfaces deviate substantially from the actual data, particularly for the MBA sample. The absolute difference index yielded a tent-shaped surface, and the squared difference yielded an inverted parabolic surface. These surfaces are obviously inaccurate for the executive sample but somewhat more accurate for the MBA sample. However, they both imply that satisfaction is the same for all points along the line where supplies equal desires, which is clearly not the case. Though the results of hierarchical analyses of the product index were not significant, the surface estimated using these results was quite close for the executive sample but highly inaccurate for the MBA sample. The close approximation for the executive sample was achieved because these analyses entered supplies and desires as separate predictors prior to the product term, thereby allowing appropriate estimation of the positive relationship between supplies and satisfaction. However, like those based on the difference indices, this surface again failed to reflect the differences between the two samples.

Given these misleading results, it is clear that alternative approaches are needed to analyse the relationship between the person, the job, and outcomes. One approach involves response surface methodology (Myers, 1971; Neter, Wasserman, & Kutner, 1989), in which models representing higher-order functions of the person and job are estimated. A simple but rather robust model uses five predictors, including the person, the job, the person squared, the job squared, and the product of the person and the job. This model represents a quadratic function of the person and job, yielding a surface that can have slope, curvature, and tilt. This model was estimated for both samples, with the three nonlinear terms entered after controlling for desires and supplies (see Table 3). For both samples, the first stage indicated a significant positive relationship between supplies and satisfaction. However, the second stage yielded significant effects only for the MBA sample. Inspection of the coefficients on the three nonlinear terms suggested an inverted asymmetric parabolic surface (cf. Edwards & Cooper, 1990). Estimated surfaces based on these results were then plotted. The model for the executive sample was first reestimated using supplies as a single predictor, since coefficients on the remaining variables were not significant. However, desires was retained in the model for the MBA sample even though it was not significant, since it is required for unbiased estimation of coefficients on the nonlinear variables

Table 3—Response Surface Analyses of the Relationship Between the Person, the Job, and Satisfaction

Index	*MBA sample (n=177)*			*Executive sample (n=165)*		
	b	ΔR^2	F	b	ΔR^2	F
J	0.531	0.223	57.26**	0.394	0.272	65.53**
P	−0.052	0.002	0.44	0.076	0.007	1.80
Both predictors		0.323	41.52**		0.327	39.44**
J^2	−0.023	0.038	10.61**	0.004	0.001	0.22
$J \times P$	0.029	0.028	7.82**	−0.004	0.000	0.10
P^2	−0.017	0.015	4.25*	0.011	0.004	1.02
All three predictors		0.054	4.97**		0.006	0.73
All five predictors		0.377	20.72**		0.333	15.88**

*$p < 0.05$; **$p < 0.01$.
Note: The three nonlinear variables (J^2, $J \times P$, P^2) were entered hierarchically, after controlling for P and J.

(Cohen, 1978). For both samples, these surfaces yielded good approximations of the data (Figures 2f and 3f). Substantively, these results indicate that, for the executive sample, supplies and satisfaction are positively related, and that desires has little influence on this relationship. In contrast, results for the MBA sample indicate that, for a given level of desires or supplies, satisfaction is highest where supplies and desires are approximately equal, but that satisfaction is much higher when both desires and supplies are high than when both are low (cf. Imparato, 1972). These interpretations differ markedly from those provided by the four fit indices analysed earlier, particularly when any given index is considered in isolation, as is typically done in P–J fit research.

From the preceding discussion, it is apparent that indices commonly used in P–J fit research provide no conceptual or empirical advantage over their constituent components and, furthermore, are prone to yield ambiguous and misleading results. Consequently, the findings of the vast majority of the studies reviewed earlier must be considered inconclusive. However, this conclusion is not as discouraging as it may seem, since most of the studies reviewed found significant relationships between fit and outcomes. Instead, it suggests that many potentially viable relationships between the person, the job, and outcomes remained to be discovered. To avoid the ambiguity inherent in the studies reviewed, future research should avoid reducing person and job measures to a single index. Instead, techniques that retain the integrity of the person and job as separate constructs, such as the response surface methodology employed here, should be adopted.

These recommendations will undoubtedly meet some resistance from researchers accustomed to using P–J fit indices, because using separate person and job variables may seem to eliminate any vestige of 'fit' from data analysis and, therefore, threaten its existence as a theoretical concept. Admittedly, the recommendations presented here not only suggest different methods of analysis, but also imply a fundamental shift in the conceptualization of P–J fit. However, rather than threatening its existence, these recommendations suggested an expanded view of fit, from a set of constraints on the relationship between the person, the job, and outcomes, to any situation in which the person and job are jointly related to outcomes. These relationships may take a variety of forms, including those implied by fit indices used in previous research, the inverted asymmetric parabolic surface found in the preceding illustration, and other more complex surfaces. The fundamental shift that will allow the discovery of these surfaces is from a two-dimensional to a three-dimensional view of the relationship between the person, the job, and outcomes. Reducing this relationship to two dimensions is inappropriate, because the person, the job, and outcomes represent three conceptually distinct constructs and should be treated as such.

The preceding recommendations were derived primarily from criticisms of difference and product indices. However, methodological problems underlying other indices used in P–J fit research, such as the conditional person and job, have been discussed elsewhere (Stone & Hollenbeck, 1984; Stone, 1988). Rather than reiterating these problems here, it will simply be noted that these indices also reduce the relationship between the person, the job, and outcomes to two dimensions. Therefore, these indices cannot adequately represent surfaces relating the person and job to outcomes, such as those found in the preceding illustration and those that may emerge in future research.

CONCLUSION AND DIRECTIONS FOR FUTURE RESEARCH

Based on the preceding review and critique, several general conclusions seem warranted. First, person and job variables, particularly employee desires and job supplies, are consistently related to many individual and organizational outcomes, most notably job satisfaction. Second, desires–supplies fit bears no consistent relationship with job performance, though these inconsistencies are probably due to the omission of theoretically relevant variables. Third, the relationship between desires–supplies fit and outcomes is apparently more consistent when desires are measured in terms of preferences (i.e. appropriate, optimal, or wanted amount) rather than importance. Finally, the relationship between the person, the job, and outcomes may take on a variety of forms, ranging from a simple sloped plane to a complex curvilinear surface. However, available evidence is inadequate to determine the relative frequency of these various forms, or whether they differ across job content dimensions, outcome measures, sample characteristics, or other factors. These ambiguities exist primarily because much of our knowledge is based on studies that examine two-dimensional relationship between fit indices and outcomes rather than three-dimensional relationships between the person, the job, and outcomes. Thus, the past 30 years of P–J fit research allows only very general conclusions regarding the relationship between the person, the job, and outcomes, and a more detailed understanding of this relationship must await future research.

To generate more conclusive evidence regarding the nature and consequences of P–J fit, the following directions for future research are offered. First, the relationship between P–J fit and outcomes should be conceptualized in three dimensions, thereby preserving the integrity of person, job, and outcome constructs. Second, techniques that allow the estimation of the resulting three-dimensional relationships, such as response surface methodology, should be employed. Third, competing hypotheses regarding the surface relating the person, the job, and outcomes should be tested. For example, it remains unclear whether employee desires operate as a moderator of the relationship between supplies and outcomes, or a standard against which job supplies are compared. If desires operate as a standard, it still must be determined whether deviations in either direction have the same effects on outcomes. Fourth, relationships involving various combinations of person and job constructs should be examined. For example, though available evidence suggests that operationalizing desires in terms of importance is inadvisable, the relative merits of other operationalizations, such as appropriate amount, optimal amount, and wanted amount, have yet to be determined. Fourth, much more research is needed regarding demands–abilities fit, given its centrality to organizational stress research. Fifth, longitudinal data should be collected to examine the cyclically recursive effects embedded in transactional and cybernetic approaches to P–J fit (e.g. Chatman, 1989; Cummings & Cooper, 1979; Edwards, 1989; Schneider, 1983, 1987; Terborg, 1981). Finally, hypotheses regarding the relationship between P–J fit constructs and those in other areas of congruence research, such as those offered by Lawler (1981) and Michalos (1985), should be examined. By incorporating these recommendations, it is hoped that future studies will avoid the pitfalls encountered in previous research, thereby generating more meaningful and definitive conclusions regarding the nature and consequences of P–J fit.

ACKNOWLEDGEMENT

This research was supported in part by the Darden Graduate Business School Foundation. The author would like to thank Arista Z. Brooks, Libby Eshbach, and Sarah Patterson for their assistance in locating and acquiring the studies reviewed, Ran Lachman, Gordon O'Brien, Paul Spector, Aharon Tziner for their clarifying comments regarding the results of selected studies, Mary Darnell and Ginny Fisher for their administrative assistance, and A. J. Baglioni, Jr, Susan Brodt, Mark Parry, and S. Gail Pearl for their helpful comments during the preparation of this chapter.

Correspondence address
Darden Graduate School of Business Administration, University of Virginia, Box 6550, Charlottesville, Virginia 22906, USA.

REFERENCES

Abdel-Halim, A. A. (1979) Interaction effects of power equalization and subordinate personality on job satisfaction and peformance. *Human Relations*, **32**, 489–502.
Aldag, R. J., & Brief, A. P. (1979) *Task Design and Employee Motivation*. Glenview, IL: Scott-Foresman.
Alderfer, C. P. (1972) *Existence, Relatedness, and Growth*. New York: Free Press.
Alutto, J. A., & Acito, F. (1974) Decisional participation and sources of job satisfaction: A study of manufacturing personnel. *Academy of Management Journal*, **17**, 160–167.
Alutto, J. A., & Belasco, J. A. (1972) A typology for participation in organizational decision-making. *Administrative Science Quarterly*, **17**, 117–125.
Alutto, J., Hrebiniak, L., & Alonso, R. (1971) Variation in hospital employment and influence perceptions among nursing personnel. *Journal of Health and Social Behavior*, **12**, 30–34.

Alutto, J. A., & Vredenburgh, D. J. (1977) Characteristics of decisional participation by nurses. *Academy of Management Journal*, **20**, 341–347.

Amerikaner, M., Elliot, D., & Swank, P. (1988) Social interest as a predictor of vocational satisfaction. *Individual Psychology*, **44**, 316–323.

Andrews, F. M., & Farris, G. F. (1972) Time pressure and performance of scientists and engineers: A five-year panel study. *Organizational Behavior and Human Performance*, **8**, 185–200.

Aranya, N., Barak, A., & Amernic, J. (1981) A test of Holland's theory in a population of accountants. *Journal of Vocational Behavior*, **19**, 15–24.

Arnold, H. J. (1982) Moderator variables: A clarification of conceptual, analytic, and psychometric issues. *Organizational Behavior and Human Performance*, **29**, 143–174.

Assouline, M., & Meir, E. I. (1987) Meta-analysis of the relationship between congruence and well-being measures. *Journal of Vocational Behavior*, **31**, 319–332.

Barak, A., & Meir, E. I. (1974) The predictive validity of a vocational interest inventory—'Ramak': Seven year follow-up. *Journal of Vocational Behavior*, **4**, 377–387.

Barrett, G. V. (1978) Task design, individual attributes, work satisfaction, and productivity. In A. Negandhi & B. Wilpert (eds), *Work Organization Research*. Kent, OH: Kent State University Press, pp. 261–278.

Bateman, T. S., & Ferris, G. R. (eds) (1984) *Method and Analysis in Organizational Research*. Reston, VA: Reston Publishing Company.

Beehr, T. A., & Bhagat, R. S. (1985) Introduction to human stress and cognition in organizations. In T. A. Beehr & R. S. Bhagat (eds), *Human Stress and Cognition in Organizations* (pp. 3–19). New York: Wiley.

Beer, M. (1966) *Leadership, employee needs, and motivation*. Columbus: Ohio State University, Bureau of Business Research.

Berger-Gross, V. (1982) Difference score measures of social perceptions revisited: A comparison of alternatives. *Organizational Behavior and Human Performance*, **29**, 279–285.

Betz, E. L. (1969) Need-reinforcer correspondence as a predictor of job satisfaction. *Personnel and Guidance Journal*, **47**, 878–883.

Betz, E. L. (1984) Two tests of Maslow's theory of need fulfilment. *Journal of Vocational Behavior*, **24**, 204–220.

Billings, R. S., & Wroten, S. P. (1978) Use of path analysis in industrial/organizational psychology: Criticisms and suggestions. *Journal of Applied Psychology*, **63**, 677–688.

Blau, G. (1981) An empirical investigation of job stress, social support, service length, and job strain. *Organizational Behavior and Human Performance*, **27**, 279–302.

Borgen, F. H., Weiss, D. J., Tinsely, H. E. A., Dawis, R. V., & Lofquist, L. H. (1968) The measurement of occupational reinforcer patterns. *Minnesota Studies in Vocational Rehabilitation*, **25**.

Brandt, J. E., & Hood, A. B. (1968) Effect of personality adjustment on the predictive validity of the Strong Vocational Interest Blank. *Journal of Counseling Psychology*, **15** 547–551.

Bryman, A. (ed.) (1988) *Doing Research in Organizations*. New York: Routledge.

Burt, R. S. (1976) Interpretational confounding of unobserved variables in structural equation models. *Sociological Methods and Research*, **5**, 3–52.

Busemeyer, J. R., & Jones, L. E. (1983) Analysis of multiplicative combination rules when the causal variables are measured with error. *Psychological Bulletin*, **93**, 549–562.

Butler, J. K. (1983) Value importance as a moderator of the value-fulfillment–job satisfaction relationship: Group differences. *Journal of Applied Psychology*, **68**, 420–428.

Cairo, P. C. (1982) Measured interests versus expressed interests as predictors of long-term occupational membership. *Journal of Vocational Behavior*, **20**, 343–353.

Campbell, D. P. (1971) *Handbook for the Strong Vocational Interest Blank*. Stanford, CA: Stanford University Press.

Campbell, D. P., & Hansen, J. C. (1981) *Manual for the Strong–Campbell Interest Inventory*, 3rd edn. Palo Alto, CA: Consulting Psychologists Press.

Caplan, R. D. (1987) Person–environment fit theory and organizations: Commensurate dimensions, time perspectives, and mechanisms. *Journal of Vocational Behavior*, **31**, 248–267.

Caplan, R. D., Cobb, S., French, J. R. P., Jr, Harrison, R. V., & Pinneau, S. R. (1980) *Job Demands and Worker Health: Main Effects and Occupational Differences*. Ann Arbor, MI: Institute for Social Research.

Chatman, J. A. (1989) Improving interactional organizational research: A model of person–organization fit. *Academy of Management Review*, **14**, 333–349.

Cherrington, D. J., & England, J. L. (1980) The desire for an enriched job as a moderator of the enrichment–satisfaction relationship. *Organizational Behavior and Human Peformance*, **25**, 139–159.

Coburn, D. (1975) Job–worker incongruence: Consequences for health. *Journal of Health and Social Behavior*, **16**, 198–212.

Cohen, J. (1978) Partialed products *are* interactions: Partialed powers *are* curve components. *Psychological Bulletin*, **85**, 858–866.

Cohen, J., & Cohen, P. (1983) *Applied Multiple Regression/Correlation Analysis for the Behavioral Sciences*, 2nd edn. Hillsdale, NJ: Erlbaum.

Cook, J., & Wall, T. (1980) New work attitude measures of trust, organizational commitment and personal need non-fulfilment. *Journal of Occupational Psychology*, **53**, 39–52.

Cooper, H. M. (1982) Scientific guidelines for conducting integrative research reviews. *Review of Educational Research*, **52**, 291–302.

Cronbach, L. J., & Furby, L. (1970) How should we measure 'change'—or should we? *Psychological Bulletin*, **74**, 68–80.

Cronbach, L. J., & Gleser, G. C. (1953) Assessing the similarity between profiles. *Psychological Bulletin*, **50**, 456–473.

Cronbach, L. J., & Meehl, P. C. (1955) Construct validity in psychological tests. *Psychological Bulletin*, **52**, 281–302.

Crosby, F. (1982) *Relative Deprivation and Working Women*. New York: Oxford University Press.

Cummings, T. G., & Cooper, C. L. (1979) Cybernetic framework for studying occupational stress. *Human Relations*, **32**, 395–418.

Cummings, L. L., & ElSalmi, S. M. (1968) Empirical research on the bases and correlates of managerial motivation: A review of the literature. *Psychological Bulletin*, **70**, 127–144.

Dawis, R. V., & Lofquist, L. H. (1984) *A Psychological Theory of Work Adjustment*. Minneapolis: University of Minnesota Press.

Desmond, R. E., & Weiss, D. J. (1973) Supervisor estimation of ability requirements in jobs. *Journal of Vocational Behavior*, **3**, 181–194.

Dolliver, R. H., Irvin, J. A., & Bigley, S. S. (1972) Twelve-year follow-up of the Strong Vocational Interest Blank. *Journal of Counseling Psychology*, **19**, 212–217.

Dorr, D., Honea, S., & Posner, R. (1980) Ward atmosphere and psychiatric nurses' job satisfaction. *American Journal of Community Psychology*, **8**, 455–461.

Doty, M. S., & Betz, N. E. (1979) Comparisons of the concurrent validity of Holland's theory for men and women in an enterprising occupation. *Journal of Vocational Behavior*, **15**, 207–216.

Drexler, J. A., & Lindell, M. K. (1981) Training/job fit and worker satisfaction. *Human Relations*, **34**, 907–915.

Dunlap, W. P., & Kemery, E. R. (1988) Effects of predictor intercorrelations and reliabilities on moderated multiple regression. *Organizational Behavior and Human Decision Process*, **41**, 248–258.

Dunnette, M. D. (1976) Aptitudes, abilities, and skills. In M. D. Dunnette (ed.), *Handbook of Industrial and Organizational Psychology*. Chicago: Rand McNally, pp. 473–520.

Dyer, L., & Theriault, R. (1976) The determinants of pay satisfaction. *Journal of Applied Psychology*, **61**, 596–604.

Edwards, J. R. (1989) A cybernetic theory of stress, coping, and well-being in organizations. Paper presented at the 49th Annual Meeting of the Academy of Management, Washington, DC, August, 1989.

Edwards, J. R., & Cooper, C. L. (1990) The person–environment fit approach to stress: Recurring problems and some suggested solutions. *Journal of Organizational Behavior*, **10**, 293–307,

Elizur, D., & Tziner, A. (1977). Vocational needs, job rewards, and satisfaction: A canonical analysis. *Journal of Vocational Behavior*, **10**, 205–211.

Evans, M. G. (1969) Conceptual and operational problems in the measurement of various aspects of job satisfaction. *Journal of Applied Psychology*, **53**, 93–101.

Feldman, S., & Meir, E. I. (1976) Measuring women's interests using Holland's vocational classification. *Journal of Vocational Behavior*, **9**, 345–353.

French, J. R. P., Jr, & Caplan, R. D. (1972) Organizational stress and individual strain. In A. J. Marrow (ed.), *The Failure of Success*. New York: Amacon, pp. 30–66.

French, J. R. P., Jr, Caplan, R. D., & Harrison, R. V. (1982) *The Mechanisms of Job Stress and Strain*. London: Wiley.

French, J. R. P., Jr, Rodgers, W. L., & Cobb, S. (1974) Adjustment as person–environment fit. In G. Coelho, D. Hamburg, & J. Adams (eds), *Coping and Adaptation*. New York: Basic Books, pp. 316–333.

Furnham, A., & Schaeffer, R. (1984) Person–environment fit, job satisfaction, and mental health. *Journal of Occupational Psychology*, **57**, 295–307.

Gay, E. G., Weiss, D. J., Hendel, D. D., Dawis, R. V., & Lofquist, L. H. (1971) Manual for the Minnesota Importance Questionnaire. *Minnesota Studies in Vocational Rehabilitation*, **28** (Bulletin No. 54).

Gilbride, T. V. (1973) Holland's theory and resignations from the Catholic clergy. *Journal of Counseling Psychology*, **20**, 190–191.

Giles, B. A., & Barrett, G. V. (1971) Utility of merit increases. *Journal of Applied Psychology*, **55**, 103–109.

Giles, W. F. (1977) Volunteering for job enrichment: Reaction to job characteristics or to change? *Journal of Vocational Behavior*, **11**, 232–238.

Goodman, P. S. (1977) Social comparison processes in organizations. In B. M. Staw & G. R. Salancik (eds), *New Directions in Organizational Behavior*. Chicago, IL: St. Clair Press, pp. 97–132.

Graen, G., & Schiemann, W. (1978) Leader-member agreement: A vertical dyad linkage approach. *Journal of Applied Psychology*, **63**, 206–212.

Graham, W. K. (1976) Commensurate characteristics of persons, groups, and organizations: Development of the Trait Ascription Questionnaire (TAQ). *Human Relations*, **29**, 607–622.

Greenhaus, J. H., Seidel, C., & Marinis, M. (1983) The impact of expectations and values on job attitudes. *Organizational Behavior and Human Performance*, **31**, 394–417.

Guzzo, R. A., Jackson, S. E., & Katzell, R. A. (1987) Meta-analysis analysis. In L. L. Cummings & B. M. Staw (eds), *Research in Organizational Behavior*. Greenwich, CT: JAI Press, pp. 407–442.

Hackman, J. R., & Lawler, E. E. (1971) Employee reactions to job characteristics. *Journal of Applied Psychology Monograph*, **55**, 259–286.

Hackman, J. R., & Oldham, G. R. (1975) Development of the job diagnostic survey. *Journal of Applied Psychology*, **60**, 159–170.

Hackman, J. R., & Oldham, G. R. (1980) *Work Redesign*. Reading, MA: Addison-Wesley.

Haire, M., Ghiselli, E. E., & Porter, L. W. (1966) *Managerial Thinking: An International Study*. New York: Wiley.

Hall, D. T., Schneider, B., & Nygren, H. T. (1970) Personal factors in organizational identification. *Administrative Science Quarterly*, **15**, 176–190.

Harrison, R. V. (1985) The person–environment fit model and the study of job stress. In T. A. Beehr & R. S. Bhagat (eds), *Human Stress and Cognition in Organizations*. New York: Wiley, pp. 23–55.

Hattie, J. (1985) Methodology review: Assessing unidimensionality of tests and items. *Applied Psychological Measurement*, **9**, 139–164.

Hener, T., & Meir, E. I. (1981) Congruence, consistency, and differentiation as predictors of job satisfaction within the nursing occupation. *Journal of Vocational Behavior*, **18**, 304–309.

Herman, J. B., & Hulin, C. L. (1973) Managerial satisfactions and organizational roles: An investigation of Porter's Need Deficiency scales. *Journal of Applied Psychology*, **57**, 118–124.

Holland, J. L. (1977) *Manual for the Vocational Preference Inventory*. Palo Alto, CA: Consulting Psychologists Press.

Holland, J. L. (1978) *The Occupations Finder*. Palo Alto, CA: Consulting Psychologists Press.

Holland, J. L. (1979) *Professional Manual for the Self-Directed Search*. Palo Alto, CA: Consulting Psychologists Press.

Holland, J. L. (1985) *Making Vocational Choices*, 2nd edn. Englewood Cliffs, NJ: Prentice-Hall.

Hollenbeck, J. R. (1989) Control theory and the perception of work environments: The effects of focus of attention on affective and behavioral reactions to work. *Organizational Behavior and Human Decision Process*, **43**, 406–430.

Hrebiniak, L. G. (1974) Effects of job level and participation on employee attitudes and perceptions of influence. *Academy of Management Journal*, **17**, 649–662.

Hrebiniak, L. G., & Alutto, J. A. (1972) Personal and role-related factors in the development of organizational commitment. *Administrative Science Quarterly*, **17**, 555–573.

Hrebiniak, L. G., & Roteman, M. R. (1973) A study of the relationship between need satisfaction and absenteeism among managerial personnel. *Journal of Applied Psychology*, **58**, 381–383.

Hughes, J. N. (1979) Consistency of administrators' and psychologists' actual and ideal perceptions of school psychologists' activities. *Psychology in the Schools*, **16**, 234–239.

Hulin, C. L., & Blood, M. R. (1968) Job enlargement, individual differences, and worker responses. *Psychological Bulletin*, **69**, 41–55.

Hulin, C. L., & Smith, P. C. (1965) A linear model of job satisfaction. *Journal of Applied Psychology*, **49**, 206–216.

Humphrys, P. (1981) The effect of importance upon the relation between perceived job attributes, desired job attributes, and job satisfaction. *Australian Journal of Psychology*, **33**, 121–133.

Hunter, J. E., & Gerbing, D. W. (1982) Unidimensional measurement, second order factor analysis, and causal models, In B. M. Staw and L. L. Cummings (eds),

Research in Organizational Behavior. Greenwich, CT: JAI Press, pp. 267–320.

Hunter, J. E., Schmidt, F. L., & Jackson, G. B. (1982) *Meta-analysis: Cumulating Research Findings Across Studies*. Beverly Hills, CA: Sage.

Huseman, R. C., Hatfield, J. D., & Miles, E. W. (1987) A new perspective on equity theory: The equity sensitivity construct. *Academy of Management Review*, **12**, 222–234.

Iachan, R. (1984) A measure of agreement for use with the Holland classification system. *Journal of Vocational Behavior*, **24**, 133–141.

Imparato, N. (1972) Relationship between Porter's Need Satisfaction Questionnaire and the Job Descriptive Index. *Journal of Applied Psychology*, **56**, 397–405.

Ivancevich, J. M. (1979) An analysis of participation in decision making among project engineers. *Academy of Management Journal*, **22**, 253–269.

Ivancevich, J. M., & Donnelly, J. H. (1974) A study of role clarity and need for clarity for three occupational groups. *Academy of Management Journal*, **17**, 28–36.

Jackson, S. E., & Schuler, R. S. (1985) A meta-analysis and conceptual critique of research on role ambiguity and role conflict in work settings. *Organizational Behavior and Human Decision Process*, **36**, 16–78.

James, L. R. (1980) The unmeasured variable problem in path analysis. *Journal of Applied Psychology*, **65**, 415–421.

Johns, G., (1981) Difference score measures of organizational behavior variables: A critique. *Organizational Behavior and Human Performance*, **27**, 443–463.

Kahn, R. L. (1970) Some propositions toward a researchable conceptualization of stress. In J. E. McGrath (ed.), *Social and Psychological Factors in Stress*. New York: Holt, Rinehart, & Winston, pp. 97–103.

Kahn, R. L., Wolfe, D. M., Quinn, R. P., Snoeck, J. D., & Rosenthal, R. A. (1964) *Organizational Stress: Studies in Role Conflict and Ambiguity*. New York: Wiley.

Karasek, R. A., Jr (1979) Job demands, job decision latitude, and mental strain: Implications for job redesign. *Administrative Science Quarterly*, **24**, 285–308.

Katzell, R. A. (1964) Personal values, job satisfaction, and job behavior. In *Man in a World at Work*. Boston, MA: Houghton Mifflin.

Kemelgor, B. H. (1982) Job satisfaction as mediated by the value congruity of supervisors and their subordinates. *Journal of Occupational Behavior*, **3**, 147–160.

Klein, K. L., & Wiener, Y. (1977) Interest congruency as a moderator of the relationships between job tenure and job satisfaction and mental health. *Journal of Vocational Behavior*, **10**, 92–98.

Korman, A. L. (1967) Relevance of personal need satisfaction for overall job satisfaction as a function of self-esteem. *Journal of Applied Psychology*, **51**, 533–538.

Kuder, G. F. (1946) *Manual, Kuder Preference Record*. Chicago: Science Research Associates.

Kuder, G. F. (1966) *Manual, Kuder Occupational Interest Survey, Form DD*. Chicago: Science Research Associates.

Kulik, C. T., Oldham, G. R., & Hackman, J. R. (1987) Work design as an approach to person–environment fit. *Journal of Vocational Behavior*, **31**, 278–296.

Kulka, R. A. (1979) Interaction as person–environment fit. In L. R. Kahle (ed.), *New Directions for Methodology of Behavioral Science*. San Francisco: Jossey-Bass, pp. 55–71.

Lachman, R., & Aranya, N. (1986) Evaluation of alternative models of commitments and job attitudes of professionals. *Journal of Occupational Behavior*, **7**, 227–243.

Laing, J., Swaney, K., & Prediger, D. J. (1984) Integrating vocational interest inventory results and expressed choices. *Journal of Vocational Behavior*, **25**, 304–315.

Lawler, E. E. (1981) *Pay and Organizational Development*. Reading, MA: Addison-Wesley.

Lawler, E. E., & Hall, D. T. (1970) Relationship of job characteristics to job involvement, satisfaction, and intrinsic motivation. *Journal of Applied Psychology*, **54**, 305–312.

Lawler, E. E., & Porter, L. W. (1967) The effect of performance on job satisfaction. *Industrial Relations*, **7**, 20–28.

Lee, T. W., Locke, E. A., & Latham, G. P. (1989) Goal setting theory and job performance. In L. A. Pervin (ed.), *Goal Concepts in Personality and Social Psychology*. Hillsdale, NJ: Erlbaum, pp. 291–326.

Lefkowitz, J., Somers, M. J, & Weinberg, K. (1984) The role of need level and/or need salience as moderators of the relationship between need satisfaction and work alienation-involvement. *Journal of Vocational Behavior*, **24**, 142–158.

Lewin, K. (1951) *Field Theory in Social Science*. New York: Harper.

Locke, E. A. (1967) Relationship of success and expectation to affect on goal-seeking tasks. *Journal of Personality and Social Psychology*, **7**, 125–134.

Locke, E. A. (1969) What is job satisfaction? *Organizational Behavior and Human Performance*, **4**, 309–336.

Locke, E. A. (1976) The nature and causes of job satisfaction. In M. Dunnette (ed.), *Handbook of Industrial and Organizational Psychology*. Chicago: Rand McNally, pp. 1297–1350.

Locke, E. A. (ed.) (1986) *Generalizing from Laboratory to Field Settings*. Lexington, MA.: D. C. Heath.

Locke, E. A., Shaw, K. N., Saari, L. M., & Latham, G. P. (1981) Goal setting and task performance: 1969–1980. *Psychological Bulletin*, **90**, 125–152.

London, M., & Klimoski, R. (1975) Self-esteem and job complexity as moderators of performance and satisfaction. *Journal of Vocational Behavior*, **6**, 293–304.

Lopez, E. M., & Greenhaus, J. H. (1978) Self-esteem, race, and job satisfaction. *Journal of Vocational Behavior*, **13**, 75–83.

Lyons, T. (1971) Role clarity, need for clarity, satisfaction, tension, and withdrawal. *Organizational Behavior and Human Performance*, **6**, 99–110.

MacKinnon, N. J. (1978) Role strain: An assessment of a measure and its invariance of factor structure across studies. *Journal of Applied Psychology*, **63**, 321–328.

McGrath, J. E. (1976) Stress and behavior in organizations. In M. Dunnette (ed.), *Handbook of Industrial and Organizational Psychology*. Chicago: Rand McNally, pp. 1351–1395.

McGrath, J. E., Martin, J., & Kulka, R. A. (eds) (1982) *Judgment Calls in Research*. Beverly Hills: Sage.

McLain, D. H. (1974) Drawing contours from arbitrary data points. *The Computer Journal*, **17**, 318–324.

Meglino, B. M., Ravlin, E. C., & Adkins, C. L. (1989) A work values approach to corporate culture: A field test of the value congruence process and its relationship to individual outcomes. *Journal of Applied Psychology*, **74**, 424–434.

Meir. E. I., & Engel, K. (1986) Interests and specialty choice in medicine. *Social Science and Medicine*, **23**, 527–530.

Meir, E. I., & Erez, M. (1981) Fostering careers in engineering. *Journal of Vocational Behavior*, **18**, 115–120.

Meir, E. I., & Melamed, S. (1986) The accumulation of person–environment congruences and well-being. *Journal of Occupational Behavior*, **7**, 315–323.

Melamed, S., & Meir, E. I. (1981) The relationship between interest-job incongruity and selection of avocational activity. *Journal of Vocational Behavior*, **18**, 310–325.

Michalos, A. C. (1980) Satisfaction and happiness. *Social Indicators Research*, **8**, 385–422.

Michalos, A. C. (1983) Satisfaction and happiness in a rural northern resource community. *Social Indicators Research*, **13**, 224–252.

Michalos, A. C. (1985) Multiple discrepancies theory. *Social Indicators Research*, **16**, 347–413.

Miles, R. H., & Petty, M. M. (1975) Relationships between role clarity, need for clarity, and job tension and satisfaction for supervisory and non-supervisory roles. *Academy of Management Journal*, **18**, 877–883.

Mobley, W. H., & Locke, E. A. (1970) The relationship of value importance to satisfaction. *Organizational Behavior and Human Performance*, **5**, 463–483.

Mount, M. K., & Muchinsky, P. M. (1978) Person–environment congruence and employee job satisfaction: A test of Holland's theory. *Journal of Vocational Behavior*, **13**, 84–100.

Mowday, R. T., & Steers, R. M. (eds) (1979) *Research in Organizations: Issues and Controversies*. Santa Monica, CA: Goodyear Publishing Company.

Murray, H. A. (1938) *Explorations in Personality*. Boston, MA: Houghton Mifflin.

Myers, R. H. (1971) *Response Surface Methodology*. Boston, MA: Allyn & Bacon.

Neter, J., & Wasserman, W., & Kutner, M. H. (1989) *Applied Linear Regression Models*, 2nd edn. Homewood, IL: Irwin.

Newton, T. J., & Keenan, A. (1987) Role stress reexamined: An investigation of role stress predictors. *Organizational Behavior and Human Decision Process*, **40**, 346–368.

O'Brien, G. E., & Dowling, P. (1980) The effects of congruency between perceived and desired job attributes upon job satisfaction. *Journal of Occupational Psychology*, **53**, 121–130.

O'Brien, G. E., & Humphrys, P. (1982) The effects of congruency between work values and perceived job attributes upon the job satisfaction of pharmacists. *Australian Journal of Psychology*, **34**, 91–101.

O'Brien, G. E., & Stevens, K. (1981) The relationship between perceived influence and job satisfaction among assembly line employees. *Journal of Industrial Relations*, **23**, 33–48.

Oldham, G. R., Kulik, C. T., Ambrose, M. L., Stepina, L. P., & Brand, J. F. (1986) Relations between job facet comparisons and employee reactions. *Organizational Behavior and Human Decision Process*, **38**, 27–47.

Orpen, C. (1974) A cognitive consistency approach to job satisfaction. *Psychological Reports*, **35**, 239–245.

Payne, R. L. (1970) Factor analysis of a Maslow-type need satisfaction questionnaire. *Personnel Psychology*, **23**, 251–268.

Pazy, A., & Zin, R. (1987) A contingency approach to consistency: A challenge to prevalent views. *Journal of Vocational Behavior*, **30**, 84–101.

Peiser, C., & Meir, E. I. (1978) Congruency, consistency and differentiation of vocational interest as predictors of vocational satisfaction and preference stability. *Journal of Vocational Behavior*, **12**, 270–278.

Pelz, D. C., & Andrews, F. M. (1976) *Scientists in Organizations: Productive Climates for Research and Development*, 2nd edn. Ann Arbor, MI: Institute for Social Research, University of Michigan.

Phillips, J. S., Barrett, G. V., & Rush, M. C. (1978) Job structure and age satisfaction. *Aging & Work*, **1**(2), 109–119.

Porter, L. W. (1962) Job attitudes in management: I. Perceived deficiencies in need fulfillment as a function of job level. *Journal of Applied Psychology*, **46**, 375–384.

Porter, L. W. (1964) *Organizational Patterns of Managerial Attitudes*. New York: American Foundation for Management Research.

Porter, L. W., & Lawler, E. E. (1964) The effects of 'tall' versus 'flat' organizations structures on managerial job satisfaction. *Personnel Psychology*, **17**, 135–148.

Porter, L. W., & Lawler, E. E. (1968) *Managerial Attitudes and Performance.* Homewood, IL: Dorsey Press.

Posner, B. Z., Kouzes, J. M., & Schmidt, W. H. (1985) Shared values make a difference: An empirical test of corporate culture. *Human Resource Management,* **24,** 293–309.

Pryor, R. G. L. (1987) Differences among differences: In search of general work preference dimensions. *Journal of Applied Psychology,* **72,** 426–433.

Rice, R. W., McFarlin, D. B., & Bennett, D. W. (1989) Standards of comparison and job satisfaction. *Journal of Applied Psychology,* **74,** 591–598.

Rice, R. W., McFarlin, D. B., Hunt, R. G., & Near, J. P. (1985) Organizational work and the perceived quality of life: Toward a conceptual model. *Academy of Management Review,* **10,** 296–310.

Rizzo, J. R., House, R. J., & Lirtzman, S. I. (1970) Role conflict and ambiguity in complex organizations. *Administrative Science Quarterly,* **15,** 150–163.

Rokeach, M. (1973) *The Nature of Human Values.* New York: Free Press.

Rosman, P., & Burke, R. J. (1980) Job satisfaction, self-esteem, and the fit between perceived self and job on valued competencies. *Journal of Psychology,* **105,** 259–269.

Rounds, J. B., Dawis, R. W., & Lofquist, L. H. (1987) Measurement of person–environment fit and prediction of satisfaction in the Theory of Work Adjustment. *Journal of Vocational Behavior,* **31,** 297–318.

Sadler, P. J. (1970) Leadership style, confidence in management and job satisfaction. *Journal of Applied Behavioral Science,* **6,** 3–19.

Salomone, P. R., & Sheehan, M. C. (1985) Vocational stability and congruence: An examination of Holland's proposition. *Vocational Guidance Quarterly,* **34,** 91–98.

Scarpello, V., & Campbell, J. P. (1983) Job satisfaction and the fit between individual needs and organizational rewards. *Journal of Occupational Psychology,* **56,** 315–328.

Schletzer, V. M. (1966) SVIB as a predictor of job satisfaction. *Journal of Applied Psychology,* **50,** 5–8.

Schneider, B. (1983) Interactional psychology and organizational behavior. In B. M. Staw & L. L. Cummings (eds), *Research in Organizational Behavior,* vol. 5, Greenwich, CT: JAI Press, pp. 1–31.

Schneider, B. (1987) $E = f(P, B)$: The road to a radical approach to person–environment fit. *Journal of Vocational Behavior,* **31,** 353–361.

Schuler, R. S. (1980) Definition and conceptualization of stress in organizations. *Organizational Behavior and Human Performance,* **25,** 184–215.

Schwab, D. P. (1980) Construct validity in organizational behavior. In L. L. Cummings and B. M. Staw (eds), *Research in Organizational Behavior,* vol. 2. Greenwich, CT: JAI Press, pp. 3–43.

Sexton, W. P. (1967) Organization and individual needs: A conflict? *Personnel Journal,* **46,** 337–343.

Sheridan, J. E., & Slocum, J. W. (1975) The direction of the causal relationship between job satisfaction and job performance. *Organizational Behavior and Human Performance,* **14,** 159–172.

Shirom, A. (1982) What is organizational stress? A facet analytic conceptualization. *Journal of Occupational Behavior,* **3,** 21–37.

Slocum, J. W. (1971) Motivation in managerial levels: Relationship of need satisfaction to job performance. *Journal of Applied Psychology,* **55,** 312–316.

Smith, P. C., Kendall, L., & Hulin, C. L. (1969) *The Measurement of Satisfaction in Work and Retirement.* Chicago: Rand McNally.

Sorensen, J. E., & Sorensen, T. L. (1974) The conflict of professionals in bureaucratic organizations. *Administrative Science Quarterly,* **19,** 98–106.

Spokane, A. R. (1985) A review of research on person-environment congruence in

Holland's theory of careers. *Journal of Vocational Behavior*, **26**, 306–343.

Stone, E. F. (1978) *Research Methods in Organizational Behavior*. Santa Monica, CA: Goodyear Publishing Company.

Stone, E. F. (1986) Research methods in industrial and organizational psychology: Selected issues and trends. In C. L. Cooper & I. T. Robertson (eds), *International Review of Industrial and Organizational Psychology*. New York: Wiley, pp. 305–334.

Stone, E. F. (1988) Moderator variables in research: A review and analysis of conceptual and methodological issues. In K. Rowland & G. R. Ferris (eds), *Research in Personnel and Human Resource Management*, vol. 6. Greenwich, CT: JAI Press, pp. 191–229.

Stone, E. F., & Hollenbeck, J. R. (1984) Some issues associated with the use of moderated regression. *Organizational Behavior and Human Performance*, **34**, 195–213.

Super, D. E. (1973) The Work Values Inventory. In D. G. Zytowski (ed.), *Contemporary Approaches to Interest Measurement*. Minneapolis: University of Minnesota Press, pp. 189–205.

Swaney, K., & Prediger, D. (1985) The relationship between interest–occupation congruence and job satisfaction. *Journal of Vocational Behavior*, **26**, 13–24.

Tannenbaum, A. S., & Kuleck, W. J., Jr (1978) The effect on organization members of discrepancy between perceived and preferred rewards implicit in work. *Human Relations*, **31**, 809–822.

Terborg, J. R. (1981) Interactional psychology and research on human behavior in organizations. *Academy of Management Review*, **6**, 569–576.

Turner, A. N., & Lawrence, P. R. (1965) *Industrial Jobs and the Worker: An Investigation of Responses to Task Attributes*. Boston, MA: Harvard University Press.

Tziner, A. (1987) Congruency issue retested using Fineman's achievement climation notion. *Journal of Social Behavior and Personality*, **2**, 63–78.

Vaitenas, R., & Wiener, Y. (1977) Development, emotional, and interest factors in voluntary mid-career change. *Journal of Vocational Behavior*, **11**, 291–304.

Vroom, V. H., & Deci, E. L. (1971) The stability of post-decision dissonance: A follow-up study of the job attitudes of business school graduates. *Organizational Behavior and Human Performance*, **6**, 36–49.

Wahba, M. A., & Birdwell, L. G. (1976) Maslow reconsidered: A review of research on the need hierarchy theory. *Organizational Behavior and Human Performance*, **15**, 212–240.

Waldman, D. A., & Spangler, W. D. (1989) Putting together the pieces: A closer look at the determinants of job performance. *Human Performance*, **2**, 29–59.

Wall, T. D., & Payne, R. (1973) Are deficiency scores deficient? *Journal of Applied Psychology*, **58**, 322–326.

Wanous, J. P. (1974) Individual differences and reactions to job characteristics. *Journal of Applied Psychology*, **74**, 616–622.

Wanous, J. P., & Lawler, E. E. (1972) Measurement and meaning of job satisfaction. *Journal of Applied Psychology*, **56**, 95–105.

Wanous, J. P., & Zwany, A. (1977) A cross-sectional test of hierarchy theory. *Organizational Behavior and Human Performance*, **18**, 78–97.

Weiss, D. J., Dawis, R. V., Lofquist, L. H., & England, G. W. (1966) Instrumentation for the Theory of Work Adjustment. *Minnesota Studies in Vocational Rehabilitation*, **21**.

West, M., & Rushton, R. (1989) Mismatches in the work–role transitions. *Journal of Occupational Psychology*, **62**, 271–286.

White, A. T., & Spector, P. E. (1987) An investigation of age-related factors in the age–job-satisfaction relationship. *Psychology and Aging*, **2**, 261–265.

White, J. K., & Ruh, R. A. (1973) Effects of personal values on the relationship between participation and job attitudes. *Administrative Science Quarterly*, **18**, 506–514.

Wiener, J., & Klein, K. L. (1978) The relationship between vocational interests and job satisfaction: Reconciliation of divergent results. *Journal of Vocational Behavior*, **13**, 298–304.

Wiggins, J. D. (1976) The relation of job satisfaction to vocational preferences among teachers of the educatable mentally retarded. *Journal of Vocational Behavior*, **8**, 13–18.

Wiggins, J. D. (1984) Personality–environment factors related to job satisfaction of school counselors. *The Vocational Guidance Quarterly*, **33**, 169–177.

Wiggins, J. D., Lederer, D. A., Salkowe, A., & Rys, G. (1983) Job satisfaction related to tested congruence and differentiation. *Journal of Vocational Behavior*, **23**, 112–121.

Wiggins, J. D., & Moody, A. (1981) *Compatibility Index Description*. Dover, DL: Training Associates.

Wolf, F. M. (1986) *Meta Analysis: Quantitative Methods for Research Synthesis*. Beverly Hills: Sage.

Wright, D., & Gutkin, T. B. (1981) School psychologists' job satisfaction and discrepancies between actual and desired work functions. *Psychological Reports*, **49**, 735–738.

Zener, T. B., & Schnuelle, L. (1976) Effects of the self-directed search on high school students. *Journal of Counseling Psychology*, **23**, 353–359.

Zytowski, D. G. (1974) Predictive validity of the Kuder Preference Record, Form B, over a 25-year span. *Measurement and Evaluation in Guidance*, **7**, 122–129.

Zytowski, D. G. (1976) Predictive validity of the Kuder Occupation Interest Survey: A 12- to 19-year follow-up. *Journal of Counseling Psychology*, **23**, 221–233.

Chapter 9

JOB SATISFACTION: DISPOSITIONAL AND SITUATIONAL INFLUENCES

Richard D. Arvey, Gary W. Carter and Deborah K. Buerkley
Industrial Relations Center
The University of Minnesota
USA

What are the determinants of job satisfaction? Intuitively, it seems that facets of the job environment, individual or person factors, and the fit between job facets and person factors should all influence the general attitude an employee holds toward his or her job. From a historical perspective, the Lewinian model suggests that behavior and attitudes are a function of both person and environmental factors $[B = f(P, E)]$. While few scholars would discount this broad functional relationship, recent discussion and research suggests debate concerning the relative importance of these two broad domains as causes and correlates of job satisfaction.

In this chapter we:

1. Discuss research streams providing evidence concerning the impact of person and situational factors on job satisfaction;
2. Discuss methods which have been used in attempts to untangle the joint influence of person and situational factors on job satisfaction;
3. Discuss potential research directions, and methodological issues relevant to this domain of inquiry.

We should note at the outset the limitations of this presentation. First, we limit our discussion to general or overall satisfaction. We do not deal here, except tangentially, with the problems and issues associated with facet satisfaction or with the relationships between job facet satisfaction and overall or general satisfaction. Second, we make no claim to be comprehensive in our discussion. Instead, we intend the discussion to be illustrative and conceptual. We adopt the perspective that the term 'situational' factors refers to variables

International Review of Industrial and Organizational Psychology 1991 Volume 6
Edited by C. L. Cooper and I. T. Robertson © 1991 John Wiley & Sons Ltd.

and constructs which are predominately associated with the job, the job environment, the job climate, organizational factors, and other 'non-person' factors. Similarly, we classify constructs such as 'dispositions' and traits as person factors.

In the sections that follow, we discuss four major research models which have been followed by researchers studying the causes and correlates of job satisfaction. The first model includes studies examining associations between *specified* psychological individual difference variables and demographic variables (e.g. personality, values, gender, age, etc.) and job satisfaction. We call this the specified person effects model because it is characterized by the identification and measurement of variables having a relationship to satisfaction. The second model subsumes studies examining associations between specified situational variables and job satisfaction (the specified situational effects model). Researchers conducting these studies identify and measure aspects of the job environment, and examine relationships between these environmental measures and job satisfaction. The third model, the interactional model, includes research examining the fit between person variables and situational variables, as well as studies positing dynamic interactions between person variables and situational variables. Finally, the fourth model involves the study of the influence of *unspecified* person variables on satisfaction. That is, it includes studies employing methods which can provide evidence of person effects without necessarily specifying the nature of the person influences involved. Studies of the stability of responses to satisfaction questionnaires over time and studies examining genetic influences on satisfaction are subsumed by this model.

THE SPECIFIED PERSON EFFECTS MODEL

The specified person effects model includes studies treating relationships between specified person variables and job satisfaction. Most researchers embracing this model have employed correlation or regression to determine the amount of variance accounted for by person variables, and have assumed that the direction of causality runs from person variables to satisfaction. However, some authors (e.g. Kornhauser, 1965) have assumed the opposite causal pathway, that is, that person variables (such as mental health and personality) are primarily influenced by satisfaction and not vice versa.

Two major classes of variables comprise the 'person variables' category—psychological individual difference variables, and demographic variables. It is important to draw a clear distinction between these classes of variables because demographic variables, theoretically, can only influence satisfaction through their influence on situational variables and/or psychological individual difference variables. For example, it is frequently found that satisfaction increases with age. Such increases could stem either from situational influences (e.g. older persons may obtain jobs with more desirable characteristics) or person influences (e.g. age-related changes in personalities or aspiration levels).

While relationships between measures of psychological individual differences and satisfaction have received increased attention in the past few years (e.g. Staw, Bell, & Clausen, 1986; Watson, Pennebaker, & Folger, 1987; Watson & Keltner, 1989; Levin & Stokes, 1989), such relationships have been discussed in the satisfaction literature for many years. In fact, most early conceptions of morale and of work adjustment, from which research in job satisfaction stemmed, were inextricably linked with conceptions of psychological adjustment and personality. As early as 1931 Fisher & Hanna (p. 27) stated:

> . . . a large part of vocational maladjustment and industrial unrest are secondary to, and but a reflection of, emotional maladjustment. . . . His maladjustment, whatever it relates to, breeds within him dissatisfaction and thwarts him in his search for happiness and success. Inasmuch as his feelings and emotions are inherent aspects of himself, he carries them with him, so to speak, into every situation which he enters . . . it is not surprising that he very frequently attaches or attributes it (his dissatisfaction) to his work or his working situation.

Over the years, researchers have established that job satisfaction is significantly associated with general mental health indices (Kornhauser, 1965; Kavanagh, Hurst, & Rose, 1981; Kasl, 1973), and with several personality variables, including locus of control (Spector, 1982), neuroticism (Capin, 1986; Furnham & Zacherl, 1986; Perone, DeWaard, & Baron, 1979) and positive and negative affectivity (e.g. Watson & Keltner, 1989; Levin & Stokes, 1989).

One particularly promising area of specified person effects research entails the examination of relationships between positive and negative affectivity and satisfaction. Positive and negative affectivity are basic, pervasive personality dimensions which arise repeatedly in measures designed to tap a variety of personality constructs and which are strongly related to major dimensions of mood (Watson & Clark, 1984; Tellegen, 1985). Positive and negative affectivity 'index the strength of the individual's disposition to experience, respectively, pleasure and pain, reward and punishment, self-enhancement and self-imperilment, and to behave and think in ways that are conducive to these experiences' (Tellegen, 1982, p. 3).

A few researchers (e.g. Brief et al., 1988; Watson & Keltner, 1989; Levin & Stokes, 1989; George, 1990) have demonstrated significant relationships between these variables and job satisfaction.

Staw, Bell & Clausen (1986) found significant relationships between a composite of Q-sort items that appears to have been a measure of negative affectivity, and job satisfaction, even when the job satisfaction data were collected almost 50 years after the dispositional data. A correlation of 0.34 was found between affective disposition in early adolescence and overall job attitude in late adulthood.

Levin & Stokes (1989) conducted both a laboratory study and a field study to examine relationships between negative affectivity and satisfaction. In the laboratory study, Levin and Stokes employed 140 subjects scoring the upper or lower quartile in an administration of the Negative Affectivity Scale (Stokes & Levin, 1989). Levin and Stokes found that subjects low in negative affectivity reported higher satisfaction with both an enriched and an unenriched task. In the field study, Levin and Stokes found a correlation of −0.29 between negative affectivity and scores on the Job Descriptive Index Work Itself Scale (Smith, Kendall, & Hulin, 1969) among 315 employees of a professional services firm. Levin and Stokes also found that a portion, though not all, of the relationship between negative affectivity and satisfaction could be explained by differences in perceptions of job characteristics. However, it is unclear whether persons differing in negative affectivity perceived similar jobs differently, or whether they held jobs with objectively different job characteristics.

In addition to research designed to explore relationships between psychological individual difference variables and job satisfaction, the specified person variables category encompasses a relatively large body of research examining relationships between demographic variables (such as education, age, and gender) and job satisfaction. Unfortunately, many researchers attempting to explain relationships between demographic variables and job satisfaction have used questionable and convoluted statistical analyses, and have explained their results so poorly that it is virtually impossible to determine whether their conclusions are justified. As a result, a significant portion of the research literature intended to explain relationships between demographic variables and job satisfaction is uninterpretable.

A modest positive association between education and job satisfaction has typically been found when the samples studied include a broad occupational range and when rewards are not held constant (Quinn & Baldi de Mandilovitch, 1977). This relationship has been shown to be nonlinear in some cases, indicative of a credentials effect (Quinn & Baldi de Mandilovitch, 1977). This positive association appears to be primarily attributable to increases in job rewards and quality of employment (including financial rewards) with increases in education. When samples including narrow occupational ranges are studied (e.g. Larsen & Owens, 1965), or when job rewards are held constant (e.g. Glenn & Weaver, 1982), the relationship between education and job satisfaction is usually nonsignificant or negative. Differences in values or frames of reference between persons of differing educational levels probably underlie such negative relationships.

The most consistent (though not universal) finding among researchers examining age–satisfaction relationships is that there is a positive relationship between age and satisfaction (Rhodes, 1983). There has been considerable debate regarding the form of this relationship, with researchers typically finding either a linear (Rhodes, 1983) or a quadratic (Kalleberg & Loscocco, 1983) relationship between age and satisfaction. Kalleberg & Loscocco (1983) found that a curvilinear model (with satisfaction increasing until middle age, then leveling off, and increasing again after about age 56) provided the best fit to the male sample of the 1972–73 Quality of Employment Survey data (Quinn & Shepard, 1974), while a linear model was most appropriate for the female sample. It is likely that age-related differences in rewards, values, and frames of reference all contribute to positive age–satisfaction relationships. Unfortunately, research conducted thus far does not permit an assessment of the relative importance of these variables in accounting for age–satisfaction relationships.

Studies examining gender–job satisfaction relationships have shown no consistent gender-related differences in satisfaction, despite marked gender-related differences in job circumstances (Herzberg *et al.*, 1957; Weaver, 1978; Campbell, Converse, & Rodgers, 1976). The underlying causes of this lack of differences are unclear, although they may reflect gender differences in both values and frames of reference.

THE SPECIFIED SITUATIONAL EFFECTS MODEL

An alternative research model is characterized by an emphasis on situational causes and correlates of job satisfaction. Many investigators conducting research subsumed by this model have taken the view that situational factors are largely responsible for job satisfaction. This view may have emanated from a broader behavioristic paradigm in psychology which questioned the scientific utility of dispositional constructs and concentrated solely on environmental contingencies or situational variables. Thus, researchers searched for, and found, a large number of external situational and contextual factors which are associated with job satisfaction. This emphasis on situational factors related to job satisfaction is evident in a number of influential streams of research, including the 'human relations' research stemming from the Hawthorne studies, and work design and redesign research.

Several investigators, including Payne, Fineman, and Wall (1976) and Schneider and Snyder (1975), have examined conceptual similarities and differences between organizational climate, a subjectively measured situational variable, and job satisfaction, a subjectively measured attitudinal variable. Payne, Fineman, & Wall (1976) conclude that job satisfaction differs from organizational climate in three important ways: first, the unit of analysis in measures of job satisfaction is the individual, while the unit of analysis in measures of organizational climate is the 'social collectivity'. Second, the element of analysis in measures of job satisfaction is the job, while in measures of organizational climate it is the organization. Third, job satisfaction measures are evaluative in nature, while measures of organizational climate are descriptive. Schneider & Snyder (1975) present evidence showing that, while correlated, measures of job satisfaction and organizational climate are empirically as well as conceptually distinguishable. For example, they show that the correlations between climate scores and job satisfaction scores were smaller than correlations among scores on different climate scales.

Researchers have also spent a large amount of time and resources investigating the impact of specific job characteristics on work attitudes and job satisfaction. Loher et al. (1985) reviewed 28 studies investigating relationships between job characteristics identified by the Hackman & Oldham (1976) Job Characteristics Model, and job satisfaction. Their results showed that, after correcting the observed correlations for statistical artifacts such as restriction in range, reliability attenuation, etc. the relationship between such subjectively measured job characteristics as task identity, task autonomy, skill variety, feedback, etc. and job satisfaction ranged from 0.24 to 0.34. Squaring these values yields estimates of the proportion of variance in job satisfaction accounted for by these variables: 0.05–0.11.

Another meta-analysis of the relationships between job characteristics and job satisfaction was reported by Fried & Ferris (1987). These researchers summarized the results of several studies, which included a total of about 20 samples. The mean correlations between various job characteristics and overall job satisfaction found by Fried and Ferris (1987) are shown in Table 1.

These results show, obviously, that facets of the job environment are associated with job satisfaction. Again, squaring these correlations suggests that these job characteristics individually account for between 4 and 9% of the variance in job satisfaction.

One criticism of the research associated with the Job Characteristics Model is that both the job characteristics data and job satisfaction reports are provided by job incumbents. That is, measures of the job environment are subjective,

Table 1—Mean Correlations Between Job Characteristics and Overall Job Satisfaction. Drawn from Fried & Ferris (1987)

Job characteristic	Total sample size	Observed mean
Skill variety	18 035	0.29
Task autonomy	18 455	0.20
Task significance	17 887	0.26
Autonomy	7 861	0.34
Job feedback	18 561	0.29

perceptually based measures provided by the same people who provide job satisfaction data. Thus, any observed correlation between these job characteristics and job satisfaction could be due to common method variance.

Other researchers have focused on more objective features of job environments as potential correlates of job satisfaction. For example, Pritchard & Peters (1974) showed that there was a sizable relationship between job duties as defined by Position Analysis Questionnaire (PAQ) scores (McCormick, Jeanneret, & Mecham, 1972) and job satisfaction for over 600 US Navy personnel in a diverse set of jobs. The correlation between a PAQ composite measure of job duties and overall satisfaction was 0.46 for this sample. The multiple R-squared value (uncorrected for shrinkage) was 0.21, suggesting that the job itself plays an important role as a determinant of job satisfaction.

Another illustration of the role the job itself plays in accounting for variance in satisfaction is provided by a simple inspection of mean satisfaction scores across different occupations based on normative information for standardized job satisfaction measures. Table 2 provides means and standard deviations of general satisfaction scores measured via the Minnesota Satisfaction Questionnaire (MSQ) across six diverse occupations as reported in the MSQ manual (Weiss et al., 1967). These mean satisfaction scores range between 67.47 and 79.82 (about a full standard deviation difference). The omega-squared value computed using these data—representing the proportion of job satisfaction variance accounted for by occupation—is 0.11. (It is important to note that this variance may be due to the influence of the job environment on job satisfaction, from the influence of person variables which are also related to occupation (as a result of self-selection into occupations), or from the influence of both person and situational variables. However, a similar observation could

Table 2—Means and Standard Deviations for Seven Occupations on the General Satisfaction Scale of the Minnesota Satisfaction Questionnaire. Drawn from Weiss *et al.* (1967)

Job title	*Mean*	*SD*	*N*
Engineers	77.88	11.92	387
Office clerks	74.48	12.45	222
Salesmen	79.82	11.82	195
Janitors/maintenancemen	78.01	11.51	242
Machinists	75.71	11.52	240
Assemblers	69.78	11.41	74
Electrical assemblers	67.47	12.26	358
Total group	74.858	11.94	1718

Sums of squares between subjects = 32 394.41.
Sums of squares within subjects = 243 996.63.
Omega squared estimate = 0.114.

be made with regard to any person or situational variable measured in isolation.)

Recently, a few researchers have employed structural equation modeling techniques in attempts to understand the nature of causal pathways linking situational variables with job satisfaction. James & Tetrick (1986), for example, tested three causal models relating job perceptions to job satisfaction, and found that only one of the models—the postcognitive-nonrecursive model—was not disconfirmed. The postcognitive-nonrecursive model specifies that job perceptions precede job satisfaction in the causal order, but that perceptions and satisfaction are reciprocally related.

The research literature exploring relationships between other environmental factors and job satisfaction is voluminous (see Locke, 1976 for a more comprehensive review). Obviously, we have summarised only a small portion of that literature. However, our limited review of the literature suggests that environmental variables influence job satisfaction in important ways, but that any single environmental factor does not explain a substantial amount of variance in job satisfaction.

While the majority of studies discussed thus far have included either person variables or situational variables, we do not intend to portray the impression that the satisfaction literature is devoid of studies which include variables from both categories. A large number of researchers have measured both individual difference variables and situational variables in studies of job satisfaction. In these studies, which frequently use a multiple regression or analysis of variance framework, the additive and unique variance in satisfaction accounted for by person and situational variables can be computed. A study conducted by O'Reilly & Roberts (1975) illustrates this approach. Subjects consisted of 578 US Navy enlisted men in a high-technology naval aviation unit. O'Reilly & Roberts (1975) obtained three measures of ability, measures of ten personality and motivational traits, measures of structural characteristics of the subjects' positions, and a measure of job satisfaction. Canonical correlation methods were used to show that when the variance in satisfaction accounted for by personality traits was partialled out, the structural variables were significantly associated with job satisfaction. However, no significant relationships were observed between personality and job satisfaction when variance accounted for by the structural variables was partialled out.

Another study following this approach is described by Colarelli, Dean, & Konstans (1987). They measured several person variables (i.e. cognitive ability, socioeconomic status, and career goals) as well as several situational variables (ie. job feedback, autonomy, and job context), using a sample of 280 entry-level accountants. Their results showed that 9% of the variance in job satisfaction was accounted for by the person factors, 30% was accounted for by the situational factors, and 39% was accounted for by the joint additive effects of these sets of variables.

THE INTERACTIONAL MODEL

An obvious advantage of measuring both situational and person variables in job satisfaction studies is that the influence of the interaction between such variables can be examined. These interactions form the basis for a third stream of job satisfaction research which stresses the joint influences of person and situational variables on satisfaction. Two avenues of research can be identified which employ an interactional model. The first, the congruence stream, stresses the importance of person–environment fit in explaining satisfaction, and the importance of mechanistic (or static) interaction between persons and situations (Weiss & Adler, 1984). The second research avenue, which has received little empirical attention by job satisfaction researchers, stresses the importance of dynamic interactions between persons and environments and of self-selection into and out of job environments (Schneider, 1987).

The basic notion underlying congruence research is that people must 'fit' their jobs or that there should be some degree of 'congruence' between person variables and situational variables in order for individuals to be optimally satisfied, perform well, maintain tenure, etc. Most congruence research entails the examination of differences in behavior and attitudes among persons exhibiting different levels of congruence, or fit, between person characteristics and job characteristics. Thus, the joint influences of person and environmental factors operating *interactively* are considered to be of primary importance in the production of job satisfaction (Terborg, 1981).

The Theory of Work Adjustment (Dawis & Lofquist, 1984) is among the most well-known models positing the importance of person–environment congruence on job satisfaction. A major tenet of this model is that job satisfaction is a function of the correspondence between the reinforcer pattern of the work environment and individual needs. Rounds, Dawis, & Lofquist (1987) present a recent test of this model using multiple operational definitions of 'fit' or congruence between job factors (occupational reinforcers) and individual occupational needs (measured by the Minnesota Importance Questionnaire (MIQ; Gay et al., 1971)). (The 'needs' measured by the MIQ are simple preferences for various job characteristics.) Their findings revealed that between 3 and 30% of the variance in general job satisfaction could be explained by various congruence indices.

Holland (1973, 1985) introduced another congruence model which has received a substantial amount of research attention. According to this model, job satisfaction depends upon the congruence between personality and the work environment. (Holland's personality constructs are based on broad interest composites and thus are closer to traditional conceptions of vocational interests than personality.) Holland's theory specifies that most persons and most environments can be categorized as realistic, investigative, artistic, social, enterprising, or conventional (Holland, 1985). Assouline & Meir (1987) present a meta-analysis of 41 studies which have tested Holland's congruence hypothesis by correlating person–environment congruence with job satisfaction. Assouline & Meir (1987) report a weighted mean correlation of 0.21 between congruence indices and satisfaction.

Another well-recognized body of research emphasizing the importance of the interaction between person variables and situational variables in the production of job satisfaction is based on the Job Characteristics Model. The Job Characteristics Model proposes that the relationships between various job characteristics and behavioral/attitudinal outcomes are moderated by growth need strength (Kulik, Oldham, & Hackman, 1987). Loher et al.'s (1985) meta-analysis summarizes research examining this hypothesized interaction. After correcting for measurement unreliability, Loher et al. (1985) showed that the average correlation between a composite index of job characteristics (MPS—Motivating Potential Score) and job satisfaction was 0.68 among persons high in growth need strength, and 0.38 among persons low in growth need strength.

Equity and frame of reference models—two important theoretical frameworks relevant to satisfaction research—could also be seen, in a sense, as congruence models. Equity theorists argue that satisfaction is a function of the match between job rewards and a person's perceived equitable level of rewards (Adams, 1963). Likewise, according to the frame of reference model, satisfaction depends on the discrepancy between perceived job characteristics and an external standard of comparison (Motowidlo et al., 1976). The perceived equitable level of rewards and the external standard influencing satisfaction are almost certainly influenced by psychological individual difference variables and demographic variables (e.g. level of education). For example, Oldham et al. (1982) found that referents, or comparison others, used by employees in evaluating characteristics of their jobs tended to be similar to the employees in terms of education, skill level, seniority, and sex.

The 'fit' or congruence framework has received substantial attention in the vocational counseling literature. An entire issue of the Journal of Vocational Behavior in 1987 was devoted to conceptual and methodological issues associated with this general model. A number of issues have surfaced in this literature, concerning topics such as the appropriateness of various congruence indices, whether the 'right' person variables have been measured, whether the environment has been adequately sampled, etc. We discuss some of these issues below. However, one issue which deserves some attention here concerns the cross-sectional nature of the vast majority of research investigating person–environment interactions. Most studies are time bound in that subjects are 'nested' within particular situations or environments at one specific time. There may be a great deal to be gained by utilizing longitudinal designs (which are inherently more powerful statistically than cross-sectional designs) to investigate relationships between satisfaction and person and situational variables.

The importance of longitudinal designs is highlighted by studies stressing the importance of dynamic interactions and of the self-selection of persons into environments. For example, Pervin (1987, p. 225) stresses the need for 'dynamic, interpretive, process models that focus on . . . the stasis and flow of behavior'. Schneider (1987) presents an attraction–selection–attrition (ASA) framework, which specifies that persons are attracted to and selected for job environments where they will 'fit', and that persons tend to leave settings where they do not fit. Moreover, Schneider (1987) asserts, the job environment is determined by the persons who are in an organization. Thus, not only is behavior a function of the person and the environment, as specified by Lewin, but environment is also a function of persons and behavior. Chatman (1989) presents a model based on the fit between individual value profiles and organizational value profiles which can be used to predict changes in behavior, norms, and values. Snyder and Ickes (1985) discuss a 'situational strategy' for examining social behavior. The situational strategy 'reflects the dynamic interactional perspective on personality and social behavior' (Snyder & Ickes, 1985, p. 933). One of the core features of the situational strategy is that 'properties of individuals (including stable traits, enduring dispositions, social attitudes, and conceptions of self) are reflected in the processes by which individuals choose to enter and to spend time in social situations and in the processes by which they influence the character of the social situations in which they find themselves' (Snyder & Ickes, 1985, p. 932).

The ASA framework, articulated by Schneider, and the related situational strategy, described by Snyder & Ickes (1985), have several important implications for job satisfaction research. First, by arguing that persons essentially create environments, including job environments, these theorists blur the distinction between person variables and situational variables (including both subjective and objective situational variables). For example, James *et al.* (1978, pp. 805–806) assert that '. . . many psychologically important situational variables, as well as individual variables, reflect reciprocal situation–individual interactions, and the measurement of variables representing one domain will often reflect, causally, the influences of the other domain'. Emmons, Diener, & Larsen (1986) go so far as to suggest that personality could be assessed by assessing situational choice. Second, self-selection into and out of environments can lead to attenuations in correlations between both person variables and situational variables and job satisfaction. Third, the ASA framework and the situational strategy offer potential explanations for correlations between certain individual difference variables and job satisfaction. For example, Snyder & Ickes (1985) discuss several studies providing evidence that persons actively gravitate toward situations congruent with their personalities. Thus, higher job satisfaction among persons high in positive affectivity (Watson & Keltner, 1989) may be due either to a tendency among such persons to evaluate any situation more favorably than persons low in positive affectivity, or to a tendency for such persons to seek out or to create environments where there is a greater opportunity to experience positive affect. There has been little empirical research within the job satisfaction domain exploring the influence of dynamic person–situation interactions over time, or exploring the impact of self-selection on relationships between job satisfaction, person variables, and situational variables. Such research could be extremely valuable.

THE UNSPECIFIED PERSON EFFECTS MODEL

The unspecified person effects model includes studies employing methods which can provide evidence of person effects without necessarily specifying the nature of the person influences involved. Interestingly, by employing this model researchers can provide evidence of person effects without specifying the nature of the person effects involved, but must specify situational variables to rule out potential alternative explanations for apparent person influences. Two streams of research fall within this framework—research examining stability in responses to job satisfaction instruments over time and research examining genetic influences on job satisfaction.[1]

Staw & Ross (1985) rekindled the debate over the importance of person variables in understanding job satisfaction when they noted that the situational aspects of job attitudes may have been overemphasized and that researchers could profit by adopting a 'dispositional' approach in explaining job attitudes and behavior. That is, individual characteristics predispose people to respond positively or negatively to job contexts and the influences of these individual characteristics on job attitudes have been underestimated. Staw & Ross (1985) conducted a study using data gathered on over 5000 men between the ages of 45 and 59 as part of the National Longitudinal Survey. Individuals completed a one-item satisfaction measure in three different time periods. Persons who had remained with the same employer were surveyed along with persons who exhibited a change in employer as well as occupation. These data revealed that there was substantial consistency in job satisfaction across the different time periods for individuals with the same employer and occupation (ranging from 0.37 to 0.48) and that this consistency in attitude was maintained, to some extent, even when persons changed employers and occupations. The correlation observed for persons who had changed both employers and occupations between the years 1966 and 1971 was 0.19; a composite index of satisfaction for 1966 and 1969 correlated 0.34 with the 1971 satisfaction

---

[1]Note that, while stability of satisfaction across time despite important situational changes provides evidence of dispositional influences, the lack of stability does not necessarily preclude dispositional influences. Trait influences produce behavioral coherence and thus behavior—or attitudes—should be predictable, but do not necessarily produce behavioral consistency (Weiss & Adler, 1984).

measure for these individuals. Staw & Ross (1985, p. 477) also found that neither pay nor job status was as good a predictor of job satisfaction as prior satisfaction level: 'Changes in pay did predict some variance when both employer and occupation changed, but the strength of its relationship with satisfaction was considerably less than that represented by prior work attitudes.'

Following up on the Staw & Ross (1985) research, Gerhart (1987) suggested that their results may have been influenced by the kind of sample used, potential unreliability of the measures, and possible restriction in range in the kinds of job changes experienced. Gerhart (1987) examined the youth cohort of the National Longitudinal Survey and used an independently derived measure of job complexity as an indicator of job change. While Gerhart's (1987) results replicated those found by Staw & Ross (1985) in that significant stability was found in levels of job satisfaction when individuals had changed both job and occupation, Gerhart (1987) found that situational changes accounted for a substantial portion of the variance in job satisfaction responses across time. Using regression analyses, Gerhart (1987) found evidence that both previous satisfaction and changes in the complexity levels of jobs over time predicted current job satisfaction. Thus, his analysis demonstrated that situational factors as well as dispositional or person factors predicted job satisfaction.

Another recent report of research in this area is provided by Gutek & Winter (1989). In one study, over 1000 employees in a financial institution responded to questions regarding their satisfaction with their current jobs and with the jobs they held two years previously (a retrospective measure). Subjects were categorized into those who had held the same job for the two years, those who had changed jobs, and those who had changed both jobs and companies. The correlations between job satisfaction measured in 1986 and the one-item retrospective measure of 1984 satisfaction for these three groups were 0.266, −0.084 (*ns*), and −0.091 (*ns*) respectively. Using the two-item satisfaction measure, the correlations between time one and time two satisfaction for the three groups were 0.246, −0.15, and −0.14 respectively. These last two correlations were significant at the 0.05 level; thus, time one satisfaction was significantly negatively associated with time two satisfaction for the latter two groups.

Gutek & Winter (1989) also report a second study using 582 employees from a number of organizations. Again, retrospective measures of job satisfaction were used and correlations between the time one and time two measures of job satisfaction for those individuals who had changed jobs and/or organizations were very low.

While the use of retrospective measures of job satisfaction in a cross-sectional study is problematic, the results of these studies are interesting in light of the results of Staw & Ross's (1985) study. It can be assumed that turnover frequently results from dissatisfaction and from the expectation that alternative employment opportunities offer greater potential for satisfaction. When people pursue alternative job options, they often expect their satisfaction levels to increase. However, as discussed earlier, there also appears to be a personality-based tendency to be satisfied or dissatisfied across situations. Thus, studies examining the stability of satisfaction over time may be confounding influences due to dissatisfaction-based turnover and dispositionally based attitudinal stability.

USING TWIN STUDIES

Better control of the factors influencing job satisfaction might be achieved by utilizing identical and fraternal twins as subjects, and by examining the correlations between job satisfaction scores within twin pairs. Rowe (1987) suggests a variety of ways in which twin studies might be utilized within the context of the person–situation debate. To date only one study of job satisfaction has been conducted employing this type of methodology. We turn now to a review of this study.

Arvey et al. (1989) noted Staw & Ross's (1985) suggestion that there might be a biologically based explanation for observed dispositional correlates of job satisfaction: 'Job attitudes may reflect a biologically based trait that predisposes individuals to see positive or negative content in their jobs. . . . Differences in individual temperament ranging from clinical depression to a very positive disposition, could influence the information individuals input, recall and interpret within various social situations, including work' (Staw & Ross, 1985, p. 471).

Following this suggestion, Arvey et al. (1989) used an unusual methodology to investigate whether biological or genetic factors are significantly related to job satisfaction. Their study involved the use of identical or monozygotic twins who had been reared apart (MZA) from an early age. Monozygotic twins reared together share the same genetic structure but also share a common environment; thus, it is difficult to separate genetic and environmental influences among twins reared together. While there are a variety of statistical procedures which permit estimations of the magnitude of such influences (usually in combination with fraternal or dizygotic twins), the use of monozygotic twins reared apart as subjects allows for more simple estimation procedures. Given the assumption of random placement with respect to any trait-relevant environments, the intraclass correlation computed between such pairs is a direct estimate of the genetic contribution to any measured variable.

The MZA twins participating in this study were part of a larger sample in the Minnesota Study of Twins Reared Apart at the University of Minnesota. Details of their recruitment and zygosity diagnosis can be found in Bouchard (1987). Thirty-four monozygotic twin pairs provided data for this study. These individuals comprise a fascinating group with rich and varied histories; a provocative article providing detailed information about these twins was published by Rosen (1987). The twins participating in this study were separated soon after birth; their mean age at separation was 0.45 ($SD = 0.79$). The mean age of the sample at the time of the study was 41.88 ($SD = 12.03$). Twenty-five of the twin pairs were female and 9 were male.

The twins were asked to complete the short form of the MSQ for the job they had held for the longest period of their lives or the job that they considered to be their 'major job'. The mean general satisfaction scale score was 78.64 ($SD = 10.78$) which was similar to the values reported for a large normative group.

The twins reported their satisfaction in a diverse set of jobs including research chemist, assembler, food processor, miner, etc. Each of these jobs was assigned several scores derived from the *Dictionary of Occupational Titles* (DOT; US Department of Labor, 1977) by Roos & Triman (1980). (These scores were also used by Gerhart (1987) in developing relatively objective indices of job characteristics.) Jobs were assigned scores based on their relative complexity, motor skills requirements, physical demands, and working conditions.

The first stage of analyses consisted of simply computing intraclass correlations for the various single-item and composite job satisfaction scores after adjusting for age and sex. The intraclass correlation is an index of the degree of similarity between the members of the twin pairs, and a direct estimate of the amount of variance accounted for by genetic factors.[2]

The intraclass value obtained by Arvey *et al.* (1989) for the compositive job satisfaction scale was 0.309 which was significant at the 0.05 level. Arvey *et al.* (1989) interpreted this value to mean that approximately 30% of the variance in job satisfaction among those in their sample is associated with genetic factors. The remaining 70% of variance is accounted for by different environments (jobs), environmentally based dispositional influences (such as personality influences that are not genetically determined), and error variance.[3] It is important to realize that this value represents a variance estimate

---

[2]The intraclass correlation is a composite based on both variance within and between the twin pairs. Any difference observed between twin pairs (the mean square between factor) reflects differences due to genetic and environmental influences whereas differences within twin pairs (the mean square within factor) reflects differences due to environmental experiences for the twins (as well as measurement error).

[3]Davis-Blake & Pfeffer (1989) discount the results of this study because the extrinsic facet satisfaction items and a one-item overall satisfaction scale failed to show significant heritabilities. However, the finding of non-significant heritabilities for the extrinsic facet satisfaction items was consistent with the hypotheses of the study. Moreover, one-item scales (such as the overall satisfaction scale used by Arvey *et al.*, 1989) are typically less reliable than longer scales, leading to attenuated intraclass correlations. Therefore, we feel that the lack of statistically significant heritabilities for these scales does not justify discounting the finding of significant heritabilities for the general and intrinsic satisfaction scales.

analogous to an R-squared value. To determine what a corresponding Pearson product–moment correlation would be, one must compute the square root of the 0.309 value, i.e. 0.55. A Pearson product–moment correlation between a variable and job satisfaction would have to be equal to or greater than 0.55 to be equal to or greater than an intraclass correlation of 0.309 in associative strength.

The second set of analyses conducted by Arvey et al. (1989) was designed to determine whether the twins sought out similar jobs and whether this job similarity could have been responsible for the significant job satisfaction heritability estimate. Arvey et al. (1989) found significant intraclass correlations for the job complexity, motor skills requirements, and physical demands of the jobs described. These data indicated that there was, indeed, a significant genetic factor associated with the kinds of jobs individuals seek and find. Subsequently, these job characteristics were partialled from the job satisfaction value and the intraclass correlation again computed to determine if a significant genetic factor still remained after these characteristics (the job environments) were controlled. The resulting intraclass value (0.289) changed very little and was still significant.

These data are quite provocative. They do, indeed, suggest that a biological component is significantly associated with job satisfaction. One way to look at the results of this study is to view the intraclass correlation as the correlation of job satisfaction between genetically identical people who happen to hold different jobs. In fact, one can use the data derived from the MSQ manual and shown in Table 2 of this chapter to obtain a feel for what these data mean. In Table 2 the mean square within subjects value reflects the amount of variation between different individuals who share the same job. This value is 142.60 (the corresponding standard deviation computed by taking the square root of this value is 11.94). The mean square within subjects value computed for the monozygotic twins which reflects the amount of variation between the twins in each pair across all twin pairs in the Arvey et al. (1989) study is 74.47 ($SD = 8.63$). Thus, there is less variability in job satisfaction between genetically identical people who hold different jobs than there is among genetically unrelated people who hold the same job.

There are several limitations associated with this study. First, it was based on a relatively small sample, so generalizations must be made with caution. Second, while the data demonstrate an association between genetic factors and job satisfaction, the genetically based dispositions leading to satisfaction are unspecified. Third, there is some concern for the precision of measurement of job characteristics—these measures were rather global and were measured at the occupational level rather than at the level of the positions held by subjects. A final point worth noting is that this interpretation of the intraclass correlation is based on the assumption that there is no genotype–environment interaction. Thus, the estimates obtained reflect an additive model rather than an interactive model. However, to the extent that an interaction exists between individual genetic structures and the job environments in which the subjects worked, the intraclass correlation is an *underestimate* of the heritability of job satisfaction.

There has been a great deal of speculation concerning the mechanisms through which this genetic influence might operate. Arvey *et al.* (1989) suggest that the pathway might be through intelligence as well as through personality. Both intelligence and personality have been shown to be strongly influenced by genetics (Bouchard, 1987; Tellegen *et al.*, 1988; Rushton *et al.*, 1986). Another possible mechanism might be through work values: If job satisfaction is seen as a function of what individuals want and value in jobs compared to what they get (Locke, 1976), and if work values are partially genetically determined, then work values could be one mechanism through which genetics influence job satisfaction. Using samples of both monozygotic (*n* pairs = 23) and dizygotic (*n* pairs = 20) twins reared apart, Keller (1989) analyzed genetic influences on work values as measured by the MIQ. Her results demonstrated significant genetic influences on several central work values. A list of these values (with estimates of the contribution of genetic factors in parentheses) follows: achievement value (0.497), comfort value (0.318), status value (0.448), altruism value (0.156), safety value (0.399), and autonomy value (0.355). Thus, there seems to be some indication that work values could underlie genetic influences on satisfaction. However, the specific linkages were not tested in the study reported by Keller (1989).

An important question which occurs within the context of these types of investigations concerns how much influence environmental interventions such as job redesign can have given that there may be a significant genetic component to job satisfaction. Both Staw & Ross (1985) and Arvey *et al.* (1989) suggest that there may not be as much plasticity among individuals as we might have once believed. For example, Staw & Ross (1985, p. 478) comment that: 'The most straightforward implication is that many situational changes such as job redesign and organizational development may not affect individuals as they are intended. Many situational interventions may be prone to failure because they must contend with attitudinal consistency or a tendency for individuals to revert back to their basic dispositions.'

We are more sanguine than Staw and Ross about the possibility of effective environmental interventions. There are three factors which lead us to a more optimistic appraisal. First, even characteristics and traits which are highly genetically based (e.g. height, weight, etc.) can show considerable change given environmental interventions (Angoff, 1988). Second, the research results reported by both Arvey *et al.* (1989) and Staw & Ross (1985) are correlational in nature. These data simply show consistency across situations and not level changes. Thus, while the rank ordering of individuals might be preserved on job satisfaction across situations, considerable level differences might be obtained. Third, while the study by Arvey *et al.* (1989) showed that a significant proportion of the variance in job satisfaction was associated with genetic factors (30%), a considerable amount (70%) was nonetheless attributable to other influences, including the job environment. Thus, there is a lot of room for 'play' in the measurement range. In sum, these lines of evidence do not tell us much about the potential impact of environmental interventions.

The unique features of twin designs make such designs immune to some of the confounding factors affecting more traditional designs used in job satisfaction studies. For example, twin designs avoid the potential confounding (mentioned earlier) between dissatisfaction-based turnover and dispositionally based attitudinal stability in studies examining the stability of satisfaction given job change. As a result, twin designs can potentially contribute valuable information concerning the consistency and stability of job satisfaction in cross-situational contexts.

SUMMARY AND DISCUSSION

Where do we stand with regard to the issue of person–environment factors and their influence on job satisfaction? It seems to us that the following summary observations, given under the headings below, are in order.

Determinants of Job Satisfaction

It is obvious that both factors associated with the individual and facets of the job environment are important determinants of job satisfaction. From the longstanding person–situation controversy in the personality domain we have learned that it is senseless to ask whether persons or situations are important (Pervin, 1968). The research reviewed above clearly demonstrates that a number of individual characteristics and a number of situational variables account for variance in job satisfaction. In order to simply operationalize and measure the job satisfaction construct one needs to have an individual working in and experiencing a job environment. It is interesting to observe that several recent treatments of this issue (e.g. Staw & Ross, 1985; Gutek & Winter, 1989) seem to imply that previous research and researchers have not considered the possibility that person factors were associated with job satisfaction. Our review reveals that these factors were among the first examined as potential correlates of job attitudes.

Partitioning Variance

We recognize that the percentage of variance in responses to job satisfaction instruments attributed to various factors can vary drastically depending upon the nature of the sample and types of situations sampled (Weiss & Adler, 1984). It would be possible to arrange studies such that virtually any amount of variance, from 0% to 100%, could be attributed to person variables, situational variables, or the interaction between the two. The proportion of variance attributed to each of these factors depends upon a number of factors, including the range and variance of variables measured. For example, a researcher could examine the relative influence of person and situational factors in extremely good and extremely poor work environments. Under this circumstance, a great deal of variance will undoubtedly be attributed to situational factors. Conversely, both psychotically depressed workers and extraordinarily happy workers could be sampled. In this case, it is likely that a large portion of variance will be attributed to person factors. Nonetheless, we feel that studies examining the importance of variables in accounting for variance in satisfaction are informative and worthwhile.

As we have noted, it is difficult to form precise estimates of the proportions of variance due to person and situational factors or their interaction. However, based on the literature we have reviewed and making a number of abstractions over different studies, our hunch is that person factors account for between 10 and 30% of the variance in job satisfaction, that 40–60% of the variance is associated with situational factors, and that interactive elements account for between 10 and 20%. We say this very tentatively. We have not performed an exhaustive review of the literature nor have we been able to sort out the effects of person–environment interactions from additive effects. Moreover, these estimates do not take complex interrelationships between person and situational factors into account (see below).[4]

Methodological Issues

There are a number of methodological issues and research questions in this arena which need clarification and development. A few of these issues and questions are discussed below.

1. There is confusion regarding which person variables should be examined. A formidable array of person variables have been discussed as possible determinants of job satisfaction in the research literature. These include

---

[4]We also recognize that there is debate regarding the appropriateness of statistical indices commonly used to partition variance between persons and situations. A discussion of the problems associated wth indices used to partition variance due to persons and situations can be found in Golding (1975) and Olweus (1977).

demographic factors such as gender, age, and race as well as psychological individual differences variables or dispositions. Seashore & Taber (1975) identify a number of person factors along a 'more stable . . . less stable' dimension. Person factors identified which are relatively stable are demographic variables, stable personality variables, and abilities, whereas person factors which they classify as relatively unstable are perceptions, cognition, and transient affective states (such as anger and boredom). More clarification is needed, however, to help identify the person fators most likely to be associated with job satisfaction.

It would be helpful if researchers would choose person variables on a theoretical basis, instead of indiscriminately including any conveniently available person variables (Weiss & Adler, 1984). Weiss & Adler (1984) advise researchers who wish to examine relationships between personality variables and organizational behavior to use variables with well-established nomological nets. This advice is particularly appropriate in the theory–barren job attitude domain, which could be greatly enriched by establishing links between satisfaction and personality constructs (such as positive and negative affectivity) which have been shown to have important affective and behavioral correlates.

2. Similarly, almost every imaginable situational variable has been discussed in this research literature. A coherent taxonomy of job environments and situations is needed to guide satisfaction research. This taxonomy should be based on theoretical as well as empirical work. Olson & Borman (1989) have begun to develop a taxonomic structure for work environments in a military setting which might be used to assess situational constraints and facilitators of performance. Perhaps this and related taxonomic structures could also be used within the context of work attitude studies.

3. Researchers need to pay greater attention to the direction of causal arrows linking person variables, situational variables, and job satisfaction by employing statistical techniques based on structural equation modeling and by undertaking longitudinal studies.

4. Greater clarification is needed concerning the interdependence of person and environmental variables. Schneider (1987), for example, argues that the environment is influenced by individuals through selection and attrition processes in organizations. The employees remaining tend to create specific work climates and environments. Arvey et al.'s (1989) finding that there is a genetic tendency for individuals to seek and work in particular occupations is consistent with this notion. Similarly, James et al. (1978) suggest that there may be reciprocal influences between people and work climates. Thus, it may be useful to think of the matrix of person–environment variables as a set of overlapping cells with redundancies built into them.

5. More work needs to be done to gain an understanding of the range of

situations which will elicit potentially different job satisfaction responses. Most research is conducted in settings where the facets of the job environment are only slight variations within an organizational milieux. It might be quite helpful to study job attitudes among persons in radically different job environments (e.g. extremely complex jobs, jobs characterized by extreme social isolation and chaotic working conditions, etc.). It is possible that the observed associations between satisfaction and environmental factors are greatly constrained due to restriction in range.

6. More research needs to be conducted in settings where the same persons receive exposure to multiple job environments. The longitudinal studies of Staw & Ross (1985) and Gerhart (1987) are important starts in this area. Cross-sectional designs are severely limited in their information yield.

7. More creative research designs need to be developed and utilized. The twin studies discussed above represent one creative approach to job satisfaction research. Another possibility might be to conduct laboratory studies where individuals are asked to work under carefully controlled and different environments, or to examine the job satisfaction of temporary help employees as they work across different work environments.

A FINAL WORD

The research issues surrounding the examination of influences on job satisfaction are fascinating, and a diverse array of research designs could be utilized in exploring these issues. There is a need for creative theory and research to gain a better understanding of the nature of job satisfaction and of other subjective reactions to the job. Hopefully, this chapter will challenge others to continue in this area.

Correspondence address
Industrial Relations Center, 574 Management and Economics Building, University of Minnesota, 271 19th Avenue South, Minneapolis, Minnesota 55455, USA.

REFERENCES

Adams, J. S. (1963) Toward an understanding of inequity. *Journal of Abnormal and Social Psychology*, **67**, 422–436.

Angoff, W. H. (1988) The nature-nurture debate, aptitudes, and group differences. *American Psychologist*, **43**, 713–720.

Arvey, R. D., Bouchard, T. J., Jr, Segal, N. L., & Abraham, L. M. (1989) Job satisfaction: Environmental and genetic components. *Journal of Applied Psychology*, **74**, 187–192.

Assouline, M., & Meir E. I. (1987) Meta-analysis of the relationship between congruence and well-being measures. *Journal of Vocational Behavior*, **31**, 319–332.

Bouchard, T. J., Jr (1987) Diversity, development and determinism: A report on identical twins reared apart. In M. Amelang (ed.), *Bericht uber den 35. Kongress der Deutschen Gesellsschaft fur Psychologie in Heidelberg 1986* [Proceedings of the 35th Congress of the German Society for Psychology]. Göttingen, Federal Republic of Germany: Hogrefe.

Brief, A. P., Burke, M. J., Atieh, J. M., Robinson, B. S., & Webster, J. (1988) Should negative affectivity remain an unmeasured variable in the study of job stress? *Journal of Applied Psychology*, **73**(2), 193–198.

Campbell, D. P., Converse, P. E., & Rodgers, W. L. (1976) *The Quality of American Life*. New York: Russell Sage Foundation.

Capin, P. H. (1986) The effects of personality and type of job on satisfaction with work. Doctoral dissertation, University of Louisville, 1985. *Dissertation Abstracts International*, **47**(3), 1311B.

Chatman, J. A. (1989) Improving interactional organizational research: A model of person–organization fit. *Academy of Management Review*, **14**, 333–349.

Colarelli, S. M., Dean, R. A., & Konstans, C. (1987) Comparative effects of personal and situational influences on job outcomes of new professionals. *Journal of Applied Psychology*, **72**(4), 558–566.

Davis-Blake, A., & Pfeffer, J. (1989) Just a mirage: The search for dispositional effects in organizational research. *Academy of Management Review*, **14**, 385–400.

Dawis, R. W., & Lofquist, L. H. (1984) *A Psychological Theory of Work Adjustment*. Minneapolis, MN: University of Minnesota Press.

Emmons, R. A., Diener, E., & Larsen, R. J. (1986) Choice and avoidance of everyday situations and affect congruence: Two models of reciprocal interactionism. *Journal of Personality and Social Psychology*, **51**(4), 815–826.

Fisher, V. E., & Hanna, J. V. (1931) *The Dissatisfied Worker*. New York: Macmillan.

Fried, Y., & Ferris, G. R. (1987) The Validity of the Job Characteristics Model: A review and meta-analysis. *Personnel Psychology*, **40**, 287–322.

Furnham, A., & Zacherl, M. (1986) Personality and job satisfaction. *Personality and Individual Differences*, **7**(4), 453–459.

Gay, E. G., Weiss, D. J., Hendel, D. D., Dawis, R. V., & Lofquist, L. H. (1971) Manual for the Minnesota Importance Questionnaire. *Minnesota Studies in Vocational Rehabilitation*, *xxviii*, University of Minnesota.

George, J. M. (1990, April) Work, time, and life satisfaction. Paper presented at the fifth annual convention of the Society for Industrial and Organizational Psychology, Inc, Miami, FL.

Gerhart, B. (1987) How important are dispositional factors as determinants of job satisfaction? Implications for job design and other personnel programs. *Journal of Applied Psychology*, **72**, 366–373.

Glenn, N. D., & Weaver, C. N. (1982) Further evidence on education and job satisfaction. *Social Forces*, **61**, 46–55.

Golding, S. L. (1975) Flies in the ointment: Methodological problems in the analysis of the percentage of variance due to persons and situations. *Psychological Bulletin*, **82**, 275–288.

Gutek, B. A., & Winter, S. (1989) Consistency of job satisfaction across situations: Fact or artifact? Unpublished manuscript.

Hackman, J. R., & Oldham, G. R. (1976) Motivation through the design of work: Test of a theory. *Organizational Behavior and Human Performance*, **16**, 250–279.

Herzberg, F., Mausner, B., Peterson, R. O., & Capwell, D. F. (1957) *Job Attitudes: Review of Research and Opinion*. Pittsburgh, PA: Psychological Services of Pittsburgh.

Holland, J. L. (1973) *Making Vocational Choices: A Theory of Careers*. Englewood Cliffs, NJ: Prentice-Hall.

Holland, J. L. (1985) *Making Vocational Choices: A Theory of Careers*, 2nd edn. Englewood Cliffs, NJ: Prentice Hall.

James, L. R., Hater, J. J., Gent, M. J., & Bruni, J. R. (1978) Psychological climate: Implications from cognitive social learning theory and interactional psychology. *Personnel Psychology*, **31**, 783–813.

James, L. R., & Tetrick, L. E. (1986) Confirmatory analytic tests of three causal models relating job perceptions to job satisfaction. *Journal of Applied Psychology*, **71**(1), 77–82.

Kalleberg, A. L., & Loscocco, K. A. (1983) Aging, values, and rewards: Explaining age differences in job satisfaction. *American Sociological Review*, **48**, 78–90.

Kasl, S. V. (1973) Mental health and work environment: An examination of the evidence. *Journal of Occupational Medicine*, **15**(6), 509–518.

Kavanagh, M. J., Hurst, M. W., & Rose, R. (1981) The relationship between job satisfaction and psychiatric health symptoms for air traffic controllers. *Personnel Psychology*, **34**, 691–707.

Keller, L. M. (1989) Genetic and environmental factors associated with work values. Doctoral dissertation, University of Minnesota, 1988. *Dissertation Abstracts International*, **50**, 483A.

Kornhauser, A. (1965) *Mental Health of the Industrial Worker*. New York: Wiley.

Kulik, C. T., Oldham, G. R., & Hackman, J. R. (1987) Work design as an approach to person-environment fit. *Journal of Vocational Behavior*, **31**, 278–296.

Larsen, J. M., & Owens, W. A. (1965) Worker satisfaction as a criterion. *Personnel Psychology*, **18**, 39–47.

Levin, I., & Stokes, J. P. (1989) Dispositional approach to job satisfaction: Role of negative affectivity. *Journal of Applied Psychology*, **74**, 752–758.

Locke, E. A. (1976) The nature and causes of job satisfaction. In M. D. Dunnette (ed.), *Handbook of Industrial and Organizational Psychology*. Chicago: Rand McNally, pp. 1297–1349.

Loher, B. T., Noe, R. A., Moeller, N. L., & Fitzgerald, M. P. (1985) A meta-analysis of the relation of job characteristics to job satisfaction. *Journal of Applied Psychology*, **70**, 280–289.

McCormick, E. J., Jeanneret, P., & Mecham, R. A. (1972) A study of job characteristics and job dimensions as based on the Position Analysis Questionnaire (PAQ) [Monograph]. *Journal of Applied Psychology*, **56**, 346–368.

Motowidlo, S. J., Dowell, B. E., Hopp, M. A., Borman, W. C., Johnson, P. D., & Dunnette, M. D. (1974) *Motivation, Satisfaction, and Morale in Army Careers: A Review of Theory and Measurement* (Contract No. DAHC19-73-C-0025). Arlington, VA: US Army Institute for the Behavioral and Social Sciences.

Oldham, G. R., Nottenburg, G., Kassner, M. W., Ferris, G., Fedor, D., & Masters, M. (1982) The selection and consequences of job comparisons. *Organizational Behavior and Human Performance*, **29**, 84–111.

Olson, D. M., & Borman, W. C. (1989) More evidence on relationships between the work environment and job performance. *Human Performance*, **2**, 113–130.

Olweus, D. (1977) A critical analysis of the 'modern' interactionist position. In D. Magnusson & N. S. Endler (eds) *Personality at the Crossroads: Current Issues in Interactional Psychology*. New York: Wiley.

O'Reilly, C. A., & Roberts, K. H. (1975) Individual differences in personality, position in the organization, and job satisfaction. *Organizational Behavior and Human Performance*, **14**, 144–150.

Payne, R. L., Fineman, S., & Wall, T. D. (1976) Organizational climate and job satisfaction: A conceptual synthesis. *Organizational Behavior and Human Performance*, **16**, 45–62.

Perone, M., DeWaard, R. J., & Baron, A. (1979) Satisfaction with real and simulated jobs in relation to personality variables and drug use. *Journal of Applied Psychology*, **64**(6), 660–668.

Pervin, L. A. (1968) Performance and satisfaction as a function of individual-environment fit. *Psychological Bulletin*, **69**(1), 56–68.

Pervin, L. A. (1987) Person–environment congruence in the light of the person–situation controversy. *Journal of Vocational Behavior*, **31**, 222–230.

Pritchard, R. D., & Peters, L. H. (1974) Job duties and job interests as predictors of intrinsic and extrinsic satisfaction. *Organizational Behavior and Human Performance*, **12**, 315–330.

Quinn, R. P., & Baldi de Mandilovitch, M. S. (1977) *Education and Job Satisfaction: A Questionable Payoff*. Washington, DC: US Dept. of Education.

Quinn, R. P., & Shepard, L. J. (1974) *The 1972–1973 Quality of Employment Survey*. Ann Arbor, MI: Survey Research Center, Institute for Social Research.

Rhodes, S. R. (1983) Age-related differences in work attitudes and behavior: A review and conceptual analysis. *Psychological Bulletin*, **93**, 328–367.

Roos, P. A., & Treiman, D. J. (1980) Worker functions and worker traits for the 1970 U.S. census classification. In A. R. Miller, D. J. Treiman, P. S. Cain, & P. S. Roos (eds), *Work, Jobs and Occupations: A Critical Review of the Dictionary of Occupational Titles* (Appendix F). Washington, DC: National Academy Press.

Rosen, C. M. (1987) The errie world of reunited twins. *Discover*, September, 36–46.

Rounds, J. B., Dawis, R. V., & Lofquist, L. H. (1987) Measurement of person–environment fit and prediction of satisfaction in the Theory of Work Adjustment. *Journal of Vocational Behavior*, **31**, 297–318.

Rowe, D. C. (1987) Resolving the person–situation debate. *American Psychologist*, **42**, 218–227.

Rushton, J. P., Fulker, D. W., Neale, M. C., Nias, D. K. B., & Eysenck, H. J. (1986) Altruism and aggression: To what extent are individual differences inherited? *Journal of Personality and Social Psychology*, **50**, 1192–1198.

Schneider, B. (1987) $E = f(P,B)$: The road to a radical approach to person–environment fit. *Journal of Vocational Behavior*, **31**, 353–361.

Schneider, B., & Snyder, R. A. (1975) Some relationships between job satisfaction and organizational climate. *Journal of Applied Psychology*, **60**(3), 318–328.

Seashore, S. E., & Taber, T. D. (1975) Job satisfaction indicators and their correlates. *American Behavioral Scientist*, **18**(3), 333–368.

Smith, P. C., Kendall, L. M., & Hulin, C. L. (1969) *The Measurement of Satisfaction in Work and Retirement: A Strategy for the Study of Attitudes*. Chicago: Rand McNally.

Snyder, M., & Ickes, W. (1985) Personality and social behavior. In G. Lindzey & E. Aronson (eds), *Handbook of Social Psychology*, 3rd edn. New York: Random House, pp. 883–948.

Spector, P. E. (1982) Behavior in organizations as a function of employee's locus of control. *Psychological Bulletin*, **91**(3), 482–497.

Staw, B. M., Bell, N. E. & Clausen, J. A. (1986) The dispositional approach to job attitudes: A lifetime longitudinal test. *Administrative Science Quarterly*, **31**, 56–77.

Staw, B. M., & Ross, J. (1985) Stability in the midst of change: A dispositional approach to job attitudes. *Journal of Applied Psychology*, **70**, 469–480.

Stokes, J. P., & Levin I. M. (1989) *The Development and Validation of a Measure of Negative Affectivity*. Manuscript submitted for publication.

Tellegen, A. (1985) Structures of mood and personality and their relevance to assessing anxiety, with an emphasis on self-report. In A. H. Tumas & J. D. Maser (eds), *Anxiety and the anxiety disorders*. Hillsdale, NJ: Erlbaum.

Tellegen, A. (1982) *Brief manual for the Multidimensional Personality Questionnaire*. Unpublished manuscript.

Tellegen, A., Lykken, D. T., Bouchard, T. J., Jr., Wilcox, K. J., Segal, N. L., & Rich, S. (1988) Personality similarity in twins reared apart and together. *Journal of Personality and Social Psychology*, **54**, 1031–1039.

Terborg, J. (1981) Interactional psychology and research on human behavior in organizations. *Academy of Management Review*, **6**, 569–576.

US Department of Labor (1977) *Dictionary of Occupational Titles*, 4th edn. Washington, DC: Government Printing Office.

Watson, D., & Clark, L. A. (1984) Negative affectivity: The disposition to experience aversive emotional states. *Psychological Bulletin*, **96**(3), 465–490.

Watson, D., & Keltner, A. C. (1989) General Factors of Affective Temperament and their Relation to Job Satisfaction Over Time. Unpublished manuscript.

Watson, D., Pennebaker, J. W., & Folger, R. (1987) Beyond negative affectivity: Measuring stress and satisfaction in the workplace. *Journal of Organizational Behavior Management*, **8**, 141–157.

Weaver, C. N. (1978) Sex differences in the determinants of job satisfaction. *Academy of Management Journal*, **21**, 265–274.

Weiss, D. J., Dawis, R. V., England, G. W., & Lofquist, L. H. (1967, Oct.) Manual for the Minnesota Satisfaction Questionnaire. *Minnesota Studies in Vocational Rehabilitation* (xxii), University of Minnesota.

Weiss, H. M., & Adler, S. (1984) Personality and organizational behavior. In B. M. Staw (ed.), *Research in Organizational Behavior*, vol. 6. London, England: JAI Press, pp. 1–50.

INDEX

Index compiled by Geoffrey C. Jones

*International Review of Industrial
and Organizational Psychology
1986*

CONTENTS

*International Review of Industrial
and Organizational Psychology
1987*

CONTENTS

International Review of Industrial
and Organizational Psychology
1988

CONTENTS

International Review of Industrial
and Organizational Psychology
1989

CONTENTS

*International Review of Industrial
and Organizational Psychology
1990*

CONTENTS